Regulation of Debt Collection in Europe

Due to the absence of due process and other procedural guarantees generally offered by judicial enforcement, informal debt collection practices (IDCPs) can become abusive, harming both consumers and the economy by threatening consumers' physical, psychological, and economic wellbeing; exposing law-abiding debt collectors to unfair competition; undermining the financial system; and negatively impacting social peace by resorting to criminal activity. The need to control and harmonize IDCPs surfaced in connection with the European Commission's Action Plan to tackle the high level of non-performing loans caused by the financial crisis and the Covid-19 pandemic – specifically the Proposal for a Directive on Credit Servicers, Credit Purchasers, and the Recovery of Collateral (CSD). Harmonizing the regulation of abusive IDCPs is vital for several reasons. First, IDCPs have a cross-border dimension due to the freedom of movement, enabling debt collection operations across the internal market. Second, the internal market's size amounts to over 450 million citizens potentially exposed to abusive IDCPs. The regulatory frameworks addressing IDCPs in the E.U. display divergent characteristics that may be difficult to navigate and require creating a level-playing field for consumers and debt collectors, especially when approaches vary at Member State level. This book addresses this gap by providing a comprehensive guide to regulating informal debt collection practices in eight Member States of the E.U. and the United Kingdom (U.K.). It serves as a comparative law instrument for implementing the recently adopted CSD. It will be important reading for students, academics, and stakeholders with an interest in debt collection practices and the law.

Cătălin-Gabriel Stănescu is Associate Professor in Law at the Faculty of Business and Social Sciences, University of Southern Denmark.

Routledge Research in Finance and Banking Law

Regulation and the Global Financial Crisis
Impact, Regulatory Responses and Beyond
Daniel Cash and Robert Goddard

Vulnerable Consumers and Fair Access to Financial Services
Present and Future Challenges
Edited by Cătălin Gabriel Stănescu and Asress Adimi Gikay

The European Sovereign Debt Crisis
Breaking the Vicious Circle Between Sovereigns and Banks
Phoebus L. Athanassiou and Angelos T. Vouldis

Global Finance in the 21st Century
Stability and Sustainability in a Fragmenting World
Steve Kourabas

Banking Regulation in Africa
The Case of Nigeria and Other Emerging Economies
Folashade Adeyemo

Crypto-Finance, Law and Regulation
Governing an Emerging Ecosystem
Joseph Lee

Regulation and Governance of Mutual Funds
United Kingdom and United States of America Perspectives on Investor Protection
Mohammed Khair Alshaleel

Regulation of Debt Collection in Europe
Understanding Informal Debt Collection Practices
Cătălin-Gabriel Stănescu

The Regulation of Megabanks
Global Systemically Important Banks and their Legal Frameworks
Katarzyna M. Parchimowicz

For more information about this series, please visit: www.routledge.com/Routledge-Research-in-Finance-and-Banking-Law/book-series/FINANCIALLAW

Regulation of Debt Collection in Europe

Understanding Informal Debt Collection Practices

Edited by Cătălin-Gabriel Stănescu

Routledge
Taylor & Francis Group
LONDON AND NEW YORK

First published 2023
by Routledge
4 Park Square, Milton Park, Abingdon, Oxon OX14 4RN

and by Routledge
605 Third Avenue, New York, NY 10158

Routledge is an imprint of the Taylor & Francis Group, an informa business

British Library Cataloguing-in-Publication Data
A catalogue record for this book is available from the British Library

ISBN: 978-1-032-38033-9 (hbk)
ISBN: 978-1-032-38034-6 (pbk)
ISBN: 978-1-003-34315-8 (ebk)

DOI: 10.4324/9781003343158

Typeset in Times New Roman
by Deanta Global Publishing Services, Chennai, India

To my daughter, Alexandra

Contents

Contributors

Cătălin Gabriel Stănescu

Tibor Tajti

Paula Poretti

David Markworth

Eleni Kaprou

Karin Sein

Candida Leone

Joanna Van Duin

Jakub Kępiński

Albert Albanezi

Hajo Michael Holtz

Jodi Gardner

Mia Gray

Agnes Horvath

Acknowledgements

This book is the outcome of an international conference entitled 'Regulation of abusive informal debt collection practices – could the Scandinavian model serve as a model for EU regulation?' that took place in at the Faculty of Law, University of Copenhagen, Denmark, in September 2021 and concluded my Marie Curie Individual Fellowship. The aim of the conference was to contribute to the improvement of the legal base and regulation of IDCPs across the E.U. by sharing and discussing some of the existing regulatory models.

I would like to thank **all those who answered the call and actively participated in the presentations and discussions** in Copenhagen and made possible both the event and this book.

My appreciation goes to the **European Commission – Marie Curie Actions** and the **Carlsberg Foundation** for their generous support, their commitment to high-quality academic research, their flexibility and responsiveness. Without them, it would have been impossible to organize the conference, bring together the participants, record all presentations, and make them available for the wider public.

I express my gratitude to **Professor Caroline Heide-Jørgensen**, the Head of the **Center for Market and Economic Law (Faculty of Law University of Copenhagen)** for her and the Center's steady support throughout my Fellowship, and for endorsing, promoting, and hosting the conference.

Finally, a special acknowledgement goes to **Siobhan Poole**, from Routledge, for her support and assistance in turning this book into a reality.

I hope the book will prove interesting and will facilitate the exchange of ideas and understanding, foster meaningful discussions, and lead to inspired solutions for the benefit of all consumers and ethical businesses involved in debt collection.

Cătălin Gabriel Stănescu

Regulating informal debt collection in the European Union

An introduction

Cătălin-Gabriel Stănescu

0.1 Background: the adoption of the Directive on Credit Servicers and the need to regulate informal debt collection practices

The financial crisis left a deep scar on the European Union (E.U.)'s economy and the lives of E.U. citizens. The aftermath saw myriad regulatory interventions trying to ensure that the crisis and its devastating effects would not repeat. The E.U. institutions aimed at the causes and consequences of over-indebtedness, even if the measures adopted to tackle them were not always the most inspired. They emphasized restoring financial stability, profitability, and the viability of financial institutions. The financial crisis generated a significant number of non-performing debts or loans (NPLs), which led to a reduction in bank lending, negatively affecting economic growth.

In July 2017, the Council of the E.U. noted that banks in some Member States still had high ratios of NPLs. It further stressed the need for a comprehensive approach combining complementary policy actions to address the existing stocks of NPLs and the emergence or accumulation of new NPLs by banks. It urged the European Commission (EC) to develop a European approach to foster the development of secondary markets for NPLs while safeguarding consumers' rights.[1]

Several policy directions were highlighted to reduce the risk of new NPL problems in the future, focused on increasing the banks' capacity to enforce their debts swiftly and efficiently by resorting to self-help methods meant to avoid judicial enforcement procedures in the E.U. The latter were seen as excessively long and inefficient. Although non-judicial (out-of-court) proceedings are faster and cheaper alternatives to judicial (in-court) proceedings, they are heterogeneous or unavailable in all Member States, affecting cross-border recovery efforts.[2] Thus,

1 Council conclusions on Action plan to tackle non-performing loans in Europe (11 July 2017) para 1, 6, 8 <https://www.consilium.europa.eu/en/press/press-releases/2017/07/11/conclusions-non-performing-loans/> accessed 13 January 2020.

2 Directorate-General for Financial Stability, Financial Services and Capital Markets Union, 'Executive Summary of the Impact Assessment. The development of secondary markets for non-performing loans by removing undue impediments to loan servicing by third parties and the transfer

DOI: 10.4324/9781003343158-1

a minimum set of harmonized rules for out-of-court procedures was advocated as the solution to create a level playing field for banks and third-party investors across the E.U., who will then be able to operate under similar conditions across the E.U. through economies of scale.[3]

In March 2018, the EC presented a package of measures designed to address the risks related to high levels of NPLs in Europe, including a proposal for a Directive on Credit Servicers, Credit Purchasers, and the Recovery of Collateral (CSD).[4] In summary, the proposal aimed to foster the development of secondary markets for NPLs by harmonizing requirements and creating a single market for credit servicing and the transfer of bank loans to third parties across the E.U. It also defined the activities of credit servicers, set common standards for authorization and supervision, and imposed conduct rules across the E.U., thereby enabling debt purchasers to operate in the internal market without separate national authorization requirements.

Empirical evidence shows that when the European Council and EC discussed the need to develop the secondary market for NPLs, the market was already thriving in the E.U.'s legal void, based solely on national rules. In 2018, three debt-buying companies in the E.U. generated over 2 billion euro in profit from consumer NPL-related activities,[5] the most significant of which was debt collection.

At the time, in line with the E.U. legislators' approach after the financial crisis, consumer protection was expected to be ensured by transparency and minimalistic legal safeguards.[6] During the consultation, consumer groups asked for consumer loans to be excluded from the scope of the proposal, arguing that there are ways to address the NPL problem without endangering consumers in distress. Although not spelled out in clear language, their arguments revolved around the risk of abusive debt collection. BEUC, the European Consumer Organization, for instance, claimed that 'market actors who maximize their profits on the back of vulnerable consumers and businesses should not be supported, but should face restrictions instead.' Finance Watch took the argument further, arguing that an NPL secondary market could be a solution, 'provided it does not undermine credit standards or *lead to aggressive and inappropriate enforcement actions*' (emphasis added).[7] This concern encompassed the potential for abusive informal debt collection.

---

of loans (Part 1/2) And Accelerated Extrajudicial Collateral Enforcement (Part 2/2) Accompanying the document Proposal for a Directive of the European Parliament and of the Council on credit servicers, credit purchasers and the recovery of collateral' (*Commission Staff Working Document,* 14 March 2018) 1 <https://ec.europa.eu/transparency/documents-register/detail?ref=SWD(2018)76&lang=en> accessed 03 February 2022.

3 Ibid.

4 The original proposal is available at: <https://ec.europa.eu/transparency/documents-register/detail?ref=COM(2018)135&lang=en> accessed 03 February 2022.

5 See section 0.1.2.3.

6 Briefing of the European Parliament, Credit servicers, credit purchasers and the recovery of collateral, p. 7, available at: <https://www.europarl.europa.eu/RegData/etudes/BRIE/2019/635514/EPRS_BRI(2019)635514_EN.pdf> accessed 19 April 2022.

7 Ibid.

The consumer stakeholders noted but failed to clearly state that the market for NPLs is inextricably linked to debt-recovery activities, with an emphasis on non-judicial debt collection. NPLs make a growing market and attract investors due to their significant return opportunities. Companies purchasing NPLs expect to recover the debts that the credit institutions failed to recover, at a percentage higher than the price paid, to make a profit. The more they recover, the more profit they make, which may encourage debt collectors to engage in abusive practices. Because the Commission's proposal emphasized informal (out-of-court) collection, the absence of an adequate regulatory framework for out-of-court enforcement carried a significant risk of ill-treatment of debtors (especially consumers). Nevertheless, at the time, the E.U. did not consider the need to harmonize fair debt collection practices, increasing the likelihood that debt buyers and debt collectors would engage in unfair behavior towards debtors in their attempts to maximize profit.

Given the extent of the E.U. debt collection market and the potential negative impacts on consumers' lives, a more extensive level of consumer protection related to NPL purchases and the subsequent debt collection efforts that follow would be expected. Nevertheless, while the EC listed several regulatory instruments to suffer modifications due to the CSD proposal, none concerned the regulation of non-judicial debt collection. In the E.U., the problem is overseen heterogeneously by only a handful of Member States.[8] In most of them, debt buyers and debt collectors operate in a quasi-complete legal void, where protection can be sought only in the traditional remedies offered by civil, administrative, or criminal law.

The need to regulate and harmonize abusive IDCPs at the E.U. level resurfaced in 2020, following the impact of the Covid-19 pandemic. Several Members of the European Parliament (MEPs) advanced amendments to the CSD proposal to tackle abusive IDCPs.[9] The amendments contained detailed provisions targeting most known abusive IDCPs but have faced criticism for lacking justification.[10] Given the differences between the original *pro-creditor* approach of the CSD proposal and the *consumer-friendly* stance of the European Parliament, on 28 June 2021, the Council of the E.U. (2021) announced its endorsement of a compromise

8 According to a survey conducted by the author in 2019–2020, which collected data from 28 Member States and Norway, only nine of the 27 E.U. Member States have sector-specific legislation concerning the regulation of fair debt collection practices: Belgium, Denmark, Germany, Greece, Finland, the Netherlands, Portugal, Romania, and Sweden. However, these vary significantly in length and coverage. Cătălin-Gabriel Stănescu, 'Regulation of Abusive Debt Collection Practices in the EU Member States: An Empirical Account' (2021) 44 Journal of Consumer Policy.

9 Committee on Economic and Monetary Affairs, 'Draft Report 2018/0063A (COD)' (*European Parliament*, 2020) amendments 204–468.

10 Michael Huertas and Holger Schelling, 'European Union: The EU's new credit servicers directive – Where are we now' (Mondaq, 19 March 2020) <https://www.mondaq.com/germany/dodd-frank-consumerprotection-act/904974/the-eu39s-new-credit-servicers-directive-where-are-we-now> accessed 20 December 2020.

text of the CSD that included only a condensed version of the amendments.[11] The CSD was adopted in November 2021 and became the first pan-E.U. instrument expressly tackling abusive IDCPs.

These recent developments highlight that E.U. harmonization of abusive IDCP regulation might become a reality in a couple of years.[12] However, the adoption of the CSD and its envisioned national transposition raises two issues that must be addressed. On the one hand, the CSD lacks details on how IDCP regulation can be harmonized. Its minimal approach transfers the task to the Member States, which will have to develop national solutions – an obvious obstacle to harmonization efforts. On the other hand, the experience of Member States that already implemented sector-specific regulation and the challenges faced by those that did not have more significance for knowledge sharing and regulatory design. However, these often remain obscured due to language barriers or little interest in the topic.

The book's primary aim is to help overcome these obstacles by juxtaposing several national experiences from current and former E.U. Member States. Most of the covered jurisdictions (e.g., Greece, Germany, the Netherlands, Romania, Sweden, and the U.K.) have regulated IDCPs, albeit to various extents. In contrast, the others (e.g., Croatia, Estonia, Poland) continue to rely on traditional remedies. As the ensuing chapters reveal, the regulatory models vary in approach and coverage. Germany treats informal debt collection not as credit servicing but as legal servicing by non-lawyers. Its concern remains primarily vested in protecting the interests of the clients (the creditors resorting to such services), while consumer protection is more of a side effect. Greece deems debt collection taboo, and credit-servicing activities are referred to as information services about debt. Sweden and the U.K. have achieved a certain level of maturity, combining detailed hard and soft law provisions, while Romania and the Netherlands (still) struggle to find a functioning formula. Nevertheless, these heterogeneous examples are representative and amply valid for any other E.U. jurisdiction looking for answers.

The Introduction serves three purposes, addressed in separate sections. The first clarifies the concepts and terminology used throughout the book regarding informal (non-judicial) debt collection. The next one addresses the most common themes arising from the country reports and national experiences gathered. The final section briefly outlines each contribution before providing conclusions.

0.2 What is informal (non-judicial) debt collection?

Debt collection has been an issue of concern throughout human history, including before the emergence of capitalism as we know it, because of its indelible

11 The latest version of the CSD is available at <https://eur-lex.europa.eu/legal-content/EN/TXT/PDF/?uri=CELEX:32021L2167&from=EN> accessed 03 February 2022.

12 CSD art 32. See also Cătălin-Gabriel Stănescu, 'A Critical Assessment of the Need for Harmonization of the Legal Framework Concerning Abusive Informal Debt Collection Practices in the European Union' (2021) 44 Journal of Consumer Policy.

connection to commerce, markets, and credit.[13] As a business, it has thrived on coercion, violence, and abuse. In Europe, evidence thereof goes back to the Roman Empire,[14] which used to 'outsource' its debt collection to public companies (*societas publicanorum*) who purchased state claims and resorted to non-judicial means to recover them.[15] Consequently, the first rules to protect debtors from abusive debt collection practices also emerged in Ancient Rome.[16]

Debt collection continued throughout the Middle Ages, an era deeply characterized by the employment of self-help mechanisms[17] like those advertised by the EC's 2018 CSD proposal. As emphasized by historical studies, creditors looking for repayment

> did not have to seek the services of the court ... they simply walked into the houses of their debtors and took all that they fancied, daring their victims to do something about it ... [W]hatever the frequency, the mere existence of the practice is a reminder that debt collection ... was hardly a monopoly of the courts of law ... The process was swift and unfussy. It may have been deeply satisfying as well.[18]

Such historical evidence is not singular and shows that the forms of economic coercion encountered today – predatory lending, payday loans, repossession of movable property or houses, evictions, the large body of repo men and debt-collection agencies – are well anchored in the past.[19] The only thing that seems to have changed is how far private debt collection can go when it comes to the physical person of the debtor.[20]

0.2.1 Informal and formal debt collection

Given the plethora of existent terms and the differences stemming from their usage in various jurisdictions, the book opts for a harmonized terminology.

13 Daniel Lord Smail, *Legal Plunder: Households and Debt Collection in Late Medieval Europe* (Harvard University Press 2016) 13.

14 Cătălin-Gabriel Stănescu, *Self-Help, Private Debt Collection and the Concomitant Risks. A Comparative Law Analysis* (Springer 2015) 17.

15 Juan Javier Del Granado, 'The genius of Roman Law from a Law and Economics Perspective' (2011) 13 San Diego International Law Journal 322.

16 Hanina Ben-Menahem and Neil S. Hecht, *Selected Topics in Jewish Law Vol 6* (1st edn, The Open University of Israel Publishing House 1993) 648.

17 For details, see Stănescu 2015 (note 14) 18–19; Celia R. Taylor, 'Self-Help in Contract Law: An Exploration and Proposal' (1998) 33 Wake Forest Law Review 1998; Douglas Ivor Brandon and others, 'SPECIAL PROJECT. Self-Help: Extrajudicial Rights, Privileges and Remedies in Contemporary American Society' (1984) 37 Vanderbilt Law Review 853.

18 Smail 2016 (note 13) 137.

19 Smail 2016 (note 13) 14.

20 Joe Deville, *Lived Economies of Default: Consumer Credit, Debt Collection and the Capture of Affect* (Taylor and Francis 2015) 80–81.

To this end, this section will discuss and define these terms to avoid potential misunderstandings.

When faced with unpaid debt, the aggrieved creditor enjoys a choice: to collect the debt themself or address the courts and seek the help of the state's apparatus.[21] Based on this choice, the debt collection process can be divided into two categories depending on whether state agents are involved or not. The first category, which constitutes the book's focus, is informal (non-judicial) debt collection, while the second category is formal (judicial) debt collection.[22] It should be noted that although the two categories are easily distinguishable, they are intertwined and often used in conjunction, as several chapters emphasize.

Informal debt collection is also known as '*non-judicial*' or '*private*' collection in the US[23] or '*extra-judicial*' recovery in some E.U. Member States.[24] Other terms used in connection with informal debt collection are '*amicable recovery*' or '*soft collection.*'[25] Notwithstanding this difference, the terms are synonymous as they cover the same phenomenon and refer to the same type of practices. Consequently, they can be used interchangeably. To illustrate, in the U.S., Spanogle refers to informal collection as 'the processes a creditor might use before going to court.'[26] At the same time, in the E.U., Advocate General Maduro defined extra-judicial debt recovery as 'any act or practice which is intended to encourage a debtor to settle an unpaid debt, with the exception of any recovery on the basis of an enforcement order.'[27]

Therefore, informal debt collection usually involves attempts to extract payment from the debtor by convincing or pressuring them. As I show in the following section, the line between permissible and impermissible pressure is relatively thin.

The classical methods used by debt collectors are letters, phone calls, and house calls.[28] Still, technological advancements have enabled them to utilize computers, social media, SMS, emails, or software in their activity.[29] Most of these methods are means of communication for reaching and convincing the debtor to

21 Smail 2016 (note 13) 137.

22 Stănescu 2015 (note 14) 196.

23 John A. Spanogle and others, *Consumer law : cases and materials* (4th edn, West Academic Publishing 2013) 747.

24 See *Commission v. Italy*, Opinion of Advocate General Poiares Maduro (OAG Maduro 2006) (14 December 2006) para 4 <https://curia.europa.eu/juris/showPdf.jsf?docid=64724&doclang=EN> accessed on 03 February 2022.

25 Deville 2015 (note 20) 143.

26 Spanogle 2013 (note 23) 747.

27 OAG Maduro 2006 (note 24) para 4 n 2. In defining extra-judiciary debt recovery, Maduro used the wording of the Belgian law of 20 December 2002 on the amicable recovery of consumer debts.

28 Spanogle 2013 (note 23) 747; Stănescu 2015 (note 14) 197.

29 Deville 2015 (note 20) 112. Deville provides extensive evidence that debt collection has been one of the most innovative businesses, employing not only digitalization but also studies in psychology and behaviorism (ibid 81–101).

repay the debt (in part or whole) or agree to a repayment schedule that might erase or settle it.[30]

The outcome of the communication is binary: successful or unsuccessful. In the latter case, the creditor will have to pursue formal debt collection or dispose of the debt by selling or assigning it to a debt purchaser who will assume all the risks associated with its recovery. As most chapters reveal, selling off non-performing debts on primary and secondary markets is a very lucrative business in the E.U., with figures amounting to billions of euros.

Formal debt collection is also known as '*judicial*,' '*litigation*,' or '*hard*' collection, mainly because the enforcement of a defaulted debt will be performed by or benefit from the backing of state authorities. These are bailiffs or sheriffs, who will either act upon the enforcement order issued by a court or enjoy such power under the law. Theoretically, this method provides the creditor and the debtor with guarantees of due process and fairness because potential 'violence' will be sanctioned by and within the boundaries of the law.

The formal venue may lack efficiency and helpfulness: proceedings can be lengthy, costly, pointless (if the value of the claim is significantly lower than the expenses incurred), and risky because any adverse outcome may result in the complete loss of the claim.[31] These aspects were also listed in the EC's 2018 CSD proposal among the reasons for promoting self-help enforcement mechanisms across the E.U., albeit, for the moment, only in business-to-business (B2B) relationships. Nevertheless, debt collectors have also learned to use and abuse the judicial venue – especially the fast-track procedure for small claims – as several chapters of this book highlight.

I will not delve more into formal debt collection since it is not within the scope of this book. Suffice to say, informal debt collection is not exclusively an alternative to judicial collection or a pre-judicial phase; in some cases, depending on the circumstances of the claim, it might be the only viable option.

0.2.2 In-house and outsourced informal debt collection

The choice between informal and formal venues is not the only one that the creditor faces. If they resort to informal means, the immediate question is whether to attempt the collection themself (personal collection) or outsource the collection process (third-party collection). Each option requires additional clarification.

Personal/in-house non-judicial debt collection means that the creditor (a natural or legal person) attempts to collect the debt independently. Two legal issues emerge. On the one hand, in an unregulated environment (such as most E.U. Member States), the absence of rules may lead the creditor to cross the thin boundary between fair and abusive debt collection. Moreover, in an unregulated environment, any method may appear abusive (giving rise to disputes), and many

30 Spanogle 2013 (note 23) 752.
31 Stănescu 2015 (note 14) 200–201; Spanogle 2013 (note 23) 474.

cases of abuse could be left unsanctioned depending on where the involved parties stand. On the other hand, even in regulated environments, the original creditors might escape liability due to improper drafting, regulatory gaps, or institutional overlaps.

Outsourced non-judicial debt collection means that the creditor resorts to the services of a third party to recoup the entirety or part of the debt. As mentioned, the outsourcing of debt collection has been used throughout history. Nevertheless, the past 50 years have turned outsourced debt recovery into a multibillion-euro business[32] taking multiple forms.

0.2.2.1 Outsourcing debt collection

In most cases, original creditors collect the debt in-house via their agents or employees.[33] Should such efforts prove unsuccessful, or the creditor not wish to use their resources for debt collection, they can hire a professional. What characterizes this option is that the legal *ownership* of the debt remains with the original creditor. Whether the debt occurs in business to consumer (B2C) or business to business (B2B) relationships is irrelevant.

Third parties can be collection agencies or law firms with debt collection as their principal or regular business.[34] Such companies operate on a contingency fee (i.e. they will be paid from the amounts they recover), which can reach 30% of the face value of the debt.[35] Such contingency-based debt recovery services are present in the U.K.[36] and E.U. Member States (e.g., Denmark, Romania, and Spain).[37]

0.2.2.2 Factoring

The creditor may employ the services of a factor. By definition, factoring is a continuing legal relationship (sale of goods or provision of services) between a financial institution (the factor) and a business concern (the obligor) whereby the

32 Lauren Goldberg, 'Dealing in Debt: The High-Stakes World of Debt Collection after FDCPA' (2006) 79 Southern California Law Review 725–729.

33 Judith L. Fox, 'Do We Have a Debt Collection Crisis? Some Cautionary Tales of Debt Collection in Indiana' (2012) 24 Loyola Consumer Law Review 357 <http://ssrn.com/abstract=2023829>.

34 The inclusion of lawyers in the definition varies from jurisdiction to jurisdiction. For instance, they are deemed debt collectors by the U.S. Fair Debt Collection Practices Act (FDCPA), but not under French, German, or Romanian law.

35 Fox 2012 (note 33) 357.

36 Deville 2015 (note 20) 113.

37 The Swedish debt collection conglomerate Intrum offers 'no cure, no pay' debt collection services for a commission payable only when and if the debt has been recovered. Based on the information available on the local websites of Intrum, contingency fee-based services are available in Denmark <https://www.intrum.dk/services/vores-services/priser/laes-mere-om-no-risk/>, Romania <https://www.intrum.ro/solutii-business/recuperare-creante/servicii-colectare-creante/>, and Spain <https://www.intrum.es/soluciones-empresariales/servicios/servicios-de-gestion-de-credito/> accessed 7 July 2020.

factor purchases the obligor's account receivables with or without recourse to the obligor and controls the credit extended to the customers (including the debt collection) and administers the sales ledger.[38] Whether ownership passes or not to the factor from the obligor is for the parties to decide and depends on the type of factoring chosen (and risks undertaken). However, beyond doubt, when the client retains ownership of the account receivables and only pays commissions to the factors, the latter are not performing factoring services but mere debt-collection services.

One specificity of factoring is the triadic relationship, in which all parties are supposed to be professional, active players in commerce.[39] This would appear to exclude consumer debts incurred by individuals in their private capacity.[40] Nevertheless, as I have already shown elsewhere, the circumstances that justified the exclusion of consumer debt have changed, and the bulk sale of such debt (e.g., uncollected parking tickets or electricity bills) is currently standard practice.[41]

Moreover, the option of factoring cannot be ignored when considering non-judicial debt collection because of a phenomenon I have labeled *pseudo*-factoring.[42] Empirical evidence demonstrates that factoring is used as a cover for debt collection services due to blurred lines between actual and *pseudo*-factoring or the exploitation of regulatory gaps. The inherent connection and overlap between factoring and debt collection has been amply discussed in two CJEU cases:[43] *Finanzamt Groß-Gerau v. MKG-Kraftfahrzeuge-Factory GmbH* (C-305/01)[44] and *Revenue and Customs Commissioners v. AXA UK Plc* (C-175/09).[45] Romanian case law also provides several examples of debt collection agencies posing as 'factors,' which were precluded from recovering consumer debt. The reason was their non-compliance with the legal requirements for factors (who

38 Peter M. Biscoe, *Law and Practice of Credit Factoring* (1st edn, Butterworths 1975) 3. This definition is consistent with the more restrictive definition of factoring accepted in the U.S.: 'a continuing arrangement between a factoring concern and a seller of goods or services on open accounts, pursuant to which the factor performs the following services with respect to the accounts receivable arising from sales of such goods and services: purchases all accounts receivable for immediate cash, maintains the ledgers and performs other book-keeping duties, collects the accounts receivable, assumes the losses which may arise from the customer's financial inability to pay.' Noel Ruddy and others, *Salinger on Factoring* (4th edn, Sweet & Maxwell 2006) 1–2.

39 Stănescu 2015 (note 14) 165.

40 Ruddy and others 2006 (note 38) 2; Biscoe 1975 (note 38) 29.

41 Stănescu 2015 (note 14) 166.

42 Ibid 167–172.

43 For an analysis of the two decisions, see ibid 168–170.

44 Judgment available at <https://eur-lex.europa.eu/legal-content/EN/TXT/PDF/?uri=CELEX:62001CJ0305&from=EN> accessed 8 January 2020.

45 Judgment available at <http://curia.europa.eu/juris/document/document.jsf;jsessionid=75809E49557586D2A421D4C3A22027CE?text=&docid=83554&pageIndex=0&doclang=en&mode=lst&dir=&occ=first&part=1&cid=6533514> accessed 8 January 2020.

could be only a bank or financial institution authorized and supervised by the Romanian National Bank).[46]

The existence of such anomalies raises two relevant issues for the topic of this book. First, factors or unlicensed businesses might collect a consumer debt by taking advantage of the lack of sector-specific debt collection legislation. In this case, the potential for abuse is significant because rogue agencies elude supervision and control. Second, if supervisory bodies tolerate debt collection agencies that perform unsupervised collection services without proper authorization, legitimate and ethical businesses are exposed to unfair competition. These two reasons justify adopting sector-specific regulation against unfair informal debt collection practices and appear to have convinced the E.U. to insist on a thorough authorization procedure for credit servicers via the CSD.[47]

0.2.2.3 Assignment of debt

The creditor can also assign or sell the debt, individually or in a bundle (portfolio) of non-performing debts. Legal ownership of the debt will pass, together with the title, from the original to the subsequent creditor. As with the first option, it does not matter whether the transferred debts arise from B2C or B2B relationships unless there is specific regulatory differentiation between the two.

Previously, delinquent debts were bundled in portfolios and sold at a bargain price only after collection (attempted in-house or via hired contingency-collection agencies) had failed.[48] The moment of the sale is no longer relevant. The buyers are either debt collection conglomerates –such as the E.U.-based Intrum,[49] EOS,[50]

46 See, for instance, Civil Decision No. 2509/05.03.2009, available in Romanian at <http://portal.just.ro/281/Lists/Jurisprudenta/DispForm.aspx?ID=32> accessed 8 January 2020.

47 CSD (fn 1) recital 9, arts 4–9.

48 In the U.S., empirical evidence shows that prices vary across geographical areas due to requirements of the FDCPA and different state laws. Fox 2012 (note 33) 357.

49 The Sweden-based group Intrum offers purchases of non-performing receivables portfolios <https://www.intrum.com/about-us/business-solutions/debt-collection-services/> that encompass a minimum of 300 written-off cases. The (non-exhaustive) list of E.U. countries where the group engages in acquisition of debt portfolios includes Belgium <https://www.intrum.be/fr/business-solutions/services/debt-sales/>, the Czech Republic <https://www.intrum.cz/nabidka-pro-klienty/sluzby/sluzby-vymahani-pohledavek/>, Denmark <https://www.intrum.dk/services/vores-services/kob-af-fordringer/>, France <https://www.intrum.fr/solutions-entreprises/services/acquisition-de-creances/>, Germany <https://www.intrum.de/business-losungen/unsere-losungen/npl-kredi-tankauf-servicing/>, Hungary <https://www.intrum.hu/szolgaltatasaink-cegeknek/uzleti-meg-bizoknak/portfolio-vasarlas/>, Poland <https://www.intrum.pl/partner-biznesowy/uslugi/kupno-wierzytelnosci/>, Romania <https://www.intrum.ro/solutii-business/recuperare-creante/achizitie-portofolii-neperformante/>, and Slovakia <https://www.intrum.sk/klienti-firemne-riesenia/nase-sluzby/odkupenie-pohladavok/> accessed 7 January 2020.

50 The Germany-based EOS Group also offers purchases of debt portfolios. See, for instance, the group's presentation in Belgium <https://es.eos-solutions.com/services.html#adquisicindedeu-das>, Denmark <https://dk.eos-solutions.com/en/?ls=1>, Germany <https://eos-deutschland.de/>, Greece <https://gr.eos-solutions.com/en/services.html#debtpurchase>, Hungary <https://hu.eos

or Kruk[51] – or investment companies and speculators looking to make a quick and hefty profit.[52]

Debt buyers acquire portfolios of receivables consisting of claims against debtors, which can be valuable if their debt collection efforts generate greater revenue than the price paid for acquisition combined with the cost of the actual collection.[53]

As mentioned, the E.U. debt purchase and debt collection markets amount to billions of euros yearly. In 2018, the Swedish group Intrum spent SEK 12 billion (approximately EUR 1.2 billion) on purchasing portfolios of overdue receivables,[54] with a return of 15%.[55] In 2019, the German group EOS announced a EUR 668 million investment in receivables and real estate and reported an increase in earnings (before interest, tax, depreciation, and amortization) of EUR 283.6 million for 2018–2019, stemming mainly from purchases of unsecured and secured debt portfolios.[56] The Polish group Kruk's reported figures are no less impressive: in the first three quarters of 2019, the company spent PLN 392 million (approximately EUR 86 million) on debt portfolios with a nominal value of PLN 4.022 billion (approximately EUR 884 million) and recovered PLN 1.307 billion (approximately EUR 287 million).[57]

While non-exhaustive, the amounts spent on the purchase of debt portfolios and the profits generated by only three E.U. companies engaged in such investments and debt collection activities provide a clear image of the industry's size and economic importance. They also reflect its impact on the lives of consumer debtors and businesses.[58] The industry grew in size as a result of the spread of

-solutions.com/services.html#bd5c8443-4786-4fe6-b171-17bacd05c985>, Poland <https://pl.eos-solutions.com/en/services.html#debtpurchase>, Romania <https://ro.eos-solutions.com/en/>, Spain <https://es.eos-solutions.com/services.html#adquisicindedeudas>, and the U.K. <https://uk.eos-solutions.com/services.html#debtpurchase> accessed 7 January 2020.

51 The Poland-based group Kruk also actively engages in acquisition of NPL portfolios. According to the information presented on its homepage, Kruk has acquired 499 NPLs in 2016, amounting to 5.6 million cases, totaling PLN 35 billion, and consisting mostly of banking and non-banking financial products <https://en.kruk.eu/business-partners/offer> accessed 7 January 2020.

52 Rick Jurgens and Robert J. Hobbs, 'The Debt Machine: How the Collection Industry Hounds Consumers and Overwhelms Courts' (*National Consumer Law Center*, 2010) 18 <http://www.nclc.org/images/pdf/pr-reports/debt-machine.pdf>.

53 Stănescu 2015 (note 14) 194.

54 Intrum, '2018 Report' (*Intrum*, 2018) 13 <https://www.intrum.com/media/5068/intrum_asr_2018_en.pdf> accessed 7 July 2020.

55 Ibid 49.

56 'EOX Group once again increases revenue and profit' (EOS Group, 18 July 2019) <https://www.eos-solutions.com/Pool-Pressreleases.html?id=5ab0abeb-9d4b-4aad-b22a-1f22024cd763> accessed 7 January 2020.

57 EOS, 'Report No. 47/2019: Expenditure on and recoveries from debt portfolios' (*EOS*, 2019) <https://en.kruk.eu/investor-relations/reports/current-reports/current-report-no-47-2019-expenditure-on-and-recoveries-from-debt-portfolios> accessed 7 January 2020.

58 An additional commonality of the abovementioned companies is their significant engagement and profits in Central and Eastern E.U. Member States, which can be explained by the absence or inadequacy of regulations.

consumer credit in the E.U., the 2008 financial crisis, and the Covid-19 pandemic, which increased the number of defaults in consumer loans (NPLs).[59]

Since investors and speculators are naturally interested in maximizing profit, the likelihood of debt collectors resorting to unfair or abusive practices to boost their returns is high. In other words, the industry might engage in regulatory arbitrage. It could favor focusing its business on areas with little or no sector-specific legislation or weak and inexperienced supervisory institutions, where debt collectors can escape liability in case of abuse. As exemplified by the chapter dedicated to the Netherlands, regulatory overlook can facilitate opportunistic behavior.

The latest legislative developments reveal that the debt purchase industry has grown sufficiently to attract the attention of E.U. institutions. The CSD proposal aimed to increase the efficiency of debt-recovery procedures and encourage the development of secondary markets for NPLs.[60] The problem, however, was to implement adequate consumer protection related to informal debt collection. The 2020 amendments to the CSD would have provided clear and thorough guidance on how to tackle abusive IDCPs. Unfortunately, the final version – a compromise text – adopted only minimal rules and left the task of developing them to the Member States.

0.3 Policy considerations and common themes concerning informal debt collection

In the previous section, I showed that the debt collection industry has been expanding and developing continuously, fueled by the devastating effects of the financial crisis and the recent Covid-19 pandemic on consumer financial resilience. Devious and abusive collection practices have emerged, particularly harassment, deception, and threats.

Creditors expect to be paid, and debt collection is a legitimate business. However, this does not mean that interested parties (creditors, subsequent creditors, or their agents) do not resort to any means to recover their debts. The creditors' expectation to be paid must be balanced with that of consumers to be treated fairly and protected from abuse. The adequate solution to achieve such balance is to regulate abusive debt collection practices via sector-specific legislation. The absence of dedicated rules or reliance on traditional remedies opens the door to unfair and opportunistic behavior.

In 1974, Sweden and the U.K. were among the first in Europe to implement sector-specific IDCP regulations, namely, the Swedish Inkassolag (Swedish Debt Collection Act) and the Consumer Credit Act 1974 (CCA 1974), with subsequent

59 Andrea Enria, 'ECB: the EU needs a regional "bad bank"' (Financial Times, 26 October 2020) <https://www.ft.com/content/cc3a9a51-4d9a-4c73-9ff0-9f623ecf4065> accessed 12 February 2021.

60 Proposal for a Directive of the European Parliament and of the Council on credit servicers, credit purchasers and the recovery of collateral, Brussels, 14.3.2018, COM(2018) 135 final, 2018/0063 (COD) (CSD proposal) <https://eur-lex.europa.eu/legal-content/EN/TXT/PDF/?uri=CELEX:52018PC0135&from=EN> accessed 7 January 2020.

amendments. Two main policy goals lay at their foundation: (a) protecting consumers from egregious debt-collection practices and (b) protecting ethical and licensed debt collectors from competitive disadvantages caused by rogue businesses engaging in unfair practices.

Nevertheless, the E.U. did not implement sector-specific legislation dedicated strictly to informal debt collection, and neither did most of its Member States. To date, two-thirds of E.U. Member States lack sector-specific IDCP rules, and more than half do not provide for any oversight or vetting procedures (via authorization, licensing, or fitness tests).[61] On the one hand, these numbers are staggering considering that the general policies stated in either the E.U.'s primary legislation (i.e., the fundamental treaties) or secondary legislation (i.e., regulations and directives) emphasize consumer protection and fair competition. On the other hand, the cross-border dimension of the E.U.'s internal market should raise concerns regarding cross-border trade, the adequate performance of services, and the protection of fair competition between service providers.

The question of why sector-specific regulation concerning IDCPs is absent in most Member States is apparent. One explanation could be that national legislatures do not see sufficient justification for adopting sectorial legislation because the traditional (civil, criminal, or administrative) remedies and EU consumer protection laws are deemed adequate to tackle any abuse. This appears to be the situation in Poland. Other possible reasons include lack of political will, regulatory blindness, regulatory capture, regulatory failure, financial lobbying, and the gravity of the perceived abuses. The multitude of approaches adopted by the existing legislation also indicates that local considerations may impact which regulatory model is chosen.

Nevertheless, common themes, widespread abusive practices, and potential solutions exist. The chapters in this book attest that informal debt collection is an E.U.-wide phenomenon, accompanied by numerous accounts of abusive practices, some more prominent than others. In other words, all covered jurisdictions acknowledge that a problem exists and needs to be addressed adequately. Thus, the national reports are consistent with the current state of the art and the empirical findings I published in 2021.[62]

0.3.1 Scope and coverage of informal debt collection laws; the parallel use of the UCPD

A major question is to determine who is to be subjected to informal debt collection regulation. Most jurisdictions that implement sector-specific legislation (e.g., Romania, Sweden, the U.K.) seem to agree that the more comprehensive the coverage, the better. Even so, contentious issues remain, especially regarding two categories of debt collectors: lawyers and public entities.

61 Stănescu 2021 (note 13).
62 Stănescu 2021 (note 13).

Lawyers are a complicated category, mainly because they are already regulated by specific legislation, subject to their own authorization procedure, supervisory bodies, and codes of ethics, which require them to behave lawfully. Nevertheless, this should not preclude the application of sector-specific legislation tackling IDPCs to lawyers. Although, generally, lawyers should not be required to obtain additional authorization to undertake debt collection operations, observing sector-specific rules would only add specificity and clarity to their activities. Failure to subject them to a unique set of rules tackling abusive debt collection would create further problems (as exemplified by the situation in Greece).

The absence of public entities is also problematic because it raises the question of a possible double standard of behavior. Are public entities allowed to abuse citizens merely because the former collect for the budget and the latter do not qualify as consumers? The issue is present in some covered jurisdictions (e.g., the Netherlands, Sweden, and the U.K.) and was publicly addressed by debt collection industry representatives.[63] A potential explanation could be that public entities are obligated to act fairly, in the interest of the citizens, and fall under public scrutiny. Their activities may already be subjected to detailed procedures (such as procedure codes); however, this should not absolve them from observing rules designed purposefully for debt-collection practices. The suggestion that a single regime should apply to all categories of debt concerning individuals acting outside their profession is not without merit.

Another aspect highlighted by the country reports concerns the role played by the UCPD in addressing unfair debt collection practices. Poland and the Netherlands apply the UCPD for this purpose, while most of the jurisdictions covered (e.g., Croatia, Estonia, Greece, Romania, and Sweden) do not.

Relying on the UCPD in this context is curious. In the case of Poland, resorting to the UCPD is motivated by the absence of sector-specific legislation. However, Estonia and Croatia do not follow suit even though they are in a similar situation, which reinforces the idea that the directive's impact on abusive IDCPs is marginal.[64]

Alternatively, the UCPD enables Member States to implement more stringent rules prohibiting unfair practices related to financial services. Sweden has maintained its sector-specific legislation, which is better suited to tackling abusive IDCPs. Thus, while the UCPD and sector-specific legislation are not mutually exclusive, MS with tailor-made rules for informal debt collection seldom use the UCPD.

63 Claus Spedtsberg (President of the Federation of European National Collection Associations), Keynote Address at the International Conference 'Regulation of Abusive Informal Debt Collection Practices: Could the Scandinavian Model Serve as a Model for EU Regulation?' (2021).

64 Cătălin-Gabriel Stănescu, 'Is the Unfair Commercial Practices Directive Fit to Effectively Tackle Abusive Debt Collection?' (2020) Journal of European Consumer and Market Law.

0.3.2 Authorization systems

There is considerable agreement that some form of prior verification and state supervision to identify rogue or unprofessional debt collectors is needed. This position is supported by contributors from Member States that have implemented sector-specific legislation concerning abusive IDCPs and authorization rules (e.g., Germany, Greece, Romania, Sweden, and the U.K.) and from Member States that did not (e.g., Croatia, Estonia, the Netherlands, and Poland). This broad consensus reflects the fact that authorization is one of the building blocks of effective IDCP regulation, as I suggested in 2015.

A further confirmation stems from the CSD's detailed provisions dedicated to the authorization of credit servicers (including debt collectors), by which the EU wants to harmonize the procedure. In truth, the harmonization of authorization has more to do with market functionality and the EC's desire to remove national obstacles and avoid duplicating administrative burdens for credit servicers.[65] Nevertheless, its effects remain the same, namely, the elimination of potentially dangerous businesses and the creation of the premise for adequate state supervision and control.[66]

0.3.3 Common abusive informal debt collection practices; the role of courts

According to the contributions gathered in this book, the most common complaints concern infringements of the debtor's privacy, the artificial inflation of the debt, and the collection of time-barred debt. Abusing the court system to obtain enforcement titles against consumers also appears to be a widespread practice.

Violations of privacy can take many forms, such as the public disclosure of the debtor's status or public stigmatization. The implementation of data protection rules at the EU level seems to have benefited aggrieved consumer debtors affected by such abusive practices, especially in Member States without sector-specific legislation (e.g., Croatia, Estonia, Poland) but not only (e.g., Greece and Sweden). Besides the competent authorities, courts have played an instrumental role in ensuring compliance with personal data protection rules.

The artificial inflation of the debt remains widespread, even in Member States with sector-specific rules. The contributors from Estonia, Germany, the Netherlands, and Sweden underscore that the existing legal framework is unsatisfactory in curbing excessive fees, which only increase the debtor's financial burden and are too high in relation to the effort put into collection. Thus, more adequate solutions remain to be found.

Collecting time-barred debt is contentious because E.U. legal systems take different stances towards it. One thing is certain: time-barred debt cannot be

65 CSD (fn 1) recitals 13, 23.
66 Ibid recitals 27, art 5.

enforced via formal debt collection using the state apparatus. However, there is no agreement as to whether it can still be collected via informal means. Member States such as Sweden have clearly stated that time-barred debt can no longer be recovered. However, some of the surveyed Member States seem to share the opinion that if the debtor is convinced to repay or revive the debt via informal debt collection, the payment or revival is valid (e.g., Poland, Romania).

The use of summary proceedings to obtain an enforcement title is also reported (e.g., in Croatia, Estonia, and the Netherlands). E.U. debt collectors seem to have learned how to use the court system to speed up collection when the debtor fails to contest the debt or make an appearance, which tends to blur the lines between informal and formal debt collection. This enables debt collectors to pressure consumers into settlements but may also result in the artificial inflation of the debt due to the European principle of 'the loser pays the costs.'

Once again, the courts have become instrumental in curbing this practice, especially after the CJEU ruled that the European Enforcement Order cannot be certified unless debt collectors and creditors observe the minimum procedural requirements set[67] and enabled national courts to apply consumer-protection measures *ex officio*.

0.3.4 Enforcement and institutional approaches

In the aftermath of the financial crisis, the EC reemphasized the need to protect consumers in its European Consumer Agenda.[68] Among other issues, the EC noted that many problems faced by consumers are not remedied because consumers do not act, mainly when the sums involved are small. Moreover, the enforcement of consumer rights was found to be hampered in cross-border situations.[69] The EC also stressed the importance of the financial services sector, but without considering the issue of abusive debt-collection services.[70] On the contrary, the UCPD, which covered some unfair debt-collection practices,[71] provided no right of action to individual consumers[72] until the adoption of the New Deal for Consumers.[73]

67 Case C-289/2017 *Collect Inkasso OU, ITM Inkasso OU, Bigbank AS v. Rain Aint, Lauri Palm, Raiko Oikimus, Egle Noor, Artjom Konjarov*.

68 European Commission, Communication on A European Consumer Agenda – Boosting Confidence and Growth, Brussels, COM (2012)225, 22 May 2012 <https://eur-lex.europa.eu/legal-content/EN/TXT/PDF/?uri=CELEX:52012DC0225&from=EN> accessed 15 January 2020.

69 Ibid 6.

70 Ibid 7.

71 UCPD recital 13. See also European Commission, Note on Guidance on the interpretation and application of Directive 2005/29/EC of the European Parliament and of the Council concerning unfair business-to-consumer commercial practices in the internal market (2021/C526/01) section 0.2.3.1 <https://eur-lex.europa.eu/legal-content/EN/TXT/PDF/?uri=CELEX:52021XC1229(05)&from=EN> accessed 3 February 2022.

72 Howells Geraint and others, *Rethinking EU Consumer Law* (Taylor and Francis 2017) 84.

73 Directive (EU) 2019/2161 regarding the better enforcement and modernisation of Union consumer protection rules.

There is broad agreement among legal professionals that laws without adequate enforcement mechanisms and effective remedies are nothing but words on paper. This is even truer when seeking to tackle abusive IDCPs, where the amounts involved are usually small and consumers lack the incentive to fight back against abusive behavior. The 2021 version of the CSD now urges Member States to implement administrative penalties and remedial measures against credit servicers (including debt collectors) that are 'effective, proportionate and dissuasive' and ensure that penalties and remedial measures are 'effectively implemented'[74] at the national and E.U. levels.[75] These provisions reflect the concern for substantive and institutional measures that make for effective enforcement.

The book's chapters confirm that the enforcement of regulation against informal abusive debt collection is challenging at the national level, which is also likely to impact cross-border enforcement negatively. The challenges stem from the heterogeneity of regulatory approaches, the absence of sector-specific legislation with clear guidelines and causes for action, the diversity of institutional frameworks, low fines lacking deterrence, overlapping competencies, and a lack of incentives and direct action for aggrieved consumers. All of this not only undermines adequate enforcement but also encourages forum shopping.

The enforcement systems reveal a fragmented and somewhat schizophrenic approach at both the national and E.U. levels, given that disparate institutions manage the supervision and enforcement of laws relating to abusive IDCPs. In Germany, it is the department of justice of each German state that oversees compliance. In Greece, the Netherlands, and Romania, the task falls mainly to the national consumer-protection authorities. In Sweden, the Authority for Privacy Protection is entrusted with prosecuting abusive IDCPs; in the U.K., the Financial Conduct Authority regulates and supervises the debt collection industry. Additionally, each country's financial supervision authorities, bailiffs, and bar associations retain competence over alleged violations of good debt collection practices by their supervisees or members.

There are several explanations for this. The first is the use of pre-existing supervisory structures to avoid the duplication of administrative burdens. In most instances, debt collection laws apply to financial institutions and lawyers when such entities seek to collect debts. However, both categories are excluded from the IDCP-specific licensing requirements because they are already subject to other registration requirements and are supervised by specially designated bodies. However, seeking to prevent additional administrative burdens on businesses transfers those to aggrieved parties, who must identify the appropriate agency to report their complaint. Likewise, this fragmentation creates a risk of conflicting

74 CSD (fn 1) art 23 paras 2, 3.
75 CSD (fn 1) art 14, corroborated by ibid art 26.

case law, undermining the clarity and effect of the law. Empirical evidence suggests that enforcement by alternative entities is somewhat lax or non-existent.[76]

Although the E.U. seems aware of the existing fragmentation,[77] it is not likely that the problem will be fixed once the CSD is transposed into national law. Clarity alone might increase as the E.U. legislator requested Member States to clarify the roles of each authority involved to ensure efficient and proportionate supervision across the Union. The CSD empowers the national authorities of a home Member State to supervise, investigate, and impose penalties on companies performing activities in a host Member State and attempts to foster cross-border cooperation. However, it is difficult to believe that such cooperation will be successful, if at all possible. On the contrary, the CSD requirement that the host state solicits the home state to act against an unethical debt collector only makes the process cumbersome, lengthy, and likely to leave the consumer without an adequate remedy.

The national experiences and the pitfalls of the CSD tell us that enforcement will remain the most significant challenge in tackling abusive IDCPs in the E.U., in either a national or a cross-border setting.

0.4 Brief overview of the ensuing chapters

The empirical data gathered during my Marie Curie-funded research into the need to harmonize IDCP regulation in the EU has revealed that only nine Member States have sector-specific legislation to tackle abusive practices: Belgium, Denmark, Finland, Germany, Greece, the Netherlands, Latvia, Romania, and Sweden (not including the now-former Member State, the U.K.).

With this starting point, Tibor Tajti notes in **Chapter 1** that sector-specific regulation concerning IDCPs is primarily present in North-Western countries (generally associated with a strong rule of law) and *quasi*-absent in the old Southern and post-socialist Central and Eastern European Member States. He observes that a strong rule of law does not make the regulation of IDCPs unnecessary. On the contrary, numerous examples from these Member States suggest the opposite.[78] He argues that sector-specific legislation tackling abusive IDCPs should become part of broader rule of law-based scrutiny beyond constitutional issues. This is even more salient when one considers the inability of generic consumer-protection laws to insulate consumer debtors from questionable or unlawful practices. A more concrete and down-to-earth substance, Tajti argues, would make the concept of rule of law more comprehensible and relatable to E.U. citizens.

76 Cătălin-Gabriel Stănescu, 'Is there a Scandinavian Model for Regulating Abusive Informal Debt Collection Practices?' in Caroline Heide-Jørgensen and others (eds), *Festskrift til Linda Nielsen* (Copenhagen 2022) 382–383.

77 CSD (fn 1) recital 48.

78 Stănescu 2022 (note 76).

Chapter 2 deals with Croatia, one of the E.U. Member States without IDCP sector-specific legislation in place. Paula Poretti stresses that the 2008 economic crisis has severely impacted the financial situation of consumers and their ability to repay their debts. According to her, informal debt collection is preferred due to the high costs associated with judicial recovery and the absence of specific protections for consumer debtors exposed to abusive practices. She cites case law and anecdotal evidence of common abusive IDCPs and evaluates the effectiveness of traditional remedies and industry self-regulation. She concludes that the adoption of sector-specific legislation would improve the protection of consumer debtors, create a level playing field for ethical debt collectors, and offer legal certainty to all stakeholders.

In **Chapter 3,** David Markworth covers the regulation of IDCPs in Germany. Informal debt collection is tightly regulated and supervised given that Germany traditionally associates the activity with out-of-court legal services, not financial ones. From this characterization stems the law's focus on the creditor rather than debtor protection. However, the industry's rapid expansion has led to heightened competition with lawyers and drawn increasing attention from legislators concerned with the stability and functioning of the legal system. Markworth questions whether the existing rules are well suited to protecting consumer debtors even though recent legal amendments consider their position. He concludes that more balance is needed between the rights and expectations of creditors and debtors. In his view, the most efficient strategy would be to strictly limit the fees charged in debt collection and expand disclosure obligations.

Eleni Kaprou provides an overview of Greek regulation in **Chapter 4**. She notes that to protect consumers from abusive practices, Greece does not allow debt collection *per se* but rather the information of debtors about their debt and arrangement of a repayment plan. In addition to overviewing the legal framework, she outlines case law developments, the activity of public enforcement agencies in their attempt to tackle abusive IDCPs, and the distinctive example of law firms engaging in debt recovery. On this basis, Kaprou concludes that besides a robust set of sector-specific rules combined with effective enforcement, improving the overall economic situation of consumer debtors is a must to tackle abusive debt collection.

Chapter 5 is dedicated to Estonia, another Member State without sector-specific legislation. Karin Sein provides a general account of the Estonian debt collection market and follows the legislative developments dealing with cost caps for the licensing of statutory debt collection and ancillary case law. Sein notes that while rules on unfair commercial practices have failed to tackle abusive informal debt collection in Estonia, data protection rules have enabled courts to offer consumer debtors respite in cases where they were subjected to privacy-intruding practices leading to their public stigmatization. She delves into the potential consequences of the increasing use of software-based solutions for both creditors and debtors. In conclusion, Sein argues that while the legislator is still considering the implementation of licensing and sector-specific rules, it is the merit of courts to have curbed some of the egregious practices of debt collectors.

Candida Leone and Joanna van Duin address the regulation of IDCPs in the Netherlands in **Chapter 6**. They underscore that growing over-indebtedness has become a pressing social issue and given birth to a controversial business model relying on aggressive debt collection practices. As their chapter reveals, the threshold between formal and informal debt collection is often blurred in the Netherlands, where local companies have quickly learned to use and abuse the legal system, especially the court procedures for small claims. Leone and van Duin contend that the recent CJEU case law on the *ex officio* application of consumer law has empowered local courts to end judicial rubber-stamping on unsubstantiated claims. They then assess the provisions of a Dutch bill on the 'quality of debt collection services' and conclude that although the proposed bill still suffers from pitfalls, particularly regarding the risk of artificially inflating the consumer's debt burden, it will offer consumers more targeted and comprehensive protection than the current situation or the CSD.

In **Chapter 7**, Jakub Kępiński provides a comprehensive overview of the traditional remedies used to tackle abusive IDCPs in Poland. Since the country does not have sector-specific legislation, these practices are brought to the attention of administrative or judicial bodies with varying degrees of success. Kępiński notes that while legislation about unfair commercial practices has been used to address abusive debt collection, it does not provide a sufficient basis for protecting consumers. He reveals that in several cases concerning infringements of the debtor's rights – dignity, freedom, and inviolability of the home – consumers have been able to resort to civil or criminal law provisions to fend off abusive debt collectors. For this reason, the Ministry of Justice argues that there is no need to implement sector-specific legislation concerning abusive IDCPs. However, given the cost and length of judicial proceedings, the lack of adequate guidelines, and low awareness of consumer rights, Kępiński concludes that a dedicated legislative initiative might be beneficial.

Stănescu and Albanezi examine Romania's struggle to regulate abusive IDCPs in **Chapter 8**. Their contribution offers a summary of the (failed) legislative attempts to implement sector-specific legislation dealing with informal debt collection and a topical analysis of the Romanian legislation on fair debt collection practices. They note that while the Romanian legislator seems to have been aware of the problems arising from abusive debt collection, it repeatedly failed to regulate it because of either regulatory capture and financial lobbying or regulatory incompetence (which calls into question the legislature's intent). The authors conclude that while the current legal framework is a decent solution and a significant step forward, it is not free of shortcomings undermining its applicability and efficacy.

Sweden was among the first to introduce a fair debt collection act in Europe and is the subject of **Chapter 9**. Hajo Holtz provides a detailed account of the Swedish legal framework concerning IDCPs, which he deems solid and balanced, albeit not free of criticism. Hajo positively assesses the clarity of existing rules, the foreseeability of results, and legal certainty and evaluates the risk of collecting fraudulent claims to be limited, although not excluded. However, enforcement is primarily administrative, which, in his view, lacks a sufficiently deterrent effect. He concludes that to preclude debt collection companies from engaging in abusive behavior, the Swedish legislator should consider introducing GDPR-like fines calculated based on the company's turnover.

The U.K. is covered by **Chapter 10**. Jodi Gardner and Mia Gray explore the British IDCPs regime and outline the legal obligations of debt collectors. They posit that although the U.K. displays robust protection against abusive practices on paper, the lack of clarity concerning the processes utilized by private-sector debt collectors and ineffective enforcement mechanisms against breaches of good conduct reveal the limitations of the existing regulation. Gardner and Gray identify financial hardship as the underlying cause of abusive debt collection and raise the provocative question of whether it is morally justified to refer small consumer debts to debt collectors in the first place. They conclude their chapter by inviting other jurisdictions to learn from the mistakes and gaps in the U.K.'s approach.

When speaking of enforcement, the recent adoption of the Directive on Representative Actions to Protect the Collective Interests of Consumers[79] comes to mind. In the U.S., class-action lawsuits have proven a helpful litigation tool in the hands of consumers subjected to systematic violations of the laws on fair debt collection practices.[80] In **Chapter 11**, Agnes Horvath asks whether E.U. representative action could combat abusive IDCPs. She thoroughly discusses the implications of the Directive for debt collection entities, focusing on the Member States where collective action is not common and whether the implementation of the Directive would provide aggrieved consumers with adequate redress measures. Her chapter reveals that assessing and enforcing fairness in settlements will be complex in E.U. Member States lacking experience with IDCP regulation or collective redress. The main reason is the absence of clear rules about what constitutes abuse and how to evaluate its impact on consumers. She concludes that since representative action has the potential to empower consumers who feel powerless or disincentivized to act on their own, legislators, consumer organizations, and courts should study the example of other jurisdictions for possible interpretations and precedents.

0.5 Conclusion

This book shows that regulating abusive informal debt collection in the E.U. remains a complex matter at the national and Union levels. Abusive IDCPs are omnipresent in the E.U., notwithstanding the local circumstances (high or low rule of law index, developed or developing economy, capitalist or former communist

79 Directive (EU) 2020/1828 of the European Parliament and of the Council of 25 November 2020 on representative actions for the protection of the collective interests of consumers and repealing Directive 2009/22/EC, OJ L 409, 4.12.2020, pp. 1–27, available at: <https://eur-lex.europa.eu/legal-content/EN/TXT/PDF/?uri=CELEX:32020L1828&from=EN> accessed 19 April 2022.

80 Stănescu 2015 (note 14) 269.

background). Thus, there is broad agreement among the contributors that regulation is needed where it is absent and improvable where it is present.

The recent adoption of the CSD and its upcoming transposal should lead to a significant legislative effort to achieve a certain degree of harmonization and legal certainty regarding the activity of debt collectors and debt purchasers across the E.U. The task is entrusted to the Member States, who have different approaches to tackling the problem.

Beneficial changes will occur. According to the CSD, debt collectors will have to be authorized to provide their services. This is a significant step forward because it will bring debt collectors under supervision and control in all Member States. The harmonization of the authorization procedure should also limit the likelihood of forum shopping; however, it will not remove it. Member States will decide which practices will be deemed abusive and what types of penalties will be applied for breaches. This may give debt collectors the possibility to choose the Member States with the least stringent regulation as their home. The mechanism provided by the CSD, which emphasizes home enforcement, is more likely to complicate than simplify an already complex web of national approaches and competent bodies.

Ultimately, E.U. Member States lacking sector-specific legislation concerning abusive IDPCs will have to design and implement one. In doing so, the experience of Member States that already have such regulations in place is of utmost importance; thus, more research should emerge in this overlooked field of law. Knowledge sharing among Member States is vital for policy choices, legal drafting, and identifying workable solutions. Our book contributes to this endeavor by making available the enclosed examples.

Bibliography

Ben-Menahem, H. and Hecht, N. S. *Selected Topics in Jewish Law*. Tel Aviv, Israel: The Open University of Israel Publishing House, 1993.

Biscoe, P. M. *Law and Practice of Credit Factoring*. London: Butterworths, 1975.

Brandon, D. I., Cooper, M. L., Greshin, J. H., Harris, A. L., Head Jr., J. M., Jacques, K. R. and Wiggins, L. "SPECIAL PROJECT. Self-Help: Extrajudicial Rights, Privileges and Remedies in Contemporary American Society." *Vanderbilt Law Review*, vol 37 (5), 845–1040, 1984.

Del Granado, J. J. "The Genius of Roman Law from a Law and Economics Perspective." *San Diego International Law Journal*, vol 13 (1), 301–350, 2011.

Deville, J. *Lived Economies of Default: Consumer Credit, Debt Collection and the Capture of Affect*. Taylor and Francis, 2015.

Fox, J. L. "Do We Have a Debt Collection Crisis? Some Cautionary Tales of Debt Collection in Indiana." *Loyola Consumer Law Review*, vol 24 (3), 355–388, 2012.

Geraint, H., Christian, T.-F. and Thomas, W. *Rethinking EU Consumer Law*. Taylor and Francis, 2017.

Goldberg, L. "Dealing in Debt: The High-Stakes World of Debt Collection after FDCPA." *Southern California Law Review*, vol 79 (3), 711–752, 2006.

Jurgens, R. and Hobbs, R. J. The Debt Machine: How the Collection Industry Hounds Consumers and Overwhelms Courts. Boston. MA: National Consumer Law Center, 2010.

Ruddy, N., Mills, S. and Davidson, N. *Salinger on Factoring*. London: Sweet & Maxwell, 2006.

Smail, D. L. *Legal Plunder: Households and Debt Collection in Late Medieval Europe*. Cambridge: Harvard University Press, 2016.

Spanogle, J. A. *Consumer Law: Cases and Materials*. Edited by Rohner, R. J., Pridgen, D., Sovern, J. and Peterson, C. L. St. Paul, MN: West Academic Publishing, 2013.

Stănescu, C.-G. *Self-Help, Private Debt Collection and the Concomitant Risks. A Comparative Law Analysis*. Switzerland: Springer, 2015.

Stănescu, C.-G. "Is the Unfair Commercial Practices Directive Fit to Effectively Tackle Abusive Debt Collection?" *Journal of European Consumer and Market Law*, Alphen aan den Rijn, The Netherlands: Kluwer Law International, vol 9 (6), 235–247, 2020.

Stănescu, C.-G. "A Critical Assessment of the Need for Harmonization of the Legal Framework Concerning Abusive Informal Debt Collection Practices in the European Union." *Journal of Consumer Policy*, vol 44 (4), 531–557, 2021.

Stănescu, C.-G. "Regulation of Abusive Debt Collection Practices in the EU Member States: An Empirical Account." *Journal of Consumer Policy*, vol 44 (2), 179–216, 2021.

Stănescu, C.-G. "Is There a Scandinavian Model for Regulating Abusive Informal Debt Collection Practices?" In *Festskrift til Linda Nielsen*, edited by Heide-Jørgensen, C., Lund-Andersen, I. and Hansen, J. L. Copenhagen: Djøf Forlag, 2022.

Taylor, C. R. "Self-Help in Contract Law: An Exploration and Proposal." *Wake Forest Law Review*, vol 33 (4), 839–908, 1998.

1 Contemporary European debt collection practices through the prism of the rule of law

Tibor Tajti (Thaythy)[1]

> *[A]side from human rights abuses, the rule of law is likely to be compromised even in purely private law matters if the leadership of a country or if privileged individuals can act arbitrarily against other.*[2]

1.1 Why scrutinize private debt collection through a rule of law lens?

1.1.1 Fact: legally questionable debt collection practices are part of the European reality[3]

If one departs from the scarce English language legal scholarship, traceable court cases, and consumer authority decisions on this topic in Europe, one may easily be misled to believe that there are no problems to discuss. If we take Denmark, which, similarly to the other Scandinavian jurisdictions has had consumer debt sectoral regulations for decades,[4] only one short English language piece is available, and that merely sketches an outline of the Danish sectoral law.[5] The same could also be stated vis-a-vis Hungary, where the efforts to pass sectoral regulations seem to have been given up with the 2012 recommendations of the Financial

1 Tibor Tajti, professor of law, CEU-Private University, Vienna – Austria. Contact: tajtit@ceu.edu.
I would like to extend my gratitude to Professors Marie-Pierre Granger (CEU-PU) and Catalin Stanescu (Syddansk Universitet, Denmark) for exchanges regarding this paper and the linguistic assistance of Joshua Haynes-Mannering, CEU doctoral candidate.

2 Dam, K.W., (2006), 'The Law-Growth Nexus: The Rule of Law and Economic Development' (Brookings, Washington D.C.), at 16.

3 Stanescu, G.C. 'Regulation of Abusive Debt Collection Practices in the EU Member States: An Empirical Account' [2021] J Consum Policy, 3.

4 See the Swedish '*Inkassolagen*' (1974:182) as amended, and the Norwegian '*Lov om onkassovirksomhet og annen inndriving av forfalte pengekrav (inkassoloven)*' (lov nr 26/26.13.05.1988); also as amended.

5 For a short English language account on the Danish 'Debt Collection Act' ("*Inkassoloven*") [Lov no 319/14.05.1997 om inkassovirksomhed. Latest update is Lav nr 498/12.06.2009.] enacted in 1997 see Chapter 3 in Werlauff, Eric, Civil Procedure in Denmark (Wolter Kluwers, 3rd ed., 2017), at 44–47, which is devoted to bailiffs and 'authorized debt collection businesses.'

DOI: 10.4324/9781003343158-2

Supervisory Authority the tasks of which were taken over by the Hungarian National Bank from 1 October 2013. The text of this soft law instrument can still be found on the website of the National Bank[6] but little can be known about its use and relevance. The situation is similar in roughly half of all European jurisdictions, and there are no initiatives for Europe-wide regulations in this sector forthcoming from Brussels, either. Consequently, the topic is neither widely discussed, nor have problems corollary to debt collection been acknowledged. As a result, policy repercussions in this area have not been adequately understood either by policy-makers, or scholars.

Questionable debt collection practices nonetheless exist. *First and foremost*, their quantity and severity have inevitably increased together with the expanding consumer-debt crisis looming large in Europe. In particular, since the spillover effects of the U.S. 2007–2008 financial crisis (Credit Crunch) reached the Old Continent and were exacerbated by local financial calamities such as the collapse of the Swiss-Franc denominate mortgage market in Croatia, Hungary, and some other regional states. The unprecedentedly severe negative effects of the COVID-19 pandemic have compounded this further.

The fact that the European Union (E.U.) itself has realized the perils that non-performing loans (NPLs) pose to the common market could be added as indirect evidence for the reasons underlying a burgeoning private (i.e. extra-judicial) debt collection industry in Europe in the last few decades. What is surprising is that this was not paralleled by an awareness of the dangers that unregulated debt collection activities might pose to consumer-debtors. While the systemic NPLs problem can supposedly be more efficiently tackled by the tools of the European Parliament's Committee on Economic and Market Affairs' (CEMA) Proposal for a '*Directive on credit servicers, credit purchasers and the recovery of collateral*' (NPLD),[7] this bill, still in the legislative process as of October 2021, unfortunately fails to adequately address the problematic practices of private debt collectors.

Second, the fact that even Europe's top rule of law countries employ sector-specific regulations in this area is persuasive evidence that sectoral regulations in this domain are needed. Scandinavian countries (the all-time champions of international rule of law rankings) passed legislation regulating this sector decades ago. Germany (which is likewise a high rule of law country) set out to revamp its laws in this area from 2008 onwards, a fact that *per se* corroborates the legitimacy of the concerns this paper is focused upon. These are perfectly expressed in the title of the German Federal Ministry of Justice and Consumer Protection's 2019 Proposal: '*Draft Law for Strengthening Consumer Protection*

6 The full title of the recommendations in English is: 'Recommendations of the Financial Supervisory Authority's President No. 14/2012 (as of 13 December) for Debt Collectors on the Consumer Protection Principles they are Expected to Apply when Engaging in Debt Collection' [*A Pénzügyi Szervezetek Állami Felügyelete elnökének 14/2012. (XII.13.) számú ajánlása a követeléskezelők számára a követeléskezelési gyakorlatuk során elvárt fogyasztóvédelmi elvekről*]. The Hungarian text is downloadable at <https://www.mnb.hu/letoltes/2012-xii-13> accessed 2 November 2021.

7 COM/2018/0135 final – 2018/063 (COD).

in the Context of Debt Collection' ['*Entwurf eines Gesetzes zur Verbesserung des Verbraucherschutzes in Inkassorecht*'].[8]

Third, harassment and other problematic debt collection practices have been empirically backed-up by a few recent reports.[9] These reports suggest that questionable practices have not merely surfaced sporadically in isolated cases. Far from being an occasional rotten apple in a proverbial basket of healthy fruits, such practices likely amount to a serious and systemic risk. As the 2020 research paper of Finance Watch succinctly concludes: 'Abusive practices are widespread throughout Europe.'[10]

Fourth, although no E.U. case has caused a major volte face in this domain as of yet, it is an encouraging development that some corollary problems, uncontested so far, were given a new interpretation by the European Court of Justice (ECJ) in its *Nemzeti Fogyasztóvédelmi Hatóság v. UPC Magyarország Kft*[11] decision. In an unusual disagreement with the sitting Advocate General Whal, the court held that communicating false information to a consumer qualifies as a 'B2C commercial practice' under the Unfair Commercial Practices Directive [UCPD][12] 'even though that information concerned only one single consumer.'[13]

This is the case where the ECJ expressed its concern with regards to a major cable television services provider's problematic business attitude, despite the miniscule size of the claim and the fact that it involved only one consumer. This is of importance because the court was willing to interpret the Directive to afford even an individual consumer a remedy despite 'recital 6 in the preamble of the UCPD, stating very clearly that, in line with the principle of proportionality, the Directive is not concerned with business conduct whose effect is negligible (*de minimis*).'[14] Although the case did not directly concern debt collection activities, one should bear in mind that thousands of low-value unpaid invoices due to major service-providers such as UCP usually are either sold to private debt collector

8 The law is already in force and was published in the German Federal Official Gazette as of 22 December 2020. The document is available at <https://www.bmjv.de/SharedDocs/Gesetzgebungsverfahren/Dokumente/RefE_Verbraucherschutz_Inkassorecht.pdf;jsessionid=C6F7628591DF9C63E2536DC583126758.2_cid334?__blob=publicationFile&v=2> accessed 23 Oct. 2021.

9 See the document published by Finance Watch and authored by Olivier Jérusalmy, Paul Fox, and Nicolas Hercelin, 'Is the Human Dignity of Individual Debtors at Risk? – A Research Paper on Debt Collectors' Practices and the Protect of Debtor Household Income' [2020] available at <https://www.finance-watch.org/wp-content/uploads/2020/01/Report_Human-dignity_final_with-annex.pdf> accessed 15 Oct. 2021.

10 ibid, at 33.

11 C-388/13 ECLI:EU:C:2015:225. [Hereinafter: ECJ UPC case].

12 Directive 2005/29/EC of the European Parliament and of the Council of 11 May 2005 concerning unfair business-to-consumer commercial practices in the internal market and amending Council Directive 84/450/EEC, Directives 97/7/EC, 98/27/EC and 2002/65/EC of the European Parliament and of the Council and Regulation (EC) No 2006/2004 of the European Parliament and of the Council ('Unfair Commercial Practices Directive').

13 Holding of the judgment in the C-399/13 case.

14 For a critique of this judgment see Bert Keirsbilck's case commentary, 'The UCPD's notion of "commercial practice": UPC Magyarország' [2016] Common Market L. Rev. 53: 527–542.

companies or the private debt collectors are hired to collect the debt on the original service-provider's behalf.

Lastly, although exposed by investigative journalists rather than by legal scholars in their law review publications, reports describing specific instances where consumer-debtors are harassed or abused, and other reports of legally (and morally) questionable debt collection practices, have indeed been published.[15] European legal scholarship's disinterest in developments in the debt collection sector may be related to the insufficiency of (and problems with access to) empirical data. The fact that data protection, bank secrecy, and other laws with similar effects interfere with and/or prevent data dissemination is also an issue compounded by the apparent lack of interest in or incentives for debt collectors' industrial associations to reveal anything about their problematic practices.

However, no less problematic is European legal scholarship's lack of any established (and therefore any widely accepted) method for the collection of comparable country-by-country data on problematic debt collection practices across Europe based upon the outcomes and the procedures used in the proceedings of consumer protection authorities and/or other competent government bodies. As there are no methods for the collection or processing of such data as of yet, it is more convenient for those who publish in (and those who edit) law reviews to avoid this fraught topic than it is for them to try to articulate complex and novel methods for the collection and processing of such data. At this stage there is still a dearth of relevant empirical evidence available for most E.U. countries, and as such, these cases might fill the gap.

1.1.2 Fact: the inertness of the European Union and the concomitant dilemmas

1.1.2.1 Raising awareness: dead-end avenues?

Although Article 265 of the Treaty on the Functioning of the European Union (TFEU)[16] contains express rules which can be invoked against E.U. bodies for their failure to act, in practice these cannot be efficiently exploited for a variety of reasons. This is mainly due to the fact that the right to bring actions is generally the exclusive privilege of Member States and E.U. bodies.[17] Natural and legal persons may complain to the court only if they can prove that the failure to act has directly caused them injury. According to the pertinent section, they must 'establish either that he, she or it is the addressee of the act which the institution complained of allegedly failed to adopt in respect of that person, or that that act

15 See note 9 supra and the references in it.

16 Consolidated Version of the Treaty on the Functioning of the European Union (TFEU), Official Journal C 326, 26/10/2012, 0001-0390.

17 TFEU Article 265(1).

directly and individually concerned him, her or it in a manner analogous to that in which the addressee of such an act would be concerned.'[18]

Formally speaking, other avenues for reaching E.U. bodies or lower-level E.U. officials exist. However, these channels cannot ensure that the citizens' voice they are supposed to serve reach those in charge within a reasonable period of time. On the European Commission's topic-by-topic navigation site there is, for example, no item devoted to 'debt collection'[19] or any similar topics. While it is true that the E.U. has a relatively successful consumer protection regulatory framework, this is unable to do a proper job as far as private debt collection is concerned, as it is neither designed to nor capable of dealing with the myriad challenges private debt collection generates. This is a valid claim notwithstanding that thanks to the 2005 Unfair Commercial Practices Directive, some modest forward-looking steps have been taken in some of the Member States.[20]

The Commission's 2018 'New Deal for Consumers' also failed to mention debt collection.[21]

1.1.2.2 Surge of non-performing loans and the European Union's responses

While as far as the protections of consumer-debtors against the problematic practices of debt collectors are concerned, no major advancement is expected on the E.U. level in the near future, Brussels has put significant emphasis on making debt collection easier and more efficient. One such recent development, still in the middle of the legislative process in autumn 2021, is the Proposal of the European Parliament's Committee on Economic and Market Affairs (CEMA) for a '*Directive on credit servicers, credit purchasers and the recovery of collateral*' (NPLD), clearly indicating in what direction the balance is being tilted. To quote from the text itself: 'the proposal will help banks to better manage NPLs by increasing the efficiency of debt recovery procedures through the availability of a distinct common accelerated extrajudicial collateral enforcement procedure (AECE).'[22]

18 See para 29 of the Order of the General Court (Eight Chamber) as of 17 Dec. 2020 in the case T-350/20 on the action of Lukáš Wagenrecht, member of the Senate of the Czech Parliament [ECLI:EU:T:2020:635]. As the ECJ has declared that he had no *locus standi* to file the claim, he had to pay also the costs of the EU Commission.

19 See the related page of the European Commission at < https://ec.europa.eu/info/about-european-commissions-web-presence_en>. For a list of EU consumer legislation see the European Commission's website at < https://ec.europa.eu/info/law/law-topic/consumers/review-eu-consumer-law-new-deal-consumers_en>. Both accessed 15 Oct. 2021.

20 Stanescu, note 3 supra, at 3.

21 European Commission, Communication from the Commission to the European Parliament, the Council and the European Economic and Social Committee – A New Deal for Consumers (11.4.2018, COM (2018) 183 final).

22 CEMA, NPLD Proposal (2018/0063 (COD)), para 16, at 19.

Once enacted, this piece of legislation would come on top of the European Account Preservation Order (EAPO)[23] introduced a few years ago to improve cross-border debt collection efficiency. Thus, debt collection is considered on the E.U. level, though it is considered asymmetrically; i.e. it is biased towards erecting a legal framework to increase the efficiency of debt collection.[24] To simplify somewhat, banks have so far been favored by the E.U. lawmaker, and this has come at the expense of consumer-debtors.

As highlighted, efficient counterbalances exist mainly in the north-western Member States that have introduced sector-specific regulations aimed at protecting consumer-debtors and subjecting the activities of differing types of private debt collectors to rules. Their regulatory patterns may differ, sometimes (partly) due to historic reasons,[25] but similarities can also be found. For example, both German and Danish laws allow debt collection not only by attorneys though at the price of subjecting them to licensing.[26]

Often though, at least in the eastern part of the continent, local parliaments are too overwhelmed with political position-making instead of legislating on the sorts of real-life problems discussed in this article.[27] If no strategic advantage can be gained from doing what parliaments are supposed to, then ill-suited topics are simply dodged, especially when there are upcoming elections. The result is that a blind eye is turned to an easily recognizable reality; while the high rule of law

23 Regulation 655/2014 of the European Parliament and of the Council of 15 May 2014 establishing a European Account Preservation Order. For a short seminal comment on the new regulation see Chapter 5 of Tibor Tajti and Peter Iglikowski, *A Cross Border Study of Freezing Orders and Provision Measures – Does Mareva Rule the Waves?* (Springer, 2018), at 83–86.

24 See also, in particular, Directive No. 2000/35/EU of the European Parliament and of the Council of 29 June 2000 on combating late payment in commercial transactions, Directive No. 2011/7/EU of the European Parliament and of the Council of 16 February 2011 on combating late payment in commercial transactions, Regulation (EC) No. 1896/2006 of the European Parliament and of the Council of 12 December 2006 creating a European order for payment procedure, Regulation (EC) No. 861/2007 of the European Parliament and of the Council of 11 July 2007 establishing a European Small Claims Procedure.

25 The aim of the German 2008 Act on Provision of Legal Services ("*Gesetz über aussergerichtliche Rechtsdienstleistungen,*" abbreviated as "*Rechtsdienstleistungsgesetz*") was to liberalize the market for legal services that remained heavily restricted based on the survival of the 1935 Act on Provision of Legal Counseling that was originally passed to exclude Jewish people from the profession. See Michael Kleine-Cosack, *Rechtsdienstleistungsgesetz – RDG Kommentar* (Heidelberg, C.F. Müller Verlag), at 26.

26 See § 10(1)(1) of RDG, which limits the provision of debt collection services ("*Inkassodienstleistung*") to licensing but opens the market to non-attorneys. See Tibor Tajti, 'A Holistic Approach to Extra-Judicial Enforcement and Private Debt Collection – A Comparative Account of Trends, Empirical Evidence, and the Connected Regulatory Challenges' – Part Two [2020] Pravni Zapisi, vol. XI, No. 1 (2020), para 4.2.2.3, at 30 et seq. [Hereinafter: Tajti Holistic Approach].

27 For example, the speaker of the Ukrainian Parliament stated in a 2009 TV show 'Freedom of Speech' that while in 2008 *the Verhovna Rada* should have worked for 151 days, it failed to work for 55 days. Stefan Messmann & Tibor Tajti, *The Case Law of Central and Eastern Europe – Enforcement of Contracts, Editors' Introduction*, note 8, at 18 (European University Press, Bochum, Germany, 2009).

north-western part of the E.U. subjects private debt collection to strict sector-specific regulation (and thus sectoral protections are in place), this is not the case for roughly half of Europe. This asymmetry does not seem to be a concern at either the E.U. or national levels of government.

1.1.3 What does a comparative account of debt collection-related regulatory responses suggest?

Outside of Europe, from the 1977 U.S. federal Fair Debt Collection Practices Act (FDCPA)[28] (as supplemented by the numerous State-level mini-FDCPAs) to the Australian Debt Collection Guide,[29] tried-and-tested models of debt collection have been in place for decades.[30] Such regulation can come in the form of either 'hard' or 'soft' law, with approaches differing considerably. For example, in comparison with the FDCPA, the German and the aforementioned Scandinavian laws are less detailed as to precisely which concrete debt collection practices are problematic. For example, in a Danish case, the courts had to clarify the meaning of the vague legal requirement that serving the debtor with a warning presumes also 'clearly stating all the information required for the debtor's assessment of the claim.'[31] In the FDCPA, this area is regulated by express provisions[32] notwithstanding that courts do play a substantial role in shaping the contours of the law[33] (as one would expect from a common law country). The point is that European regulatory patterns compared to the U.S. FDCPA and its State-variants might be the right basis for the future common European regulatory framework.

28 Fair Debt Collection Practices Act, as amended by Public Law 111-203, title X, 124 Stat. 2092 (2010). Consolidated text available at <https://www.ftc.gov/enforcement/rules/rulemaking-regulatory-reform-proceedings/fair-debt-collection-practices-act-text#801> accessed 15 Oct. 2021.

29 Australian Competition & Consumer Commission (ACCC), *Debt Collection Guide: For Collectors and Creditors* (April, 2021), text available at <https://www.accc.gov.au/publications/debt-collection-guideline-for-collectors-creditors> accessed 15 Oct. 2021.

30 For a more detailed account of various national approaches, see Tajti, Holistic Approach, at 271–335.

31 Eric Werlauff, *Civil Procedure in Denmark* (Wolters Kluwer, 2010), at 39. For FDCPA see § 809 'Validation of debt', and § 809(a) on 'notice of debt; contents.'

32 For example, it prohibits harassment tactics but provides concrete examples to clarify the term's meaning. Such examples include using obscenities or calling past 10:00 p.m. Warren, E., Westboork, J.L, Porter, K., and Pottow, J.A.E., *The Law of Debtors and Creditors – Text, Cases, and Problems* (Wolters Kluwer, 8th ed., 2021), at 27.

33 In the 2017 case of *Henson v. Santander Consumer USA, Inc.* 137 S. Ct. 1718 (2017) the issue revolved around the question of who exactly qualifies as a 'debt collector' for the purposes of the FCDPA. The question arose when Santander Consumer USA purchased defaulted loans from CitiFinancial Auto (a company in the business of financing consumer car purchases) and then sought to collect them. According to the petitioner, Santander did qualify as a debt collector under the FDCPA, and its collections were in contravention of the Act. The Supreme Court held, however, that those 'who seek only to collect for themselves loans they originated,' even if 'purchased for [their] own account' are not caught by the FDCPA.

However, methods of assessing the development of the rule of law in different jurisdictions or industries may also assist in the task of making these problems visible. We turn to this aspect of the topic below.

1.2 Why scrutinize the debt collection practices through the prism of the rule of law?

1.2.1 The unprecedented prestige of the rule of law in Europe

The rule of law has become a top priority in Europe during the last years. There is no need to read law journals to realize this; turning on the television, reading a newspaper, or scrolling through social media suffices. For the legal community, even for those who are not constitutional lawyers, this should be more obvious still. The related debates, however, tend to remain focused on what could be conveniently termed 'big politics,' rather than focusing on down-to-earth issues such as debt collection practices.

This paper aims to fill this gap by showing that some debt collection practices cannot be reconciled with the rule of law, or more precisely, one or more of its constituent parts. The primary motivation for embarking on this unorthodox exercise is the conclusion of the train of thought outlined above.

1.2.2 The big picture: a word on the political dimensions of rule of law in the European Union

The history of the rule of law in the E.U. and its predecessors is far from a story of linear growth even though '[a]dherence to [the rule of law] has always been praised as an essential feature of the E.U.'s constitutionalism.'[34] The fact that aspirations to rule of law are not necessarily backed up in reality has been increasingly emphasized as of late, primarily as a political question generated by the realization that the E.U. possesses 'no competence to intervene in the cases when backsliding [has] occurred at the national level.'[35]

Paradoxically, emergent and subsequently deepening populism has been a key factor not only behind the growing prestige of the rule of law as populism's antipode, but also behind a realization that definitions and understandings of the concept itself vary widely across the continent. Furthermore, as constitutional scholars admit, the past few years have thus brought about 'significant advances in understanding the Rule of Law.'[36] Some new developments though have been criticized, like the European Court of Justice's attempts to position

34 Kochenov, Dimitry Vladimirovich, 'Upgrading Rule of Law in Europe in Populist Times' [2021] XII/1 Pravni Zapisi, pp. 16–29, at 16. Available at < http://www.pravnizapisi.rs/en/ > accessed 15 Oct. 2021.

35 Kochenov, ibid.

36 Kochenov, ibid, at 18.

itself as the ultimate arbiter of the rule of law's definition,[37] or its controversial position that compliance with E.U. law is somehow 'the essence of the rule of law' in and of itself.[38]

What matters for us here is that the concept of the rule of law extends beyond foundational building blocks of constitutional law such as checks and balances or the basic constitutional architecture of the E.U., and is broad enough to be invoked to tackle infringements of a systemic nature traditionally perceived as private or commercial law problems. Thus, it should reach less political matters, and this includes the regulation of private debt collection as a distinct burgeoning market niche of Europe.

1.2.3 The concept of the rule of law described

Defining the rule of law is an elusive task comparable to opening Pandora's Box. Tamanaha justifiably spoke of it as an 'excessively elusive notion.'[39] Faced with this problem, Dam,[40] juxtaposing the rule of law and the predominantly non-constitutional topic of economic development, refrained from delving into the matter but admitted that '[i]t would be a diversion in this discussion of economic development to go further, although [admitting that] a great deal of elaboration and extension of rule-of-law principles is possible.'[41] A similar avoidance of definitional dilemmas is equally appropriate here, limiting our elaboration to highlighting the following points.

Krygier rightly understood the rule of law to be primarily a 'political ideal'[42] rather than a legal concept: the two obviously being the two sides of the same coin. This matters, as it explains the doctrine's intrinsic instability when contrasted with the comparatively precise standards through which private and commercial law operates. Its malleability cannot but result often even in diametrically opposed interpretations, and thus any elucidation of the concept will inevitably

37 As Kochenov noted, 'With the latest case-law from Danish, Czech, and, crucially, German highest courts, the limited, if not myopic, nature of this picture is clear: not all the 'participants in the dialogue' believe that the ECJ is, indeed, the court to lead the pack. In the absence of such a belief, self-referentialism can become dangerous and, indeed, end up denying the very essence of the rule of law.' Kochenov, ibid, at 27.

38 Kochenov, ibid, at 27.

39 Brian Z. Tamanaha, *On the Rule of Law* (Cambridge Univ. Press, 2004), at 3.

40 Kenneth W. Dam, *The Law-Growth Nexus: The Rule of Law and Economic Development* (Brookings Institution Press, Washington D.C., 2006). Dam recommended the following works containing 'fine discussions of the rule-of-law concept': Lon L. Fuller, *The Morality of Law* (Yale University Press, 1964); Joseph Raz, *The Authority of Law: Essays on Law and Morality* (Oxford University Press, 1983), at 210–229; Summer, Robert S., 'The Principles of the Rule of Law' [1999] Notre Dame L. Rev. 74:1691–1712; Cass Sunstein R., 'Problems with Rules' [1995] Cal. L. Rev. 83:953–1023, at 968–969; and Hayek F.A., *the Constitution of Liberty* (University of Chicago Press, 1960). Dam, note 9, at 16.

41 Dam, at 16.

42 Krygier, at 1.

invite critique. Therefore, it ought to be underlined that 'there is no consensus on what 'the rule of law' stands for, even if it is fairly clear what it stands against.'[43]

Due to its political facet, it is also a concept that politicians may twist to fit their short and long-term needs and aspirations.[44] It is a *cause célèbre* of politicians for a reason. To quote Tamanaha: 'the notion of the rule of law is perhaps the most powerful and often repeated political ideal in contemporary global discourse. Everyone, it seems, is for the rule of law. The rule of law is a major source of legitimation for governments in the modern world. A government that abides by the rule of law is seen as good and worthy of respect.'[45]

It could be described also as a legal construct made of more identifiable building blocks which behave like a set of open-end legal definitions, while the task of shaping the concept's contents based on constantly changing realities is left to constitutional courts or other courts performing comparable functions.

Although the rule of law is first and foremost the cherished child of constitutional law today, it is relevant to the myriad dilemmas surrounding debt collection as the penumbras of the rule of law (as with other comprehensive constitutional doctrines) inevitably extend into other areas of law. Thus, to greater or lesser extents, the rule of law affects various areas of private, commercial, and even regulatory law to varying extents; areas which are all of relevance to the economic activity of debt collection.

Dam also noted that the concept is not limited to 'the sphere involving the structure of government and its relation to economic actors,' human rights, or 'the second sphere involving relations among economic actors.'[46] He stressed that 'aside from human rights abuses, the rule of law is likely to be compromised even in purely private law matters if the leadership of a country or if privileged individuals can act arbitrarily against other.'[47] However, he also argued that '[j]ust as in the case of the public law side involving the relation between government and the people, achieving the property-contract rule-of-law goal in private and commercial law has proved to be more of an evolutionary process than a simple exercise in decision-making and legal drafting.'[48] Dam backs up these arguments with selected references from the French Civil Code.

It should be borne in mind that the rule of law could be utilized as a legal tool to unearth debt collection practices that are simply irreconcilable with the vast

43 Rosenfeld, Michel, 'The Rule of Law and the Legitimacy of Constitutional Democracy' [2001] 74 S. Cal. L. Rev. 1307, at 1307.

44 See, e.g., Sajó, András, 'The Rule of Law as Legal Despotism: Concerned Remarks on the Use of Rule of Law in Illiberal Democracies' [2019] Hague J on the Rule Law 11(2–3):371–376, and Gianluigi Palombella, 'The Abuse of the Rule of Law' [2020], Hague J. on the Rule of Law (2020) 12:387–397.

45 Tamanaha, Z. Brian, 'The History and Elements of the Rule of Law' 2012 Sing J Legal Stud 232, at 232.

46 Dam, at 16.

47 Dam, at 16.

48 Dam, at 87–88.

majority of definitions, descriptions, or elucidations of the rule of law. This article is a modest attempt to demonstrate that.

1.2.4 The benchmark: Krygier's four building blocks of the rule of law

The literature on the rule of law is abundant; myriad theories, explanations, and comments are available. A stable orientation point – a sort of benchmark – is therefore needed to apply the concept in a given analysis. Such an explanation would preferably enumerate what the building blocks of the rule of law are. These building blocks must be concrete enough for the essence of the concept to be grasped and for the concept's applicability in the business world to be comprehensible to those who are not constitutional lawyers.

These criteria are adequately satisfied by Martyn Krygier's[49] description, which appeared in a 2001 collection which focused on developments in Central and Eastern Europe. The article successfully and clearly explains the concept and its building blocks in a manner accessible even to an audience unfamiliar with constitutional law. The paper properly summarizes prevailing contemporary views, the fundamentals of which remain up to date, thus serving as a valuable reference.

Krygier's explanation of the rule of law's building blocks and their ramifications go into the depths of its constituent concepts. Of relevance for the analysis of the problematic debt collection practices is the **scope**, **character**, **authoritativeness**, and the **social embeddedness of law**.[50] Each of these identifiable propositions coalesces together, and like pieces of a mosaic constitute elements of the overarching concept of the rule of law. These are obviously not equally relevant to problems surrounding private debt collection, but they are relevant nonetheless, as will be demonstrated below. Here, only a short account should suffice, highlighting those facets most readily applicable to assessing the compatibility of concrete debt collection practices with the rule of law.

The question of the **scope** of laws potentially applicable to debt collection is crucial from the perspective of the rule of law for the following two reasons. Krygier stressed not only the most obvious expectation that 'there should be no privileged groups or institutions exempt from the scope of the law,' but also – of more direct relevance to debt collection – that 'there must exist legal ways of challenging and forcing the government and political officials, even the very highest, to submit to the law.'[51] Although these propositions apply primarily to public officials, in particular the consumer protection authorities that are supposed to protect consumer debtors against debt collectors' harassment, private debt collectors are equally required to remain within the boundaries of law: boundaries that are even

49 Krygier, Martin, 'Transitional Questions about the Rule of Law: Why, What, and How?' In: Adam Czarnota (ed.), East Central Europe/L'Europe du Centre Est: Eine Wissenschaftliche Zeitschrift, vol. 28, part 1 (2001), Special Issue: Ius and Lex in East Central Europe Socio-Legal Conditions of the Rule of Law amid Post-Communist Transformation, pp. 1–34.

50 Krygier, at 9.

51 Krygier, ibid, at 9.

in the lack of express sectoral regulations set ultimately exactly by constitutional law. The non-existence of express provisions prohibiting harassment of debtors obviously does not entitle debt collectors to engage in practices that might amount to that.

As far as the **character of the laws** is concerned, the rule of law first and foremost requires that 'people will be able to be guided by it.'[52] Although this ideal cannot be fully attained in practice, and precisely what should be defined as part of the 'character of laws' is contestable, the key criteria for assessment revolve around the publicity, understandability, and relative clarity of laws, including the requirement that laws should be determinate and relatively stable. For Krygier, however, this building block also entails 'judgment with an eye to its purpose [instead of] the mechanical application of an imported and inviolable set of rules,'[53] as vividly illustrated by the above-mentioned UPC case especially on the point of the treatment of the *de minimus* rule.

The reason that the **authoritativeness of law** is of heightened relevance for our exercise is that this particular building block requires institutions (courts, regulatory bodies, police, and consumer protection authorities) to take the law seriously, enforce it fairly, and administer it 'in ways that conform to its publicly announced terms.'[54] Here, the private debt collectors' attitude to law is one issue, but the dismissive behavior of consumer protection authorities, especially when facing exorbitant number of claims for opening proceedings, is perhaps a more serious concern.

If the authoritativeness of law applies to institutions enforcing law, then the fourth building block, **the social embeddedness of law**, aims to assess whether, and to what extent, does law matter to citizens and others.[55] This building block becomes typically more visible in extraordinary situations such as outbreak of wars, as could be witnessed with the Balkan wars of the 1990s, starting in Slovenia, and continuing in Croatia from 1991 and in Bosnia and Herzegovina from 1992. Virtually overnight, the value and relevance of contracts, no matter how well-drafted, fell drastically as the likelihood of repayment came to depend more on the quality of personal ties with debtors or their staff than upon compliance with the law. Instead of lawyers, companies' sales teams and other personnel came to dominate the scene as the usefulness of litigation and subsequent enforcement proceedings became highly uncertain.

Let us see through selected examples how these building blocks could be used to scrutinize debt collection practices and the legal framework destined to protect consumer-debtors against harassment and overreach.

52 Krygier, ibid, at 10.
53 Krygier, ibid, at 11.
54 Krygier, ibid, at 11.
55 Krygier, ibid, at 14.

1.2.4 Questionable debt collection and debt collection-related practices: capita selecta

1.2.4.1 Charging for unearned services

If unregulated, the charges collected by private debt collectors are not subject to government- or industry-controlled tariffs. Hence, it is often uncertain how much collectors are permitted to charge consumer-debtors, and further, the basis upon which the charges are calculated is often highly opaque. Concretely, may they collect the mere principal, or also interest and costs?

Using a concrete European case as the point of departure for reflection, we once again refer back to the ECJ UPC case.[56] As previously noted, the questionable practice in the UPC case did not directly concern debt collection but instead UPC's issuance of an erroneous invoice charging an individual consumer (Mr. Szabó) the costs of an extra four days of services preceding the formal termination of his cable television subscription. The case was nonetheless instructive on debt collection because large telecommunications companies such as UPC and other companies with thousands of consumer-debtors tend to either sell such invoices (including those erroneously issued) to established debt collection companies, or alternatively employ such companies to collect such debts. In case of sale, the debts are sold at a deep discount. For example, the activities of the giant European debt collector companies – Intrum Justitia and EOS – were noted in Hungarian media because the city of Budapest sold the former tens of thousands of unpaid parking tickets dating from the first years of the 21st century's first decade. It would be mistaken to perceive such business practices as isolated individual cases.

Ever since the parking ticket cases, these giants and other local private debt collection companies have continued to grow in Hungary. And as hundreds of consumer-debtors could have realized: they do collect and charge costs. The rule of law question is simple: as there is no regulation fixing the limits of collectible costs by private debt collectors, on what basis are such costs calculated?

The range of questions that could be formulated based on the UPC case does not stop here. Namely, as superbly illustrated by the judgment itself, courts and consumer authorities alike often work with unsubstantiated presumptions, which may be completely out of sync with reality. The Budapest Hight Court presumed that the erroneous invoice was an isolated administrative error (without demanding any evidence or explaining how such an error may have occurred). They also uncritically assumed that the consumer-victim, Mr. Szabo, could have checked the correctness of the invoice 'from several other sources.' The ECJ, contrary to this assumption, correctly recognized that it would have been 'extremely difficult to [expect Mr. Szabo as an individual consumer]' to assess the invoice's correctness. [57]

56 ECJ UPC case [2015].

57 See paras 20 and 46 of the ECJ judgment in the UPC case.

1.2.4.2 Collection of 'zombie debts'

Even though European empirical data on the collection of so-called 'zombie debts' is scarce, they must be addressed as they represent one distinct class of problematic collection practices. This strange-sounding epithet is a collective term for debts for which the prescription time (statute of limitations) has passed, debts that have been settled with the creditor, or debts which have been discharged in bankruptcy proceedings; i.e. debts which are no longer legally collectible.[58] Thanks to new technologies, debts arising from identity theft may also be included.[59]

Private debt collectors may nonetheless try to enforce them as no sanctions are provided for attempts to collect such debt in the absence of express regulatory language. Exploiting their superior strategic position, expertise in law, and carefully designed tactics, many collectors successfully manage to make a considerable number of consumer-debtors pay for (legally) unenforceable debt in order to avoid an endless deluge of telephone calls, emails, or changing-colored mail. Consumer-debtors often feel compelled to pay for these (legally) unenforceable debts out of fear, embarrassment, and ignorance of law. One may presume, for example, that many elderly, less educated, and other vulnerable classes of consumer-debtors even have difficulty distinguishing private debt collectors from court bailiffs. As a result, they are inclined to pay rather than embarking on a lengthy game of tug-of-war and subsequent litigation with private debt collectors.

The U.S. Federal Trade Commission, for example, has educational pages warning consumers how to detect zombie debts,[60] which is a good practice not necessarily followed by other countries. My own personal experience in Hungary, which is detailed in the next sub-section and which also involves an alleged debt owed to UPC, resulted in debt collection companies vexing me for 11 years with their warning letters despite all relevant prescription times elapsing long ago.

The point here is that private debt collectors can do all the above especially when sector-specific regulations are lacking, and moreover, as the U.S. experiences suggest, even with one in place.[61] What should be stressed insofar as zombie debts are concerned is that debt collection companies, the ones active in Hungary, just as the U.S. ones, have engaged in the collection of these peculiar debts despite the fact that they are obviously fully aware of the laws on statutes of limitations. Consequently, the collection of zombie debts, presumably ongoing in much of Europe and beyond, cannot be reconciled with the rule of law regardless of the building block being used as the reference point.

58 See, e.g., Hebert Amy, 'When Dead Debts Come Back to Life' (28 Oct. 2015) at <https://www.consumer.ftc.gov/blog/2015/10/when-dead-debt-comes-back-life> accessed 15 Oct. 2021.

59 Hebert (2015), ibid.

60 Hebert (2015), ibid.

61 See Debt Buyers: Last Week Tonight with John Oliver, show of 6 June 2016 at <https://www.youtube.com/watch?v=hxUAntt1z2c> last accessed 23 Oct. 2021.

1.2.4.3 Intentional or negligent disregard of applicable law

As an internet subscriber of UPC, I was exposed to similar misfortunes as Mr. Szabó in the aforementioned UPC case. The exact basis of the claim has never been clarified as the claim was quickly transferred to a private debt collection company, and later was further passed on to two other professional collection companies before the case – that had been started in 2008 – was finally satisfactorily concluded in 2019. As Hungary had no sector-specific regulation in place throughout the 11 years in question, it cannot be unequivocally determined whether mailing colored envelopes containing repeated demands for the payment of specified amounts (again, arbitrarily divided and labelled as principal, interest, and costs) roughly every second month constitute harassment. As an alleged consumer-debtor, I certainly felt harassed by unsubstantiated claims, especially after the prescription period had elapsed.

Part of the saga is that after about three years still having regularly received the mailed demands to pay coupled with threats to sue, I turned to the competent first instance consumer protection authority requesting an investigation into these debt collection practices and a prohibition of their continuation.[62] Unexpectedly, the body terminated proceedings without a hearing or request for any further documentation or evidence. They did this on the basis of a single argument: the contractual nature of the case and the enforceability of the claim in civil proceedings (litigation).[63] This position was not only mistaken but also rather ironic considering that it was taken by the governmental body entrusted with protecting consumer rights, especially considering the existence of a High Court decision rejecting this simplistic argument that had been published online since 2006 in Hungarian databases of selected High Court decisions.[64]

While it is true that in those days High Court decisions formally had only persuasive force, the process leading to the elevation of High Court decisions to the level of primary sources of law which culminated in the 2020 introduction of a ‘limited precedential system’[65] (‘*korlátozott precedensjog*’) was already in progress. A consumer protection authority, in other words, should not have disregarded that decision.

If this argument made on the basis of case law is insufficiently persuasive, let us add that the UCPD itself proclaims that, as reiterated in the UPC case, it is

62 Case No. FK-I-5041/2011 (filing No/Ikt./Ref.: 27263/2/2011) as of 29 April 2011; not published, on file with the author.

63 For a detailed account of the procedural steps, including the holding of passed decisions, see Tajti, ‘A Holistic Approach,’ part one [2019] X/2 Pravni Zapisi 275, at 307–323.

64 EBH 2006.1477. The key sentence, as translated by me, reads in English as follows ‘The duty of the consumer protection agency to conduct consumer protection proceedings exists regardless of whether a civil claim could also be pursued on the basis of the same cause of action.’

65 See articles 72–74 of the *2019. évi CXXVII. Törvény az egyes törvényeknek az egyfokú járási hivatali eljárások megteremtésével összefüggő módosításáról* [Act No. CXXVII of year 2019 on the amendment of various laws related to the introduction of single-level county official proceedings].

'*without prejudice to individual actions brought by those who have been harmed by an unfair commercial practice.* It is also without prejudice to Community and national rules on contract law.'[66] [Emphasis added.] Therefore, the first instance Hungarian consumer protection agency has disregarded a Hungarian High Court decision and the UCPD itself. Whether this was a one-time occurrence caused by incompetence of the staff member handling the case, or worse, an intentional act, cannot be proven. True, neither can be excluded either.

Through the prism of the rule of law, the fact that governmental bodies such as the consumer protection authority have the sorts of attitudes outlined above seems to be problematic at least under the axiom that 'institutions charged with administering the law take it seriously and enforce it fairly.'[67]

1.2.4.4 Embeddedness of law and debt collectors

Private debt collectors work on a for-profit basis and take advantage of their superior strategic and tactical position in their dealings with consumers-debtors with a lower degree of bargaining power. This leads one to formulate the simple and logical presumption that whether (and to what extent) the directors, officers, and staff performing debt collection are bound by effective legal standards is crucial. Where sectoral regulations are in place, the division between the legal and illegal is much clearer than in jurisdictions which rely on generic consumer protection laws and traditional areas of law such as contract, tort, or penal laws.

Bearing the aforementioned Hungarian case in which the consumer protection agency intentionally or negligently failed to apply the law, the same question should be raised whenever the rule of law and its building blocks are at stake. Assuming that other national consumer protection authorities behave similarly, with some of them functioning more like the circumlocution offices described by Charles Dickens in *Little Dorrit* that frighten off the consumers for whose protection they owe their existence, are these not the rule of law issues? Such questions already involve much more than an individual or few customers potentially having their constitutional rights infringed. This is because these sorts of failures of governmental bodies can only be described as systemic, as such bodies form an inseparable part of the institutional framework of a constitutional system. What they do should also be of relevance to all who care for the rule of law.

Finally, the EJC's UPC case – properly remedying the *de minimis* rule of European consumer laws – does suggest that the law and courts cannot be completely insensitive to the superior strategic position of debt collectors and their adversaries (or sometimes victims), the consumer-debtors. In fact, a closer look at available empirical evidence (including the more thoroughly processed data from the U.S. and the European systems possessing sectoral regulations) reveals that

66 ECJ UPC case, para 3(9).
67 Krygier, at 11.

the severity of problematic collection practices are on a par with problems corollary to adhesion contracts, special regulatory protections of inherently weaker franchisees, or the myriad tools securities regulations are filled with.

1.3 Epilogue

The above, hopefully, does show that scrutiny of debt collection-related empirical evidence through the prism of the rule of law pays as it could result in unearthing concrete problems faced by European citizens and placing them in the limelight instead of sweeping them under the carpet. Yet it is perhaps of even bigger importance that this process may allow the concept of the rule of law to be filled with new concrete contents, which are more comprehensible and relatable to European citizens than the often abstract constitutional debates dominating the political stratosphere of Europe today. This could reduce the risk of this fundamental constitutional doctrine gradually deteriorating in the eyes of European citizens into an ineffable *flatus vocis* that is comprehensible only to a narrow group of constitutional law experts.

Hard laws (statutory and sub-statutory law)

Denmark

'Debt Collection Act' ("Inkassoloven") [Lov no 319/14.05.1997 om inkassovirksomhed] (Last amendment: Lav nr 498/12.06.2009).

European Union

Directive No. 2000/35/E.U. of the European Parliament and of the Council of 29 June 2000 on combating late payment in commercial transactions.

Directive 2005/29/E.C. of the European Parliament and of the Council of 11 May 2005 concerning unfair business-to-consumer commercial practices in the internal market and amending Council Directive 84/450/EEC, Directive 97/7/EC, 98/27/E.C. and 2002/65/E.C. of the European Parliament and of the Council and Regulation (E.C.) No 2006/2004 of the European Parliament and of the Council ('Unfair Commercial Practices Directive').

Directive No. 2011/7/EU of the European Parliament and of the Council of 16 February 2011 on combating late payment in commercial transactions.

Regulation (E.C.) No. 1896/2006 of the European Parliament and of the Council of 12 December 2006 creating a European order for payment procedure.

Regulation (E.C.) No. 861/2007 of the European Parliament and of the Council of 11 July 2007 establishing a European Small Claims Procedure.

Regulation 655/2014 of the European Parliament and of the Council of 15 May 2014 establishing a European Account Preservation Order.

Treaty on the Functioning of the European Union (TFEU), Official Journal C 326, 26/10/2012, 0001-0390.

The Consumer Credit Directive (Directive 2008/48/E.C.).

The Mortgage Credit Directive (Directive 2014/17/E.U.).

Germany

Act on Provision of Legal Services (2008) ("Gesetz über aussergerichtliche Rechtsdienstleistungen," abbreviated as "Rechtsdienstleistungsgesetz").

Hungary

2019. évi CXXVII. Törvény az egyes törvényeknek az egyfokú járási hivatali eljárások megteremtésével összefüggő módosításáról [Act No. CXXVII of year 2019 on the amendment of various laws related to the introduction of single-level county official proceedings].

Norway

'Lov om onkassovirksomhet og annen inndriving av forfalte pengekrav (inkassoloven)' (Lov nr 26/26.13.05.1988) as amended.

Sweden

'Inkassolagen' (1974:182) as amended.

The United States of America

Fair Debt Collection Practices Act, as amended by Public Law 111-203, title X, 124 Stat. 2092 (2010).

Soft law

Australia

Australian Competition & Consumer Commission (ACCC), Debt Collection Guide: For Collectors and Creditors (April, 2021), text available at <https://www.accc.gov.au/publications/debt-collection-guideline-for-collectors-creditors>.

European Union

European Commission, Communication from the Commission to the European Parliament, the Council and the European Economic and Social Committee – A New Deal for Consumers (11.4.2018, COM (2018) 183 final).

Proposal of the European Parliament's Committee on Economic and Market Affairs (CEMA) for a 'Directive on credit servicers, credit purchasers and the recovery of collateral' (NPLD) COM/2018/0135 final – 2018/063 (COD).

Germany

German Federal Ministry of Justice and Consumer Protection, 'Draft Law for Strengthening of the Protection of Consumers in the Context of Debt Collection' ["Entwurf eines Gesetzes zur Verbesserung des Verbraucherschutzes in Inkassorecht "].

Soft law

Hungary

A Pénzügyi Szervezetek Állami Felügyelete elnökének 14/2012. (XII.13.) számú ajánlása a követeléskezelő számára a követeléskezelési gyakorlatuk során elvárt fogyasztóvédelmi elvekről.

Court and agency (authority) cases

European Court of Justice

Order of the General Court (Eight Chamber) as of 17 Dec. 2020 in the case T-350/20 on the action of Lukáš Wagenrecht, member of the Senate of the Czech Parliament [ECLI: E.U.:T:2020:635].

Nemzeti Fogyasztóvédelmi Hatóság v. UPC Magyarország Kft (C-388/13 ECLI:EU:C:2015:225).

Hungary

Case No. FK-I-5041/2011 (filing No/Ikt./Ref.: 27263/2/2011)) as of 29 April 2011; not published, on file with the author.

EBH 2006.1477.

United States

Henson v. Santander Consumer USA, Inc. 137 S. Ct. 1718 (2017).

Books, monographs, dictionaries

Dam, W. Kenneth, *The Law-Growth Nexus: The Rule of Law and Economic Development* (Brookings Institution Press, 2006).

Kleine-Cosack, Michael, *Rechtsdienstleistungsgesetz – RDG Kommentar* (C.F. Müller Verlag, 1st ed., 2008).

Tajti, Tibor and Iglikowski, Peter, *A Cross Border Study of Freezing Orders and Provision Measures – Does Mareva Rule the Waves?* (Springer, 2018).

Tamanaha, Brian Z., *On the Rule of Law* (Cambridge University Press, 2004).

Warren, E., Westbrook, J.L., Porter, K., and Pottow, J.A.E., *The Law of Debtors and Creditors – Text, Cases, and Problems* (Wolters Kluwer, 8th ed., 2021).

Werlauff, Eric, *Civil Procedure in Denmark* (Wolter Kluwers, 3rd ed., 2017).

Edited books

Messmann, Stefan and Tajti (Thaythy), Tibor, *The Case Law of Central and Eastern Europe – Enforcement of Contracts, Editors' Introduction* (European University Press, 2009).

Law journals and law reviews

Keirsbilck, Bert, 'The UCPD's Notion of 'Commercial Practice': UPC Magyarország' (2016) Common Market L. Rev. 53: 527–542.

Kochenov, Dimitry Vladimirovich, 'Upgrading Rule of Law in Europe in Populist Times' (2021) XII/1 Pravni Zapisi 16–29.

Krygier, Martin, 'Transitional Questions about the Rule of Law: Why, What, and How?' In: Adam Czarnota (ed.), *East Central Europe/L'Europe du Centre Est: Eine Wissenschaftliche Zeitschrift*, vol. 28, part 1 (2001), Special Issue: Ius and Lex in East Central Europe Socio-Legal Conditions of the Rule of Law amid Post-Communist Transformation, pp. 1–34.

Palombella, Gianluigi, 'The Abuse of the Rule of Law' (2020) Hague J. on the Rule Law 12: 387–397.

Rosenfeld, Michel, 'The Rule of Law and the Legitimacy of Constitutional Democracy' (2001) S. Cal. L. Rev. 74: 1307.

Sajó, András, 'The Rule of Law as Legal Despotism: Concerned Remarks on the Use of Rule of Law in Illiberal Democracies' (2019) Hague J. on the Rule Law 11(2–3): 371–376.

Stanescu, G. Catalin, 'Regulation of Abusive Debt Collection Practices in the E.U. Member States: An Empirical Account' (2021) Journal of Consumer Policy.

Sunstein, Cass R., 'Problems with Rules' (1995) Cal. L. Rev. 83: 953–1023, at 968–969; and Hayek, F.A., *The Constitution of Liberty* (University of Chicago Press, 1960).

Tajti (Thaythy), Tibor, 'A Holistic Approach to Extra-Judicial Enforcement and Private Debt Collection – A Comparative Account of Trends, Empirical Evidence, and the Connected Regulatory Challenges' – Part One (2019), Pravni Zapisi, vol. X, no. 2, pp. 275–331, and Part Two (2020), Pravni Zapisi, vol. XI, no. 1, pp. 17–69.

Tamanaha, Z. Brian, 'The History and Elements of the Rule of Law' (2012) Sing J Legal Stud 232.

Newspaper articles

Industrial publications

Jérusalmy, Olivier, Fox, Paul, and Hercelin, Nicolas, 'Is the Human Dignity of Individual Debtors at Risk? – A Research Paper on Debt Collectors' Practices and the Protect of Debtor Household Income' (2020) available at https://www.finance-watch.org/wp-content/uploads/2020/01/Report_Human-dignity_final_with-annex.pdf.

[Other] Internet-based sources

Hebert, Amy, 'When Dead Debts Come Back to Life' (28 October 2015) available at https://www.consumer.ftc.gov/blog/2015/10/when-dead-debt-comes-back-life.

2 Regulation of abusive informal debt collection practices in Croatia

Paula Poretti[1]

2.1 Introduction

The Croatian economy is, without doubt, one of the weakest in the EU and, therefore, Croatian consumer-debtors among the most indebted. The Financial Crisis in 2008 caused the loss of jobs and decrease of personal income. The low resilience of the Croatian economy also heightened the issues with the repayment of the debt for many of them.[1]

The problems many over-indebted consumers faced were recognized, and a set of measures aimed at facilitating their position were introduced in the Croatian Enforcement law in 2017 and 2018. They were to remove systematic deficiencies in the functioning of the enforcement system. However, the reform was limited, and several aspects were left untackled. Among them, how the costs of the enforcement proceedings are collected, and the conduct of court and FINA[2] remained generators of costs and the further rise of debt for the debtors. In addition, the detected absence of a regulation against abusive informal (non-judicial) debt collection was overlooked entirely. Due to the narrow and unilateral approach, which directed the reform only towards resolving particular issues faced by consumer-debtors and their creditors, a market for abusive debt collection practices remained out of the legislative reach.[3]

1 Paula Poretti, PhD, Associate Professor and Vice-dean for education and students, Faculty of Law Osijek, J.J. Strossmayer University of Osijek, pporetti@pravos.hr. This paper is a product of work that has been fully supported by the Faculty of Law Osijek Josip Juraj Strossmayer University of Osijek under the project nr. IP-PRAVOS-10 'The contemporary trends in development of Croatian civil judiciary.'

2 Financial Agency (Fina) is a legal person whose founder and owner is the Republic of Croatia. It is the body competent to carry out and coordinate enforcement against pecuniary assets, along with participation of the Croatian National Bank (*Hrvatska narodna banka* – HNB) and commercial banks.

3 For a detailed overview of measures introduced in Croatian Enforcement law in 2019 see Poretti, Paula, 'Debt Collection Practices under Croatian enforcement law – Is there a way out for over-indebted consumers,' Journal of European Consumer and Market Law (EuCML), C.H. Beck/Kluwer Law International, Nomos (2018), 233–241.

DOI: 10.4324/9781003343158-3

This further deteriorated the position of over-indebted consumers by exposing them to abusive collectors. Namely, at the time, only 6,248 of over-indebted consumers were exempted from their total debt (for the debt up to 10,000 kn; approx. 1,333 euro) through Government measures, which meant that a total number of 325,254 over-indebted citizens still faced enforcement, whether by means of a judicial or non-judicial debt collection. It was evident that a portion of that debt will end up being enforced by private debt collection agencies. The reform did not incentivize banks to exempt the debtors from their debt, and, thus, facilitated selling it off to the agencies, for a part of its value.

The specific path of non-judicial, informal debt collection practice has been present in Croatia since 2010. It offered creditors a more convenient approach to debt collection, especially in situations where, due to over-indebtedness, judicial methods had a limited or no chance of success. At the same time, it offered no legal protection for consumer debtors since informal debt collection is not specifically regulated under the current Croatian legal framework. This became especially obvious when a new health and economic crisis emerged in 2020, which required even more efforts to help citizens struggling with their inability to repay the debt and the often-abusive debt collection practices they are exposed to.

Before discussing the lack and the need for an effective sector-specific regulation of abusive informal debt collection practices, an overview of the current situation of indebtedness will be presented. An insight into the informal debt collection in Croatia will be offered, coupled with the current (abusive) practices. Finally, arguments in favor of regulating debt collection agencies and their activities will be provided.

2.2 Current situation of indebtedness and debt collection during Covid-19 pandemic in Croatia

To understand the current situation and the impact the Covid-19 pandemic has had on the overall indebtedness of citizens in Croatia, it is necessary to provide both a quantitative and qualitative analysis.

On 17 April 2020, AEAMA[4] was introduced and entered into force a day after. The introduced emergency measures temporarily stopped enforcement against monetary assets of natural person debtors, except in case of maintenance and other similar claims. The Act was to be applied during the period of special circumstances, for the subsequent three months, or exceptionally, for a more extended period, if the legislator finds it necessary.[5] The introduced moratorium

4 Act on amendments of the Act on enforcement against monetary assets (Zakon o dopuni Zakona o provedbi ovrhe na novčanim sredstvima) Official Gazette 47/20.

5 arg. *ex* Article 2 of the Act on amendments of the Act on enforcement against monetary assets.

on enforcement proceedings lasted for six months (the longest period in EU) and was lifted in October 2020.[6]

When the moratorium was lifted and approximately 1.4 million enforcement proceedings were initiated in Croatia (16 billion HRK), out of which 1.2 million were previously initiated proceedings and 200,000 new ones.[7]

More than half a year after the emergency measures ceased, on 31 July 2021, there were 242,626 over-indebted consumers in enforcement proceedings, 0.6% more than in June 2021, and 4.8% more than in December 2020. The overall debt was 17.9 billion HRK/approx. 2.38 billion euro and 6.7 billion HRK/approx. 0.8 billion euro interests (2% more than in June 2021 and 5.7% more than in December 2020 (Table 2.1).[8] The increase in the number of over-indebted consumers shows that the Covid-19 pandemic generated further debt repayment problems. Therefore, one could conclude that the emergency measures – although welcome as a provisional measure – should not mark the end, but rather the beginning of designing support and solutions to fight and overcome problems consumer-debtors face in the Croatian legal system.

Concerning the structure of debt, it is notable that its most considerable portion, approx. 733,000,000 million euro (without interests), is consumer debt towards banks and 853,000,000 million euro towards other financial institutions.[9] These figures depict the comprehensiveness of the problem and the danger faced by consumers. Namely, if the banks or other financial institutions are unsuccessful in recovering the debt they might choose to transfer or sell their claims to private debt collection agencies. The figures alone should be sufficient incentive for exploring the topic of informal debt collection in Croatia. Undoubtedly, there are additional ones. One can be that, although informal debt collection cannot be considered novel, since it first emerged in Croatia over a decade ago, it is still an unregulated path. Also, it is interesting to note that there was no significant legal research, and it remained largely unexplored in Croatian legal literature. As such, one can only presume that it offers creditors a convenient approach to maximize collection or at least to minimize the loss due to inability of the consumer-debtors to repay their debt. At the same time it provides weak or no guarantees to the rights of over-indebted consumers in the process. To explore whether and to what extent this presumption is accurate, it is necessary first to define the notion of

6 Under the Act, on 18 April 2020 Croatian Financial Agency (FINA) interrupted enforcement proceedings for 244,865 natural persons, out of which for a prevailing number of 234,587 over-indebted consumers.

7 Information retrieved from the official webpage of FINA: <https://www.fina.hr/-/zastoj-ovrhe-na-novcanim-sredstvima-mjera-pomoci-fizickim-osobama-uslijed-pojave-epidemije-bolesti-covid-19>.

8 Information retrieved from the official webpage of FINA: <https://www.fina.hr/-/zastoj-ovrhe-na-novcanim-sredstvima-mjera-pomoci-fizickim-osobama-uslijed-pojave-epidemije-bolesti-covid-19>.

9 Information retrieved from the official webpage of FINA: <https://www.fina.hr/gradani/ovrha-na-novcanim-sredstvima>.

Table 2.1 Consumer Overindebtedness in Croatia

Date	*Number of consumers*	*Main debt HRK/euro*	*Interests*	*Total HRK/europ*
31.12.2020.	231.602	16.960.120.142/2.261.466.670	6.299.030.872/840.000.000	**23.259.151.014/3.101.333**
30.06.2021.	241.086	17.571.443.398/2.342.933.333	6.495.150.710/866.133.333	**24.066.594.108/3.208.933**
31.07.2021.	242.626	17.920.713.727/2.389.333.333	6.708.545.637/894.400.000	**24.629.259.364/3.284.000**

Source: Financial Agency FINA – the Register

informal debt collection and consult the existing legal framework under which debt collectors currently operate in Croatia.

2.3 Informal debt collection in Croatia

2.3.1 The (lack of) sector-specific regulation on informal debt collection

In the Croatian legal system, the legal gap concerning informal debt collection is not merely a lack of a definite legal rules but a complete absence of its specific regulation. In this sense, there are difficulties in defining and understanding it without referring to its notion in foreign legal literature and legislation. According to legal literature, along with the traditional method of judicial enforcement, the creditors may resort to non-judicial debt collection.[10] Informal debt collection is the recovery of debt without the participation of state authorities, the judiciary, or other state agents (bailiffs, sheriffs, or police officers). As a form of private enforcement, it is mentioned in various legal documents (the Draft Common Frame of Reference, the Fair Debt Collection Practices Act in the U.S., or the Consumer Credit Sourcebook in the U.K.).[11] Similarly, Advocate General Maduro[12] defined it as an act or practice, which is intended to encourage a debtor to settle an unpaid debt, with the exception of any recovery based on an enforcement order. For reasons such as duration, procedural fees, and (in)efficiency of judicial procedure, non-judicial debt collection can even seem like a more attractive option to the creditor.[13] At the same time, the lack of a due process requirement and other procedural guarantees allow the non-judicial debt collection to become abusive, which results in violations of consumer-debtors' legal rights.

The debt collectors act as agencies that provide debt recovery for a client and charge a fee based on their success. In other cases, they operate as debt collectors based on assignment (*cession*). Their income is earned based on the residual of the purchasing price for the debt (inclusive of the operative costs) and the collected debt. According to the Croatian National Bank (CNB),[14] for the credit institution to be allowed to sell the debt, the sale has to be economically feasible. The

10 See Stănescu, Catalin-Gabriel, 'Regulation of Abusive Debt Collection Practices in the EU member States: An Empirical Account,' Journal of Consumer Policy, 44(2021), 179–216, at p. 180.

11 Harmonization of Regulation of Abusive Non-Judicial Debt Collection in the European Union: Models, Benefits and Challenges, available at <https://cordis.europa.eu/project/id/798912>.

12 *Commission of the European Communities v. Italian Republic*, Case C-134/05, ECLI:EU:C:2007:435 (*Commission v. Italy*).

13 See Spanogle, J. A., Rohner, R. J., Pridgen, D., Sovern, J., & Peterson, C. L. (2013). *Consumer law. Cases and materials* (4th ed.). (2013), St Paul in: Stănescu, Catalin-Gabriel, Regulation of Abusive Debt Collection Practices in the EU member States: An Empirical Account, Journal of Consumer Policy, 44(2021), 179–216, at p. 180.

14 Petričić, Darko, Deset koraka kako na sudu pobijediti agencije koje su ilegalno kupile vase dugove, available at a web portal Otvoreno.hr: <https://otvoreno.hr/gospodarstvo/novac/deset-koraka-kako-na-sudu-pobijediti-agencije-koje-su-ilegalno-kupile-vase-dugove/370873>.

feasibility of the debt sale is obvious from the inability of the credit institution to collect the debt from the consumer-debtor in a timely way.

A bank considers a bank loan as defaulted if the debtor cannot repay a loan instalment or is behind with payment for more than 90 days. This is per Regulation 575/2013[15] and applied by banks in all Member States.[16] There are several steps which the banks and other credit institutions take in order to collect the defaulted debt. In the early stage, the debtor is informed that he is behind with payments (via text messages, written warnings, or a call center for debt collection). In the second stage, the bank or other credit institution cooperates with the consumer-debtor to establish the reasons for the default and find a possible solution (adjustment of the repayment plan). If the second stage is unsuccessful, one of the exit strategies is employed (enforcement, settlement, partial dismissal of the debt). The enforcement proceedings are initiated only if there are no other available methods. Judicial enforcement is considered long, inefficient, and overburdensome for both the bank or other credit institution and the consumer-creditor.[17]

With the debt sale, the consumer debtor's obligation does not cease to exist. The person (natural or legal) who purchases the debt becomes the new creditor to whom the consumer-debtor must repay the debt. In some cases, the bank that sold the debt as a prior creditor continues collecting monthly instalments for the new creditor. This ensures no obvious changes for the consumer-creditor in the debt repayment.

Debt collection agencies have developed specific informal debt collection practices in the Croatian market which raise serious concerns regarding their permissiveness. Regardless, they are still allowed to conduct business by applying a bare minimum of legal rules provided under a fragmented general legal framework,[18] without licensing or supervision.

15 Regulation (EU) No 575/2013 of the European Parliament and of the Council of 26 June 2013 on prudential requirements for credit institutions and investment firms and amending Regulation (EU) No 648/2012 Text with EEA relevance, OJ L 176, 27.6.2013, pp. 1–337.

16 Ploh, Matija, Naplata neprihodonosnih kredita u bankama, Privredna kretanja i ekonomska politika, 25(2017)2, 39–69.

17 Pavlović, Andrea, Upravljanje NPL plasmanima u okruženju", rad prezentiran na konferenciji "18. znanstveno-stručna konferencija Hrvatsko novčano tržište" u organizaciji Tržišta novca Zagreb, Opatija, 8. svibnja 2015 in: Ploh, Matija, Naplata neprihodonosnih kredita u bankama, Privredna kretanja i ekonomska politika, 25(2017)2, 39–69.

18 This includes the Civil Obligations Act (Zakon o obveznim odnosima), Act on Enforcement of Monetary Funds (Zakon o ovrsi na novčanim tražbinama), Enforcement Act (Ovršni zakon), Act on Credit Institutions (Zakon o kreditnim institucijama), Consumer Protection Act (Zakon o zaštiti potrošača), Act Against Money Laundering and Financing of Terrorism (Zakon o sprječavanju pranja novca i financiranja terorizma), General Data Protection Regulation (Uredba o GDPR-u), Consumer Credit Act (Zakon o potrošačkom kreditiranju), and Insolvency Act (Stečajni zakon). The list of applicable general legislation retrieved from the official web page of Croatian Association for Debt Collection (HUAN): <https://huan.hr/zakonska-regulativa/>.

In 2008, the Croatian Association for Debt Collection (HUAN) was established. It gathers eight out of 20 agencies estimated to operate in Croatia.[19] HUAN has been a member of the Federation of European National Collection Associations (FENCA) since 2011.[20] Although most agencies that are members of FENCA adhere to national legal rules and strict licensing regimes, Croatian agencies are under no such requirement. Namely, apart from complying with self-proclaimed ethical standards, which are to some extent derived from the international FENCA practices, there is no other similar obligation for members of HUAN.[21] In addition, although HUAN declares that its members comply with ethical standards (information published on the official website of the association)[22] there is no further information as to what these standards are. The standards are not published, or publicly available. There is no mention of the FENCA Code of conduct[23] either. Unlike other national collection agencies in Europe, HUAN has not addressed the possibility of self-regulation.[24]

Namely, from the very beginning, there were no attempts of systematic regulation of debt collection provided by debt collection agencies at the national level. Instead, their business activity was enabled by a Decision of the CNB on loan sale of credit institutions from 2013,[25] under Article 160a para 7 of the Credit Institutions Act.[26] According to a CNB statement, there was no formal initiative for issuing such a decision from the Government. Instead, the Decision was issued based on the CNB's assessment and in accordance with its legislative powers. It is important to note that under the relevant Croatian legislation, the powers of CNB concerning regulation of loan sales and monitoring of financial/credit institutions are prescribed, but not in detail.[27] *Argumentum a contrario*: since they are not financial institutions, collection agencies cannot fall under the CNB's juris-

19 It is very interesting to mention that there is a disclaimer at the official web page of the Association that it can only guarantee that the agencies which are members of the said association act in accordance with the ethical principles, but also offers a telephone number at which debtors can report an unethical act, in case it occurs. However, it is not obvious what would be the consequence of unethical behavior by an agency, since there is no legal regulation prescribing their business conduct. See HUAN official webpage <https://huan.hr/o-udruzi/>.

20 See HUAN official webpage <https://huan.hr/o-udruzi/>.

21 See HUAN official webpage <https://huan.hr/o-udruzi/>.

22 See HUAN official webpage <https://huan.hr/o-udruzi/>.

23 For more on FENCA Code of Conduct see the official webpage of FENCA: <https://fenca.eu/news/fenca-congress-2018>.

24 According to research into the regulation on abusive debt collection in EU, there are currently 10 Member States in which debt collectors have adopted Codes of Conduct. See Stănescu, Catalin-Gabriel, 'Regulation of Abusive Debt Collection Practices in the EU member States: An Empirical Account, Journal of Consumer Policy,' 44(2021), 179–216, at p. 208.

25 Decision on loan sale of credit institutions (Odluka o kupoprodaji kreditnih plasmana) Official Gazette 67/2013.

26 Credit Institutions Act (Zakon o kreditnim institucijama) Official Gazette 159/2013.

27 See relevant Croatian legislation (Act on Credit Institutions Official Gazette 159/13, 19/15, 102/15, 15/18, 70/19, 47/20, 146/20 and Act on Croatian National Bank Official Gazette 75/2008, 54/2013, 47/2020).

diction to monitor and control their activity. Hence, it is questionable whether the CNB had the authority to issue the Decision from 2013. Namely, it has no mechanisms to ensure that in the process, the debtors' rights will be respected under the existing national legislation, as was prescribed under Article 14 of the Decision.[28] The same provision to Article 14 of the Decision was also introduced under subsequent amended Decisions on loan sales of credit institutions which provided for sales of non-performing loans (NPLs) in Croatia, including the most recent Decision from 2021.[29] However, until now, no adequate means have been introduced in order to ensure its application.

For the bank or other credit institution to sell the NPL, it has to notify the CNB[30] and deliver the required documentation.[31] From the wording of the Decision from 2021, it is not apparent whether the CNB is entitled to approve the agreement's signing after the receipt and control of the documentation. The bank/credit institution and the buyer sign the agreement following Article 2 para 1 of the Decision from 2021. The agreement stipulates the conditions of the NPLs sale, including the managing and collection of monetary claim (debt). The Decision from 2021 prescribes that in case the buyer provides the managing and collection of debt, the seller must stipulate the obligation of debt collection with respect and regard for the protection of the debtor's integrity and reputation (arg. *ex* Article 10 para 3 Decision). The agreement should also include a requirement of no further deterioration of the position of the debtors (arg. *ex* Article 10 para 3 Decision). This requirement also includes collecting debt through collaterals (arg. *ex* Article 10 para 4 Decision). According to the 2021 Decision's wording (as well as previous Decisions on the matter), the agreement provides fundamental obligations for the buyer in their further conduct towards the debtor and debt collection.

Regardless of those mentioned above, according to official information provided by HUAN, the legal background for collection activities of debt collectors is provided under provisions of the COA[32] on assignment of claims (cession) (Article 80–89) and several other general acts on enforcement of claims. There is no mention of the agreements on the NPL sale based on the CNB's Decision. Furthermore, as the case law of Croatian courts shows, in the course of disputes with consumer-debtors, the agencies collecting the debt refer to COA prescribing assignment of claim (cession) and disclose merely information on the assignment. If the question of the existence and terms of the agreement on the NPL sale arises,

28 The Decision on the loan sale of credit institutions stipulates that the seller is obligated to ensure that consumers do not find themselves in an unfavorable position with the buyer or a third person to whom the loan has been transferred, compared to their position with the bank (Article 14 Decision of loan sale of credit institutions). However, it is not obvious how the CNB controls whether the seller of a third person complies with these obligations.

29 Decision on loan sale of credit institutions (Official Gazette 127/2014, 24/2018 and 26/2021).

30 Arg. *ex* Article 8 para 1 Decision on loan sale of credit institutions from 2021.

31 Arg. *ex* Article 12 Decision.

32 Civil Obligations Act (Zakon o obveznim odnosima) Official Gazette 35/05, 41/08, 125/11, 78/15, 29/18, 126/21.

the agencies invoke their confidentiality and refuse to disclose the details as to their obligations under them.[33] However, without the access to both agreements, it is impossible to understand their relationship and the nature of the transfer of the same debt, first by way of a NPL sale and afterwards by way of an assignment.[34] In addition, this agreement provides information to the consumer debtor on the conditions of the NPL sale and stipulates the obligation of consumer protection of both the seller and the buyer. Namely, Article 14 of the Decision from 2021 prescribes the seller's obligation to ensure that the position of consumer-debtors does not deteriorate as a result of the transfer. It also provides for a solidary obligation of the seller, the buyer, or a third person (a person who bought the debt from the buyer) for any damage incurred to the consumer-debtor for falling into a factually or legally more adverse position than the one he held previously. In addition, the undertaken analysis of available court practice indicates that, although examined agreements do not stipulate the possibility of further NPL sale to third persons, nevertheless, the sale was undertaken.[35]

Even though the debt collectors rely on provisions of the COA on assignment (Article 80–89 COA), the overall approach towards the next steps and the possibility of offering the debtor co-signing the assignment agreement along with the seller and the buyer is unharmonized. It is essential to note that, while providing information to the debtor on the assignment is required, his consent is not a prerequisite of the validity of the assignment agreement.[36] However, in many cases, the consumer debtors try to (unsuccessfully) rely on the missing consent as a reason for invoking nullity of the agreement before the court.[37] Although there is no formal requirement, when a seller and a buyer conclude the assignment, to ensure that the debtor is informed (arg. *ex* Article 82 para 1 COA),[38] as a rule, it

33 In a case before the Municipal Court in Osijek, Povvr-267/2017, the plaintiff (the agency) explained that it would be impossible to produce the agreement since it is written in English, refers to the sale of 2,000 different debts and it would be considered as a violation of privacy if the information on 2,000 consumer-debtors contained in the agreement would be made available to the court and the defendant.

34 The issue of the nature of the relationship, as well as the validity of such debt transfer, has arisen in case Povvr-267/2017 before the Supreme Court of the Republic of Croatia, but unfortunately did not meet the criteria to be examined.

35 Petričić, Darko, Deset koraka kako na sudu pobijediti agencije koje su ilegalno kupile vase dugove, available at a web portal Otvoreno.hr: <https://otvoreno.hr/gospodarstvo/novac/deset-koraka-kako-na-sudu-pobijediti-agencije-koje-su-ilegalno-kupile-vase-dugove/370873>.

36 County Court in Velika Gorica 13 Gž Zk-638/2021-2. According to Article 82 para 1 COA consent of a debtor is not a prerequisite for the assignment, but the creditor as seller is required to notify (inform) the debtor of the assignment. However, as accurately confirmed by the first instance court in his decision, it is not a prerequisite of validity of a loan sale agreement.

37 High Commercial Court of the Republic of Croatia, Pž 1395/2018-2, from 8 June 2020; County Court in Varaždin, 35 Gž-162/2021-2 – 22 July 2020; County Court in Split 22 Gž-2140/19-3 from 22 April 2020.

38 The debtor has to be informed of the assignment, but his consent is not required in order for the assignment to be legal. See also 13 Gž Zk-638/2021-2. However, in the case at hand the County Court has ruled that providing information to the debtor is not a requirement.

would be advisable for the debtor to co-sign it along with the parties.[39] However, in most cases the parties to the agreement avoid providing the consumer-debtor with that possibility. They fail to consider that a signature is an acknowledgment of debt and provides a buyer with proof of its entitlement. This is both recognized and confirmed by existing case law.[40]

Under the COA, after the assignment of the claim, the buyer is a controller of the processing of personal data and provisions of the GDPR[41] apply.

As for the CPA[42] in which provisions of the UCPD[43] are transposed, according to the information obtained in research conducted recently, the agencies as buyers are not aware of the existing body of applicable E.U. law or available remedies for the protection of consumer-debtors.[44] The same is also confirmed concerning Croatia, within the same research.[45] Conversely, the official webpage of HUAN refers to provisions of the CPA as part of the relevant legal framework under which its members operate in Croatia.

Since some of the agencies also resort to legal action in debt collection, as an initial step, they tend to initiate enforcement proceedings under the provisions of EA[46] in order to collect the debt. In 2020, due to the coronavirus epidemic, a set of measures aimed at relaxing the position of indebted citizens and companies was introduced by the Croatian Government (already in March 2020). It was decided that the credit institutions would render decisions and not employ coercive payment measures (enforcement orders) towards natural and legal persons for three months starting from 20 April 2020, in case they are unable to pay the credit loan

39 Pž 1480/2019-2 from 13 March 2020. 'By determining that within an assignment (cession) agreement from 1 March 2017, the trader (N.T.m.d.o.o.) transferred his claim of 5.379,02 HRK to the buyer and that the agreement was signed by the seller, the buyer and the debtor, the court of first instance concluded that the buyer is a new creditor under Article 80 para 1 COA (Official Gazette 35/05, 41/08, 125/11 and 78/15).'

40 Pž 1480/2019-2 from 13 March 2020. 'In order for the third person to be able to request fulfilment of a claim as a creditor, he has to provide evidence that it has been transferred to him by the previous creditor. In case the debtor signed the assignment agreement, the agreement serves as evidence of the existence of a claim. This is based on the fact that, by signing the agreement, the debtor confirms the existence of the debt towards the previous creditor.'

41 Regulation (EU) 2016/679 of the European Parliament and of the Council of 27 April 2016 on the protection of natural persons with regard to the processing of personal data and on the free movement of such data, and repealing Directive 95/46/EC, OJ L 119, 4.5.2016, pp. 1–88. (arg. *ex* Article 4 para 7 GDPR).

42 Consumer Protection Act (Zakon o zaštiti potrošača) Official Gazette 41/14, 110/15, 14/19.

43 Directive (EU) 2019/2161 of the European Parliament and of the Council of 27 November 2019 amending Council Directive 93/13/EEC and Directives 98/6/EC, 2005/29/EC and 2011/83/EU of the European Parliament and of the Council as regards the better enforcement and modernisation of Union consumer protection rules, OJ L 328, 18.12.2019, pp. 7–28.

44 See Stănescu, Catalin-Gabriel, 'Regulation of Abusive Debt Collection Practices in the EU member States: An Empirical Account, Journal of Consumer Policy,' 44(2021), 179–216, p. 189.

45 Study for the Fitness check of EU consumer and marketing law, Final report part 3 – Country reporting, DG for Justice and Consumers 2017, pp. 152–155.

46 Enforcement Act (Ovršni zakon) Official Gazette 112/12, 25/13, 93/14, 55/16, 73/17, 131/20, (hereinafter EA).

instalments regularly. This measure would apply only if the debtors' creditors in question were not brought into an unequal position in comparison to other creditors. The debtors needed to request that the measure be applied in each case. On 17 April 2020, AEAMA[47] came into force and introduced emergency measures of the second stage. Although in the other Member States, debt collectors voluntarily suspended recovery during the pandemic, in Croatia, members of HUAN only suspended enforcement of the pending proceedings and initiation of new proceedings at the part of Croatia affected by an earthquake in December 2020.[48] All other suspension was statutory.

2.3.2 Abusive non-judicial debt collection practices

Non-judicial (informal) debt collection is not monitored closely by a regulatory body in Croatia. In addition, the CNB has no authority to oversee the activities of debt collection agencies.[49] Consequently, there are no overview reports to give an insight into their activities or practices. The only publicly available evidence on abusive debt collection practices is provided in the yearly reports submitted by the Ombudswoman of Croatia. For several years now, the Ombudswoman has repeatedly been warning of the abusive practices of collection agencies and problems indebted consumers face. The evidence she provided includes detailed submissions her office received from consumer-debtors affected by such practices.[50] Most common complaints refer to consumer-debtors' inability to get information from the agency on the amount of their debt. Some of them also express concern that the agencies practice double debt collection, which is impossible to establish without insight into the outstanding debt calculation. Consumer-debtors complain of the inability to negotiate the manner of debt repayment or arrange for more favorable conditions. A specific category of abusive practices reported by consumer-debtors refers to exercising force, intimidation, and repeated phone calls and visits to the debtor, his family members, friends, or even neighbors.[51] Although the Ombudswoman has no legal competence to investigate these prac-

47 Act on amendments of the Act on enforcement against monetary assets (Zakon o dopuni Zakona o provedbi ovrhe na novčanim sredstvima) Official Gazette 47/2020.

48 See Varošanec, Suzana, Do daljnjega bez straha od ovrha za građane Gline, Petrinje i Siska, kreću prvi otpisi dugova, available at the web portal Poslovni dnevnik: <https://www.poslovni.hr/hrvatska/clanice-huan-a-obustavile-provedbu-novih-ovrsnih-postupaka-na-potresom-pogodenim-podrucjima-4267407>.

49 This is also confirmed in the Ombudswoman of Croatia annual reports which detect the lack of legal framework defining standards and rules on conduct of debt collectors as one of the main reasons behind the abusive practices that consumer-debtors face. Available at the official webpage of Ombudswoman's office: <https://www.ombudsman.hr/hr/siva-zona-naplate-dugova-nedostatak-pravila-duznike-cini-dodatno-ranjivima/>.

50 See the Ombudswoman's report for 2019 on finances available at the official webpage of the Ombudswoman's office: <https://www.ombudsman.hr/hr/financije/>.

51 Ombudswoman's report for 2020, pp. 134–135, available at the official webpage of the Ombudswoman's office: <https://www.ombudsman.hr/hr/izvjesca-puckog-pravobranitelja/>.

tices, in the reports, she emphasizes that her office advises consumer-debtors on the legal assistance they can acquire within the legal system.[52]

The annual reports of the Croatian Agency[53] also mention complaints from the consumer-debtors and third persons against debt collection agencies for violations of personal data protection rules. One such example is a complaint against the debt collection agency, which contacted a woman on her private mobile phone number in order for her to take a message for her neighbor regarding the debt owed to the agency. She was surprised that the debt collection agency asked numerous questions about the neighbor. The woman confirmed to the Agency that she is not a consumer-debtor and has no obligations towards the debt collection agency. After an investigation into the facts of the case, the Agency established that the complaint was founded and that the woman was contacted without any legal foundation regarding her neighbor's debt. The employee of the debt collection agency was unable to collect the information on the debtor from the available public registries, so instead, he contacted the said woman. The Agency decided against the debt collection agency and prohibited the debt collection agency from collecting or processing personal data of the woman in question or any other person for whom it is not established beyond doubt that he/she is a debtor. Since a violation of rules on personal data protection was established, the Agency also recommended that the debt collection agency improves its GDPR compliance and raise the level of implementation of the technical and organizational measures regarding personal data protection by Article 18 of the Act on the Implementation of the GDPR.[54] In addition, the debt collection agency was warned of the necessary measures to be introduced in order for the personal data of the debtors not to be revealed to third persons and the personal data to be processed fairly and legally. It was advised that processing operations referred to in Article 36(2) of the GDPR

52 According to the information provided on the official pages of Ombudswoman of Croatia, the office advises consumer-debtors that after HUAN and Croatian association of debtors (Blokirani) signed a cooperation agreement in March 2019, they regularly conciliate positions on questions of debt repayment, respect for ethical norms and communication which contributed to resolving 10,000 problems and situations of frozen accounts. <https://www.ombudsman.hr/hr/financije/>. At best, this can be considered as helpful information, but can not be classified as legal advice provided to consumer-debtors.

53 The Croatian Personal Data Protection Agency (the Agency) is the only independent public supervisory authority in the Republic of Croatia within the meaning of the provision of Article 51 of the Regulation (Eu) 2016/679 of the European Parliament and of the Council of 27 April 2016 on the protection of natural persons with regard to the processing of personal data and on the free movement of such data, and repealing Directive 95/46/EC (General Data Protection Regulation) and the Act on the Implementation of the General Data Protection Regulation (Official Gazette 44/2018). The Agency as a supervisory authority has investigative, corrective, and advisory powers. <https://azop.hr/about-the-agency/>.

54 Act on the Implementation of the GDPR (Zakon o provedbi Opće uredbe o zaštiti podataka) Official Gazette 42/2018.

should be put in place and codes of conduct drawn up pursuant to Article 40(1), which provide sufficient safeguards, under Article 40(5) of the GDPR.[55]

Similarly, Croatian newspapers and news portals regularly publish information on abusive practices of debt collection agencies. Since debt collection agencies started operating in Croatia, it is estimated that the overall debt purchased, in the largest number of cases from the banks, is 36 billion HRK/approx. 5 billion euro (one-quarter of the Croatian state budget). Although inquiries have been made to the CNB on the number of loan sales since 2013, instead of a concrete reply, the CNB only refers to its financial reports (which provide no particular information on the sales number). Nevertheless, from the reports it is possible to estimate that, on average, the debt is sold for 30–50% of its worth. At least, these are the official figures. It is impossible to establish whether they match the figures of the undertaken sales.

The debt collection agencies buy the debt from banks or other legal persons (credit institutions, utility companies) regardless of whether the enforcement proceedings have already been initiated or if a portion of the debt has already been repaid. Even if FINA has frozen the bank accounts of the consumer-debtor, the agencies still call the debtors inviting them to repay the debt. Although the consumer-debtors should first receive information on the assignment from the previous creditor, the agencies regularly send an additional notification immediately after the previous creditor has done so and start to contact the debtor over the telephone.[56]

Moreover, in numerous cases, the agencies tend to use open items statements, which they issued, as enforcement titles, which is contrary to Croatian enforcement law.[57] In order for the agencies as buyers to use open items statements as enforcement titles, they should be certified by an independent, competent entity. The trend of requesting direct enforcement of the total debt before it is due is also becoming more apparent. It is triggered by changes in circumstances of the debtor. The agencies initiate direct enforcement before FINA, or, more often, the debtors' employer, forcing the repayment of the whole debt at once instead of following the repayment plan previously agreed on by the bank and the consumer-debtor.[58] Although such practice is contrary to E.U. law, unfortunately, it is not adequately sanctioned in the Croatian legal system.

55 Mišljenja, primjeri i preporuke Agencije za obradu osobnih podataka; Prilog godišnjem izvješću o radu Agencije za zaštitu osobnih podataka za razdoblje 1. siječnja 2018. do 31. prosinca 2018., Agencija za zaštitu osobnih podataka, 2019, available at <https://sabor.hr/sites/default/files/uploads/sabor/2019-04 02/154603/PRILOG_AZOP_2018_MISLJENJA_PRIMJERI_PREPORUKE.pdf str. 38>.

56 Milojević, Tatjana, Agencije za naplatu potraživanja, PRO BONO Bilten pravne klinike Pravnog fakulteta u Zagrebu, 11(2019), 4–8. Available at <https://www.pravo.unizg.hr/_download/repository/Pro_bono_11.pdf>.

57 Enforcement titles are prescribed under Article 23 EA.

58 Petričić, Darko, Deset koraka kako na sudu pobijediti agencije koje su ilegalno kupile vase dugove, available at a web portal Otvoreno.hr: <https://otvoreno.hr/gospodarstvo/novac/deset-koraka-kako-na-sudu-pobijediti-agencije-koje-su-ilegalno-kupile-vase-dugove/370873>.

Some agencies request the debt repayment after the limitation period (prescription) has expired to trick the consumer-debtor into acknowledging the debt. For instance, if the consumer-debtor acknowledges the debt by repaying a portion of it, under Article 240 in connection to Article 244 COA, the limitation period is interrupted, and the agency can enforce the entire debt.[59]

According to Article 129 SA[60] a person inheriting the estate becomes an heir at the moment of the deceased's death. Although the heirs become liable for the deceased's debts (arg. *ex* Article 139 para 1 SA), the liability is limited to the value of the inherited estate (arg. *ex* Article 139 para 3 SA). If the heirs refuse to receive the estate, they are no longer liable for the debts (arg. *ex* Article 139 para 2 SA). However, when the agencies learn of the heirs, they attain the necessary information from the public notary competent to conduct succession proceedings or the state registry office and contact them. They request the repayment of the debt from the heirs of the indebted estate. Often, the heirs are unaware of the possibility of refusing the acceptance of the estate. The agencies take advantage of this fact and burden the heirs with the obligation of repaying a debt which is not theirs. Many such cases, described as fraudulent behavior on the part of the agencies, are reported in Croatian media and online.[61]

2.4 Remedies – available and desired

For the consumer-debtors, as a first step, it would be important to confirm if the agreement on bank loan concluded with the bank permits for the debt to be sold to a third person and under what conditions (arg. *ex* Article 80 para 2 COA). There is an established court practice on the validity of the debt purchase in cases where such stipulation was not in the original agreement.[62] Since it is often the case that the provisions of these agreements are contrary to general principles of the COA – such as fairness and diligence in performance and counter-performance – consumer-debtors should also check whether they could request the annulment of the agreements. If the agencies would not submit the agreement voluntarily,

59 According to the provisions of Article 244 COA, it shall not be sufficient for interruption of prescription for the creditor to request performance from the debtor in writing or by word of mouth. Prescription shall be interrupted by filing of a suit or any other action by the creditor against the debtor before a court or other competent body for the purpose of ascertaining, securing, or effecting a claim (Article 241 COA). However, actions against the debtor are connected with the risk of the court dismissal of the suit. Hence, Article 240 allows for the prescription to be interrupted if the debtor voluntarily repays a portion of the debt.

60 Succession Act (Zakon o nasljeđivanju) Official Gazette 48/03, 163/03, 35/05, 127/13, 33/15, 14/19.

61 See different webpages: <https://www.progreso.hr/blog/naplata-potrazivanja/; https://legalis.hr/topic/115887-agencija-za-naplatu-potra%C5%BEivanja/>; <https://dnevnik.hr/vijesti/hrvatska/provjereno-donosi-ispovijest-obitelji-zukanovic-i-pricu-o-nezaustavljivom-placanju-dugova---544304.html>.

62 High Commercial Court of the Republic of Croatia, Pž 1395/2018-2 from 8 June 2020.

there are mechanisms within the civil proceedings that ensure that the consumer-debtors can acquire it.

Similar to the Danish model where a contested debt purchased by an agency is considered illegal to collect,[63] in the aftermath of the CJEU judgment C-407/18,[64] Croatian civil courts, on application by the consumers, suspended the enforcement of a mortgage contract concluded between a bank and a consumer. The enforcement is suspended until the conclusion of civil proceedings against a bank for determining the potential unfairness of the contractual terms. Recently, the Supreme Court of the Republic of Croatia, in its judgment Rev-3375/2018 from 24 November 2021 confirmed that the courts may determine *ex officio* whether the terms of a mortgage contract are unfair, not only in separate court proceedings but also in the proceedings for declaring the enforcement inadmissible. These developments in the case law have had a direct influence on the proceedings initiated by consumer-debtors against debt collection agencies. The first issue the courts had to resolve was whether the consumer-debtor could initiate proceedings directly against the debt collection agency, request the terms of the mortgage contract to be declared unfair, and solicit the return of the over-paid amounts. The debt collection agencies claimed that they are not original creditors, which signed a contract with the consumer-debtor and they cannot be held liable for the unfair terms or the return of the over-paid amounts. The County Court in Pula[65] confirmed that, if the terms of a mortgage contract are declared unfair, the consumer-debtor is entitled to request the restitution of the amounts collected by the agency based on the assignment agreement with the bank (arg *ex* Article 84 para 2 COA).

The second issue was declaring the enforcement initiated by the debt collection agency against the consumer-debtor as inadmissible. On 22 October 2020, the Municipal Court in Čakovec found that the enforcement is inadmissible since the terms of the mortgage contract from which the debt purchased by the agency originates are unfair. In addition, the court found that the total amount owed by the consumer-debtor should be reduced significantly since, due to the unfair terms, a portion of the debt was over-paid. As a result, the consumer-debtor had to repay only half of the total amount of the debt purchased by the debt collection agency from a bank as the debtor's previous creditor.[66] The County Court in Varaždin[67] also warned that the assignment does not automatically transfer the overall legal position of the previous creditor from the contract (a bank or other credit institution) to the debt collection agency as the new creditor (arg. *ex* Article 80–89

63 See Stănescu, Catalin-Gabriel, 'Regulation of Abusive Debt Collection Practices in the EU member States: An Empirical Account, Journal of Consumer Policy,' 44(2021), 179-216, p. 189.

64 *Aleš Kuhar and Jožef Kuhar v. Addiko Bank d.d.*, Case C-407/18, ECLI:EU:C:2019:537.

65 County Court in Pula, Gž-426/2020-2 from 21 May 2020.

66 Information retrieved from the official webpage of Večernji list: <https://www.vecernji.hr/vijesti/prva-presuda-u-kojoj-je-zbog-nistetnosti-odredaba-umanjeno-potrazivanje-agencije-za-naplatu-1442307>.

67 County Court in Varaždin in his judgment also warned that the assignment of the claim Gž-1261/2017-2 from 23 October 2017.

COA). Namely, the contract term defining the court's jurisdiction in case of a dispute did not apply in the case of a dispute between a debtor and a new creditor.

These cases are evidence that relief to consumer-debtors could be made available through civil law remedies before civil courts in many situations. However, there are concerns of serious obstacles to their application. Pursuing legal protection before civil courts requires time, and generates high costs of legal representation and court fees. In many cases, this causes rational apathy of consumer-debtors to acquire any legal protection before courts. This is additionally intensified with the possibility of appeal and revision procedures, which further contribute to the duration and uncertainty of the outcome for the consumer-debtor.

Contrary to civil proceedings, ADR mechanisms are considered as more attractive, less costly, less complex, and more convenient. However, ADR mechanisms available to consumers in the Croatian legal system would not be suitable for resolving consumer-debtors' disputes with debt collection agencies (arg. *ex* Article 105 Consumer Protection Act in connection with the Croatian Act on Alternative Consumer Dispute Resolution[68]). There is no sector-specific legislation which the consumer-debtors could rely on. In addition, the decision of the competent ADR entity has no binding effect on the parties, which also undermines its effectiveness in comparison to other available legal paths.[69]

As to the collective redress mechanism available to consumers (Article 106 Consumer Protection Act), there are changes that would have to be introduced in its regulation to initiate such collective redress proceedings in Croatia. The upcoming implementation of the Directive (EU) 2020/1828 of the European Parliament and of the Council of 25 November 2020 on representative actions for the protection of the collective interests of consumers and repealing Directive 2009/22/EC[70] could be an opportunity for such legislative intervention.

Another available legal path for consumer-debtors to tackle the abusive practice of agencies is an administrative remedy. The consumer-debtor is allowed to file an objection against the buyer as a new creditor to the Market Inspection[71] with the State Inspectorate of the Republic of Croatia, which conducts inspec-

68 Act on Alternative Consumer Dispute Resolution (Zakon o alternativnom rješavanju potrošačkih sporova) Official Gazette 121/16, 32/19.

69 For comparison of civil proceedings and ADR in providing justice for consumers in Croatian legal system see Poretti, Paula, *Sudska zaštita prava potrošača – (naj)bolji put?*, Zbornik Pravnog fakulteta Sveučilišta u Rijeci, 39(2018)1, pp. 535–570; Mišćenić, Emilia; Tomljenović, Vesna, National Report (Croatia), Implementing EU Consumer Rights by National Procedural Law in: Hess, Burkhard; Law, Stephanie; (eds.). Oxford, Chicago, Baden-Baden: Beck/Hart/Nomos, 2019, 4–25.

70 Directive (EU) 2020/1828 of the European Parliament and of the Council of 25 November 2020 on representative actions for the protection of the collective interests of consumers and repealing Directive 2009/22/EC, OJ L 409, 4.12.2020, pp. 1–27.

71 See more on Market Inspection at the official webpage of the State Inspectorate of the Republic of Croatia: <https://dirh.gov.hr/o-drzavnom-inspektoratu/trzisna-inspekcija/85>; for regional offices of the Market Inspection see: <https://dirh.gov.hr/kontakti/podrucni-uredi-dezurne-inspekcije/131>.

tions in the field of consumer protection. In addition, the consumer-debtor may deliver detailed information on the credit institution which sold the debt to the Office for following the consumer protection at the CNB,[72] which is entitled to examine further the circumstances of every reported case.[73] However, this is only available if, prior to informing the Office for following the consumer protection, the consumer-debtor filed an objection to the credit institution and received no response or was unable to resolve the dispute. Upon receiving the information, the CNB offers remedies of a limited effect. Namely, the CNB is only entitled to check if the credit institution upholds internal acts, agreements, and applicable legal framework for consumer protection; ensure transparent and timely proceedings upon objections to the institution; and analyze objections regarding illegality and misconduct of the credit institution.[74] In contrast, the CNB is not allowed to influence business decisions of the credit institution; signing of bilateral or other agreements between a credit institution and consumers; intervene in or decide disputes between credit institutions and consumers; or order a credit institution to conduct activities other than those set as obligations under the agreement.[75]

There is also an available administrative relief in case of personal data protection rules violations, which are regularly applied against the debt collection agencies. Anyone who considers that their rights guaranteed by the GDPR and the Act on the Implementation of the GDPR have been violated, may submit a complaint to the Agency. The Agency shall decide on the violation of rights by a ruling. The ruling of the Agency shall be an administrative act. No appeal shall be allowed against the ruling of the Agency. However, an administrative dispute may be instituted by lodging a complaint before a competent administrative court (arg. *ex* Article 34 Act on the Implementation of the GDPR).

There is no published statistical data on the number of initiated criminal proceedings against debt collection agencies, but the available anecdotal evidence indicates certain trends. Cases are reported of consumer-debtors initiating criminal proceedings against debt collection agencies through a private lawsuit (arg. *ex* Article 60 Criminal proceedings Act[76]). In one such case, the consumer-debtor initiated civil proceedings against the agency for damages incurred due to the col-

72 The Croatian National Bank conducts its consumer protection policy by contributing to the development of the legal framework, exercising supervision of credit institutions within its competence with regard to the application of regulations governing consumer protection, and by conducting financial education activities. Information retrieved from the official webpage of the CNB: <https://www.hnb.hr/en/about-us/consumer-protection>.

73 Petričić, Darko, Deset koraka kako na sudu pobijediti agencije koje su ilegalno kupile vase dugove, available at a web portal Otvoreno.hr: <https://otvoreno.hr/gospodarstvo/novac/deset-koraka-kako-na-sudu-pobijediti-agencije-koje-su-ilegalno-kupile-vase-dugove/370873>.

74 Information retrieved from the official webpage of CNB: <https://www.hnb.hr/o-nama/zastita-potrosaca/prijavite-pitajte>.

75 Information retrieved from the official webpage of CNB: <https://www.hnb.hr/o-nama/zastita-potrosaca/prijavite-pitajte>.

76 Criminal Proceedings Act (Zakon o kaznenom postupku) Official Gazette 152/08, 76/09, 80/11, 121/11, 91/12, 143/12, 56/13, 145/13, 152/14, 70/17, 126/19, 126/19.

lection of an inexistent debt. The first instance court decided in favour of the consumer-debtor. However, the agencies kept calling the debtor inviting him to repay the debt. The debtor received more than 250 phone calls and messages in a short period. The consumer-debtor reported an offense to the Municipal State Attorney Office in Zagreb, which dismissed it on 30 October 2017. He filed a private lawsuit and initiated criminal proceedings against the agency and the responsible person for intrusive behavior. The first instance criminal court decided that there was no offence, since the period of duration of the behaviour was not sufficient for it to be considered intrusive.[77]

2.5 Conclusion

Looking at the available comparative solutions, two approaches to regulating the activities of debt collection agencies stand out as ubiquitous; self-regulation and statutory regulation.[78] In relation to self-regulation, the current situation and the lack of interest within the business should be understood as a clear indicator of the likelihood of its success in Croatia. Occasional media appearances of HUAN or its members, which emphasize the need for some kind of regulation and welcome possible future arrangements, can hardly be considered significant.[79] Even in the case of opting for self-regulation, the experience with it in relation to the UCPD has had only a minimal effect at the national level. Conduct codes are still the most widely introduced self-regulation mechanisms. However, the research into their effectiveness in prohibiting unlawful practices shows that they do not impose sufficiently deterrent sanctions and are not accompanied by mechanisms to remove agencies with such practices from the market.[80] Therefore, self-regulation is not an acceptable approach.

Conversely, sector-specific legislation would provide an answer to all the observed shortcomings, which the existing general regulation is not able to do. Regardless of the announced activities of the Ministry of Finance and the CNB,

77 Information retrieved from the official webpage of Vecernji list: <https://www.vecernji.hr/vijesti/stotine-sms-ova-i-250-poziva-sud-to-nije-nametljivo-ponasanje-1219194>.

78 The research shows that 79% of business associations found self- and co-regulation initiatives to be either 'very effective' or 'rather effective' in protecting consumer rights. In contrast, only 30% of consumer associations and 33% shared this view. A small minority of businesses agree that such initiatives were not effective in protecting consumer rights. The indicated reasons for the success of such initiatives included ensuring strong enforcement mechanisms such as public monitoring or impartial compliance procedures, and maintaining backing for such initiatives at the E.U. and Member State level. Study for the Fitness check of EU consumer and marketing law, Final report Part 1-Main report, DG Justice and Consumers, 2017, p. 94.

79 Rad agencija za naplatu potraživanja reguliran je nizom zakona i podzakonskih akata Republike Hrvatske, a članice HUAN-a podržavaju dodatnu regulaciju te su otvorene za suradnju u procesu donošenju ciljanog zakonskog okvira, u skladu s propisima EU. <https://huan.hr/zakonska-regulativa/>

80 Study for the Fitness check of EU consumer and marketing law, Final report part 3 – Country reporting, DG for Justice and Consumers 2017, pp. 154–155.

the faith of the Proposal of an Act on the protection of the debtor in specific cases of assignment from 2017 does not inspire confidence that such legislation would be introduced any time soon in Croatia. So far, only amendments to the income tax legislation have been introduced, to motivate the banks to write off/deduct portions of defaulted credit loans, rather than to sell the debt to the debt collection agencies. However, the effect of this recently introduced measure is still not apparent. The financial reports of the debt collection agencies suggest that their profit remains extremely high (even record profit for some).[81]

Still, the analysis above shows that a full-functioning body of the legislature, available and able to end abusive practices and offer legal certainty to the consumer-debtors, needs to be provided, without delay. It would also afford a level playing field to debt collection agencies whose business model is not based on abusive or aggressive debt collection. Fortunately, recent adoption of the Directive on Credit Servicers, which contains an extensive framework of rules concerning authorization and control of debt collectors, opened the pathway towards its introduction. It is now for the Croatian legislator to take the first step on this new and promising route.

Bibliography

Milojević, Tatjana, Agencije za naplatu potraživanja, PRO BONO Bilten pravne klinike Pravnog fakulteta u Zagrebu, 11(2019), 4–8. Available at https://www.pravo.unizg.hr/_download/repository/Pro_bono_11.pdf.

Mišćenić, Emilia and Tomljenović, Vesna, National Report (Croatia), *Implementing EU consumer rights by national procedural law* in: Hess, Burkhard and Law, Stephanie (eds.). Oxford, Chicago, and Baden-Baden: Beck/Hart/Nomos, 2019, 4–25.

Pavlović, Andrea, Upravljanje NPL plasmanima u okruženju", paper presented at 18. znanstveno-stručna konferencija Hrvatsko novčano tržište" organized by Tržišta novca Zagreb, Opatija, 8 May 2015 in: Ploh, Matija, Naplata neprihodonosnih kredita u bankama, Privredna kretanja i ekonomska politika, 25(2017)2, 39–69.

Petričić, Darko, Deset koraka kako na sudu pobijediti agencije koje su ilegalno kupile vase dugove, available at a web portal Otvoreno.hr: https://otvoreno.hr/gospodarstvo/novac/deset-koraka-kako-na-sudu-pobijediti-agencije-koje-su-ilegalno-kupile-vase-dugove/370873.

Ploh, Matija, Naplata neprihodonosnih kredita u bankama, Privredna kretanja i ekonomska politika, 25(2017)2, 39–69.

Poretti, Paula, Debt collection practices under Croatian enforcement law – Is there a way out for over-indebted consumers, Journal of European Consumer and Market Law (EuCML), C.H. Beck/Kluwer Law International, Nomos (2018).

Poretti, Paula, *Sudska zaštita prava potrošača – (naj)bolji put?*, Zbornik Pravnog fakulteta Sveučilišta u Rijeci, 39(2018)1, 535–570.

81 EOS Matrix emphasizes that its biggest investments in defaulted credit loans in 2021 was in Russia, Poland and Croatia: <https://b2kapital.hr/poslovanje-b2-kapitala-nastavlja-s-rastom-na-trzistima-hrvatske-i-sredisnje-europe/>. Also B2 Kapital reports record profit: <https://b2kapital.hr/poslovanje-b2-kapitala-nastavlja-s-rastom-na-trzistima-hrvatske-i-sredisnje-europe/>.

Spanogle, J. A., Rohner, R. J., Pridgen, D., Sovern, J., and Peterson, C. L., *Consumer law. Cases and materials* (4th ed.). (2013), St Paul in: Stănescu, Catalin-Gabriel, Regulation of abusive debt collection practices in the EU member states: An empirical account, Journal of Consumer Policy, 44(2021), 179–216, p. 180.

Stănescu, Catalin-Gabriel, Regulation of abusive debt collection practices in the EU member states: An empirical account, Journal of Consumer Policy, 44(2021), 179–216.

Varošanec, Suzana, Do daljnjega bez straha od ovrha za građane Gline, Petrinje i Siska, kreću prvi otpisi dugova, available at the web portal Poslovni dnevnik: https://www.poslovni.hr/hrvatska/clanice-huan-a-obustavile-provedbu-novih-ovrsnih-postupaka-na-potresom-pogodenim-podrucjima-4267407.

Study for the Fitness check of EU consumer and marketing law, Final report part 3 – Country reporting, DG for Justice and Consumers 2017.

Study for the Fitness check of EU consumer and marketing law, Final report Part 1-Main report, DG Justice and Consumers, 2017.

Ombudswoman's report for 2019 on financies available at the official webpage of the Ombudswoman's office: https://www.ombudsman.hr/hr/financije/.

Ombudswoman's report for 2020, p. 134-135, available at the official webpage of the Ombudswoman's office: https://www.ombudsman.hr/hr/izvjesca-puckog-pravobranitelja/.

Harmonization of Regulation of Abusive Non-Judicial Debt Collection in the European Union: Models, Benefits and Challenges, available at https://cordis.europa.eu/project/id/798912.

Mišljenja, primjeri i preporuke Agencije za obradu osobnih podataka; Prilog godišnjem izvješću o radu Agencije za zaštitu osobnih podataka za razdoblje 1. siječnja 2018. do 31. prosinca 2018., Agencija za zaštitu osobnih podataka, 2019, available at https://sabor.hr/sites/default/files/uploads/sabor/2019-04 02/154603/PRILOG_AZOP_2018_MISLJENJA_PRIMJERI_PREPORUKE.pdf.

Act on amendments of the Act on enforcement against monetary assets (Zakon o dopuni Zakona o provedbi ovrhe na novčanim sredstvima) Official Gazette 47/20.

Act on Alternative Consumer Dispute Resolution (Zakon o alternativnom rješavanju potrošačkih sporova) Official Gazette 121/16, 32/19.

Act on the Implementation of the General Data Protection Regulation; GDPR (Zakon o provedbi Opće uredbe o zaštiti podataka) Official Gazette 44/2018.

Act on credit institutions Official Gazette 159/13, 19/15, 102/15, 15/18, 70/19, 47/20, 146/20.

Act on Croatian National Bank Official Gazette 75/2008, 54/2013, 47/2020).

Civil Obligations Act (Zakon o obveznim odnosima) Official Gazette 35/05, 41/08, 125/11, 78/15, 29/18, 126/21.

Consumer Protection Act (Zakon o zaštiti potrošača) Official Gazette 41/14, 110/15, 14/19.

Credit Institutions Act (Zakon o kreditnim institucijama) Official Gazette 159/2013.

Criminal Proceedings Act (Zakon o kaznenom postupku) Official Gazette 152/08, 76/09, 80/11, 121/11, 91/12, 143/12, 56/13, 145/13, 152/14, 70/17, 126/19, 126/19.

Decision on loan sale of credit institutions (Odluka o kupoprodaji kreditnih plasmana) Official Gazette 67/2013.

Decision on loan sale of credit institutions Official Gazette 127/2014, 24/2018 and 26/2021.

Enforcement Act (Ovršni zakon) Official Gazette 112/12, 25/13, 93/14, 55/16, 73/17, 131/20.

Succession Act (Zakon o nasljeđivanju) Official Gazette 48/03, 163/03, 35/05, 127/13, 33/15, 14/19.

Directive (EU) 2019/2161 of the European Parliament and of the Council of 27 November 2019 amending Council Directive 93/13/EEC and Directives 98/6/EC, 2005/29/EC and 2011/83/EU of the European Parliament and of the Council as regards the better enforcement and modernisation of Union consumer protection rules, OJ L 328, 18.12.2019, p. 7–28.

Directive (EU) 2020/1828 of the European Parliament and of the Council of 25 November 2020 on representative actions for the protection of the collective interests of consumers and repealing Directive 2009/22/EC, OJ L 409, 4.12.2020, p. 1–27.

Regulation (EU) No 575/2013 of the European Parliament and of the Council of 26 June 2013 on prudential requirements for credit institutions and investment firms and amending Regulation (EU) No 648/2012 Text with EEA relevance, OJ L 176, 27.6.2013, p. 1–337.

Regulation (EU) 2016/679 of the European Parliament and of the Council of 27 April 2016 on the protection of natural persons with regard to the processing of personal data and on the free movement of such data, and repealing Directive 95/46/EC, OJ L 119, 4.5.2016, p. 1–88.

Official web page of Croatian Association for Debt Collection (HUAN): https://huan.hr/zakonska-regulativa/.

Official webpage of FENCA: https://fenca.eu/news/fenca-congress-2018.

Official webpage of FINA: https://www.fina.hr/-/zastoj-ovrhe-na-novcanim-sredstvima-mjera-pomoci-fizickim-osobama-uslijed-pojave-epidemije-bolesti-covid-19.

Municipal court in Osijek, 2 Povvr-267/2017-33.

County court in Velika Gorica 13 Gž Zk-638/2021-2.

County court in Pula, Gž-426/2020-2 from 21 May 2020.

County court in Varaždin in his judgment also warned that the assignment of the claim Gž-1261/2017-2 from 23 October 2017.

13 Gž Zk-638/2021-2.

Pž 1480/2019-2 from 13 March 2020.

High Commercial Court of the Republic of Croatia, Pž 1395/2018-2, from 8 June 2020; County court in Varaždin, 35 Gž-162/2021-2 – 2 22 July 202; County court in Split 22 Gž-2140/19-3 from 22 April 2020.

High Commercial Court of the Republic of Croatia, Pž 1395/2018-2 from 8 June 2020.

Aleš Kuhar and Jožef Kuhar v Addiko Bank d.d., Case C-407/18, ECLI:EU:C:2019:537.

Commission of the European Communities v Italian Republic, Case C-134/05, ECLI:EU:C:2007:435 (Commission vs. Italy).

Official webpage of the CNB: https://www.hnb.hr/en/about-us/consumer-protection.

Official webpage of CNB: https://www.hnb.hr/o-nama/zastita-potrosaca/prijavite-pitajte.

Official webpage of Ombudswoman's office: https://www.ombudsman.hr/hr/siva-zona-naplate-dugova-nedostatak-pravila-duznike-cini-dodatno-ranjivima/.

Official webpage of Ombudswoman of Croatia https://www.ombudsman.hr/hr/financije/.

Official webpage of the State Inspectorate of the Republic of Croatia: https://dirh.gov.hr/o-drzavnom-inspektoratu/trzisna-inspekcija/85.

Regional offices of the Market Inspection https://dirh.gov.hr/kontakti/podrucni-uredi-dezurne-inspekcije/131.

https://www.progreso.hr/blog/naplata-potrazivanja/;

https://legalis.hr/topic/115887-agencija-za-naplatu-potra%C5%BEivanja/;

https://dnevnik.hr/vijesti/hrvatska/provjereno-donosi-ispovijest-obitelji-zukanovic-i-pricu-o-nezaustavljivom-placanju-dugova---544304.html;

https://www.vecernji.hr/vijesti/prva-presuda-u-kojoj-je-zbog-nistetnosti-odredaba-umanjeno-potrazivanje-agencije-za-naplatu-1442307.

https://www.vecernji.hr/vijesti/stotine-sms-ova-i-250-poziva-sud-to-nije-nametljivo-ponasanje-1219194.
https://huan.hr/zakonska-regulativa/
https://b2kapital.hr/poslovanje-b2-kapitala-nastavlja-s-rastom-na-trzistima-hrvatske-i-sredisnje-europe/.

3 Debt collection services in Germany

A sector in turmoil

David Markworth[1]

3.1 Informal debt collection under German law

The law on debt collection as a so-called legal service can be found in the Act on Out-of-Court Legal Services (*Rechtsdienstleistungsgesetz* or in short *RDG* in German) of 12 December 2007 that has been amended several times since then.[2]

3.1.1 Introduction

In art 2 of the RDG,[3] debt collection practices[4] are defined as 'the collection of third-party claims or claims assigned for the purpose of collection for account of a third party.' According to art 2 of the RDG, debt collection practices are considered a legal service[5] if the debt collection is conducted as an independent, stand-alone business. Since it is considered an out-of-court legal service, debt collection services cannot be provided by just anyone. Instead, the provision (like that of all out-of-court legal services) is only permissible to the extent provided for under the RDG or by other laws (s. art 3 RDG).[6] Offering debt collection services requires a license, or 'registration,' as the law puts it, natural as well as legal

1 *Dr. David Markworth* is a Senior Academic Researcher at the Institute of Labour and Commercial Law, University of Cologne, Cologne, Germany, mail: d.markworth@uni-koeln.de, twitter: @D_Mark_law.

2 Federal Law Gazette I 2007, p. 2840. English translation of an older version of the statute: <https://www.gesetze-im-internet.de/englisch_rdg/index.html>.

3 Para 2.

4 *Inkassodienstleistungen* in German.

5 Para 2. Legal service according to art 2 para 1 RDG: any activity related to the concrete affairs of others as soon as it requires a legal assessment of the individual case.

6 This legislative technique is known as a prohibition with the reservation of permission (*Verbot mit Erlaubnisvorbehalt*). Before the RDG came into force, it was considered to rely on an 'information model' (see 3.4.) instead, where the clients should have been enabled to make informed decisions in regard to whom they trust with their need for legal service rather than services being banned by law (see C Deckenbrock/M Henssler/*Martin Henssler*, Commentary on the RDG, 5th edn, C.H. Beck 2021, Introduction no 30; Barbara Grunewald, *Die Zukunft des Marktes für Rechtsberatung* [On the future of the legal services market], Anwaltsblatt [AnwBl] 2004, pp 208–211).

DOI: 10.4324/9781003343158-4

persons and companies without legal personality can and must apply for.[7] In addition to this, professional titles which include the term '*Inkasso*' or confusingly similar titles may only be used by license holders.[8] Non-licensed legal service providers or providers who act outside their license, therefore, will be prosecuted.

3.1.2 What debt collection as a legal service means

Germany might have one of the most or even the most rigid regulations of debt collection practices in the whole world. The tight regulation is considered to be justified because the practice is seen as an out-of-court 'legal service,' somewhere between what lawyers do and everyday legal counseling. Therefore, the German discussion about debt collectors and especially the relevant case law by the German Constitutional Court[9] revolves mainly around the extent of legal services debt collectors are entitled to, in comparison to the 'full' legal services only lawyers may provide.[10] Especially the recent changes in the German legislation on debt collection services cannot be fully grasped if this vital point is not taken into account.

3.1.2.1 Distinction from lawyers

In general, lawyers are regarded as the only 'full' legal professionals in Germany[11] and may therefore perform all activities related to collecting debt. Some legal services were always regarded as being exclusively 'reserved' to them, (among numerous other legal services) primarily legal services that are provided 'in court.' The relevant legislation at least proclaims that the parties to disputes before the regional courts[12] and the higher regional courts[13] must be represented by lawyer.[14] In turn, lawyers are heavily regulated. For once and

7 Art 10 para 1 no. 1, para 2 RDG.

8 Art 11 para 4 RDG.

9 *Bundesverfassungsgericht, BVerfG.*

10 In regard to this, see also German Constitutional Court (*Bundesverfassungsgericht, BVerfG*), 20 February 2002, 1 BvR 423/99 (see <https://www.bundesverfassungsgericht.de/SharedDocs/Entscheidungen/DE/2002/02/rk20020220_1bvr042399.html>, available in German only); German Constitutional Court (*Bundesverfassungsgericht, BVerfG*), 14 August 2004, 1 BvR 725/03, both proceeding following a constitutional complaint (*Verfassungsbeschwerde*) and on what defines debt collection as a legal service (see <https://www.bundesverfassungsgericht.de/SharedDocs/Entscheidungen/DE/2004/08/rk20040814_1bvr072503.html>, available in German only).

11 See art 3 para 1 and 2 Federal Lawyers' Act (*Bundesrechtsanwaltsordnung, BRAO*): 'The lawyer is the appointed independent adviser and representative in all legal matters. His right to appear before courts, arbitral tribunals or government agencies in legal matters of any kind can only be restricted by a federal law'; furthermore: C Deckenbrock/M Henssler/*Martin Henssler*, Commentary on the RDG, 5th edn, C.H. Beck 2021, Introduction no 31.

12 *Landgerichte.*

13 *Oberlandesgerichte.*

14 Section 78 para 1 Code of Civil Procedure (*Zivilprozessordnung, ZPO*). Claiming a debt in court is considered a civil dispute over which the ordinary courts have the jurisdiction (art 13 Courts

generally speaking, they could – and for the most part, up to this day still can – neither offer contingency fees (quota litis)[15] nor litigation funding.[16] Secondly, no equity participation by outsiders in law firms is allowed.[17] This, for example, means that alternative business structures (ABS) as they exist in Great Britain are not possible under German law.[18]

3.1.2.2 Recent developments

That being said, it has to be acknowledged that – backed by extensive case law – the range of work debt collectors offer has dramatically expanded recently. 'Atypical' debt collection companies have begun to offer their services towards consumer creditors, especially when it comes to the collection of small claims. According to a 2021 ruling by the German federal court,[19] it can now be considered (more or less) undisputed that registered debt collection services cannot only involve an attorney to claim a debt for their clients in court if they were unsuccessful in collecting it themselves informally. Debt collection services shall also be allowed to claim 'disputed' debt, meaning claims regarding which the debtor will certainly – under no circumstances – pay up voluntarily but instead it seems inevitable that a court ruling has to be obtained.[20] This means that registered debt

---

Constitution Act [*Gerichtsverfassungsgesetz*]). Disputes concerning claims involving an amount not exceeding the sum of 5,000 euro are assigned to the Local Courts (*Amtsgerichte*) and the parties to the dispute may, in general, pursue the legal dispute themselves (art 79 para 1 Code of Civil Procedure [*Zivilprozessordnung, ZPO*]).

15 Art 49b para 2 Federal Lawyers' Act (*Bundesrechtsanwaltsordnung, BRAO*) and art 4a Act on the Remuneration of Lawyers (*Rechtsanwaltsvergütungsgesetz, RVG*). It has to be noted, though, that the Act to Promote Consumer-oriented Offers in the Legal Services Market (*Gesetz zur Förderung verbrauchergerechter Angebote im Rechtsdienstleistungsmarkt*) of 10 August 2021 (in force: 1 October 2021) amended the relevant provisions. Lawyers now may agree on quota litis in more cases.

16 See also Art 49b para 2 Federal Lawyers' Act (*Bundesrechtsanwaltsordnung, BRAO*).

17 Only lawyers and members of other liberal professions (*Freie Berufe*) may be partners of a law firm (*Berufsausübungsgesellschaft*) (see art 59c para 1 Federal Lawyers' Act [*Bundesrechtsanwaltsordnung, BRAO*], in force: 1 August 2022). Additionally the transfer of shares requires the other shareholders' consent and shares cannot be held by trustees (see art 59i para 1 and 2 Federal Lawyers' Act [*Bundesrechtsanwaltsordnung, BRAO*], in force: 1 August 2022).

18 See C. Deckenbrock/M Henssler/*Martin Henssler*, Commentary on the RDG, 5th edn, C.H. Beck 2021, Introduction no 21; Matthias Kilian, *Alternative Business Structures ante portas?*, Neue Juristische Wochenschrift (NJW) 2014, pp. 1766–1770.

19 *Bundesgerichtshof* or *BGH*.

20 See *inter alia* German Federal Court (*Bundesgerichtshof, BGH*), 27 November 2019, VIII ZR 285/18 on a debt collection service's authority to offer quota litis arrangements (see <http://juris.bundesgerichtshof.de/cgi-bin/rechtsprechung/document.py?Gericht=bgh&Art=en&nr=101936&pos=0&anz=1>, available in German only); German Federal Court (*Bundesgerichtshof, BGH*), 13 July 2021, II ZR 84/20 on a debt collection service's authority to provide an informal collective action lawsuit for consumers, thereby acting through lawyers (*Sammelklage-Inkasso*) (see <http://juris.bundesgerichtshof.de/cgi-bin/rechtsprechung/document.py?Gericht=bgh&Art=en&sid=988087d1ccd21eb83d0d35e876892356&nr=120886&pos=0&anz=1>, available in German only).

collection services are even allowed to offer consumers the enforcement of their claims in court (= exclusively in-court legal services) in return for a contingency fee, thereby acting through lawyers and with the help of litigation financiers and have done so in prominent cases for example in the wake of the Volkswagen emission scandal. The legislator, therefore, recently took considerable measures to re-establish the regulatory balance between the legal professions. Most prominently, lawyers now can negotiate contingency fees if the value of a debt does not exceed 2,000 euro. In the meantime, though, debt collection services still face almost no restrictions regarding fee agreements.[21] The collector just has to provide even more information towards a customer client in this case.[22] Furthermore, the agreement *inter alia* has to be in writing and a court may lower the fee if it is considered excessive. In conclusion, it can be said that lawyers still face more competition than ever before when it comes to providing legal services in Germany. The future will tell what the long-term consequences for the legal services market will be.

3.1.2.3 Legal services with lesser state supervision

At the same time, debt collection as a legal service must still be distinguished from other legal services that need lesser state supervision in the legislator's opinion.[23] This includes legal services that are provided inside of family, neighborly, or similarly close personal relationships,[24] legal services which are not related to any paid activity,[25] legal services that are provided by professional or other associations established to safeguard common interests,[26] and legal services provided (*inter alia*) by court-appointed or officially appointed persons within the context of their field of activity and area of responsibility.[27]

3.2 Regulatory targets

The ongoing struggle about what debt collection services are allowed to do is directly reflected in the relevant statute: the aforementioned Act on Out-of-Court Legal Services. The general train of thought underlying the legislation is that legal services generally touch critical economic issues and there is an asymmetry of information between providers and consumers of legal services exists.[28]

21 For details see art 4a sentence 1 of the German Lawyers' Fees Act (*Rechtsanwaltsvergütungsgesetz, RVG*).
22 See the new art 13c RDG.
23 When it comes to these types of legal services see C Deckenbrock/M Henssler/*Martin Henssler*, Commentary on the RDG, 5th edn, C.H. Beck 2021, Introduction no 55.
24 Art 6 para. 2 RDG.
25 Art 6 para. 1 RDG.
26 Art 7 RDG.
27 Art 8 RDG.
28 See German Bundestag Official Record (*Bundestags-Drucksache*) 16/3655 of 30 November 2006, p. 45: 'As the highest-ranking common good, the law must not fall into the hands of unqualified persons, as it is, in its characteristic as "lived law", significantly influenced and developed by the

Therefore, the traditional focus of the regulation has always lain on consumer protection against unqualified legal services that could, for example, result in such disadvantages as a loss of rights. In connection with this, the legislator has focused on the functionality of the legal system as a whole.[29] In other words: when it comes to the law's role to protect consumers in the debt collection sector, it has to be kept in mind that this means – in the first place – the protection of the creditors (the debt collector's contractual partner or client). It even used to be commonly accepted, though this aspect is heavily disputed in recent times and the perception of the legal services market has changed significantly over the years, that the legislation was intended to shield lawyers, as 'full' legal professionals from competition by professionals with lower legal qualifications.[30]

However, when it comes to the regulatory targets of the German legislator concerning the debt collection sector, it is imperative to take into account that there have been major modifications over the years. The most prominent one occurred in the wake of the transition from the old Legal Advice Act, which still had its roots in the old Abuse of Legal Advice Act[31] enacted in 1935,[32] to the RDG in 2007. Nonetheless, the RDG has also been changed a lot recently. There were major reform projects in 2013[33] as well as in 2020[34] and even in 2021,[35] whereby the latest changes have only come in force in October 2021. The most recent amendments to the RDG can be regarded as a direct response to the shift mentioned above in the debt collectors' business model: the much bigger role they now play on the market for consumer-oriented legal services. Furthermore, when

persons who apply it professionally'; see also C Deckenbrock/M Henssler/*Christian Deckenbrock*, Commentary on the RDG, 5th edn, C.H. Beck 2021, art 1 no 3.

29 See art 1 para 1 RDG on the 'Scope of the Act': '[the RDG] serves to protect the consumers of legal services, legal relations and the legal system from unqualified legal services.'

30 So-called lawyers' monopoly or *Anwaltsmonopol* in German. See C Deckenbrock/M Henssler/*Martin Henssler*, Commentary on the RDG, 5th edn, C.H. Beck 2021, Introduction no 18, 34.

31 *Rechtsberatungsmißbrauchsgesetz, RBMG.*

32 The RBMG was intended as a monopolization of legal advice with the lawyers because of their bad economic situation but also to destroy the livelihood of Jewish legal advisors that were denied licenses to provide legal services and later (if they were lawyers) disbarred (see C. Deckenbrock/M Henssler/*Martin Henssler*, Commentary on the RDG, 5th edn 2021, Introduction no 5, 6; Simone Rücker, *Rechtsberatung*, Mohr Siebeck 2007; Simone Rücker, *Das Ende der Rechtsberatung durch jüdische Juristen* [The end of legal services by Jewish advisors], Anwaltsblatt [AnwBl] 2007, pp. 801–808).

33 Act to combat dubious business practices (*Gesetz gegen unseriöse Geschäftspraktiken*) of 1 October 2013 (serves as an amendment to the RDG), Federal Law Gazette I 2013, p. 3714 (available in German only).

34 Act on the Improvement of Consumer Protection in Debt Collection Law and on the Amendment of Further Provisions (*Gesetz zur Verbesserung des Verbraucherschutzes im Inkassorecht und zur Änderung weiterer Vorschriften*) of 22 December 2020 (serves as an amendment to the RDG, in force: 1 October 2021), Federal Law Gazette I 2020, p. 3320 (available in German only).

35 Act to Promote Consumer-oriented Offers in the Legal Services Market (*Gesetz zur Förderung verbrauchergerechter Angebote im Rechtsdienstleistungsmarkt*) of 10 August 2021 (latest amendment to the RDG, in force: 1 October 2021), Federal Law Gazette I 2021, p. 3415 (available in German only).

we look at the amendments, we can see a slight shift in the regulatory focus. The legislator emphasizes the need for better client protection and clearly also the protection of debtors against 'dubious business practices' (as the 2013 act was called) or fraudulent debt collection practices, an issue he had traditionally not spotlighted primarily.[36]

3.3 Licensing requirements

Natural and legal persons and companies without legal personality may provide debt collection services only if they are registered with the competent authority.[37] Registration shall be made upon an application.[38] Article 12 RDG – which has been amended numerous times in the last couple of years – states the requirements for registration as a debt collector. They can be divided into three categories: (1) personal suitability and reliability; (2) theoretical and practical expertise; and (3) the need for professional indemnity insurance.

Personal reliability is generally lacking where a person is – not just temporarily – incapable of adequately performing debt collection services for health reasons.[39] Furthermore, when a person has been issued with a final sentence for a serious criminal offense[40] or for a less serious criminal offense[41] on the exercise of their profession in the course of the last three years before applying.[42] In this context, art 12 RDG also takes into account if an applicant for a license stands in opposition to the German basic democratic order, meaning that he is fighting it in a punishable manner, has forfeited one of his Basic Rights[43] according to a decision of the German Federal Constitutional Court,[44] or has lost his capacity to hold public office as a result of a criminal court conviction.[45]

Additionally, it plays a role in whether a person's finances are in disorder.[46] This is generally the case if insolvency proceedings have been opened against a person's assets or the insolvency court has even refused a request to open insolvency proceedings because the debtor's assets would probably be insufficient to

36 See however German Bundestag Official Record (*Bundestags-Drucksache*) 16/3655 of 30 November 2006, p. 45: 'the protection of the legal profession from unqualified legal advisors is also a valuable common good. The opponents of those seeking justice must also be from the unqualified provision of legal services.'

37 Art 10 para 1 RDG.

38 Art 10 para 2 RDG.

39 Art 12 para 1 no. 1 a) RDG.

40 *Verbrechen*.

41 *Vergehen*.

42 Art 12 para. 1 no. 1 e) aa) RDG.

43 *Grundrechte*.

44 *Bundesverfassungsgericht, BVerfG*.

45 Art 12 para. 1 no. 1 d) RDG in connection with art 7 Federal Lawyers' Act (*Bundesrechtsanwaltsordnung, BRAO*).

46 Art 12 para. 1 no. 1 c) RDG.

cover the costs of the proceedings.[47] Because of the direct connection between the two legal professions, revocations or withdrawals of an admission as a lawyer are also taken into account as well as the corresponding procedures that lead to the prohibition of working as a tax advisor, certified accountant, public notary, judge, or judicial officer.[48,49]

When it comes to the theoretical and practical expertise applicants for registration as debt collector need to provide, a special expertise in the fields of law which are important for the collection activity for which the application is being made is required.[50] In particular, this addresses knowledge in civil law, commercial, securities, and company law, the law of civil procedure, including debt recovery, and insolvency law, as well as cost law.[51] Proof of theoretical expertise is to be furnished to the competent authority through certificates.[52] Practical expertise generally presupposes at least two years of professional activity under instruction or practical professional training. Generally, the professional activity or training must have been pursued in Germany for at least 12 months.[53] Where a person is authorized to pursue informal debt collection or a comparable profession in another Member State of the European Union, in another state party to the Agreement on the European Economic Area, or in Switzerland, proof of the expertise may also be furnished taking into account the existing professional qualification using at least a six-month adaptation course.[54]

Finally, as indicated before, professional indemnity insurance with a minimum insurance cover of 250,000 euro for each insured event is required (art 12 para 1 no. 3 RDG).

Most of the requirements mentioned above can only be fulfilled by natural persons. That is why art 12 para 4 RDG addresses debt collection companies separately. Legal persons and companies without legal personality must designate

47 Art 12 para. 2 RDG. The latter occurrence leads to a person being registered in a debtors' register (*Schuldnerverzeichnis*) (see art 26 para 1, 2 Insolvency Statute [*Insolvenzordnung*] and art 882b Code of Civil Procedure [*Zivilprozessordnung, ZPO*]).

48 *Rechtspfleger*.

49 Art 12 para. 1 no. 1 e) bb) RDG. Art 12 RDG furthermore uses to also point out that reliability might be lacking where, in the last three years before submitting the application, a previous registration as a debt collector has been revoked. But in the last rounds of amendments to the RDG the legislator deemed this 'lockout period' to not be expedient since an application should always be assessed from the current point of view. This still does not mean that an application for a new license immediately after the old one was revoked for fair reasons has good chances to succeed (see C. Deckenbrock/M Henssler/*Wolfgang Dötsch*, Commentary on the RDG, 5th edn, C.H. Beck 2021, art 12 no 96c).

50 Art 12 para 1 no. 2 RDG.

51 Art 11 para 1 RDG.

52 Art 12 para 3 RDG.

53 Art 12 para 3 RDG.

54 On foreign legal service providers‘ capabilities in Germany see *C. Deckenbrock, M. Henssler, Christian Deckenbrock*, Commentary on the RDG, 5th edn, C.H. Beck 2021, para 10 no 15 ff. Germany is not very protectionistic in this regard. E.g., foreign providers do not need a branch office in Germany.

at least one natural person who fulfils all the conditions regarding personal suitability and reliability as well as theoretical and practical expertise (a so-called qualified person). The qualified person must be in the permanent employ of the company, must be capable of acting independently and issuing instructions on all matters concerning the company's legal services, and must be authorized to represent the company externally. Registered private individuals may also designate qualified persons.[55]

3.4 Disclosure and information

When it comes to the regulation of licensed debt collectors, the legislator established requirements that – as a whole – form a system that can be regarded as an 'information model.' This German information model has two pillars.

3.4.1 Legal Services Register

For once, everyone is entitled to inspect a Legal Services Register, free of charge (art 16 para 1 RDG).[56] The Legal Services Register is supposed to provide information to the consumers of legal services, persons providing legal services, public agencies, and legal relationships in general.[57] Concerning licensed persons permitted to provide debt collection services, the register makes public their family and first name, their company name,[58] including the company's legal representatives and the court of registration, and the registry number under which it has been entered in the register of companies, partnerships, cooperatives, or associations. Furthermore, the year a debt collection service was established, the service's business address, including the addresses of all branch offices and the qualified persons designated per art 12 para 4 RDG, stating their family name and first name. Finally, the register makes the specific content and scope of the authorisation to provide legal services, including any imposed requirements public. (Only) if the debt collector agrees, his telephone number and email address are also made available. The register also provides information about licensed debt collectors who have been temporarily banned from providing their services (up to five years, see art 9 para 1 RDG).[59]

3.4.2 Information requirements

The second pillar of Germany's information model consists of information requirements licensed debt collectors have to fulfill, both towards the debtors

55 See art 12 para 4 RDG for details.

56 *Rechtsdienstleistungsregister*. On the internet, it can be found using the URL <www.rechtsdienstleistungsregister.de>, see art 16 para 3 RDG.

57 Art 16 para 1 RDG.

58 *Firma*.

59 See art 16 para 2 sentence 1 no. 2 RDG, art 9 para 2 RDG.

and the creditors (meaning their clients). In recent years, one of the main legislative goals was to alter the transparency of claims, asserted by debt collectors. In the legislator's opinion, the situation for debtors has improved significantly due to new obligations to present and provide information introduced in 2013.[60] However, the obligations were amended again recently because the level of transparency still was not regarded as satisfactory.[61] Debt collectors asserted claims without the debtors knowing who owned the claim and if they really had to pay.

When asserting a claim against a natural person against whom a claim is being made which is not linked to his or her commercial or independent professional activity (see art 13a para 5 RDG), registered persons performing collection services according to art 13a RDG must communicate the following information in a clear and comprehensible manner upon first asserting the claim:

- the client's name or the name of the client's company as well as their address, unless it is shown that the disclosure of the address would prejudice the overriding interests of the principal which are worthy of protection,
- the basis of the claim, if contracts have been concluded including a precise description of the subject matter of the contract and the date of conclusion of the contract, in the case of tortious acts with a statement of the nature and date of the act,
- if interest is being claimed, a calculation of the interest together with the claim on which interest is to be paid, the rate of interest, and the period for which interest is being calculated,
- if a rate of interest is being claimed over and above the statutory rate of default interest, special reference to that fact and information regarding the circumstances on the basis of which the higher rate of interest is being claimed,
- if remuneration for collection or other costs for collection are being claimed, information regarding the type, amount, and basis of that remuneration or those costs,
- if value added tax is being claimed together with the collection fee, a declaration to the effect that it is not tax deductible,
- if the address of the private individual has not been provided by the creditor but has been determined otherwise, an indication of this and of how any errors that may have occurred can be asserted, and
- the name, address, and electronic contact details of the supervisory authority responsible for them.

In circumstances the legislator regards as especially dangerous for the debtor – a deferral or an instalment agreement or an acknowledgement of the debt – even more information must be disclosed.[62] Finally, regarding some more pieces of

60 See German Bundestag Official Record (*Bundestags-Drucksache*) 19/20348 of 24 June 2020, p. 1.
61 See German Bundestag Official Record (*Bundestags-Drucksache*) 19/20348 of 24 June 2020, p. 1. Tatjana Halm, *Erreicht das Inkassogesetz das gesteckte Ziel?*, BRAK-Mitt. 2021, p 282.
62 Art 13a para 3 and 4 RDG.

information, the legislator has decided that they only have to be provided upon request by a private individual.[63] These new measures might reduce the number of cases in which debt collectors threaten or intimidate debtors while still providing the collectors with means to show debtors the seriousness of their situation.

3.4.3 Information requirements towards the clients

Since the latest amendment of the RDG in October 2021, licensed debt collectors must provide extensive information towards the claimants – meaning their clients – if the client is a consumer (see the new art 13b RDG[64]), which, as mentioned before, has become a common occurrence recently. With the new requirements, the legislator reacts to the emergence of 'atypical' debt collection services specializing in a kind of 'informal' class action suit, previously unknown in Germany. If the debt collector and client agree upon a contingency fee (quota litis), meaning arrangements where the collector, when he is successful in claiming the debt, receives part of the sum as his fee, the collector has to disclose alternative measures to collect the debt that might be cheaper for the consumer. If the risk of claiming the debt is secured by litigation funding, the collector has to disclose the relevant provisions with the financier. Furthermore, the law also requires more client information if the debt collection service is trying to reach a settlement with the debtors. The idea behind this being that the collection service has much more to gain from a settlement than the single claimant, who in the process has to give up on part of his claim, because it represents numerous clients at once.[65] Additionally, the consumer clients have to also be provided with information on the relevant enforcement authority. Finally, debt collection services even have to tell consumers why they do not want to enter into an agreement with them and whether this decision was based upon a legal assessment or an automated procedure.[66]

3.5 Collection fees

The prevention of over-imposing fees charged for the collection of debt on the debtors themselves plays another significant role in Germany's regulation of debt collection services.[67] The provisions on collection fees that are being passed on from the claimant – as the debt collector's contractual client – onto the debtor have been continuously expanded, the reason behind this being that up to as recently as 2020,

63 E.g. the essential circumstances relating to the conclusion of a contract (see art 13a para 2 RDG).

64 Art 13b RDG was part of the Act to Promote Consumer-oriented Offers in the Legal Services Market (*Gesetz zur Förderung verbrauchergerechter Angebote im Rechtsdienstleistungsmarkt*) of 10 August 2021 (in force: 1 October 2021).

65 See *C. Deckenbrock, M. Henssler, Wolfgang Dötsch*, Commentary on the RDG, 5th edn, C.H. Beck 2021, para 13a nF no 74.

66 Art 13b para 2 RDG.

67 This should not be confused with the provisions on handling external funds (= the debt they have claimed) by debt collection services. In this regard, see art 13g RDG that dictates the collector to immediately hand out those funds to the entitled person or deposit them in a separate account.

the legislator viewed the situation regarding collection costs being claimed by debt collectors as being 'still very unsatisfactory.' The legislator himself considered the collection fees as usually being far too high concerning the effort put into the collection process.[68] As being especially problematic in this context he identified fees in connection with industrialized or mass debt collection that relies heavily on automatization and therefore does not generate many costs.[69] At the same time, it is regarded as unsatisfactory that some debtors have to bear costs even though they are fully willing to pay.[70] Finally, debtors in the past had to bear collection costs that were even higher than the amount they owed. If the debtor then agreed to payment by low installments, due to a bad financial situation, she risked never to fully recover.[71]

3.5.1 Passing on debt collection fees

Therefore, there are two general rules for passing on debt collection fees. Firstly – and obviously – if the claim does not exist, collection costs cannot be passed on either. Secondly, the claimant can only pass on collection fees if they present damages on their part.[72] There is a lot of case law dealing with this second rule.[73] Some details are still disputed up to this day. In theory, the second provision means that claiming higher costs must be considered fraud, but it is scarcely prosecuted.

Furthermore, if a debt is outstanding, but the debtor is not in default, he must only pay the outstanding debt and not the costs associated with the involvement of a debt collector.[74] As a general rule, this means that the creditor has to first try to collect the debt on his own. If he fails to do this, the costs associated with a debt collector are not reimbursed. In the case of contractual claims, the debtor is in default upon a reminder after the performance is due, unless the reminder is even exceptionally dispensable (s 286 para 1 BGB). But the debtor of a claim for payment shall already be in default at the latest if he does not make payment within 30 days of the due date and receipt of an invoice or equivalent payment schedule. This shall only apply to a consumer debtor if a specific reference has been made to these consequences in the invoice or payment schedule.[75]

According to the German Federal Court case law, the injured party can only claim compensation for necessary and expedient expenses for protection and enforcement of his rights.[76] The necessity is not determined by the organizational possibilities

68 See German Bundestag Official Record (*Bundestags-Drucksache*) 19/20348 of 24 June 2020, p. 1, 22.

69 German Bundestag Official Record (*Bundestags-Drucksache*) 19/20348 of 24 June 2020, p. 22.

70 See German Bundestag Official Record (*Bundestags-Drucksache*) 19/20348 of 24 June 2020, p. 1.

71 Tatjana Halm, *Erreicht das Inkassogesetz das gesteckte Ziel?*, BRAK-Mitt. 2021, p 282.

72 See *Münchener Kommentar zum BGB*, Christian Ernst, 8th edn, C.H. Beck 2019, para 286 no 167.

73 See recently *inter alia* German Federal Court (*Bundesgerichtshof, BGH*), 10 June 2020, VIII ZR 289/19 on the limited reimbursability of an energy provider's debt collection fees (see <https://juris.bundesgerichtshof.de/cgi-bin/rechtsprechung/document.py?Gericht=bgh&Art=en&sid=071a092eb89d25afabe813fe2996dbb2&nr=108378&pos=0&anz=1>, available in German only).

74 See German Bundestag Official Record (*Bundestags-Drucksache*) 19/20348 of 24 June 2020, p. 1.

75 Art 286 para 3 German Civil Code (*Bürgerliches Gesetzbuch, BGB*).

76 See Münchener Kommentar zum BGB, *Christian Ernst*, 8th edn, C.H. Beck 2019, para 286 no 167.

but by the actual organization of the creditor. Beyond the creditor's obligations, the debtor must accept the creditor's actual form of organization. One should note that the debtor can easily avoid the commissioning of a legal service provider if he settles the claim at the latest on the second reminder or declares and proves his willingness to pay to the creditor, disclosing his (temporary) inability to pay.

3.5.2 Equating debt collectors' and lawyers' fees

In 2013, the legislator tried to stop disproportionately high out-of-court debt collection costs by passing the law against dubious business practices.[77] Since then, it has been regulated that debt collectors may not charge more than lawyers for such services.[78] Additional costs might be charged to the creditor but do not have to be reimbursed by the debtor.

To lawyers – and therefore to debt collectors as well – the German Lawyers' Fees Act[79] applies. The lawyer's fees regulated there, therefore, represent a maximum limit for the collection costs. The amount of the collection costs depends on the amount of the claim. For example, if the claim amounts to up to 50 euro, from October onwards, the remuneration is limited to 30 euro.[80] In addition, the calculation of the amount of the collection costs considers how extensive and complex the work of the debt collector was. This can vary in each case and depends, for example, on whether the debt collector first had to ascertain the debtor's address. Since October 2021, the debt collector's fee is strictly limited if a claim is undisputed, especially when met at the first request.[81] Thereby, consumers are favoured that succumb to pressure by the collectors immediately, even though they might have doubts in regard to the validity of the claim, whereas consumers disputing a claim are disadvantaged. The new legislation has therefore rightfully been criticized.[82]

In addition to the debt collectors' claims being considered too high, the legislator has targeted unnecessary duplications of costs.[83] In Germany, in many cases, a creditor decides to rely on a debt collector first but after that still finds the need to commission a lawyer. For example, because the debtor is unwilling to pay voluntarily even when confronted by a debt collection service. In this case, a civil dispute is needed, meaning the (presumed) debt has to be claimed in court because then a formal execution title, that a bailiff can later act on, needs to be obtained. To react to this common occurrence, the legislator introduced a rule that states that if the creditor commissions first a debt collection service provider and then a lawyer to collect the debt, he may only claim compensation for the costs incurred by him as damages up to the amount that would have been incurred if he had

77 *Gesetz gegen unseriöse Geschäftspraktiken.*
78 See the new s 13b RDG (in force: 1 October 2021).
79 *Rechtsanwaltsvergütungsgesetz, RVG.*
80 See art 13 para 2 German Lawyers' Fees Act (*Rechtsanwaltsvergütungsgesetz, RVG*).
81 German Bundestag Official Record (*Bundestags-Drucksache*) 19/20348 of 24 June 2020, p. 23.
82 Tatjana Halm, *Erreicht das neue Inkassogesetz das gesteckte Ziel?*, BRAK-Mitt. 2021, p 282.
83 German Bundestag Official Record (*Bundestags-Drucksache*) 19/20348 of 24 June 2020, p. 2.

only commissioned the lawyer.[84] This applies to all instructions to collect the debt regardless of whether the collection should take place out-of-court or in-court. The only case in which the debtor can be double-charged for a debt collector's and a lawyer's fees is if the debtor has disputed the claim only after commissioning a debt collection service provider and the dispute has given rise to the commissioning of a lawyer.

3.6 Licensing, supervision, and enforcement

To complete the picture of the German regulation of the debt collection sector, the provisions on supervision and enforcement have to be taken into account.

3.6.1 Competent government agencies

Responsible for overseeing compliance with the provisions set out in the RDG are the departments of justice[85] in each German state.[86][87] The German states are free when it comes to assigning which agencies these are. The result of this legislation has been a fragmentation of control. There are approximately 36 different government agencies involved in the oversight procedures, many of which are courts. This, in turn, has led to forum shopping: service providers that in one state were denied a registration or have been subjected to specific conditions regarding their activities turn to the department of justice of another one. At least in theory, this competition between state enforcement agencies may lead to a downward spiral and the RDG's provisions – over time – being watered down. The fragmentation of control mentioned above, therefore, is heavily criticized. A centralized enforcement agency would probably be far more effective. In regard to this criticism, the German federal government has recently been given time to evaluate this matter further. In this context, it has also to be taken into account that the number of licensed debt collectors in Germany has – at least traditionally – never been very high,[88] so one agency would presumably still be able to keep up with the market's development.

3.6.2 Duties

The government agencies competent under the aforementioned provisions are tasked with registering debt collectors, stopping unlicensed debt collection, and supervising licensed collectors.

84 See the new art 13c RDG (in force: 1 October 2021).
85 *Landesjustizverwaltungen*.
86 *Bundesland*.
87 Art 13a para 1, s 19 para 1 RDG.
88 Now, there are around 2,100 licensed debt collectors; see German Bundestag Official Record (*Bundestags-Drucksache*) 19/20348 of 24 June 2020, p. 21.

3.6.2.1 Registration procedure

The application for registration as a debt collector must be submitted to the authority competent at the person's principal place of business in Germany (art 13 RDG[89]). When applying for registration, the applicant must produce everything to enable the competent authority to verify the licensing requirements in section 3.3. The applicant has to provide a summary of his course of professional training and previous professional practice, a certificate of good conduct per the German Federal Central Criminal Register Act,[90] a declaration as to whether insolvency proceedings are pending or whether an entry has been made in a record of debtors according to the aforementioned art 882b Code of Civil Procedure[91] within the last three years before applying, and finally documents providing proof of theoretical and practical expertise (art 13 para 1 RDG). At the same time, an applicant has to explain in detail the content of the services he intends to provide, especially in which fields of the law he wants to practice.[92] The states' departments of justice are then given a deadline of three months to decide on an application.[93]

3.6.2.2 Debt collection without proper registration

Where debt collection as a legal service is provided without the required registration or without temporary registration, the competent authority may stop the activities (art 15b RDG). Whoever provides it additionally commits a so-called regulatory offense,[94] and a fine of up to 50,000 euro may be imposed on him.[95] A contract between the creditor and a debt collector is considered invalid[96] if the debt collection is offered without registration or outside the parameters of the RDG. This may result in the creditor forfeiting his claim.[97]

3.6.2.3 Case-by-case measures

Additionally, the competent authorities may take case-by-case measures against persons or companies licensed as debt collectors. In particular, they may order or amend the requirements laid down in the RDG and other statutes (art 13h para. 1 RDG). In particular, the competent authority may temporarily fully or partially prohibit persons from providing legal services where well-founded facts justify the assumption that

89 Para 1.
90 See art 30 para 5 Federal Central Criminal Register Act (*Bundeszentralregistergesetz*).
91 *Zivilprozessordnung, ZPO.*
92 Art 13 para 2 RDG.
93 Art 13 para 3 RDG.
94 *Ordnungswidrigkeit.*
95 Art 20 para 1 no. 2 and para 3 RDG.
96 Pursuant to art 134 German Civil Code (*Bürgerliches Gesetzbuch, BGB*).
97 The reason for this being that the claim has become time-barred in the meantime.

- a registration requirement has ceased to apply or
- significant or permanent breaches of duty are being committed.[98]

According to art 14 RDG, the justice departments even have the authority to revoke a debt collector's license. This cannot be done light-heartedly, however. Rather, a revocation of a license can only be an *ultima ratio* measure because it deeply interferes with the constitutional right to choose a certain career path (see art 12 of the Basic Law for the Federal Republic of Germany:[99] 'All Germans shall have the right freely to choose their occupation or profession, their place of work and their place of training. The practice of an occupation or profession may be regulated by or under a law.') Well-founded facts must justify the assumption that the licensed person or a qualified person no longer possesses the requisite personal suitability or reliability to revoke a license. A license may also be revoked where the registered person no longer maintains professional indemnity insurance or where well-founded facts justify the assumption that unqualified legal services are being provided on a permanent basis to the detriment of the consumers of legal services or of legal relations. This shall generally be the case where the registered person is providing a substantial volume of legal services over and above the registered person's authorization or persistently fails to comply with requirements imposed or disclosure and information requirements. Finally, a legal person or company without legal personality might lose its license when it does not designate a qualified person within six months of the departure of the only other qualified person it had assigned.

3.6.2.4 Inspection of business premises and (electronic) documents

In so far as it is necessary to fulfill the tasks assigned to the competent government agency in its capacity as supervisory authority, companies or persons providing legal services must permit the authority and those acting on its behalf to enter their business premises during normal operating hours. Furthermore, upon request, they have to present the relevant books, records, receipts, papers, and other documents in an appropriate form for inspection, including those kept electronically, to provide information and the required assistance.[100] The person obliged to provide information may refuse to do so if, by doing so, that person would put himself or herself or one of their relatives at risk of prosecution for a criminal offense or proceedings under the Act on Regulatory Offences. The person is to be informed of this right.[101]

98 Art 13h para. 4 RDG. See for example V.G. Berlin, 25 August 2011, 1 K 5.10 on the revocation of a debt collector's licence because of the failure to check the existence of claims brought forward to him (available in German only).

99 *Grundgesetz, GG.*

100 Art 13a para 4 RDG.

101 Art 13a para 4 RDG.

3.7 Conclusions

In Germany, debt collection, defined as 'the collection of third-party claims or claims assigned for the purpose of collection for account of a third party' (*Inkassodienstleistung*), is tightly regulated, mainly because it is regarded not purely as a financial service but rather as an out-of-court 'legal service'. According to the Act on Out-of-Court Legal Services of 2007, it may only be exercised with a permit and is permissible only to the extent provided for under the RDG. The provision without a proper license is considered a regulatory offense and will result in a fine.

Recently, the debt collection sector in Germany has gone into turmoil and the legislator has yet to find the appropriate measures on how to react. Debt collection services have expanded their range of services considerably. They now offer their services towards consumers and have started to compete with lawyers, who traditionally have been the only 'full' legal professionals recognized by German law, especially when collecting small claims. According to a 2021 ruling by the German Federal Court, registered debt collection services are even allowed to offer consumers the enforcement of their claims in court (= exclusively in-court legal services) in return for a contingency fee, thereby acting through lawyers and with the help of litigation financiers.

At the same time, a shift in the main focus of legal service regulation in Germany can be observed. Traditionally, the legislative focus has lain on protecting the legal system and the creditors (the consumers of legal services or the debt collectors' contractual partners) but the latest reinforcements of the applicable legislation have clearly emphasized the protection of debtors from abusive debt collection practices. These reinforcements need to be evaluated thoroughly since it still remains unclear whether the measures towards debtor protection suit their purpose.

The most effective strategy to protect debtors from abusive debt collection practices seems to be a strict limitation of the fees charged for debt collection that can be imposed on debtors. In contrast, extensive information obligations seem more fitting when it comes to the protection of consumer creditors. The German regulation has very recently experienced many changes that follow these findings. Though, when the legislative system tailored towards the provision of legal services is viewed in its entirety, it now seems to be more unbalanced than ever before.

Bibliography

Act to Combat Dubious Business Practices (*Gesetz gegen unseriöse Geschäftspraktiken*) of 1 October 2013, Federal Law Gazette I 2013, p. 3714 (available in German only).

Act on the Improvement of Consumer Protection in Debt Collection Law and on the Amendment of Further Provisions (*Gesetz zur Verbesserung des Verbraucherschutzes im Inkassorecht und zur Änderung weiterer Vorschriften*) of 22 December 2020, Federal Law Gazette I 2020, p. 3320 (available in German only).

Act to Promote Consumer-Oriented Offers in the Legal Services Market (*Gesetz zur Förderung verbrauchergerechter Angebote im Rechtsdienstleistungsmarkt*) of 10 August 2021, Federal Law Gazette I 2021, p. 3415 (available in German only).

Deckenbrock C, in Deckenbrock C/Henssler M, *Commentary on the RDG*, 5th edn, C.H. Beck 2021, art 1.

Dötsch W, in Deckenbrock C/Henssler M, *Commentary on the RDG*, 5th edn, C.H. Beck 2021, art 12.

——— in Deckenbrock C/Henssler M, *Commentary on the RDG*, 5th edn, C.H. Beck 2021, art 13a nF.

Ernst C, in Säcker J/Rixecker R/Oetker H/Limperg B, *Münchener Kommentar zum BGB*, 8th edn, C.H. Beck 2019, vol 2, para 286.

German Bundestag Official Record (*Bundestags-Drucksache*) 16/3655 of 30 November 2006.

German Bundestag Official Record (*Bundestags-Drucksache*) 19/20348 of 24 June 2020.

German Constitutional Court (*Bundesverfassungsgericht, BVerfG*), 20 February 2002, 1 BvR 423/99 (see <https://www.bundesverfassungsgericht.de/SharedDocs/Entscheidungen/DE/2002/02/rk20020220_1bvr042399.html>, available in German only).

German Constitutional Court (*Bundesverfassungsgericht, BVerfG*), 14 August 2004, 1 BvR 725/03 (see <https://www.bundesverfassungsgericht.de/SharedDocs/Entscheidungen/DE/2004/08/rk20040814_1bvr072503.html>, available in German only).

German Federal Court (*Bundesgerichtshof, BGH*), 27 November 2019, VIII ZR 285/18 (see <http://juris.bundesgerichtshof.de/cgi-bin/rechtsprechung/document.py?Gericht=bgh&Art=en&nr=101936&pos=0&anz=1>, available in German only).

German Federal Court (*Bundesgerichtshof, BGH*), 10 June 2020, VIII ZR 289/19 (see <https://juris.bundesgerichtshof.de/cgi-bin/rechtsprechung/document.py?Gericht=bgh&Art=en&sid=071a092eb89d25afabe813fe2996dbb2&nr=108378&pos=0&anz=1>, available in German only).

German Federal Court (*Bundesgerichtshof, BGH*), 13 July 2021, II ZR 84/20 (see <http://juris.bundesgerichtshof.de/cgi-bin/rechtsprechung/document.py?Gericht=bgh&Art=en&sid=988087d1ccd21eb83d0d35e876892356&nr=120886&pos=0&anz=1>, available in German only).

Grunewald B, Die Zukunft des Marktes für Rechtsberatung [On the future of the legal services market], *Anwaltsblatt [AnwBl]* 2004, pp. 208–211.

Halm T, Erreicht das neue Inkassogesetz das gesteckte Ziel?, *BRAK-Mitt* 2021, p. 282.

Henssler M, in Deckenbrock C/Henssler M, *Commentary on the RDG*, 5th edn, C.H. Beck 2021, Introduction.

Kilian M, Alternative Business Structures ante portas?, *Neue Juristische Wochenschrift (NJW)* 2014, pp. 1766–1770.

Rücker S, *Rechtsberatung*, Mohr Siebeck 2007.

———, Das Ende der Rechtsberatung durch jüdische Juristen [The end of legal services by Jewish advisors], *Anwaltsblatt [AnwBl]* 2007, pp. 801–808.

V.G. Berlin, 25 August 2011, 1 K 5.10.

4 Abusive informal debt collection practices in Greece

Eleni Kaprou

4.1 Introduction

The impact of the financial crisis in Greece has been the focus of literature from a macro-economic perspective or sovereign debt perspective. There has also been much attention on the issue of over-indebted households and the impact of the financial crisis on individual citizens.[1] However, an aspect that has been less researched is the mechanisms employed to collect private debt and their impact on debtors. This chapter aims to shed light on the issue of informal debt collection in Greece, setting out the legislative framework and offering an insight into how companies offering debt recovery services work in practice.

The recent financial crisis exposed the importance of consumers as drivers of the economy and their heightened risk of suffering detriment.[2] As a country that was severely impacted by the crisis and by high levels of household over-indebtedness, Greece is a poignant example of this. Consumer credit in Greece skyrocketed in the 90s and 2000s, along with the Greek economy. It went from 5% of Greece's GDP in 2000 to 16% in 2008 and mortgages followed suit with 51% of Greece's GDP.[3] This easy access to credit was unprecedented for the unaccustomed Greek consumers, many of whom became over-indebted.[4] As the effects of the crisis became apparent, many consumers became unemployed and unable to service their loans, which amounted to a significant economic and social crisis.

The Greek legislator took bold steps to protect debtors during this tumultuous period. The most important measures were the introduction of N.3869/2010

1 See for example, Irina Domurath, Guido Comparato and Hans W. Micklitz, 'The Over-Indebtedness of European Consumers A View from Six Countries' EUI Working Papers Law 2014/10; Ioannis Glinavos, *Redefining the Market–State Relationship: Responses to the Financial Crisis and the Future of Regulation* (Routledge 2014);Dorothee Bohle, 'To Pay or Not to Pay? Debt Cultures and the Politics of Debt in Europe's Periphery' [2018] Stato e Mercato 61.

2 Olivier Jérusalmy, Paul Fox and Nicolas Hercelin, 'Is the Human Dignity of Individual Debtors at Risk ?' (Finance Watch January 2020) 11.

3 Πρακτικά Βουλής, ΙΒ' Περίοδος Προεδρευομένης Δημοκρατίας, Σύνοδος Β', Συνεδρίαση ΡΙΒ' (30 March 2009), 7519.

4 Ibid.

DOI: 10.4324/9781003343158-5

on over-indebted households and a moratorium on foreclosures.[5] N.3869/2010 allowed debtors to file an application in court to settle their debt, a procedure that many debtors followed and which created a high number of applications, many of which are still awaiting trial in 2021.[6] This law has been very influential in Greece's practice and academic discourse.[7] To protect, in particular, the debtors' first residence for properties with a value of up to 200,000 euro, the Greek government decided to impose a moratorium on foreclosures in 2008.[8] The emergency measure of the moratorium on foreclosures was extended for 2014, and with strikes and other measures lasted until 2019 the foreclosure procedure is still disrupted.[9]

N.3758/2009 on companies that inform debtors belongs to the same category of legislative measures aimed at protecting debtors.[10] With that law, private debt collection in Greece became illegal. The existing debt collection companies, which have been operating since 2005, were transformed into companies that inform debtors about their debt.[11] This non-standard category of debt notification companies is the closest relative to a debt collection company in the Greek system and, as such, is the main focus of the analysis of this chapter. During the financial crisis, as the traditional avenue of foreclosure became unavailable, these companies whose primary function was to call debtors to notify them about their outstanding debt, convince them to make payments, and, when necessary, negotiate a new repayment plan with debtors became popular.

Informal debt collection practices raise important consumer protection issues as they can become abusive in their efforts to make the debtor pay.[12] The same is true for companies that inform debtors. Evidence shows that abusive practices

5 N.3869/2010, Ρύθμιση των οφειλών υπερχρεωμένων φυσικών προσώπων και άλλες διατάξεις, ΦΕΚ Α΄130/3.8.2010; N. 3714/2008, Προστασία δανειοληπτών και άλλες διατάξεις, ΦΕΚ 231/Α'/7.11.2008.

6 N.3869/2010, art 4; for the deadlines for debtors to apply electronically to redefine their trial date see <http://www.keyd.gov.gr/epanaprosdiorismos/> (accessed December 2021).

7 See for example, Μ Αθανασίου, Α Αλεξανδρόπουλος, Ν Κωστάκου et al, *Υπερχρεωμένοι οφειλέτες από τις οφειλές προς τις τράπεζες στις οφειλές προς το δημόσιο*, (Εκδόσεις Σάκκουλα 2016); Α Γαλανοπούλου-Μητροπούλου, *Υπερχρεωμένα νοικοκυριά- Νομική Αντιμετώπιση*, (3rd ed. Εκδόσεις Σάκκουλα 2014); Α Κρητικός, *Ρύθμιση των οφειλών υπερχρεωμένων φυσικών προσώπων*, (4th ed. Εκδόσεις Σάκκουλα 2016).

8 N.3714/2008, Προστασία δανειοληπτών και άλλες διατάξεις, art 5.

9 N.4224/2013 Κυβερνητικό Συμβούλιο Διαχείρισης Ιδιωτικού Χρέους Ελληνικό Επενδυτικό Ταμείο Αξιοποίησης Περιουσίας του Δημοσίου και άλλες επείγουσες διατάξεις; 49214/21-7-2015 Κοινής Υπουργικής Απόφασης «Αναστολή πράξεων αναγκαστικής εκτέλεσης, καταβολής δικαστικών παραβόλων, εγγυοδοσιών και χρηματικών ποσών από μετατροπή ποινών.

10 N.3758/2009, Εταιρείες Ενημέρωσης οφειλετών για ληξιπρόθεσμες απαιτήσεις και άλλες διατάξεις, ΦΕΚ Α' 68/05-05-2009.

11 N.3758/2009, art 4.

12 C. Stanescu, 'Is the Unfair Commercial Practices Directive Fit to Tackle Effectively Abusive Debt Collection? A Critical Evaluation' European Consumer and Market Law Review, (2020) 9(6), 235–247.

in the sector are widespread in the E.U., and Greece is no exception.[13] Given the unique characteristics of Greece in this case, as both a country that has a high number of non-performing loans (NPLs), has legislated extensively in the field and has made the unusual choice of banning private debt collection, this chapter offers a first of its kind in-depth analysis of the Greek framework for abusive debt collection practices.

It is important to note that the main instrument for regulating unfair practices on an E.U. level is Directive 2005/29/EC (the Unfair Commercial Practices Directive).[14] With its broad scope, the Directive can catch practices that are taking place after the conclusion of a contract, in this case a credit agreement. Indeed, many of the practices employed by debt collection agencies, such as harassing calls, threatening to take action that cannot legally be taken, and providing misleading information, would be caught by the Directive.[15] However, the Directive was not designed to tackle debt collection practices, and as such, there are gaps in protection.[16] In Greece, in particular, the UCPD does not seem to be applied in the context of abusive debt collection practices, with regulators and courts using the Greek law N.3758/2009, which regulates companies that inform debtors instead. Apart from N.3758/2009 being the *lex specialis*, it also includes more detailed provisions which make enforcement easier. Therefore, as the impact of the UCPD is limited, the focus will be on the Greek framework, which is more relevant in practice.

The structure of the chapter is as follows: section 4.2 focuses on how companies that inform debtors are regulated by N.3758/2009, covering unfair practices, informational duties, record-keeping duties, and enforcement issues. Section 4.3 looks into the phenomenon of law companies acting as debt collection companies and their treatment by the law. Section 4.4 discusses the regulation of debt management companies, a more recent development in Greece, by N.4354/2015, while section 4.5 concludes.

4.2 Companies that inform debtors

As mentioned above, informal debt collection is not allowed in Greece. It has been replaced by companies that inform consumers about their debt, which are the only lawfully operating firms in the sector. Usually, the lender hires

13 Olivier Jérusalmy, Paul Fox and Nicolas Hercelin, 'Is the Human Dignity of Individual Debtors at Risk ?' (Finance Watch January 2020), 33.

14 Directive 2005/29/EC of the European Parliament and of the Council of 11 May 2005 concerning unfair business-to-consumer commercial practices in the internal market and amending Council Directive 84/450/EEC, Directives 97/7/EC, 98/27/EC and 2002/65/EC of the European Parliament and of the Council and Regulation (EC) No 2006/2004 of the European Parliament and of the Council (Unfair Commercial Practices Directive).

15 Dir 2005/29/EC, art 7–9.

16 C. Stanescu, 'Regulation of Abusive Debt Collection Practices in the EU Member States: An Empirical Account', (2021) 44(2) Journal of Consumer Policy, 179, 182.

these companies when the loan becomes non-performing to either convince the consumer to make a payment to the bank or negotiate a payment plan. These companies operate extra-judicially and are not allowed to collect the debt, nor is the debt transferred to them. They cannot take any legal action or initiate foreclosure proceedings against the debtor.[17] The debt management companies receive a percentage of the recovered debt from these accounts for their services. The sector's most prominent companies have their own business association, ESEDA, a member of the Federation of European National Collection Associations (FENCA).[18]

ESEDA was formed in 2005, prior to the introduction of N.3758/2009, when the members were the largest debt collection companies at the time. ESEDA has been vocal in expressing its views regarding the sector's regulation. Prior to the introduction of N.3758/2009, ESEDA was positive to regulating the sector and in their position paper set out their suggested requirements for the companies of the sector, such as companies being organized as public limited companies, minimum capital of 500,000 euro, a minimum of 50 employees, and minimum technological infrastructure such as a call center, customer relationship management software, and computer telephony integration.[19] Some of these suggestions were adopted by N.3758/2009. Their suggestions aimed at upgrading the sector and removing smaller, perhaps less reputable players from the market with consumer protection not being a major concern beyond the value of informing consumers about their debt.[20]

In 2010, only one year after the introduction of N.3758/2009, there were rumors about a law reform. ESEDA was concerned about the prospect of a reform, pointing out that further regulation of their activities would result in the reluctance of debtors to service their debt, financial uncertainty for the lenders, and an increase in judicial debt collection.[21] The reform took place a couple years later with the adoption of N.4038/2012, which addressed unfair practices and modernized aspects of the law relating to data protection.[22] One may argue whether it became overly difficult for lenders to collect their debt in the years of the crisis. However, the Greek legislator made the arguably necessary choice to protect debtors and, as a result, maintain social cohesion.

17 N.3758/2009, art 3.3.

18 <https://fenca.eu> (accessed November 2021).

19 ΕΣΕΔΑ, 'Πρόταση προς το Υπουργείο Ανάπτυξης', (13 May 2008), available online at <https://www.eseda.gr/el/legal-framework-comments/of-eseda> (accessed December 2021), 14.

20 Ibid, 7.

21 ΕΣΕΔΑ, 'ΑΠΟΨΕΙΣ ΤΟΥ Ε.Σ.Ε.Δ.Α (Σχετικά με τις «προαναγγελθείσες», δια του τύπου, τροποποιήσεις του N.3758/2009)'(Athens, 20 September 2010), available online at <https://www.eseda.gr/Uploads/pdf/theseis/THESEIS_ESEDA.pdf> (accessed December 2021).

22 N.4038/2012, Επείγουσες ρυθμίσεις που αφορούν την εφαρμογή του μεσοπρόθεσμου πλαισίου δημοσιονομικής στρατηγικής 2012–2015, ΦΕΚ Α'14/02/02/2012.

ESEDA has also adopted a code of conduct that considers Greek legislation and the FENCA code of conduct.[23] The ESEDA code of conduct contains measures for the protection of debtors, including forbidding the use of threats, offensive language, and psychological pressure, and threatening to take measures that cannot legally be taken.[24] In no way does the ESEDA code exceed the standard required by the law, and its provisions are less detailed than those of N.3758/2009.

The companies that inform debtors, despite not being able to collect debts or take legal action against debtors, are frequently referred to, especially by media, as debt collection companies, a reminder of their previous debt management activities. According to consumer complaints to the regulator, they play an essential role in the NPLs market and continue to engage in unfair commercial practices.[25]

4.2.1 Legal Framework of N.3758/2009

N.3758/2009 was introduced during the crisis to regulate the activity of debt collection companies for the first time. It is worth looking into the background of the introduction of N.3758/2009 and the reasons behind introducing a prohibition on debt collection, as these were set out in the parliamentary debate of the proposed law.

In 2009, debt collection companies had been already active in Greece, and it was widely known that there were many consumer complaints to the Consumer Ombudsman and the General Secretariat of Consumer protection about the abusive practices employed by the debt collection companies.[26] Debt collection companies would threaten debtors, visit them at their home, visit their family members, or mislead them by presenting themselves as bailiffs.[27] The unscrupulous informal debt collection made it obvious that there was a legal gap in protection that needed to be addressed. Oddly enough, there was no mention, either during the debate or in the law itself, of Directive 2005/29/EC (the Unfair Commercial Practices Directive), which had been transposed into Greek law since 2007.[28] This can point either to low awareness of the Directive's provisions and their potential to catch the practices employed by the debt collection companies or to the need for a more tailored solution.

The law's main objective was to turn the debt collection companies into companies that inform debtors. The rationale behind this choice is that if the

23 Κώδικας Δεοντολογίας του Ελληνικού Συνδέσμου Ενημέρωσης και Διαπραγμάτευσης Απαιτήσεων, (Athens January 2010), available online at <https://www.eseda.gr/Uploads/pdf/CODIKAS_DEONTOLOGIAS_ESEDA.pdf> (accessed December 2021)

24 Ibid, art 5.

25 See below, s 4.2.1.1.

26 Πρακτικά Βουλής, ΙΒ' Περίοδος Προεδρευομένης Δημοκρατίας, Σύνοδος Β', Συνεδρίαση ΡΙΒ' (30 March 2009), 7519.

27 Ibid.

28 Τροποποίηση και συμπλήρωση του ν. 2251/1994 «Προστασία των καταναλωτών», όπως ισχύει – Ενσωμάτωση της οδηγίας 2005/29 του Ευρωπαϊκού Κοινοβουλίου και του Συμβουλίου, ΦΕΚ Α'152/10.07.2007.

companies could not collect the debt, there would be no incentive for them to engage in abusive practices, such as looking for debtors in their relatives' houses and exerting psychological pressure.[29] Protection of debtors from abusive informal practices was the priority for N.3758/2009, which set out appropriate trading standards for companies that inform debtors and regulate their relationships with borrowers and lenders.[30]

The parliamentary debate also reveals that banks were heavily criticized by MPs of all parties for using the debt collection companies. The point was made that if lenders wish to collect their debt, they should do so in court or have their in-house debt notification services.[31] The implication was that outsourcing debt collection to third companies allowed banks to reap the benefits of abusive practices towards debtors while keeping their hands 'clean.' Debt collection was viewed negatively in the Parliament, with opposition MPs in particular calling for even stricter measures, such as debtors being able to deny any further communication with the company or a general prohibition of passing the claim to third parties.[32]

While it was not able to eliminate the use of abusive practices, N.3758/2009 provided much-needed clarity in informal debt collection, with detailed rules. It was a measure designed to protect consumers beyond regulating efforts in other E.U. Member States. This early stance against debt collection for consumer debt, which helped households avoid further abusive practices, has changed with N.4354/2015, which created the Greek framework for the secondary market for NPLs, examined below in section 4.4.[33]

Next, some of the key aspects of the law will be examined, namely, unfair practices, informational and record-keeping duties of the companies, and enforcement issues.

4.2.1.1 Unfair and misleading practices

N.3758/2009 dedicates art 5 to unfair and misleading practices.[34] That article forbids common misleading and aggressive practices, including physical violence and psychological pressure, threatening to take measures that cannot legally be taken, and presenting themselves or their agents as lawyers or bailiffs.[35] To a large extent, there is an overlap between this article and the UCPD's provision on misleading and aggressive practices. One of the differences is the prohibition of visits to the debtor's home or place of work and other private spaces, such as hospitals.[36] Such visits are forbidden as they would put additional pressure

29 Ibid, note 28.
30 N.3758/2009, art 4.
31 Ibid, note 28, 7519, 7524,7529.
32 Ibid, note 28, 7520, 7521.
33 See below, s 4.4.
34 N.3758/2009, art 5.
35 N.3758/2009, art 5.1, 5.2., 5.6., 5.10.
36 N.3758/2009, art 5.8.

on the debtor and amount to an unfair practice. It would also make it easier for companies to cross the line into debt collection. The law is also concerned with maintaining the reputation of the debtor. Therefore, companies are not allowed to contact the debtor's family members or defame the debtor to his family or social environment, as that would increase the psychological pressure on the debtor to pay and harm their dignity.[37]

As seen above, companies that inform debtors are not allowed to visit debtors in their home or business, meaning the only allowed forms of communication are phone calls and written communication. The most effective measures against unfair practices are listed in art 4 N.3758/2009 on principles for informing debtors. These measures aim to ensure that debtors do not receive multiple harassing calls from companies that inform debtors. Borrowers may assign an account only to one company at a time, and thus debtors should not receive calls from multiple companies simultaneously.[38] The agreement between the borrower and the company that informs the debtor must be recorded in a durable medium.[39]

The principles define the timing and frequency of the company's calls to the consumer in a detailed manner. It is worth noting that the provisions became more detailed after the 2012 reform of the law.[40] The 2012 reform, only three years after introducing the law, seems to be motivated by the need for greater clarity in the provisions.[41] Rather than a significant change in the market, it points to inadequacies when drafting the initial law. Companies need to comply with the following conditions when communicating with the debtor:

1) Initiate communication with the debtor only ten days after the debt has become outstanding. If a settlement has been reached or the statute of limitations has expired, communication should cease.[42]
2) Communication can take place only on working days between 9.00 am and 8.00 pm.[43]
3) Communication can take place only once every second day.[44]

37 N.3758/2009, art 5.4., 5.9.
38 N.3758/2009, art 4.2.
39 N.3758/2009, art 4.5.
40 For example, see art 4.4, abstract phrasing such as 'communication with the debtor should take place within reasonable time' has been replaced with the more precise 'communication with the debtor should take place 10 days after the debt becomes outstanding.'
41 Πρακτικά Βουλής, ΙΓ' Περίοδος Προεδρευομένης Δημοκρατίας, Σύνοδος Γ', Συνεδρίαση ΞΓ' (18 January 2012),3452.
42 N.3758/2009, art 4.6.
43 N.3758/2009, art 4.4.
44 N.3758/2009, art.4.4; in practice, companies that inform debtors have call centers which use a dialer programme which calls debtors multiple times a day until they answer, which may cause distress to the debtors but does not breach the rules, as an unanswered call does not qualify as a communication. The use of dialer programmes does not seem to be forbidden under the law.

However, in practice, things look different. In 2018, some of the most common abusive practices reported to the General Secretariat for Consumer Protection were companies calling debtors before the ten-day deadline expired, companies calling debtors in their place of work, often even if the debtor did not list these numbers, companies breaching rules regarding the frequency of the calls and providing misleading information.[45] The most recent official evidence from the General Secretariat for Consumer Protection for 2019–2020 does not indicate there is much cause for optimism when curbing the use of abusive practices. The General Secretariat received 185 consumer complaints in 2019 and 274 in 2020.[46] Some of the most common practices continue to be calling debtors before the ten-day deadline has expired, and companies calling debtors in their place of work.[47] In addition to that, offensive language and providing misleading information are also featured.[48]

Another widespread abusive practice is calling debtors over a debt that has been settled judicially. As mentioned above, one of the most critical legislative interventions for protection of debtors in Greece has been N.3869/2010 on the settlement of debts of over-indebted natural persons, which allows over-indebted physical persons to file an application in court to write off part of their debt and to receive a court-mandated repayment plan, binding for all parties.[49] When debtors apply to the court to benefit from that law, they should no longer be receiving calls from companies that inform them about their debt as they are in the process of settling their debt. However, it is a widespread practice, as reported by the Greek Consumer Ombudsman, that companies ignore this and continue to call these debtors in an attempt to get them to make payments in a debt that may well end up being written off by the court.[50]

45 Γενική Γραμματεία Εμπορίου και Προστασίας Καταναλωτή, 'Διοικητικές κυρώσεις που επιβλήθ ηκαν σε εταιρείες ενημέρωσης οφειλετών κατά την διάρκεια του πρώτου εξαμήνου του 2018 με βάση τις διατάξεις του ν.3758/2009' (Press release 3 July 2018), available online at <https://www .mindev.gov.gr/διοικητικές-κυρώσεις-που-επιβλήθηκα/> (accessed December 2021).

46 Γενική Γραμματεία Εμπορίου και Προστασίας Καταναλωτή, 'Επιβολή διοικητικών κυρώσεων σε εταιρείες ενημέρωσης οφειλετών για ληξιπρόθεσμες οφειλές κατά τη διετία 2019-2020' (Press release 24 December 2020), available online at <https://www.mindev.gov.gr/επιβολή-διοικητικών-κυρώσεων-σε-εται/> (accessed December 2021).

47 Ibid.

48 Ibid.

49 Νόμος 3869/2010, Ρύθμιση των οφειλών υπερχρεωμένων προσώπων και λοιπές διατάξεις, ΦΕΚ Α' 130/3.08.2010.

50 Σύσταση της Ανεξάρτητης Αρχής «Συνήγορος του Καταναλωτή», 'Μη ενδεδειγμένη δράση και λειτουργία Τραπεζικών Ιδρυμάτων και Εταιρειών Ενημέρωσης Οφειλετών', (5325/27.02.2013), available online at <http://www.synigoroskatanaloti.gr/docs/reports/2013-02-28.Σύσταση-Εισπρα κτικες.pdf> (accessed December 2021).

4.2.1.2 Informational duties

Companies must disclose certain information to the debtor. They must not call from an unknown number. The company's representatives calling the debtor must state their name, their capacity as a representative of the company, the company's registration number, and the reason for the call.[51] In any case, they should not present themselves as the lenders or use any of their credentials. In other words, if a representative of a company calls a debtor and presents itself as its client Bank ABC they will be in breach of this law, as they will be misleading the debtor and perhaps pressure them to make a payment. If the debtor requests it, the company must provide a detailed analysis of their debt in writing and for free within ten days from the first communication.[52] It is doubtful whether debtors are aware of this measure, but they will likely ask for more information if contacted by the company.

4.2.1.3 Record keeping duties

One of the measures from the 2012 reform that has had a significant impact in curbing abusive practices is the duty of companies to record all communications with the debtors. In particular, the date and time of the communication and the debt in question must be recorded.[53] The debtor and the General Secretariat on Consumer Protection may request a copy of these records, which the company must provide within ten days.[54] These records are valuable evidence for proving the existence of abusive practices as they can be used to show the frequency and timing of communication and whether misleading or aggressive practices were employed. The obligation to keep such a record and inform debtors of these recordings appears to act as a deterrent for companies that inform debtors because they know that both individual debtors and public authorities can easily build a case against them. The records are not meant to be used against the debtors, but they can be helpful to companies as well, as they can be used to prove that debtors consented to a settlement of their debt by phone, provided that the settlement does not place them in a worse position.[55]

4.2.1.4 Enforcement issues

N.3758/2009 is enforced by the General Secretariat for Consumer Protection, which falls under the Ministry for Development and Investments. As such, the

51 N.3758/2009, art 6.2.
52 N.3758/2009, art 6.3.
53 N.3758/2009, art 6.7.
54 N.3758/2009, art 6.7.
55 N.3758/2009, art 6.8.

Ministry has the power to administer fines to the companies that inform debtors and the lenders, usually banks.[56] The fines can range from 5,000 to 500,000 euro.

The General Secretariat is also responsible for keeping the register for companies that inform debtors. Companies in the field must be inscribed in this register; otherwise, they cannot commence their economic activities.[57] The register is freely accessible from the General Secretariat for Consumer Protection website, and as of 06 October 2021, 12 companies were inscribed in the register.[58] The Ministry also has the power to order that a company is deleted from the register of companies that inform debtors for one to six months or permanently.[59]

According to the data published by the Ministry of Development and Investment, in 2018, they issued 21 fines totalling 160,000 euro. In 2019, that figure went up to 49 fines with a total value of 470,000 euro while in 2020, there were 19 fines of 231,000 euro.[60] The decline in the number of fines in 2020 is most likely attributed to the moratorium on loan repayments due to the covid-19 pandemic implemented in Greece and the other E.U. countries.[61] Having data concerning enforcement activities available publicly online is a relatively recent phenomenon. While there is information on the total amount of fines administered, the breakdown of this amount to individual companies or the identity of the companies is not publicly available. Not announcing the identity of the offenders means that these announcements do not act as a 'name and shame' list. However, the deterring effects of such lists have proven elusive in other jurisdictions.[62] It is also difficult to know whether these fines have been paid, as most companies would appeal the ministerial decision to administer a fine. It would usually take several years until the decision becomes final. While the relatively high fines show the willingness of the enforcement agency to go after companies that inform debtors on account of their abusive practices, it is difficult to tell whether these fines indeed have a deterring effect on the companies.

56 N.3758/2009, art 10.1.

57 N.3758/2009, art 7.4.

58 Μητρώο εταιρειών ενημέρωσης οφειλετών, available online at <https://www.mindev.gov.gr/προστασία-του-καταναλωτη/#1557918450200-4565ea14-a21b> (accessed December 2021).

59 Ibid.

60 Γενική Γραμματεία Εμπορίου και Προστασίας Καταναλωτή, 'Διοικητικές κυρώσεις που επιβλήθηκαν σε εταιρείες ενημέρωσης οφειλετών κατά την διάρκεια του πρώτου εξαμήνου του 2018 με βάση τις διατάξεις του ν.3758/2009' (Press release 3 July 2018), available online at < https://www.mindev.gov.gr/διοικητικές-κυρώσεις-που-επιβλήθηκα/> (Accessed December 2021); Γενική Γραμματεία Εμπορίου και Προστασίας Καταναλωτή, 'Επιβολή διοικητικών κυρώσεων σε εταιρείες ενημέρωσης οφειλετών για ληξιπρόθεσμες οφειλές κατά τη διετία 2019-2020' (Press release 24 December 2020), available online at <https://www.mindev.gov.gr/επιβολή-διοικητικών-κυρώσεων-σε-εται/> (accessed December 2021).

61 European Banking Authority, 'First Evidence on the Use of Moratoria and Public Guarantees in the EU Banking Sector (November 2020), EBA/Rep/2020/31, 16.

62 For an analysis of the use of the 'name and shame' technique in the Netherlands see J. Van Erp, 'Regulatory Disclosure of Offending Companies in the Dutch Financial Market: Consumer Protection or Enforcement Publicity' (2010) Law and Policy 32(4), 407.

In specific issues that touch on data protection, such as the duty of the companies to keep a record of all communications and the duty to verify the debtor's identity in communications, the relevant enforcement authority is the Hellenic Data Protection Authority.[63]

The Data Protection Authority has been quite active in enforcing and interpreting the law for companies that inform debtors. It has also called for reform of N.3758/2009 to bring it up to date with the General Data Protection Regulation as in its opinion, GDPR should apply to data protection issues between the debtors and the companies, and data protection provisions should be removed from N.3758/2009 which would be left to cover most topics of unfair practices of the companies.[64] However, it seems that the 2018 plans to update N.3758/2009 have been put on hold, as so far there have not been any changes to the law.

The case law on companies that inform debtors has primarily focused on a data protection issue, namely how banks disclose to their consumers, for them to consent, that they will share their personal data with companies that inform debtors. In particular, do banks need to specifically mention companies that inform debtors in the relevant term in their credit agreements or does a more general mention suffice?

In such an appeal case decided by the first instance court in Athens, a debtor brought a lawsuit against the bank and the company that informs debtors (a sister company of the bank) alleging that the bank had shared her data with a company that informs debtors without her consent and she was now receiving harassing calls from said company.[65] The decision was not based on N.3758/2009, though it was for a loan agreement concluded in 2013, but on N.2472/1997, which transposes the now-repealed Directive 95/46/EC into Greek law.[66] An important aspect to consider is the penalties, as those from N.3758/2009 are much stricter than those of N.2472/1997 transposing the e-privacy Directive into Greek law. Respectively, if the GDPR were applied in these cases, penalties would be even stricter. The court found that the relevant term in the agreement was vague, as it mentioned companies that inform debtors in general, as opposed to the specific company the data was passed to and included many other recipients, thus unduly broadening the recipients of the personal data of the debtor.[67] The court concluded that the bank had not adequately informed the debtor who would process their

63 N.3758/2009, art 10.1.

64 Αρχή Προστασίας Δεδομένων Προσωπικού Χαρακτήρα, 'Προσχέδιο τροποποίησης του ν. 3758/2009 «Εταιρείες Ενημέρωσης Οφειλετών για ληξιπρόθεσμες απαιτήσεις και άλλες διατάξ εις» – Παρατηρήσεις Αρχής', (Athens 30/04/2018) Γ/ΕΞ/2964-1/30-04-2018, available online at <https://www.dpa.gr/sites/default/files/2020-03/ΓΕΞ2964_2018.pdf> (accessed December 2021).

65 ΜΠρΑθ 9179/2017.

66 N. 2472/1997, Προστασία του ατόμου από την επεξεργασία δεδομένων προσωπικού χαρακτήρα, ΦΕΚ Α'50 /10.4.1997; Directive 95/46/EC of the European Parliament and of the Council of 24 October 1995 on the protection of individuals with regard to the processing of personal data and on the free movement of such data, [1995], OJ L 281, 23.11.1995, pp. 31–50.

67 Ibid.

data, and the bank owed the debtor 6,000 euro in damages. Concerning the debt information company, even though the court recognized that it breached the communication frequency rules of N.3758/2009, it was not held responsible as it was not the one that had to get the debtor's consent for the processing of the data.[68]

In a recent decision, the Supreme Court of Greece (Άρειος Πάγος) decided on the same issue in plenary session.[69] The credit agreement stated that 'the bank or those acting on behalf of the bank and its name will process the personal data of the debtor.' Following that, the terms stated that debt collection companies, lawyers, notaries, and bailiffs might be recipients of the data. It must be noted that the credit agreement in question was from 2004 and therefore preceded the introduction of N.3758/2009 and, in fact, the legal recognition of companies that inform debtors. For that reason, the decision was made based on N.2472/1997 on data protection instead of N.3758/2009. The Supreme Court decided, by majority vote, that the disclosure of the bank was sufficient, as debt information companies did not exist at the time of the contract. Therefore the customer couldn't be explicitly informed about debt information companies.[70]

Ten judges out of 27 dissented in the controversial judgment and stated that since the companies that inform debtors were not included in the categories set out in the credit agreement, the bank had not fulfilled its obligations. It should have informed the debtor before sharing their data with the debt information company.[71] Ultimately, the Supreme Court decided to maintain the status quo as a different decision would have caused a significant disruption in the activities not only of debt information companies but also of banks who rely on them to recover debt, as it would have opened the way for more debtors to go against them in court.

The Data Protection Authority has also issued a decision on the topic, which diverges from that of the Supreme Court and sides with the minority opinion. The Data Protection Authority decided that banks should inform their customers in the following ways: (1) at the stage of the conclusion of the contract that the lender has the right, should the debt become outstanding to share their data with companies that inform debtors, to inform them as per N.3758/2009. If the terms are vague or inaccurate, they should be amended. As for older customers who signed their credit agreement before N.3758/2009 came into force, they should be notified appropriately, for example, with a letter or along with their bank statement. (2) Along with the last written notification that their debt has become outstanding, should the debtor not promptly make a payment, their data will be shared with a company that informs debtors.[72]

68 Ibid.
69 ΑΠ Ολ 3/2020.
70 Ibid
71 Ibid.
72 Απόφαση 98/2017 (Αρχή Προστασίας Δεδομένων Προσωπικού Χαρακτήρα), available online at <https://www.dpa.gr/sites/default/files/2019-10/98_2017anonym.pdf> (accessed December 2021).

This section has examined enforcement of N.3758/2009, a key aspect for its success. Public enforcement by the General Secretariat for Consumer Protection has been quite active in issuing fines; however, there is little transparency as to the effect of these fines.

Conversely, case law has been limited to issues of data protection of debtors, not offering guidance regarding other unfair practices, which is unfortunate, as abusive practices employed by traders were in no way limited to data protection. The case law of the Supreme Court on the issue points to an attitude that is not supportive of debtors, as it allowed banks to provide only a general disclosure to consumers, instead of the name of specific companies, missing out on an opportunity to disrupt the outsourcing model employed by banks.

4.3 Law firms acting as debt collection companies

As mentioned above, for companies that inform debtors to operate lawfully, they must be listed in the registry kept by the General Secretariat for Consumer Protection and adhere to the provisions of N.3758/2009.[73] As the field of debt collection grew and before the introduction of N.3758/2009, law firms operated the field, with debt collection being their main if not sole area of practice. As the sector became regulated, debt collection was transformed to informing debtors, and companies that informed debtors became subject to more requirements; law firms that operated in the same field enjoyed the advantage of not being subjected to the additional legal requirements of N.3758/2009, giving them far greater flexibility. The foremost example of such a law firm, though the only one, is Sioufas and Partners. Sioufas and partners commenced its activity in 2005 and has grown into a large company of 350 employees and offices outside Greece, a size unusual for the small Greek market. Their main field of activity has been in the debt notification sector, with the firm operating call centers both with lawyers and non-lawyers calling debtors to inform them of their debt along with other legal work. As one of the first firms in the field, it soon built up an extensive portfolio of accounts from the major Greek banks.

In 2014, the Athens Bar Association issued a decision condemning the model where law firms act like companies that inform debtors and make repeated calls to debtors in a manner that breaches lawyers' code of ethics.[74] The Bar Association clarified that there would be zero tolerance for such policies, and lawyers that breach them would be prosecuted for disciplinary offences. Sioufas and partners have been scrutinized for their practices and their law firm's structure, to the extent

73 N.3758/2009, art 11.

74 Δικηγορικός Σύλλογος Αθηνών, 'Απόφαση για τις πρακτικές δικηγορικών-εισπρακτικών εταιρειών' (14/11/2014), available online at < https://www.dsa.gr/δελτία-τύπου/γραφείο-τύπου/απόφαση-δσ-του-δσα-για-τις-πρακτικές-των-δικηγορικών-«εισπρακτικών»-εταιρ> (Accessed December 2021).

that it has been questioned whether it indeed is a law firm. Their cases are now in the Greek Council of State following disciplinary hearings and a long legal battle.

The Disciplinary Council for Lawyers had imposed on the two founders of the law firm and their head of legal services the penalty of one year and six months' suspension from practising law and a fine of 15,000 euro for illegal practices against debtors.[75] The reasoning behind these penalties was that the law firm was operating as a debt collection service that is not compatible with the function of a lawyer and its conduct was closer to that of a debt collection service than that of a law firm.[76]

The founders and head of legal services and the law firm as a legal person filed interlocutory injunctions against the decision to suspend them from practising law. The injunction application of the founders and their head of legal services and their claim that the decision would cause irreparable damage to their professional reputation and would endanger their livelihood was rejected.[77] However, for the injunction of the law firm the court accepted that as the law firm has 42 active mandates from banks and other creditors along with other open legal cases, it should not be dissolved due to their suspension as that would cause irreparable damage if the decision were overturned in the last instance court.[78] Similar to the data protection cases examined above, Greek courts are reluctant to do anything that would disrupt the functioning of the banks.[79]

The case of law firms acting as debt collection companies is indicative of the high-profit margins in the field of debt collection or debt notification and the incentives for firms to do whatever is necessary to achieve their set goals, even if that means operating in a grey area or breaching the law.

4.4 Debt management companies

In the last few years, the market for NPLs has been transformed by the entrance of debt management companies and servicers of NPLs. Their activity in Greece is regulated by N.4354/2015.[80] This law signifies a change in the consumer credit landscape and a profound shift in the legislator's approach towards debt collection. The Greek legislator's desire to protect debtors at the height of the financial crisis that led to a total ban on private debt collection and N.3758/2009 has been curbed to accept the new player on the market for NPLs, debt management companies. Their activities are expanding judging by their number, as there are

75 ΣΤΕ 60-61/2021.
76 Ibid.
77 Ibid.
78 Ibid.
79 See above s 4.2.1.4.
80 N.4354/2015 Διαχείριση των μη εξυπηρετούμενων δανείων, μισθολογικές ρυθμίσεις και άλλες επείγουσες διατάξεις εφαρμογής της συμφωνίας δημοσιονομικών στόχων και διαρθρωτικών μεταρρυθμίσεων.

23 such companies active in Greece, organized in a business association.[81] This presents a significant change compared to the four systemic Greek banks that were previously handling these accounts, as not the same workload is divided, perhaps reducing the need for banks to outsource to companies that inform debtors.

Debt management companies are placed under the supervision of the Bank of Greece, which is the Greek central bank.[82] This marks a difference compared to companies that inform debtors which are under the supervision of the General Secretariat for Consumer Protection.[83] N.4354/2015 sets out the criteria for a debt management company to be approved by the Bank of Greece to operate lawfully. The requirements include providing information on the company statute, business plan, shareholders, and members of the board of directors' identity.[84] One of the authorization requirements relevant for abusive practices is to submit a comprehensive report on the basic principles and methods for debt management.[85] Special mention must be made to the provisions for debtors belonging to vulnerable groups, as defined by the code of conduct of art 1.2 of N.4224/2013.[86]

The aforementioned code of conduct is issued by the Bank of Greece, is binding for banks and debt management companies, and applies to credit agreements that were terminated post-2015.[87] The code of conduct sets out a procedure for resolving payments in arrears, distinguishing between natural persons and professionals on the one hand and legal persons on the other hand.[88] The code requires financial institutions to have a formalized procedure for resolving payments in arrears and informational leaflets for debtors. It also requires financial institutions to follow five stages of resolving late payments of debtors, including two mandatory warnings to the debtor, followed by an assessment of their financial situation, and finally, the suggestion of a solution.[89] When it comes to communication with debtors, the code's provisions are general, stating that it should be honest, in the spirit of good cooperation, and at a suitable time.[90] These provisions leave a lot to be desired compared to the highly specific N.3758/2009 for companies that inform debtors.

The main benefit of the code of conduct in curtailing abusive practices lies in setting out distinct stages, including when and how to communicate with the debtor regarding their late payments and thus delaying the escalation of the procedure and judicial enforcement. However, there is evidence that debt

81 <https://eedadp.com/melh/#ta-melh-mas> (accessed December 2021).
82 N.4354/2015, art 1(β).
83 See above, s 4.2.1.4.
84 N.4354/2015, art 1.2.
85 N.4354/2015, art 1.2(ζ).
86 Ibid.
87 N.4224/2013 Κυβερνητικό Συμβούλιο Διαχείρισης Ιδιωτικού Χρέους Ελληνικό Επενδυτικό Ταμείο Αξιοποίησης Περιουσίας του Δημοσίου και άλλες επείγουσες διατάξεις, art 1.2.
88 Τράπεζα της Ελλάδος, Κώδικας Δεοντολογίας του N.4224/2013,(2016), available online at <https://www.nbg.gr/el/law-4224> (accessed December 2021), ch 2, 3.
89 Κώδικας Δεοντολογίας του N.4224/2013, ch 2.
90 Κώδικας Δεοντολογίας του N.4224/2013, ch 2(A)(1).

management companies often do not adhere to the code of conduct. In a recent case between a company that had taken out a loan and a debt management company, the court stated that the debt management company breached the code of conduct as it prioritized quick debt settlement over achieving a viable solution for both parties.[91] In the same case, the debt management company gave a deadline of five days to the debtor to respond otherwise they would proceed to terminate the agreement and take legal action, a practice that breaches the code of conduct.[92] This example shows that the current legal framework does not seem to prevent debt management companies from engaging in abusive practices. They are distinguished from banks by their aim to liquidate claims quickly and may leave debtors worse off.

The issue of regulating the secondary market for NPLs is addressed by the Proposal for a Directive on Credit Servicers, whose first parliamentary reading was completed in 19 October 2021.[93] However, as the Proposal will not apply to existing NPLs, it will not impact current issues.[94] The Proposal contains measures that to an extent mirror the Greek framework, such as authorization requirements, but in terms of protecting debtors, it sets out the obligations of the credit servicers in greater detail.[95] In its initial form the Proposal lacked adequate measures for protection of debtors, instead placing weight on licensing requirements, an issue that the European Parliament has partially addressed.[96] Hopefully, if the Proposal is adopted, it will signal a positive development for debtors in the E.U.

4.5 Conclusions

To sum up, this chapter has examined the Greek legal framework for private debt collection, its particular characteristics, and the reasons behind these choices. Greece is an interesting case as a country that has been heavily impacted by the financial crisis, with a high number of NPLs, which makes the issue of debt collection prominent.

N.3758/2009 was introduced during the crisis forbidding debt collection and allowing only informing debtors about their debt, thus creating a new category, the companies that inform debtors. The chapter analysed the provisions of this law, especially regarding abusive informal debt collection. N.3758/2009 contains

91 ΜΠρΑθ 753/2020.

92 Ibid.

93 European Commission, 'Proposal for a Directive of the European Parliament and of the Council on credit servicers, credit purchasers and the recovery of collateral' COM/2018/0135 final, art 34–35.

94 Ben Schuijling, Vincent van Hoof and Tom Hutten, 'Non-Performing Loans and the Harmonisation of Extrajudicial Collateral Enforcement across Europe' (2019) 28 International Insolvency Review 340, 351.

95 COM/2018/0135 final, art 10.

96 C. Stănescu, 'A Critical Assessment of the Need for Harmonization of the Legal Framework Concerning Abusive Informal Debt Collection Practices in the European Union: Is Harmonization Possible and How Can It Best Be Attained?' (2021) 44 Journal of Consumer Policy 531, 549.

detailed provisions on the place and timing of communications of companies to consumers as well as the allowed content of the calls. It also places duties on companies to provide accurate information to debtors as to their identity, the capacity in which they are calling, and the debt in question. To achieve greater transparency and facilitate the discovery of evidence, N.3758/2009 also requires that companies record all communications with debtors.

Despite the legislative intervention and detailed measures, abusive practices remain a big issue. Public enforcement has been active in administering relatively high fines, while case law has been limited to issues of data protection which have ultimately not been helpful to debtors.

The chapter has also covered other actors in the debt collection field, namely law firms, which have benefitted from the gap in protection, as they fall outside the scope of N.3758/2009, to act as debt collection companies, under the guise of legal work, a practice which is being addressed by Greek courts.

Finally, the chapter analysed the legal framework for debt management companies regulated by N.4354/2015. A new player in Greece, debt management companies are growing in numbers and are incentivized to achieve quick payments from consumers. Unfortunately, N.4354/2015 does not seem well-equipped to tackle abusive practices, focusing instead on the financial viability of such companies. This stance mirrors E.U. developments with the proposed Directive on Credit Servicers.

Ultimately, Greece made bold choices in regulating the field of debt collection by banning informal debt collection and providing detailed measures for tackling abusive practices, placing debtor protection front and center. However, the practice has shown that abusive informal debt recovery remains a critical issue, perhaps motivated more by the sheer size of NPLs rather than the law itself. In recent years, as seen in the regulation of debt management companies, protection of debtors is starting to take a secondary role in the efforts to tackle NPLs.

It is important to not lose track of the potential harm for debtors that informal debt collection may cause and be vigilant about maintaining high levels of consumer protection. This complex issue goes beyond consumer law and needs a holistic approach to ensure success.

Bibliography

Books

Αθανασίου Μ, Αλεξανδρόπουλος Α, Κωστάκου Ν, et al., *Υπερχρεωμένοι οφειλέτες από τις οφειλές προς τις τράπεζες στις οφειλές προς το δημόσιο* (Εκδόσεις Σάκκουλα 2016).

Γαλανοπούλου-Μητροπούλου Α, *Υπερχρεωμένα νοικοκυριά- Νομική Αντιμετώπιση* (3rd ed. Εκδόσεις Σάκκουλα 2014).

Κρητικός Α, *Ρύθμιση των οφειλών υπερχρεωμένων φυσικών προσώπων* (4th ed. Εκδόσεις Σάκκουλα 2016).

Glinavos I, *Redefining the Market–State Relationship: Responses to the Financial Crisis and the Future of Regulation* (Routledge 2014).

Journal articles

Bohle D, 'To Pay or Not to Pay? Debt Cultures and the Politics of Debt in Europe's Periphery' (2018) Stato e Mercato 61.

Domurath I, Comparato G, Micklitz HW, 'The Over-Indebtedness of European Consumers: A View from Six Countries' EUI Working Papers Law 2014/10.

Schuijling B, van Hoof V, Hutten T, 'Non-Performing Loans and the Harmonisation of Extrajudicial Collateral Enforcement across Europe' (2019) 28 International Insolvency Review 340.

Stanescu C, 'Is the Unfair Commercial Practices Directive Fit to Tackle Effectively Abusive Debt Collection? A Critical Evaluation' (2020) 9(6) European Consumer and Market Law Review 235.

———, 'Regulation of Abusive Debt Collection Practices in the EU Member States: An Empirical Account' (2021) 44(2) Journal of Consumer Policy 179.

———, 'A Critical Assessment of the Need for Harmonization of the Legal Framework Concerning Abusive Informal Debt Collection Practices in the European Union: Is Harmonization Possible and How Can It Best Be Attained?' (2021) 44 Journal of Consumer Policy 531.

Van Erp J, 'Regulatory Disclosure of Offending Companies in the Dutch Financial Market: Consumer Protection or Enforcement Publicity' (2010) 32(4) Law and Policy 407.

Other sources

Αρχή Προστασίας Δεδομένων Προσωπικού Χαρακτήρα, 'Προσχέ διο τροποποίησης του ν. 3758/2009 «Εταιρείες Ενημέρωσης Οφειλετών για ληξιπρόθεσμες απαιτήσεις και άλλες διατάξεις» – Παρατηρήσεις Αρχής' (Athens 30/04/2018) Γ/ΕΞ/2964-1/30-04-2018, available online at https://www.dpa.gr/sites/default/files/2020-03/ΓΕΞ2964_2018.pdf (accessed December 2021).

Πρακτικά Βουλής, ΙΒ' Περίοδος Προεδρευομένης Δημοκρατίας, Σύνοδος Β', Συνεδρίαση ΡΙΒ (30 March 2009), 7519.

Πρακτικά Βουλής, ΙΓ' Περίοδος Προεδρευομένης Δημοκρατίας, Σύνοδος Γ', Συνεδρίαση ΞΓ' (18 January 2012), 3452.

European Banking Authority, 'First Evidence on the Use of Moratoria and Public Guarantees in the EU Banking Sector' (November 2020), EBA/Rep/2020/31.

Jérusalmy O, Fox P, Hercelin N, 'Is the Human Dignity of Individual Debtors at Risk ?' (*Finance Watch*, January 2020).

5 Abusive debt recovery practices in Estonia[1]

Karin Sein

5.1 Introduction

This paper discusses abusive debt recovery practices and the legislative and judicial responses to them in B2C relationships in Estonia. Although the Estonian banking sector recently claimed that their loan portfolios are in excellent shape and there have never been so few persons in default for more than 60 days,[2] the leading Estonian debt recovery company estimates that in February 2021, Estonian natural persons had altogether 235,594 defaults whereas 55% of the debtors had more than one defaulted payment and 15% even five or more defaults. According to their statistics, a typical natural person debtor in Estonia is an Estonian male of 42 years with two debts of 2,900 euro in total.[3] With the global economy currently in tension and the price level as well as the number of defaulting consumers rising, the threat of a negative scenario for Estonian consumers is evident.

The chapter starts with a general description of the Estonian debt collection market and the lack of sector-specific public law regulation. It gives an overview of the different authorities responsible for the supervision of the debt recovery industry. It also describes how the government has only recently started considering enacting some sector-specific public law, licensing obligation among them. Next, the paper follows the development of the legislative response setting forth statutory limits for debt recovery costs and claims that these legislative changes were very much induced by the so-called SMS-loan boom and the resulting over-indebtedness of consumers back in the 2000s and 2010s. Thereafter, the chapter addresses the quite detailed and nuanced rules setting forth statutory limits for

1 The work leading to this paper has been partially funded by the Estonian Research Council grant no PRG 124.

2 'Pangaliit: laenumaksetega hädasolijaid on rekordiliselt vähe' *Postimees* (Tallinn, 4 October 2021) <https://majandus.postimees.ee/7352842/pangaliit-laenumaksetega-hadasolijaid-on-rekordiliselt-vahe> accessed 24 October 2021.

3 Erik Aru, 'Võlanõuetega kimbutamine: Eesti kaalub inkassofirmade tegevuse rangemat reguleerimist' *Postimees* (Tallinn, 21 May 2021) <https://majandus.postimees.ee/7254924/volanouetega-kimbutamine-eesti-kaalub-inkassofirmade-tegevuse-rangemat-reguleerimist> accessed 24 October 2021.

DOI: 10.4324/9781003343158-6

debt collection costs and their application in judicial practice. As the unfair commercial practices rules have proven to be inefficient to tackle abusive debt collection practices in Estonia, the paper further discusses data protection violations in debt recovery practices and claims that at least some obviously illegal privacy-intruding practices leading to the stigmatization of debtors have been banned in the Estonian case law. Finally, the technological development and increasing use of software solutions in Estonian debt recovery practices are described – from both the industry side as well as the consumer side.

5.2 Lack of sector-specific public law regulation

There is currently no specific public law regulation in force for debt recovery companies in Estonia: these enterprises are not subject to a licensing obligation nor any other specific rules banning or restricting certain types of debt recovery behavior. For example, there are no rules concerning the hours suitable for contacting debtors or whether approaching their relatives or employers should be acceptable or not. However, very recently, the government has started to analyze whether enacting some sector-specific public law rules would be necessary.[4] The Estonian Ministry of Finance has initiated a study about the existing problems on the market and possible solutions, the results of which are expected by the end of 2021. Moreover, the Ministry is waiting for the proposal's outcome for an E.U. directive on credit servicers and credit purchasers[5] to see whether its rules would also affect debt recovery practices in Estonia.[6]

As there is no licensing obligation nor are there any requirements for the managers of debt recovery enterprises, the number of market participants is quite high although there is no reliable data as to the exact numbers. According to the Estonian public news service, several hundred companies in Estonia use the word *inkasso* (debt collection agency) in their name.[7] However, the market is rather concentrated and split between only a small number of enterprises. The biggest one – Julianus Inkasso, which is the market leader in Estonia and the whole Baltic region – admits that the amount of their competitors is unknown even to them but estimates that there are only up to five more prominent players on the market.[8] Debt recovery companies are currently not organized at industry level in Estonia and, accordingly, no industry-adopted code of conduct exists. In Estonia, debt recovery is primarily used in the domestic context (credit, parking fees, communication, and utilities contracts); cross-border cases are not common.

4 Aru (note 2).

5 Commission, 'Proposal for a Directive of the European Parliament and of the Council on credit servicers, credit purchasers and the recovery of collateral' COM/2018/0135 final.

6 Aru (note 2).

7 Huko Aaspõllu, 'Loodetavasti saab ministeerium inkassodele päitsed pähe panna' *Eesti Rahvusringhääling* (Tallinn, 15 December 2020) <https://www.err.ee/1208449/huko-aaspollu-loodetavasti-saab-ministeerium-inkassodele-paitsed-pahe-panna> accessed 24 October 2021.

8 Ibid.

As the debt collection companies are not subject to licensing obligations nor sector-specific rules, there is no specific supervisory authority overseeing debt recovery companies in Estonia. However, as they have to follow the general consumer protection rules, the Estonian Consumer Protection and Technical Regulatory Authority has the competence to supervise debt recovery companies, including the right to issue precepts and apply fines of up to 32,000 euro if unfair contract terms or unfair commercial practices are used or excessive debt recovery costs charged from consumers.[9] Yet, the Authority has not been very harsh when taming debt recovery companies: it has issued some guidance for the consumers[10] but has not imposed strict measures on the enterprises. In particular, there is no case law where unfair commercial practices rules[11] have been used to combat abusive debt collection practices. Consequently, one can say that unfair commercial practices regulation has not proven particularly useful against abusive debt recovery practices in Estonia. While the Consumer Protection and Technical Regulatory Authority is responsible for tackling consumer law breaches, supervising data protection violations, which are sadly not uncommon in debt collection practices in Estonia, is the responsibility of the Estonian Data Protection Inspectorate.[12] Unfortunately, the Data Protection Inspectorate has also taken a relatively moderate stance, concentrating on raising awareness of the importance of privacy rules, but until now has refrained from imposing hefty fines.[13]

5.3 Regulation of debt recovery costs

5.3.1 Statutory limits on debt recovery costs: historical development

The problem with high-rate debt recovery costs in Estonia occurred together with the development of instant consumer credit (the so-called SMS-loans) in the 2000s and 2010s.[14] The excessive debt recovery costs charged from consumers and other abusive debt collection practices were greatly related to the boom of high interest rate instant loans that were a prevalent and widespread business model at that time. Already in 2007, the Estonian Consumer Protection Authority

9 Consumer Protection Act (Tarbijakaitseseadus) RT I, 04.01.2021, 14. See § 61, 64, 65(2) and 72 of the Act.

10 See <https://www.ttja.ee/inkasso> accessed 2 November 2021.

11 The maximum fine for using unfair commercial practices is 50,000 euro, see § 70 of the Consumer Protection Act.

12 Data Protection Inspectorate (*Andmekaitseinspektsioon*) is the independent supervisory authority in Estonia within the meaning of art 51 of the General Data Protection Regulation (GDPR) and hence competent for monitoring the application of data protection rules in Estonia.

13 See in more detail in s 5.5.

14 On the business model and legal issues of the so-called SMS-loans in Estonia, see Kalev Saare, Karin Sein, Mari Ann Simovart, 'Protection of Consumer Rights in SMS Loan Agreements' (2010) 18 (1) European Review of Private Law 129, 129–142; Karin Sein, Urmas Volens, 'Legal Problems and Regulations related to Easy-access Non-secured Consumer Loans in Estonia' (2014) 22 Juridica International 120, 120–137.

reported on such problems in its yearbook, stating that in most cases, creditors engaged debt collection agencies who, in turn, claimed disproportionately high debt recovery costs, penalty payments, and penalty interests from the consumers.[15] Electronic credit providers' usurious and irresponsible lending practices created tensions and led to substantial socio-economic problems for consumers. To a great extent, these problems stemmed from the usurious nature of the loans as it was not uncommon in Estonia for the annual percentage rate of charge (APRC) of an electronic consumer loan to exceed 1,000%.[16] High rate debt collection fees, of course, only added to the overall consumer indebtedness.

The Estonian Supreme Court (*Riigikohus*) intervened in such practices at the beginning of 2009 and tried to protect consumers against disproportionately high debt collection costs via unfair terms rules. The case that reached the Supreme Court concerned a classical situation where a consumer had concluded a high-interest consumer credit contract, defaulted and the claim was passed on to a debt collection company. The Court ruled that disproportionately high debt recovery cost clauses may be considered unfair and thus void under § 42(3)(5) of the Estonian Law of Obligations Act (LOA)[17] as they set forth a disproportionately high fixed-sum damages payment.[18] The legislator aimed to codify the ruling in 2011, stipulating in § 113(5) second sentence of the LOA that in addition to the delay interest, the creditor can demand 'reasonable' debt recovery costs caused by the delayed payment – with the hope that such a restriction will keep debt collection costs reasonable.

Neither the case law of the Supreme Court nor the legislative change codifying it proved to be effective in practice. There was, for example, no consistent understanding of when debt collection costs can be considered unreasonable and the respective contract clauses thus void. There was no common standard for this neither on the market nor in the judicial system. In 2013, one could find decisions where the court had deemed debt collection costs of 166 euro unreasonably high and, therefore, ruled that the consumer does not have to bear them or must compensate for them only to a reduced extent. On the other hand, there were decisions where the court declared such clauses valid and ordered the consumer to pay collection costs in considerable amounts.[19]

As a result of growing tensions, the Ministry of Justice initiated a thorough empirical and comparative study in 2013 aimed at mapping the actual situation on the market and proposing legislative solutions. The study analysed the terms and conditions of 24 service providers (including several SMS-loan providers) in Estonia and came to the conclusion that while the amount of fixed debt recovery

15 Tarbijakaitseamet, *Aastaaruanne 2007* (Consumer Protection Authority, Annual Report 2007) (Tallinn 2008) 180.
16 Karin Sein, 'Protection of Consumers in Consumer-Credit Contracts: Expectations and Reality in Estonia' (2013) XX Juridica International 32.
17 Law of Obligations Act (Võlaõigusseadus), RT I, 04.01.2021, 19.
18 Decision of the Estonian Supreme Court of 14 January 2009 no 3-2-1-120-08 para 15.
19 Sein (note 16) 38 with further references.

costs varied across these service providers, the costs were often unreasonable, did not depend upon real costs of the creditor, and even exceeded the ones applied in Finland where the living standard and costs in general are considerably higher.[20]

Moreover, a study of more than 400 cases in the first instance courts highlighted that judicial control over debt collection fees had remained inefficient mainly due to procedural reasons. First, in many cases the creditor had hidden the debt recovery costs in the principal amount of the debt. Second, in nearly all cases the court afforded the creditor exactly the same amount that it had claimed in the action without any further explanations as to why the amount is justified in the court's opinion. This, in turn, was mainly due to the fact that many of the judgments were rendered *in absentia*, that is, without the debtor's presence, in which case the court may presume that the debtor has acknowledged the debt. Again, in several cases the debt collection costs awarded to the creditors exceeded the maximum amount of 210 euro allowed under Finnish law in force at that time.[21]

On top of that came the well-known problem that many natural person debtors suffer from financial illiteracy, are not prepared to assert their rights in court, and do not possess the financial means to do so.[22] Moreover, consumer-credit norms are often highly complicated and consumers, as a rule, cannot resort to them, at least not without professional legal aid.[23] Overall, only in 8% of the cases did the court reduce the debt recovery costs.[24] Therefore, the conclusion that different factors have led to a situation where judicial control over high rate debt collection fees is not functioning and consequently debtors are not able to find protection in the court system[25] does not seem to be exaggerated. As for the possible solutions, the study suggested following the example of several European countries and introducing statutory caps for debt collection fees to protect the interests of the defaulting consumers.[26] A similar plea was also published in the legal literature.[27]

At the same time, the Estonian Ministry of Economic Affairs and Communications also launched a study on the Estonian instant credit (SMS-loans) market, the results of which were published in February 2014.[28] Similar to the study conducted by the Ministry of Justice, the study regarded high debt

20 Kaisa Margus, 'Võla sissenõudmiskulude regulatsiooni muutmise vajalikkus tarbijaõigussuhetes' (2014) 2 Juridica 120, 120–122.

21 Margus (note 20) 123.

22 See, for example, Tanja Jørgensen, The Way to Over-indebtedness—Intensive Marketing, Easy Access to Loans, and Insufficient Legislation (Denmark), 22 (2014) Juridica International 71, 89-90 and Villu Kõve, Tsiviilkohtumenetluse kiirendamise võimalused ja nendega seotud ohud (2012) 9 Juridica 670–671.

23 Sein (note 16) 33.

24 Kristiina Koll, 'Tarbija kaitsmine tarbijakrediidilepinguga seotud ebamõistlike kulude eest' (2015) 4 Juridica 251, 254.

25 Margus (note 20) 124.

26 Margus (note 20) 126.

27 Sein (note 16) 38–39.

28 Majandus- ja Kommunikatsiooniministeerium, *Kiirlaenuturg – analüüs ja ettepanekud* (Tallinn, 2014).

collection fees as part of a bigger problem and suggested introducing statutory caps for debt collection costs.[29]

These two studies launched by the Ministry of Justice and the Ministry of Economic Affairs and Communications became the basis for the legislative changes adopted in 2015,[30] despite heavy critique from the industry.[31] During the legislative process, the number of natural-person debtors in 2015 rose up to 37,244, a considerable number in a population of 1.3 million. The new rules set forth statutory caps both for the consumer credit APRC as well as for the debt collection fees.[32] Yet, the changes did not introduce a licensing obligation for debt recovery companies nor any other public law restrictions. The possible explanation is that the focus of the amendments was to tackle abusive and usurious credit practices and not so much debt recovery practices. In other words, the legislator was interested in regulating debt recovery only to tackle the usurious consumer credit practices and the resulting consumer over-indebtedness.

5.3.2 Statutory limits on debt recovery costs

5.3.2.1 General issues

When introducing debt recovery cost caps, the Estonian legislator followed the Scandinavian, more precisely the Finnish *laki saatavien perinnästä* and Danish *Bekendtgørelse af lov om renter ved forsinket betaling m.v.* as the main blueprints.[33] The new rules in the added § 113² of the LOA apply to the claims from B2C contractual relationships after 1 October 2015. They are, however, not applicable to employment contracts.[34] All the provisions are mandatory, i.e. they may not be derogated from to the consumer's detriment.[35]

The law distinguishes between the costs for reminder letters and other recovery costs whereas the maximum amounts of these costs, in turn, depend upon the extent of the debt. In addition, the same maximum amounts may be claimed from the consumer for every surety giver or other solidary debtor,[36] provided that the creditor has also sent reminder letters to them. On the other hand, the maximum limits to the recovery costs apply despite the creditor having assigned the claim to a new creditor.[37]

Only in exceptional cases, in particular if the collection activities have turned out to be highly complicated, does § 113²(4) of the LOA allow to claim additional

29 Majandus- ja Kommunikatsiooniministeerium (note 28) 62.
30 The added § 113² of the LOA regulating the compensation for collection costs by consumers entered into force on 1 October 2015.
31 Koll (note 24) 255.
32 See § 406² of the LOA for the APRC caps and § 113² of the LOA for the debt collection costs caps.
33 Paul Varul and others, *Võlaõigusseadus I. Kommenteeritud väljaanne* (Juura 2016) 579.
34 Decision of the Estonian Supreme Court of 28 March 2017 no 3-2-1-178-16 para 13.
35 § 113²(6) of the LOA.
36 § 113²(1) second sentence and (2) of the LOA.
37 Varul and others (note 33) 582.

recovery costs. These extremely complicated cases may involve circumstances where the debtor's residence is unknown or abroad or where the debtor has provided wrong information about his or her whereabouts,[38] as well as a situation where the creditor has to use the bailiff in order to service the documents.[39] Until now, the courts have been rather strict when affording additional debt recovery costs; for example, the debtor's death has not been qualified as an exceptionally complicated situation for the debt collection company.[40]

As the law sets forth caps for out-of-court debt collection costs in general, they are equally applicable, regardless of whether the debt is recovered by a debt collection agency or a lawyer. They are, however, not applicable to bailiffs as a separate legal act determines their fees.[41]

Debt collection costs are recoverable only if there is a respective agreement between the parties and the costs have been incurred in reality and not calculated on an abstract basis: from the dogmatical point of view, the amounts outlined in the law do not constitute a statutory 'price list' but should rather be considered fixed-sum contractual penalties or damages.[42] In practice, the courts usually check whether the recovery costs have really been incurred and refuse to oblige debtors to pay abstract costs without any evidence.[43]

First, the law distinguishes between debt recovery costs incurred during the contract period and after the contractual relationship has ended. Second, the law also distinguishes between the costs for reminder letters and other recovery costs.

5.3.2.2 Costs for reminder letters

Sending reminder letters is typical conduct of debt recovery and, therefore, much of the regulation in the LOA deals with these letters. The law does not foresee any formal requirements for the reminder letter and therefore reminding the consumer by SMS or email (but not by phone) should also suffice; however, just stating the debt on the next month's invoice should not qualify as a reminder letter.[44] There are different restrictions on compensating for the reminder letters during the contract period and after the contract has expired or has been terminated.

The creditor may demand up to five euro of debt collection costs relating to only one reminder letter sent per each obligation fallen due during the contract period. The threshold of five euro was chosen because according to the price list of the Estonian postal services valid at the time of the legislative amendments in 2015, this amount covered all postal expenses including the expenses for using

38 Koll (note 24) 260; Varul and others (note 33) 583.

39 See § 113^2 (4) of the LOA with the reference to § 48 of the Bailiffs Act.

40 Decision of Tartu County Court of 18 May 2018 no 2-18-2288.

41 Bailiffs Act (Kohtutäituri seadus), RT I, 09.04.2021, 7.

42 Varul and others (note 33) 580.

43 See eg the decision of Pärnu County Court of 27 September 2021 no 2-21-9462.

44 Koll (note 24) 259; Varul and others (note 33) 580.

registered mail or sending notices abroad.[45] The first reminder letter, though, must be sent free of charge for the consumer.[46] For credit agreements, utilities, or subscription contracts, this regulation means that if the consumer is in default, but the contract has not yet been terminated because of it, then the creditor is only entitled to five euro for the second reminder letter and no further debt collection fees can be claimed from the debtor.

After termination of the contract, the caps for reminder letter costs depend upon the amount of the claim being asserted against the consumer; when assessing the amount of the claim, accessory claims such as interest and penalty interest should also be taken into account.[47] All in all, the creditor is entitled to claim compensation for a maximum of three reminder letters and the maximum amounts are set forth as follows: (i) up to 15 euro may be demanded for the first reminder sent to the consumer and five euro each for two subsequent letters if the debt is up to 500 euro; (ii) up to 20 euro may be demanded for the first reminder sent to the consumer and five euro each for two subsequent letters if the debt is more than 500 euro but up to 1,000 euro, and (iii) up to 25 euro may be demanded for the first reminder sent to the consumer and five euro each for two subsequent letters if the debt is over 1,000 euro.[48] The maximum amount for the first reminder letter is set higher to allow the debt collector to also compensate for its general costs, such as the office personnel costs.[49]

In addition, the regulation contains a time limitation as to when the reminder letters may be sent in order to avoid misuse: the first reminder letter may be sent only after seven days have passed from the termination of the contract. Moreover, there must be at least seven days between sending the first, second, and third letters.[50]

5.3.2.3 Other debt recovery costs

Although sending reminder letters is probably the most typical debt collection activity, there are also other costs necessary for out-of-court debt recovery. The compensation for these costs is regulated in § 113(3) of the LOA and again the maximum statutory amounts depend upon the amount of the debt. Other recovery costs within the meaning of § 113^2 LOA include all possible costs for recovery, such as costs of phone calls, personal meetings with the debtor, making inquiries in registers, etc.[51] As noted above, other debt collection costs are only recoverable after the termination of the contractual relationship: the legislator aimed to allow

45 Koll (note 24) 259; Varul and others (note 33) 581.
46 § 113^2(1) of the LOA.
47 Varul and others (note 33) 582.
48 § 113^2(3) of the LOA.
49 Varul and others (note 33) 582.
50 § 113^2(3) of the LOA.
51 Varul and others (note 33) 582.

only the recovery of reminder letter costs until the contractual relationship (e.g. credit contract) is still ongoing and not terminated.[52]

The maximum amounts of other recovery costs except for the reminder letter costs are set as follows: (i) 30 euro if the debt is up to 500 euro; (ii) 40 euro if the debt is more than 500 euro but up to 1,000 euro, and (iii) 50 euro if the debt exceeds 1,000 euro. These maximum amounts include the recoverable costs for reminder letters; hence, if the debt is up to 500 euro and the creditor has sent two reminder letters (the first one for 15 euro and the second for five euro), then he may additionally claim 10 euro for other debt collection costs. If the creditor has sent only one reminder letter and claimed 15 euro for it, he may additionally claim 15 euro for other recoverable debt collection costs. The decision on how high the maximum amounts should be set, was influenced, *inter alia*, by the statutory caps in force in the Scandinavian countries but keeping in mind that the cost of living in Estonia is generally lower.[53]

5.3.2.4 Reduction of debt recovery costs

In certain situations, the court may reduce the maximum amounts of debt collection fees described above. The consumer is entitled to demand reduction of the debt recovery costs if the costs are unreasonably high, taking into account in particular the extent to which the obligation has been performed by the party, the legitimate interests of the other party, and the economic situation of the parties.[54] Moreover, any extra-judicial objections of the consumer to the claims or earlier recognition of the claim shall be taken into consideration as well.[55] When looking at the case law, we notice that in several cases the weak financial situation of the debtor has been accepted as a reason justifying the reduction of the costs.[56] Moreover, there have been cases where lower-level courts have reduced the debt collection costs even on their own motion (*ex officio*).[57]

Unsurprisingly, the statutory limits of debt collection costs have provoked criticism by the industry. Representatives of debt recovery enterprises have complained in the media that the real costs of debt collection are actually higher than

52 Varul and others (note 33) 581.
53 Koll (note 24) 260.
54 § $113^2(5)$ and § 162 of the LOA.
55 See § $113^2(5)$ second sentence of the LOA.
56 See, for instance, the decision of Harju County Court of 24 May 2018 no 2-17-127156 where the court argued that not reducing the costs would have a considerable negative impact on the coping of the consumer whereas reduction of the costs would have little impact upon the economic situation of the creditor. Similar arguments can be found in the decision of Harju County Court of 7 December 2017 no 2-17-117428 where the income of the disabled consumer was only a little more than 300 euro per month; hence the court found that 30 euro of debt collection fees were disproportionate and reduced them to zero.
57 Therefore, the second instance court Tallinn Circuit Court repealed the decision of the first instance court in case no 2-19-139288.

the limits imposed by the law.[58] Given that the industry is still operating with considerable profits, these arguments should probably be taken with some reservations. For example, the commentaries on the provision, written, *inter alia*, by a Supreme Court justice, suggest that the statutory caps also legitimize the seemingly low penalty payments recoverable from the consumers and therefore may well be in the interests of the debt collection industry.[59]

5.4 Debt recovery practices and data protection concerns

One area of debt recovery practices that constantly creates problems for consumers relates to their privacy and protection of their personal data. It has been common practice for debt recovery companies to use public pressure and stigmatization to motivate consumers to pay off their debts. For instance, the names of indebted persons have been published either in business-oriented newspapers or on special websites,[60] but there have also been cases where debtors' names were printed on huge posters hanging on the walls of several-storey buildings[61] or on big posters set up on the cross-roads in the centre of the Estonian capital Tallinn.[62] Usually, the defaulting consumers are also listed in the privately owned credit registries: this is one of the most effective ways of exerting pressure upon them as having a notification of a payment default in such a registry makes it more or less impossible for the debtor to obtain consumer credit (including a car lease and a credit card) or even a mobile phone subscription.

Such privacy-breaching practices are not rare on the Estonian market. On the contrary: in its audit completed in 2013, the Estonian Data Protection Inspectorate found that debt recovery companies published the names of the debtors without determining whether the alleged debt even existed and that almost all debt recovery companies breached the law in one way or another.[63] Two years later, in 2015, a similar audit found that only two out of 20 debt recovery companies were

58 Aru (note 2).

59 Varul and others (note 33) 579.

60 Such as the digital platform 'volaturg,' which was the object of dispute in the decision of the Supreme Court of 25 September 2013 no 3-2-1-80-13 but has ceased to exist by now.

61 The representative of the debt recovery company CKE Inkasso claimed that this had proven to be a very efficient means to make debtors pay. Eiris Teeveere, 'Inkassofirma riputas võlgnike nimed tänavale üles' *Õhtuleht* (Tallinn, 6 January 2009) <https://www.ohtuleht.ee/310504/inkassofirma-riputas-volgnike-nimed-tanavale-ules> accessed 24 October 2021.

62 This was the case which led to the first privacy-and-debt recovery-related Supreme Court decision in 2010. The names of the debtors were printed on a huge poster with the additional text: 'Persons who do not fulfill their obligations duly.' See the decision of the Supreme Court of 21 December 2010 no 3-2-1-67-10.

63 Indrek Kald, 'Pea kõik inkassofirmad rikuvad seadust' *Äripäev* (Tallinn, 28 November 2012) <https://www.aripaev.ee/article/2012/11/28/andmekaitse-pea-koik-inkassofirmad-rikuvad-seadust> accessed 24 October 2021.

compliant with the data protection law in their activities.[64] Quite incredibly, even in 2020, the biggest debt collection company Julianus Inkasso, when confronted with the order of the Data Protection Inspectorate to stop the publication of a debtor's details in the payment default registries – in a situation where the creditor (an Estonian mobile phone company) had destroyed all the documents related to the allegedly once-existing debt – tried to argue that it is not up to them to prove the existence of the debt but rather the debtor should prove that he has paid all the invoices.[65]

The extensive, stigmatizing and uncontrolled debt recovery practices were already criticized in the legal literature in 2004.[66] Some years later, the court system also started taking measures in order to put an end to the privacy-breaching practices of debt recovery enterprises. In 2010, the Supreme Court ruled that payment defaults may be published if there is no dispute as to the existence of the debt, and the debtor has been notified and given an additional term for payment before the publication. Moreover, the context of the publication must remain within the boundaries of decency and should not violate good morals.[67] In 2013, the Supreme Court once again stressed that when publishing the names of debtors, creditors must obey the data protection rules and that publishers are not entitled to make humiliating assessments.[68]

A specific abusive debt recovery practice relates to debts that have already been prescribed. It is common practice that debt recovery agencies try to enforce a prescribed debt, alleging that although the defendant can raise the defence of prescription in court and is therefore not obliged to pay, the claim still exists and can therefore be asserted out of court.[69] In such cases, debt recovery agencies repeatedly report the debtors in publicly available (often online) blacklists or privately owned credit registries, trying to exert psychological pressure on the debtors.[70] These practices were assessed by the Estonian Supreme Court in 2011 when the court allowed publication of the default payment fact in a credit registry for 13 years after the default, as a

64 Andmekaitse Inspektsioon, 'Andmekaitse Inspektsioon seiras inkassoteenuse osutajaid' (Tallinn, 11 September 2015) <https://www.aki.ee/et/uudised/andmekaitse-inspektsioon-seiras-inkassoteenuse-osutajaid> accessed 24 October 2021.

65 Decision of the Estonian Data Protection Inspectorate. Vaideotsus 18.06.2020 avaliku teabe asjas nr 2.1.-3-20-1624 Andmekaitse Inspektsioon – Julianus Inkasso OÜ.

66 Ivo Pilving, 'Sugupuud müügiks ja roolijoodikud häbiposti? Isikuandmetega seonduvad piirangud avaliku teabe avaldamisel' 2004 (2) Juridica 75ff.

67 Decision of the Supreme Court of 21 December 2010 no 3-2-1-67-10 para 22.

68 See the decision no 3-2-1-80-13 (note 60) para 38.

69 Under the Estonian law, the usual prescription period for contractual claims is three years. In case of wilful breaches, the prescription period is ten years. Prescription does not make the claim non-existent; instead, the debtor becomes entitled to raise a defense of prescription in the court proceedings which makes the claim non-enforceable. The court is not entitled to apply prescription *ex officio*. See Paul Varul and others, *Tsiviilseadustiku üldosa seadus. Kommenteeritud väljaanne* (Juura 2009) 442.

70 See e.g. the 2012 Yearbook of the Estonian Data Protection Inspectorate describing such practices. Andmekaitse Inspektsioon, *Aastaraamat 2012* (Tallinn 2013) 47.

rule.[71] The new Estonian Data Protection Act (in force since 2019) has not reduced this rather long period.[72] However, there have recently been first instance court judgments ruling that publishing prescribed payment defaults for more than five years is disproportionate for the debtor and therefore illegitimate under § 10(2)(3) of the Data Protection Act.[73] The new Data Protection Act also clarifies that data about a payment default may not be made available to third persons before 30 days have passed from the breach of contract and that payment defaults may stay publicly visible in a credit registry for five years after the debt has been paid off.[74]

In recent years, one has also seen specific discussions on whether condominiums are entitled to publish the names of the debtors on the condominium corridor notice boards or even on monthly invoices. Already in 2012, the Estonian Data Protection Inspectorate expressed the opinion that apartment owners are entitled to get information from the condominium administrators about the debts of the other apartment owners, but it is not legitimate to publish the names of the debtors on the corridor notice boards or online.[75] Just recently, in 2021, the Data Protection Inspectorate published guidelines on data processing in condominium relationships and held that the publication of personal data in a public room (the commonly used hallway of the condominium) requires consent of the data subject because such rooms are also accessible to third parties. However, the other apartment owners are entitled to information on the debtors based on their legitimate interest to make economic decisions related to the administration of the condominium. Such information may only be made accessible on the invoices, at the owners' meetings, or in a closed mailing list or social media group but not in public rooms or spaces.[76]

5.5 Technological developments and debt recovery practices

In recent years, we have seen a straightforward and rapid development of the Estonian debt collection business model – the technological innovation. In 2020, a representative of the biggest Estonian debt recovery company, Julianus Inkasso, claimed that a contemporary debt recovery enterprise must function as a technology company as it is not possible to recover debts efficiently without advanced technological backup.[77] For example, they have linked their information systems

71 See the decision of the Supreme Court of 12 December 2011 no 3-3-1-70-11 para 22.

72 Data Protection Act (Isikuandmete kaitse seadus), RT I, 04.01.2019, 11.

73 See e.g. the decisions of Harju County Court of 27 October 2020 no 2-20-10157 and Viru County Court of 16 April 2021 no 2-20-16579.

74 See § 10(2)(4) and (5) of the Data Protection Act.

75 Tarbijakaitseamet, *Aastaaruanne 2010* (Consumer Protection Authority, Annual Report 2010) (Tallinn) 59; Andmekaitse Inspektsioon (note 63) 35.

76 See the guidelines on the webpage of the Estonian Data Protection Inspectorate. Andmekaitse Inspektsioon, 'Isikuandmete töötlemine korteriühistus' (Tallinn, 16 March 2021) <https://www.aki.ee/et/uudised/isikuandmete-tootlemine-korteriuhistus> accessed 24 October 2021.

77 'Julianus Inkasso: tänane inkassoettevõte võrdub sisuliselt tehnoloogiafirmaga' *Äripäev* (Tallinn, 30 January 2020) <https://www.aripaev.ee/juubel/2020/01/30/julianus-inkasso-tanane-inkassoettevote-vordub-sisuliselt-tehnoloogiafirmaga> accessed 24 October 2021.

directly with the Estonian electronic population registry and the Estonian digital payment order system,[78] of which they make extensive use. Arguably, up to 40% of all payment orders in Estonia are initiated by the debt collection agency with the most significant market share.[79] Consequently, there is a clear trend in Estonia towards more and more automation in debt collection, surely motivated by financial reasons as automation enables faster debt collection, helps to manage more cases and reduces the costs.

Debt collection agencies develop increasingly sophisticated digital solutions: for example, they use debtor profiling based on their age, marital status, earlier payment behavior, amount of debt, etc. Based on this information, the algorithm decides what kind of communication and which communication channel to use in relation to a particular debtor.[80] Whether and to what extent these kinds of profiling practices will be considered legitimate under the data protection rules by the courts remains to be seen. In addition to such high-level technological solutions, some simpler digital options include sending a ready-to-pay invoice with an online banking link to debtors or setting up a digital environment where debtors can apply for pay-in-installments online, have proven to be efficient in practice.[81]

Yet, technology is used not only by the debt recovery industry but also by defaulting consumers. Namely, an Estonian legal tech company HUGO.legal has created a legal chatbot InkassoAbi, which assists natural persons with debt-recovery related issues for a charge of only five euro. After identifying the problem of the consumer via web-chat, the chatbot generates a document that the consumer can use to contest the illegitimate claim of the debt recovery company.[82] Arguably, the chatbot is especially helpful in cases where the debt recovery company claims enormous but already prescribed debts: it is common practice in Estonia for debt recovery companies to try to trick consumers into accepting a small part of the claim with the negative legal consequence for the consumer of waiving the defence of prescription or prolonging the prescription period.[83] The legal tech company claims that 4,000 persons have already used such a chatbot and document generator and it has helped to avoid unfounded payments of hundreds of thousands of euro to the debt recovery industry.[84] Of course, one chatbot alone cannot put an end to the abusive industry practices, but it still shows that

78 On the description and functioning of the Estonian public digital payment order system, see in-depth Piia Kalamees, Karin Sein, 'Effective protection of consumers by the UCTD in order for payment procedure: the Estonian example' (2020) 6 (1) International Comparative Jurisprudence 46.
79 'Julianus Inkasso: tänane inkassoettevõte võrdub sisuliselt tehnoloogiafirmaga' (note 78).
80 'Julianus Inkasso: tänane inkassoettevõte võrdub sisuliselt tehnoloogiafirmaga' (note 78).
81 'Julianus Inkasso: tänane inkassoettevõte võrdub sisuliselt tehnoloogiafirmaga' (note 78).
82 See HUGO.legal <https://hugo.legal/oigusrobotid/inkassoabi/> accessed 24 October 2021.
83 See the decision of the Estonian Supreme Court of 21 December 2016 no 3-2-1-129-16 para 49.
84 Aru (note 2).

technology and legal tech companies may be of considerable help for the consumers when they try to defend their rights against unfounded claims.

5.6 Conclusions

Abusive debt collection practices, including charging disproportionately high debt collection costs and collecting already prescribed debts, have been common in Estonia since the regaining of independence in the 1990s. These practices were co-developed with the boom of the so-called instant loans (small non-secured consumer loans obtainable online or via mobile phones). Providing usurious consumer loans and high fees for debt collection resulted in serious consumer over-indebtedness and social problems in the 2010s. To tackle these problems, the Estonian legislator intervened in 2015 and set forth statutory limits for debt recovery costs, among other measures. Inspired by the Finnish and Danish legislation, the aim of these rather detailed rules is to protect consumers against disproportionately high debt collection costs in the B2C contractual relationships. As the courts have been rather strict when applying the rules, one can claim that the statutory limits have been a positive measure and have helped to protect the Estonian consumers against high debt collection costs. On the other hand, there is no public law regulation in Estonia: debt collection companies are not subject to a licensing obligation or any other requirements. Still, the government is currently scrutinizing possible public law restrictions so the situation might look different in the near future.

While the unfair commercial practices rules have proven to be inefficient to tackle abusive debt collection practices in Estonia, at least some obviously illegal privacy-intruding practices leading to the stigmatization of debtors have been banned in the Estonian case law. However, the threshold for publishing already prescribed debts is relatively low compared to some other European countries (e.g. in the Scandinavian countries).[85] Nevertheless, it is very much the merit of the Estonian court system that debt recovery companies have been obliged to respect at least the most important data protection rules. Finally, both the industry as well as the consumers are increasingly using different software solutions. Hence, technological development is part of effective debt collection practices as well as defence against unfounded claims.

Bibliography

Andmekaitse Inspektsioon, *Aastaraamat 2012* (Tallinn 2013) 47

Andmekaitse Inspektsioon, 'Andmekaitse Inspektsioon seiras inkassoteenuse osutajaid' (Tallinn, 11 September 2015) <https://www.aki.ee/et/uudised/andmekaitse-inspektsioon-seiras-inkassoteenuse-osutajaid> accessed 24 October 2021

85 In Finland, for example, the retention periods for credit-data-register entries are two to five years, depending on the type of the credit-data-register entry. Antti Makkonen, Instant Loans: Problems and Regulations in Finland, (2014) 22 Juridica International 96, 106.

Aru E, 'Võlanõuetega kimbutamine: Eesti kaalub inkassofirmade tegevuse rangemat reguleerimist' *Postimees* (Tallinn, 21 May 2021) <https://majandus.postimees.ee/7254924/volanouetega-kimbutamine-eesti-kaalub-inkassofirmade-tegevuse-rangemat-reguleerimist> accessed 24 October 2021

Jørgensen T, 'The Way to Over-Indebtedness—Intensive Marketing, Easy Access to Loans, and Insufficient Legislation (Denmark)' (2014) 22 Juridica International 71

Julianus Inkasso, 'Tänane inkassoettevõte võrdub sisuliselt tehnoloogiafirmaga' *Äripäev* (Tallinn, 30 January 2020) <https://www.aripaev.ee/juubel/2020/01/30/julianus-inkasso-tanane-inkassoettevote-vordub-sisuliselt-tehnoloogiafirmaga> accessed 24 October 2021

Kalamees P, Sein K, 'Effective Protection of Consumers by the UCTD in Order for Payment Procedure: The Estonian Example' (2020) 6(1) International Comparative Jurisprudence 46

Kald I, 'Pea kõik inkassofirmad rikuvad seadust' *Äripäev* (Tallinn, 28 November 2012) <https://www.aripaev.ee/article/2012/11/28/andmekaitse-pea-koik-inkassofirmad-rikuvad-seadust> accessed 24 October 2021

Koll K, 'Tarbija kaitsmine tarbijakrediidilepinguga seotud ebamõistlike kulude eest' (2015) 4 Juridica 251

Kõve V, 'Tsiviilkohtumenetluse kiirendamise võimalused ja nendega seotud ohud' (2012) 9 Juridica 670

Majandus- ja Kommunikatsiooniministeerium, *Kiirlaenuturg – analüüs ja ettepanekud* (Tallinn, 2014)

Makkonen A, 'Instant Loans: Problems and Regulations in Finland' (2014) 22 Juridica International 96

Margus K, 'Võla sissenõudmiskulude regulatsiooni muutmise vajalikkus tarbijaõigussuhetes' (2014) 2 Juridica 120

'Pangaliit: laenumaksetega hädasolijaid on rekordiliselt vähe' *Postimees* (Tallinn, 4 October 2021) <https://majandus.postimees.ee/7352842/pangaliit-laenumaksetega-hadasolijaid-on-rekordiliselt-vahe> accessed 24 October 2021

Pilving I, 'Sugupuud müügiks ja roolijoodikud häbiposti? Isikuandmetega seonduvad piirangud avaliku teabe avaldamisel' (2004) 2 Juridica 75

Saare K, Sein K, Simovart MA, 'Protection of Consumer Rights in SMS Loan Agreements' (2010) 18(1) European Review of Private Law 129

Sein K, Volens U, 'Legal Problems and Regulations Related to Easy-Access Non-Secured Consumer Loans in Estonia' (2014) 22 Juridica International 120

Sein K, 'Protection of Consumers in Consumer-Credit Contracts: Expectations and Reality in Estonia' (2013) XX Juridica International 32

Tarbijakaitseamet, *Aastaaruanne 2007* (Consumer Protection Authority, Annual Report 2007) (Tallinn 2008)

Tarbijakaitseamet, *Aastaaruanne 2010* (Consumer Protection Authority, Annual Report 2010) (Tallinn 59, 2011)

Teeveere E, 'Inkassofirma riputas võlgnike nimed tänavale üles' *Õhtuleht* (Tallinn, 6 January 2009) <https://www.ohtuleht.ee/310504/inkassofirma-riputas-volgnike-nimed-tanavale-ules> accessed 24 October 2021

Varul P, Käerdi M, Kõve V, Kull I, *Tsiviilseadustiku üldosa seadus. Kommenteeritud väljaanne* (Juura 2009)

Varul P, Kull I, Kõve V, Käerdi M, Sein K, *Võlaõigusseadus I. Kommenteeritud väljaanne* (Juura 2016)

6 Doubling down on debt?

Legal responses to private debt as a business model in the Netherlands

Candida Leone and Joanna van Duin

6.1 Introduction

The market for informal (extra-judicial) debt collection in the Netherlands is flourishing; recent research established its yearly turnout at 15–20 billion euro.[1] An estimated 7–8% of Dutch residents are faced with a collection action every year; the large majority find themselves up against commercial debt collectors.[2] Not only credit institutes, but all sorts of providers resort to outsourcing of their credits – from dentists to energy and telecommunication companies to webshops. According to Government documents, the market is divided between debt collection agencies, bailiffs and so-called 'incasso-lawyers,' who – we can assume – enter the picture when the outstanding amounts are more significant. Next to this distinction, as in other countries, some agencies will engage in the direct purchase of claims and the subsequent collection as new creditors rather than contractors of the original creditor, a problem which here and there emerges in the Dutch discussion.[3] The preponderance of debt collection unconnected to traditional (mortgage or personal) credit, however, has kept the debates on debt collection and non-performing loans largely separated.

The debt collection business has been largely unregulated so far; self-regulation initiatives have appeared in recent years, but it seems that their impact on the market

1 *Kamerstukken* II 2020-2021, 35733, nr. 3 (hereinafter: *Memorie van Toelichting*) para 2.2 ('Nature and significance of claim collection services'), p. 15. This chapter was closed in January 2022. The Memorie van Toelichting (explanatory memorandum) pertains to the legislative proposal on 'Quality of debt collection services' discussed in this chapter; the law has been approved on 22 May 2022.

2 *Kwantitatief onderzoek naar de aard en omvang van incassoproblematiek onder consumenten* (ACM/Motivaction 2014). See also *Memorie van Toelichting* section 2.2, with further references.

3 See Autoriteit Financiële Markten, *Consumenten en Incassotrajecten. De verantwoordelijkheden van aanbieders van consumptief krediet bij betalingsachterstanden*, 15 November 2016 (update: 19 december 2018). In 2020, the Dutch Supreme Court confirmed that it is possible, in particular, for banks to sell their claims to non-banks, in fact legitimising the cession model (see *Hoge Raad* 10 July 2020, ECLI:NL:HR:2020:1274 en ECLI:NL:HR:2020:1276). This gives rise to the question to what extent the original creditor's duties and obligations are transferred to the debt collector. See e.g. N.J.H. Huls, 'Hoe barmhartig is het burgerlijk recht voor de consument?', *Tijdschrift voor Consumentenrecht en handelspraktijken* 2019/2, at p. 87.

DOI: 10.4324/9781003343158-7

has been limited or at least slow to gain traction. The two main 'quality marks'[4] have so far registered a somewhat limited uptake,[5] while complaints keep being made to the enforcement authorities. Societal attention on questions of debt has been constant – and possibly growing – throughout the post-crisis decade, with the last government having resigned over *public* enforcement of credits viz suspected fraudsters.[6] The policy initiatives around debt collection are thus part of a broader policy agenda loosely titled 'integral approach to debt' (*brede schuldenaanpak*).[7]

Since 2012, the *costs* that can be charged to debtors are regulated in a governmental decree that caps them at a certain percentage of the concerned credit but also establishes a *minimum* compensation of 40 euro per advanced claim.[8] For very small credits (government report: a significant proportion of all claims), this has the effect that it is in fact lucrative – indeed, a business model – to immediately advance a claim as allowed charges may be several times the outstanding amount.[9] Taking the example of a cheap phone subscription that may cost a few euro per month, the same claim can be repeated several times in a row if a consumer fails to pay successive monthly installments, quickly leading to debt consisting of a few tens of euro in principal and a few hundred in collection charges. This is already poignant if the consumer simply forgot to pay, but particularly so if they do not have the money, and also if they have a disagreement with the original creditor about the delivered products or services or about the claimed amount (thus, if the claim is contested).[10]

Over the past decade, thus, stories of consumers confronted with piling debt, aggressive letters, and confusing messages have kept appearing[11] – although, as

4 'Incasso Keurmerk' by the association of Debt collectors and the independent benchmark 'Sociaal verantwoord incasseren,' see *Memorie van Toelichting* section 2.1.

5 Figures in *Memorie van Toelichting* section 2.2 indicate that around ten percent of the active debt collectors are associated with the one or the other quality marks. The figures may have changed since the *Memorie* was written, but they give a good idea of the limits encountered by the initiatives.

6 See BBC 15 January 2021, Dutch Rutte government resigns over child welfare fraud scandal, <https://www.bbc.com/news/world-europe-55674146>.

7 See 'Actieplan brede Schuldenaanpak,' <https://www.rijksoverheid.nl/onderwerpen/schulden/schulden-aanpakken>.

8 Besluit buitengerechtelijke incassokosten, art 2(2). Art 6:96(2)(c) of the Dutch Civil Code (*Burgerlijk Wetboek*; BW) stipulates that collection charges can be claimed as damages (on the basis of the debtor's contractual liability). Pursuant to art 6:96(5)–(7), the rules laid down in the governmental decree are mandatory in case the debtor is a consumer; the compensation can only be claimed 14 days after the consumer-debtor has received due notice; and the notice must encompass all claims, the aggregated amount of which is used to calculate the compensation.

9 Extra salient is that sending an automated notice can already qualify as a debt collection measure that warrants compensation; see also R.R.M. de Moor, 'Wettelijke normering van buitengerechtelijke incassokosten: alleen maar 'voordeel' voor de consument?', Tijdschrift voor Consumentenrecht en handelspraktijken 2012/5, at p. 202. In one extreme case, an amount 240 euro was claimed for legal costs whereas the original claim was only 0.05 euro: see Rb. Amsterdam 7 November 2019, ECLI:NL:RBAMS:2019:8244.

10 ACM/Motivaction 2014 (see note 2).

11 See e.g. <https://www.groene.nl/artikel/routinematige-intimidatie> ('Habitual harassment'), *Dossier De Schuldenindustrie: wie verdient er aan mensen met schulden?* ('The debt industry: who profits from people in debt?') <https://www.platform-investico.nl/dossiers/de-handel-schulden/>.

we see, less so after intervention based on unfair commercial practices rules. Next to rogue traders demanding payments of e.g., unsolicited goods and services or otherwise ungrounded claims, inflated claims and claims based on partially invalid contracts were not uncommon in an economy characterized by heavy reliance on delayed payment.

Adding pain to injury was the possibility for creditors/debt collectors to enforce a claim through court proceedings in default of appearance of the debtor, based on little documentary evidence and for the very reasonable cost of 79 euro per claim. This situation blurred the boundaries between informal and judicial debt collection, allowing creditors to have their claims rubber-stamped by local courts without, in most cases, ever going beyond merely *alleging* a claim. While the situation has changed over the past ten years (see section 6.2.1), the current state is not free from controversy and does not, of course, address the 'genuinely' informal side of the collection business.

With this background in mind, in 2020–2021 the Dutch government has been discussing a proposal entitled the 'Quality of debt collection services' (*Wet kwaliteit incassodienstverlening*, henceforth WKI), which aims to address the problem by regulating both access to the market and the way in which collection services need to be performed, in particular requiring careful communication and the provision of transparent information to debtors. The main elements in this proposal will be discussed in the second part of the paper. We will conclude by reflecting on the relationship between the Dutch proposal and the 2021 Directive on credit servicers and credit purchasers (hereinafter 2021 Credit Servicers Directive),[12] in particular with a view to exploring whether criticism raised in the Dutch debate against the pending proposal can be seen as addressed by the Directive.

6.2 First part: reigning in abusive debt collection via 'regular' (consumer) instruments

6.2.1 Blurred boundaries between informal and judicial collection and spill-over effects of ex officio *control*

Unlike in other E.U. Member States, notably Spain and Poland,[13] there is no separate order for payment procedure in the Netherlands. It is possible to file a monetary claim in summary proceedings (dubbed '*incassokortgeding*'[14]) insofar as

12 Directive (EU) 2021/2167 of the European Parliament and of the Council of 24 November 2021 on credit servicers and credit purchasers and amending Directives 2008/48/EC and 2014/17/EU.

13 See e.g. CJEU 14 June 2012, Case C-618/10 *Banco Español de Crédito v. Calderón Camino* ECLI:EU:C:2012:349; CJEU 18 February 2016, Case C-49/14 *Finanmadrid v. Albán Zambrano and Others* ECLI:EU:C:2016:98; CJEU 13 September 2018, Case C-176/17 *Profi Credit Polska v. Wawrzosek* ECLI:EU:C:2018:711 CJEU 28 November 2018, Case C-632/17 *PKO Bank Polski v. Michalski* ECLI:EU:C:2018:963.

14 Specific requirements apply, in particular a balance between urgency (*spoedeisendheid*) and recovery risk if the interim measure is revoked (*restitutierisico*). See, critically, R.P.J.L. Tjittes, 'De geest van het incassokortgeding terug in de fles', *RM Themis* 2002/3, pp. 161–163.

it is plausible that the creditor has an urgent interest – for which the threshold is relatively low – and the claim is likely to be granted. The case can be adjudicated quickly, especially if the debtor does not contest the claim or does not appear in court. The latter happens often: approximately 70% of the cases – also in ordinary (i.e., not summary) proceedings – are decided in default of the defendant's appearance.[15] Default proceedings are thus the default route. In the absence of a contentious debate, the court will usually only dismiss the claim when it appears to be manifestly unjust or unfounded.[16] This means that, in practice, the court is effectively asked to 'rubber-stamp' the claim without assessing the merits of the case.

This poses a particular problem in debt collection cases. First, the threat of court proceedings and accompanying costs, including the risk of a cost order based on the 'loser pays' principle,[17] may coerce debtors into a settlement before the case reaches the court, even if the claim is unfounded. Whilst empirical research has shown that litigants always make a cost/benefit-analysis, legal costs are constantly mentioned as one of the main factors deterring them from going to court.[18] Second, the writ of summons usually contains very little information to substantiate the claim; the underlying contract or a breakdown of the claim's components – e.g., installments, interest, penalties, costs – are often not provided. Third, of the cases that do make it to court, many are uncontested, even if there would be grounds to challenge them. This increases the risk of claims being granted that, on a closer look, are insufficiently substantiated and/or lack a factual or legal basis.

In recent years, lower courts have started exercising more scrutiny in respect of such claims. An example can be found in a case where a debt collection agency had filed a claim based on a – as it turned out – non-existent contract. The Subdistrict Court in Amsterdam considered this to be an 'aggressive commercial practice' and an 'abuse of procedural law': the agency in question knew (or should have known) the claim had no chance of success, but it still brought the claim while being aware that the threat of legal costs would very likely pressure the debtor into paying. The court subsequently dismissed the claim and imposed a much higher cost order than usual.[19]

15 De Rechtspraak, *Rapport incassozaken* 2018, p. 7.

16 Art 139 Dutch Code of Civil Procedure (*Wetboek van Burgerlijke Rechtsvordering*; Rv).

17 On legal costs and other barriers to going to court, see e.g. *Study for the Fitness Check of EU consumer and marketing Law – Final report Part 1: Main report*, European Commission 29 May 2017, available at <https://ec.europa.eu/newsroom/just/items/59332/en> (accessed 24 September 2021); Burkhard Hess and Stephanie Law (eds), *Implementing EU Consumer Rights by National Procedural Law. Luxembourg Report of European Procedural Law: Volume II* (Beck 2019).

18 M.J. ter Voert and M.S. Hoekstra, *Geschilbeslechtingdelta* 2019, WODC I&O Research, Cahiers 2020-18.

19 Rb. Amsterdam 16 October 2017, ECLI:NL:RBAMS:2017:7577, r.o. 6-12 (Direct Pay Services B.V./gedaagde). See further J.M.L. van Duin, 'Wie betaalt de rekening? De kostenveroordeling in de context van het EU-consumentenrecht', Tijdschrift voor Consumentenrecht en handelspraktijken 2018/4, p. 180.

E.U. consumer law has been an important driver to question the courts' 'rubber-stamping' role in uncontested cases, especially in light of the CJEU's case law on the *ex officio* application of the Unfair Contract Terms Directive.[20] In 2013, the Dutch Supreme Court confirmed that the duty of *ex officio* control of unfair terms equally applies in default proceedings.[21] If the necessary factual and legal information is available for the court to suspect that a clause falls within the scope of the UCTD and is unfair, the court must investigate this, even if it has not been brought up by the parties themselves. When it comes to granting leave for the enforcement of arbitral awards against consumers, the Supreme Court held in 2019 that the court must exercise *ex officio* control as well, and also in respect of the arbitration clause on which they are based.[22] The duty of *ex officio* control is not limited to unfair terms: in respect of collection charges, for instance, the court must check if the creditor has sufficiently substantiated the charges and whether the mandatory rules on collection charges have been observed.[23] The Supreme Court's judgments fit in a long line of CJEU case law, which has more recently focused on the prerequisite of the court acquiring the necessary information.[24] Dutch courts have the (discretionary) power to request information of their own accord,[25] which gives rise to the question how and to what extent they should exercise this power in default proceedings.[26]

In 2010, a report was published by a special working group of (sub)district courts containing guidelines; second and third versions of the report followed in 2014 and 2018.[27] The report intended to formulate a common judicial position on applying the CJEU's case law in practice; it contains recommendations to all lower courts dealing with consumer cases. One of those recommendations is to

20 See more elaborately e.g. C. Leone and J.M.L. van Duin, 'The real (New) Deal: levelling the odds for consumer-litigants', *European Review of Private Law* 2019/6, 1227; Werbrouck and Dauw 'The national courts' obligation to gather and establish the necessary information for the application of consumer law - the endgame?', *ELRev* 2021, 46(3), 325.

21 *Hoge Raad*, judgment of 13 September 2013, ECLI:NL:HR:2013:691 (*Heesakkers/Voets*), paras 3.6.3, 3.9.2 and 3.6.1 respectively. Both in appeal and in default proceedings, Dutch civil courts must examine compliance with rules of public policy: M. van Rossum and E. van der Minne, 'De (on)mogelijkheid van ambtshalve toetsing van het Unierecht in hoger beroep' [2017] Tijdschrift voor de Procespraktijk 98, 101.

22 *Hoge Raad* 8 November 2019, ECLI:NL:HR:2019:1731 (*Intermaris*), para 2.8.7.

23 *Hoge Raad* 25 November 2016, ECLI:NL:HR:2016:2704. In the context of art 139 Rv all mandatory rules – so not only public policy – must be applied *ex officio*.

24 See e.g. CJEU 9 November 2010 (Grand Chamber), Case C-137/08 *VB Pénzügyi Lízing v Ferenc Schneider* ECLI:EU:C:2010:65; CJEU 17 May 2018, C-147/16 *Karel de Grote – Hogeschool Katholieke Hogeschool Antwerpen v. Kuijpers* ECLI:EU:C:2018:320 and the case law cited in note 17 above; further discussed in Leone and J.M.L. van Duin (note 20).

25 Art 22 Rv.

26 C. Seinen and A. Ancery, 'Vorderingen in b2c-verstekken: toetsen of toewijzen?', Tijdschrift voor Civiele Rechtspleging 2015/3, 77.

27 Full title: *Ambtshalve toetsing III. Herzien rapport van de LOVCK&T redactieraad*, May 2018. The report will hereinafter be referred to as '2018 LOVCK Report.' It can be found (in Dutch) at <https://www.rechtspraak.nl/SiteCollectionDocuments/rapport-at-III-31-juli-2018.pdf>.

use a presumption that the defendant is a consumer, if they are a natural person and there are no indications of a business transaction, unless the claimant proves otherwise. When the writ of summons does not provide sufficient information, the court must take further instruction measures. Especially where 'repeat players' are involved – i.e., creditors who repeatedly bring similar claims in a standardized manner – lower courts already tended to impose stricter requirements. The 2018 report sanctions this: the claim should be dismissed if the claimant does not comply with the court's instructions.[28] And in case of 'repeat players' who continuously fail to substantiate the claim sufficiently, it can be dismissed immediately (without taking measures of instruction or giving the claimant an(other) opportunity to be heard).[29] A legal basis for this can be found in a violation of the duty to provide complete and truthful information to the court.[30] The 2018 report also contains a 'model instruction form,' requiring claimants to submit *inter alia* the underlying contract and terms and conditions, invoices, correspondence with the defendant, and a specification of the main claim, interest, and penalties.[31] Furthermore, the form asks specific questions, like how and where the contract has been concluded (e.g. at a distance), what products or services it pertains to, whether information duties have been complied with, and whether the claim is based on standard terms and conditions. The idea behind the form was that it contributes to streamlining the handling of debt collection cases and offering effective judicial protection to consumers.[32] From 2019 onwards, (sub)district courts have indeed dismissed claims because the creditor did not comply with the instructions.[33] As per mid-2020, bailiffs and collection agents are supposed to submit the required information by themselves, i.e. without the need for judicial intervention.

The form is not uncontroversial: it has tightened the requirements for claims resulting in default proceedings and endorses dismissal of the claim if those requirements are not met.[34] Common objections are that claimants do not know in

28 On the basis of art 21 and 111 Rv.

29 2018 LOVCK Report, pp. 49–51. In November 2021, the Supreme Court held that if there are uniform (non-binding) guidelines available for the adjudication of consumer cases, the claimant can be required to present its views in advance – in this case on (partial) annulment of the contract to sanction a violation of information duties – and does not need to be heard separately in default proceedings: Hoge Raad 12 November 2021, ECLI:NL:HR:2021:1677, para 3.1.18.

30 Art 21 and 111 Rv; see further C. Seinen, 'De waarheidsplicht en de geraden gevolgtrekking anno 2020: een zoektocht naar proportionaliteit' [2020] *Tijdschrift voor Civiele Rechtspleging* 33, pp. 39–40.

31 The eight-page long form (in Dutch, and by now in version 2.0) can be found here: <https://www.rechtspraak.nl/SiteCollectionDocuments/landelijk-informatieformulier-ambtshalve-toetsen-consumentenzaken21.pdf>.

32 Seinen and Ancery (note 35). C. Seinen and A. Ancery, 'Vorderingen in b2c-verstekken: toetsen of toewijzen?', *Tijdschrift voor Civiele Rechtspleging* 2015/3, pp. 77–88.

33 See <https://www.rechtspraak.nl/Organisatie-en-contact/Organisatie/Raad-voor-de-rechtspraak/Nieuws/Paginas/Rechter-eist-meer-informatie-in-consumentenzaken.aspx>. See e.g.Rb. Amsterdam 21 October 2019, ECLI:NL:RBAMS:2019:7985; Rb. Noord-Holland 22 April 2020, ECLI:NL:RBNHO:2020:3155.

34 See also Opinion of *Procureur Generaal bij de Hoge Raad* 16 August 2021, ECLI:NL:PHR:2021:757, paras 1.4–1.5.

advance if the defendant will appear in court (hence there should be no distinction between default and contentious proceedings), that a more elaborate assessment increases the burden on courts (to the detriment of efficiency), and that dismissing the claim (in its entirety) is disproportionate.

In addition, the Royal Federation of Bailiffs has called for more clarity and unity in the way courts assess claims in the interest of trade and legal certainty.[35] They also have doubts about the definition of 'consumers' and 'repeat players,' which some courts understand as including bailiffs. Due to the wide variety of criteria, the Federation asserts, it is impossible to develop an automated process for claims potentially involving consumers, making debt collection more costly. They observe a mismatch between the court taking into account all individual circumstances of the case and creditors focusing on large-scale processes. Moreover, when the claim is too small, a decision in a concrete case cannot be appealed, even if it impacts the overall process. In general, the introduction of the form has increased administrative costs for creditors, which makes it less worthwhile – a 'destruction of capital' – to pursue smaller claims. According to the Federation of Bailiffs, the effect of the form is thus that less claims are being brought.

Some of these criticisms would concern all judicial guidelines, such as the question whether they undermine or actually contribute to efficiency. In a recent judgment, the Supreme Court tended towards the latter: not only do guidelines enable the claimant to appreciate which information must be provided at an early stage, they also make the applicable rules more manageable and may enhance legal certainty and equality.[36]

The form essentially establishes clearer boundaries between informal and formal debt collection practices. Creditors must think twice before they seek to enforce their claim in court. The upside is that they are actively discouraged from bringing 'bad' claims, such as claims that are based on unfair terms or entail excessive charges. On the other hand, the downside may be a rise of informal enforcement, pushing creditors to look for alternative solutions.

This turns debt collection into a pressing access to justice issue, not only for creditors[37] but also and especially for consumer-debtors. Recent years have seen a decline in small claims brought before (sub)district courts.[38] Possible explanations concern an increase in court fees, efforts of municipalities and other organisations

35 <https://www.kbvg.nl/nieuws-en-opinie/kbvg-nieuws/kbvg-presenteert-rapport-over-de-ambtshalve-toetsing-door-de-rechtspraak>.

36 *Hoge Raad* 12 November 2021, ECLI:NL:HR:2021:1677, para 3.1.19.

37 Calls have even been made to introduce a national order for payment procedure for uncontested claims: M. van Zanten, 'Voorstel voor een nieuwe procedure bij onbetwiste vorderingen', *Beslag, executie & rechtsvordering in de praktijk* 2021/6, 15–19. For consumer cases, such a procedure would be hard to reconcile with the CJEU's case law on the requirement of effective judicial protection. Apart from the bailiff not being an independent judicial organ, it is highly questionable whether consumer-debtors who are confronted by a bailiff (operating on behalf of a creditor) are able to fully apprehend the claim, let alone the consequences of not contesting it. See further J.M.L. van Duin, *Effective Judicial Protection in Consumer Litigation* (Intersentia 2022), at p. 85.

38 *Rapport incassozaken* 2018, p. 7.

to prevent (further) indebtedness, as well as the rise of out-of-court debt collection mechanisms, e.g. via digital arbitration.[39] As the controversy that has arisen over one such mechanism (e-Court) shows,[40] out-of-court disputes may impair the effective (judicial) protection of consumer-debtors on a whole new level, and puts the efficacy of court intervention into perspective. Meanwhile, however, debt collection was also on the agenda of public enforcement.

6.2.2 Tackling abusive providers via unfair commercial practices

In 2015, the Authority for Consumers and Markets (ACM) announced its concerns regarding debt collection practices. A joint investigation by the ACM and the Financial Markets Authority revealed a practice of collecting non-existing or unfounded claims, charging excessive fees and exerting undue pressure on consumers.[41] In response to these findings, the ACM adopted a particularly comprehensive approach: next to the classical instruments of warnings, commitments, and fines (on which more in the next paragraph), it addressed debt collection service providers as well as creditors who used collection services, who were sensitized to choose and act responsibly.[42] Additionally, it set up an educational campaign – including a 'toolkit' – addressed not only at consumer-debtors but also, perhaps most importantly, at social workers (*schuldhulpverleners*) possibly assisting them.[43] The toolkit is meant to help debtors and their caseworkers to (1) verify the legitimate nature of the claim; (2) calculate whether the fees and interest charged are in line with Dutch law; (3) check the language of the demands for aggressiveness; (4) prepare an appropriate response letter, by making use of specifically dedicated sample letters. It appears that empowering individual consumers via information and education was considered insufficient in the case of debt collection due to the 'fear factor' that can prevent consumers from taking care of their interests in debt contexts.[44]

39 See e.g. Emma van Gelder, 'Online Dispute Resolution: een veelbelovend initiatief voor toegang tot het recht?' [2018] *Maandblad voor Vermogensrecht* 262.

40 See <https://www.groene.nl/artikel/vonnis-te-koop>; Dorien Thiescheffer, *E-court naast overheidsrechtspraak. Online rechtspraak als alternatieve geschilbeslechting en de garanties voor consumenten* (Celsus juridische uitgeverij 2018).

41 See <https://www.acm.nl/nl/publicaties/publicatie/14892/Oneerlijke-praktijken-bij-incassobureaus>.

42 See in particular the intervention viz telecom service providers, who were found to carry out several illegitimate behaviors in collecting their credits – from demanding excessive fines to setting too short terms and providing misleading information; see <https://www.acm.nl/nl/publicaties/telecombedrijven-passen-incassopraktijk-aan-na-onderzoek-van-acm>. Hierover ook B.B. Duivenvoorde, 'Oneerlijke handelspraktijken 2018-2019', *Tijdschrift voor Consumentenrecht en handelspraktijken* 2020/1, p. 26.

43 <https://www.acm.nl/nl/publicaties/nieuwe-toolkit-van-acm-maakt-actie-komen-tegen-oneerlijke-incassopraktijken-makkelijker>.

44 P.T. Dijkstra and A.A.M. Tuinstra-Karel, 'Toepassing van gedragsinzichten in het consumentenrecht door de Autoriteit Consument en Markt', Tijdschrift voor Consumentenrecht en handelspraktijken 2017/6, 279.

Taking an intertemporal look at the published interventions towards providers, one can see a bifurcation between two groups of infringers: on the one hand, collectors of genuine credit which were using excessively stark manners or charging excessive fees; on the other hand, companies acting as debt collectors which were effectively part of aggressive telemarketing networks or connected to shady websites pushing doubtful claims (rogue traders).[45] This bifurcation may be connected to empirical research conducted on behalf of the Authority during the intervention period to assess 'compliance-readiness' in the industry, which was published in 2017.[46] The research, in fact, had concluded that the vast majority of operators in the debt collection business were open to changing their behavior when confronted with their misdeeds. However, a smaller subset of the industry was made up of rogue traders which should simply be taken out of the market.

Examples of the breaches that were contested against the genuine providers are easy to summarise: the 'sample letter' published on the Authority's website to show consumers what *not* to give in to includes

1) failure to put consumers on notice before claiming collection charges,
2) inflated costs,
3) illegitimately charging VAT,
4) excessive interest rates, and
5) aggressive or misleading language (e.g. suggesting that the debt collector may directly deliver a summons notice).[47]

These genuine providers were ostensibly issued a demand that they adapt their collection practices.[48] In one case, a particularly large actor which had been the object of many complaints has been put under reinforced supervision until the ACM was satisfied that its practices had been sufficiently reformed.[49] While the ACM makes a point of avoiding legalistic language in its communications with both service providers and consumers, it is clear that they treated attempts at excessive collection as an unfair commercial practice under the general rules in the Dutch civil code; hardly any fines were issued.

45 In both scenarios, either via phone or via a website, consumers would be lured into vaguely agreeing to some kind of service provision, on the basis of incomplete and confusing information, making it likely that no binding contract had effectively been concluded. The debt collectors would then, possibly months or years later, get in touch with the consumer to claim payment.

46 ACM, *Incasso, Faciliterend of aggressief* ('Debt collection: helpful or aggressive?'), 2017, <https://www.acm.nl/nl/publicaties/onderzoek-naar-de-nalevingsbereidheid-de-incassosector>.

47 See <https://www.acm.nl/nl/onderwerpen-verkoop-aan-consumenten-toolkit-incasso-voor-schuldhulpverleners/foute-incassobrief>.

48 See e.g. <https://www.acm.nl/nl/publicaties/hendriks-incasso-past-agressieve-werkwijze-aan>.

49 <https://www.acm.nl/nl/publicaties/incassobureau-intrum-nederland-niet-langer-onder-verscherpt-toezicht>.

After the years 2015–2018, the Authority seems to have concentrated on rogue traders, issuing warnings to consumers[50] rather than to the traders themselves as well as imposing fines. Such fines were reserved for particularly egregious cases: in some cases, the claim collection activities appear to be pure scam, unconnected to any presence of service provision – as for Unitedcall[51] and Credit Invest;[52] in the case of De Reisplanner BV, a company that offered consumers a sort of timeshare contract and started billing before any written contract had been signed and before consumers had received any comprehensive information, the debt collection seemed connected to pretty extreme forms of telemarketing.[53]

Imposing a fine, which is of course subject to judicial review, requires extensive investigations and evidence collection; consumer warnings are, then, sometimes an interim measure, sometimes the only measure the ACM will manage to adopt.[54] Companies of this kind seem to fall squarely in the definition of traders that, according to the 2017 study, could not fruitfully be addressed for compliance but should rather be taken out of operation. While fines under unfair commercial practices rules can be one way to try and achieve such a result, regulating the debt collection market is perhaps the most obvious approach.

The second part of this chapter is thus devoted to recent developments seeking to establish comprehensive rules on consumer debt collection in the Netherlands, which are finally assessed and analyzed against the recently approved Credit Servicers Directive in the chapter's conclusions.

6.3 Second part: a more targeted regulatory framework? Towards specific rules for debt collection agencies

When the previous Dutch government took office in 2017, combating abuse in the debt collection industry was one of its declared policy goals.[55] A proposal to regulate debt collectors (WKI: *Wet kwaliteit incassodienstverlening*) was introduced on 16 February 2021 and is currently pending, its discussion in Parliament going

50 <https://www.acm.nl/nl/publicaties/acm-waarschuwt-voor-incasso-cc-jacobs-bemiddeling-en-herms-incasso, https://www.acm.nl/nl/publicaties/acm-waarschuwt-voor-incassobureaus-lootsma-en-partners-smits-en-co-en-inter-payment-service>.

51 <https://www.acm.nl/nl/publicaties/acm-beboet-unitedcall-voor-agressieve-incassopraktijken>.

52 <https://www.acm.nl/nl/publicaties/uitspraak-boetezaak-incassobureau-credit-invest>.

53 See <https://www.acm.nl/nl/publicaties/acm-beboet-dereisplanner-voor-incasso-onterechte-rekeningen-huur-vakantievillas>.

54 While the Authority sometimes makes a commitment to consumer indemnification, part of its negotiations with observed companies or otherwise expressly requires reimbursements to take place, there is no sign that something like this has happened (on large scale) in this investigation.The only trace we could find concerns the reimbursement of telephone expenses incurred for calling a non-existing debt collector: <https://www.acm.nl/nl/publicaties/publicatie/12448/Consumenten-krijgen-geld-terug-voor-bellen-naar-0900-nummer-Corpus-Justitia>.

55 In 2016, two Members of Parliament had already launched a draft legislative proposal (<https://www.christenunie.nl/incassowet>), in response to – *inter alia* – ACM reports on abusive debt collection practices.

forward as this chapter is finalized.[56] With the current government being to a large extent a continuation of the previous one, the WKI proposal has good chances of being approved, despite a degree of controversy and, as we will see, the possibility that more rules on similar issues will be required by the E.U. Credit Servicers Directive. The present section discusses some salient aspects of the proposal: the scope and contours of its registration requirement and procedure, quality requirements, enforcement, and overall regulatory philosophy.

6.3.1 Introducing a registration requirement

The WKI proposal introduces for the first time a registration requirement for collection in respect of individual debtors, next to some quality requirements and liminal rules. The registration requirement applies to all companies targeting individual Dutch residents/debtors.[57] This specific aspect seems designed to catch foreign debt collectors known to be active on the Dutch market. Dutch companies operating abroad, in contrast, are not covered by the regulations.

The government's records show that research has been conducted to secure compatibility of this aspect of the WKI proposal with EU law, in particular with the 2006 Services Directive.[58] According to the government, introducing a registration requirement for service providers established in other MS is justified in light of public policy, particularly with a view to the vulnerability of the groups to which the service is directed. These concerns should anyhow be largely solved by the adoption of the new Credit Servicers Directive.

The registration requirement and accompanying rules are, furthermore, only applicable to *private* debt collectors, which has prompted some questions in light of public entities' rather well-known misgivings in debt collection over the past decade.[59] Further excluded are the debt collection activities carried out in-house by providers of consumer services. While the move has drawn some criticism from the ACM,[60] the Authority's own enforcement activities suggest that in-house collection by regular (i.e. non-rogue) traders has not been a point of major contention – which could make sense to the extent that, unlike external claim collectors, providers of goods and services have an interest in maintaining a harmonious commercial relationship with the consumer.

56 Full reference can be found at the end of this chapter. The law has been adopted on 22 May 2022, see note 1.

57 Thus to the exclusion of collection viz companies; individual professionals, in contrast, fall under the scope of the envisaged regime.

58 Directive 2006/123/EC on services in the internal market. See Memore van Toelichting 3.7.1.

59 <https://www.socialevraagstukken.nl/driegesprek-rijksincassobeheer-wordt-menselijker-overheid/>.

60 The ACM's advice is included as an annex to the Memorie van Toelichting; see full reference at the end of this chapter.

Applications to the registry of debt collectors are not automatically accepted.[61] They must show how the company intends to comply with the quality requirements set out in the proposed law (see infra), provide information concerning their personnel composition and address any potential reasons that may lead to rejecting the request (e.g. in case the legal record of key employees contains previous charges or an insolvency).[62] The proposal criminalizes the unlicensed operation of collection services[63] and clearly states that debtors need not pay when approached by an unlicensed collector.[64] It also introduces fines and other administrative sanctions (suspension or, possibly, removal from the registry)[65] in case of severe breaches by registered providers. The combination of a register and a prohibition of acting without registration, including criminal sanctions, seems designed to address the problem highlighted above, namely the existence of rogue traders and trade practices, whereby aggressive claim collection is only one part of an overall abusive scheme.

6.3.2 Quality requirements and dispute resolution

Article 13 in the WKI proposal articulates a number of quality requirements directly connected to the performance of the collection services. These requirements concern personnel, transparency, ethical behavior, dispute resolution, and procedure.

Transparency, dispute resolution, and professional ethics requirements seem to be the most actionable points from a consumer's point of view and will be briefly elaborated upon here. As concerns transparency, the proposal seems to try to incorporate the lesson from the 2015 enforcement exercise: providers must take care that the build-up of the enforced monetary claim is clear to the consumer. Such clarity is of cardinal importance for consumers to challenge the claim or resist collection, for instance, because the amounts claimed are incorrect or have partially been repaid. The proposal further requires that providers secure a 'correct handling' in respect of both debtors and creditors. In this respect, the proposal can be seen to expand upon the requirements descending from consumer protection legislation – unfair commercial practices rules mainly target behavior towards *consumers* (here: debtors), leaving out the professional *creditors*. Besides this, the primary purpose of incorporating the requirement in the WKI proposal would be to make breaches actionable within the sanctioning system that the proposal also suggests putting in place. Further quality requirements would be articulated in a regulation to be adopted after approval of the proposed legislation.[66]

61 See art 7 detailing reasons for refusal.
62 See art 12 WKI proposal.
63 Art 25.
64 Art 18.
65 See art 9 and 10 (suspension or removal), 15–16 (fines and orders subject to penalty).
66 Art: 13.

As to dispute resolution, providers must establish a complaint procedure and take part in a dispute resolution scheme: this requirement makes sense from the Dutch perspective since in the Netherlands ADR is generally provided by sector-specific private dispute resolution bodies.[67] Currently, only collectors associated with the National Association of Debt Collectors provide for a generally applicable dispute resolution procedure attached to an easily identifiable dispute resolution body.[68] The establishment of a generally competent dispute resolution body may provide an indirect behavioral incentive for providers, even though it is not entirely clear to what extent consumers may directly benefit from it. This becomes quite apparent if one looks at the current regulations for the existing ADR body *Klachten Instituut Gecertificeerde Incasso Diensten (KIGID)* (Complaint Institute for Certified Debt Collection Services), which clarify that they are only competent for complaints concerning the behavior of credit collectors (thus excluding any check of the underlying claim and putting the burden on consumers to challenge debt collection practices) – raising the question of what kind of claims a consumer could submit and, crucially, what remedy they could expect. This question is not really addressed by the WKI proposal, which does not provide consumers with a specific remedy in case an authorised collector breaches the proposed quality requirements.

This means that in practice consumers are not expected to play a significant role in the enforcement of the proposed rules. The ADR body can also be seized by competitors, who may more easily benefit from this opportunity; the procedure is currently somewhat accessible, with a filing fee of 50 euro – possibly a non-negligible amount for a troubled debtor, but very affordable for a competing company. It is worth mentioning here that the most straightforward remedy is placed outside the remit of ADR, as it is provided exclusively against unregistered debt collectors. The proposal, in fact, makes clear that debtors do not have to pay if the collector is not authorized.[69] These providers will, quite self-evidently, almost necessarily not be part of the dispute resolution scheme.[70] As this remedy is left essentially to self-enforcement (the consumer refusing to pay) and relies on the consumer checking the status of the collector via the official register, it is possible to doubt whether, at least initially, information asymmetries and pressure will not prevent consumers from making use of this possibility.

67 E.N. Verhage, 'The implementation of the Consumer ADR Directive in the Netherlands'. In: Cortes P. (Ed.) *The New Regulatory Framework for Consumer Dispute Resolution.* Oxford: Oxford University Press 2016, 229.

68 See <https://www.nvio.nl/geschillenregeling>.

69 The lack of further civil law consequences has been critically highlighted by the ACM in its response to the government's request for input in early 2020. The government's accompanying text explains that connecting civil law consequences to the unauthorized performance of debt collection was considered a sufficient means to discourage abuse.

70 Furthermore, this straightforward solution addresses the 'inversion of the dispute' issue that arises when the debtor is expected to bring a case instead of the creditor.

6.3.3 Supervision and enforcement

One of the points in the WKI proposal which has drawn the most (obvious) criticism is fragmentation in the supervision and enforcement competences. Since the proposal distinguishes between three categories of service providers – bailiffs, claim lawyers, and debt collectors pur sang – it is perhaps no surprise that enforcement is also split. The Bar Association is competent for supervision in respect of registered lawyers; the Royal Federation of Bailiffs is in charge of bailiffs; finally, an office at the Ministry of Justice has direct supervision over the newly registered debt collection providers.[71]

Given that the main sanctions associated with violations of the proposal's substantive rules are suspensions or disbandment and given that the law creates different registration channels for lawyers and bailiffs, it is consistent to establish that such providers would also be supervised by their respective disciplining bodies. On the other hand, the risk of uneven enforcement seems more than material with three different bodies in charge, two of which have previously established customs that may or may not transfer well to these new competences. This risk seems a direct consequence of the choice not to establish one single register for all service providers in the debt collection industry.

6.3.4 Reluctance to tackle debt collection as a business model

As mentioned above, a governmental decree in place since 2012 regulated the costs that can be charged to debtors. These are capped at a certain percentage of the concerned credit, but collectors can still charge the *minimum* fee set at 40 euro per advanced claim for very small claims. This is seen as particularly problematic for small amounts, for instance, a subscription to a web or smartphone service, which could be only a few euros per month. The WKI proposal seeks to address this arguably disproportionate profit margin by establishing, in essence, that the minimum fee can only be charged once in six months, provided that the sum of the outstanding payments for which collection is started stays below the threshold of the higher collection charges; a lower charge of 20 euro can then be levied for following unpaid claims.[72]

This specific provision has been subject to criticism from various corners.[73] There seems to be consensus among stakeholders that the provision will be difficult to implement for providers and difficult to enforce for the competent

71 A specific provision addresses the relationship between the different supervision and enforcement bodies, see art 19 WKI proposal.

72 Art 21 of the WKI proposal, adding an eighth paragraph to art 6:96 BW.

73 See *Kamerstukken* 35733-5, 17 May 2021 (parliamentary debate records, henceforth: *Verslag*), reporting sustained criticism from the Liberals on the complexity of the rule, as well as from the Christian Democrats and the more socially oriented Christian Union on substance; all three parties are part of the governing coalition (*Verslag* section 4). Previous criticism had been expressed by various stakeholders, including the ACM, in the 2020 consultation round.

authorities, as it requires both process-tracking and frequent (re)calculations. The government explains that the WKI proposal may bring collection charges down from 240 to 140 euro over a six-month period – but fails to address the underlying possibility that this would be for a principal of close to zero significance.[74]

The most charitable interpretation of this proposal is that its complexity could provide collectors a nudge to wait a few months before initiating a collection action – which could be good to the extent that it prevents them from repeatedly charging the minimum fee, but also problematic to the extent that delayed action may let consumers inadvertently pile up higher debt. Cutting the minimum fee to a lower amount or further diversification of the allowed principal/collection fees rule would likely have been a simpler solution. However, it is quite clear from the parliamentary history that the proposal expressly does not want to undercut profit-making in consumer debt collection but just to curb abuses.[75] This approach evidently stands in the way of more far-reaching intervention on collection charges.

6.4 Conclusions

In conclusion, we would like to highlight several salient points and possible lessons learned that the Dutch experience could offer and reflect on the relationship between the WKI proposal and the 2021 Credit Servicers Directive.

First, a consumer-centred approach to abusive debt collection may require looking into the ease with which abusive claim collection can make use of judicial channels. The sanguine reaction of claim collection interest groups to the introduction of a relatively straightforward questionnaire asking them to detail the basis of their claim functions as a clear indication that the previously lax enforcement standards were essential in enabling the business to flourish – with significant negative impacts on consumer debtors. Notwithstanding all controversies, the form set up by Dutch courts could be seen as a good practice that other national judiciaries may consider adopting to increase procedural protection of consumer rights. At the same time, judicial intervention can only do so much regarding informal debt collection practices, especially if there is spill-over into out-of-court debt collection mechanisms such as arbitration.

Far-reaching enforcement interventions based on the UCPD have proven possible and were only partially facilitated by the existence of fee caps and other

74 See *Memorie van Toelichting* section 4 ('Undesired cumulation of charges'), p 34. At p 32, the *Memorie* expressly rejects an alternative rule for excessively limiting the allowed charges, reflecting the government's concern with not interfering with the business model as such.

75 See also *Memorie van Toelichting* section 2.2., explaining the advantages of debt collection services for small service providers (such as, in the government's example, care professionals), who are relieved of administrative concerns and can better concentrate on their core tasks. Next to justifying the existence of claim collection services, this argument is indirectly used by the government, in the same document and section, to dismiss proposals to allow consumers to 'buy back' their claims from credit purchasers.

Netherlands-specific rules.[76] The ACM has intervened on the assumption that both misleading and aggressive actions could be identified when consumers were, respectively, asked to fulfill unsubstantiated or inflated claims or intimidated by the use of unnecessarily harsh language. This proactive attitude and comprehensive approach on the side of the Dutch Authority could be again of interest to other regulators. Next to its actions targeted to creditors, collectors, and consumers, commissioning research on the relevant market has probably also helped persuade the government to propose new legislation targeted at cleaning up the market.

Second, despite the developments above, and even in a country which relies heavily on self-regulation, it ultimately appeared that regulation was necessary: on the one hand, the uptake of self-regulation by legitimate traders was disappointing; on the other, perhaps more importantly, self-regulation is by its nature inadequate to target rogue traders, while in a non-regulated system consumers have no way to tell whether the trader is or is not a *bona fide* undertaking. The register should make it easier for consumers to identify scammers, whilst also leveling the playing field for honest traders.

From a consumer debt perspective, the WKI proposal has limited potential to end the effect of debt collection on overall indebtment. While the proposal has been criticized for the fact that only private debt collection agencies are covered, its contents suggest that an extension to public collectors would not make much difference: it seems unlikely that personnel requirements would be relevant to public agencies and requiring a form of self-regulation can probably be achieved without legislation.

Debt collection charges are in fact one of the main problems with debt collection as a business model – something which the proposal has been very reluctant to address. This problem, one may add, is made even worse in light of the envisioned growth of markets for non-performing loans: if the claim is bought for a fraction of the original amount, the profit margins can be huge, creating a huge incentive for companies to go after distressed debtors. In the Dutch debate, some voices have proposed allowing consumer debtors to buy back their debt at the same rate that factoring agencies would pay.[77] This suggestion has not met particular favor with the government, and it seems unlikely to be taken up[78] – in par-

76 For instance, the requirement that consumers are put on a 14-day payment notice before any collection costs are charged – this requirement is seen as a consequence of article 6:96(6) BW, under which the notice is a prerequisite for claiming any pecuniary damages – see M.K.M. Enderink, A. al Mansouri, 'Nieuwe regeling buitengerechtelijke kosten', *Tijdschrift voor de Procespraktijk* 2014/5, 134.

77 *Verslag*; see for a reflection of the debate Huls (note 3) p. 86, noticing how the government's coalition agreement had settled for a combination of introducing a register and addressing business models based on high cost and high interest. A similar question had emerged in the context of Spanish unfair terms control cases, where national courts had tried to suggest that the Unfair Terms Directive should be understood to entitle consumers to buy back their debt under similar conditions: see CJEU 7 August 2018, Joined Cases C-96/16 and C-94/17 *Escobedo Cortés v. Banco de Sabadell*, ECLI:EU:C:2018:643. The CJEU declared the Directive not applicable to questions of claims assignment.

78 Despite having again been raised by some groups in parliament, see the position of the Christian Union at section 2.2 *Verslag*, with reference to previous parliamentary initiatives.

ticular, it seems hardly compatible with stimulating markets for NPLs (on which see more later in these conclusions).

From a Dutch perspective, the recently adopted Credit Servicers Directive poses some implementation puzzles which can perhaps explain why adoption of the proposed legislation has somewhat been stalled. The scope of the Dutch act is at once broader – covering credit collection at large rather than credit agreements only – and more limited than the Directive's, which covers both consumer and business debt with no restrictions. In view of this choice, it is perhaps no surprise that the European proposal only seems of limited added value from the perspective of the present analysis.[79] We will now quickly explain why this is the case.

The reconstruction above has singled out, in the ongoing debate, three main points of criticism that were raised against the Dutch proposal and that seem most relevant *from the perspective of consumer protection*: the exclusion of certain actors from the scope; the lack of private law consequences for breaches of the envisaged rules; the limited willingness to question debt collection as a profitable business model and its role in furthering consumer indebtment. None of these concerns seems to be addressed by the Directive.

As concerns the first question – which actors are regulated – the Directive allows Member States to enact a differential treatment for lawyers and bailiffs and does not seem to cover businesses keeping claim collection in house or public entities.[80]

As to the second highlighted problem, namely the lack of private law consequences, the Commission's increased attention to remedies since the 2018 New Deal for Consumers may have raised the hope that it would not ignore the connection between this area of sectoral regulation and its own intervention to secure individual remedies for unfair commercial practices.[81] This expectation is readily disappointed when one reads the Directive, which does not at all address the individual position of debtors in its one provision devoted to administrative penalties and remedial measures.[82] In this respect, the Dutch proposal exempting debtors from paying to non-registered collectors seems already a step forward, notwithstanding the failure to establish further remedies.

As concerns the third and arguably most serious problem with the WKI proposal, namely the facilitation of debt collection as a profitable business model and its role in furthering consumer indebtedness, the Directive's declared aim

79 We have elsewhere argued that an intervention establishing basic principles of procedural protection, on the other hand, would be of great use. See van Duin and Leone [2019]. The Dutch debates on the form introduced by the Dutch judiciary for repeat players further shows how harmonization of *ex officio* duties would be of significance.

80 See the definition of credit servicers at art 3(8), for what is most directly relevant here: 'a legal person that, in the course of its business, manages and enforces the rights and obligations related to a creditor's rights under a non-performing credit agreement.'

81 See art 11a UCPD, introduced by the so-called Modernization Directive (as part of the New Deal for Consumers).

82 Art 23, which – somewhat bizarrely – also doesn't seem to consider it necessary to remind Member States to establish penalties for acting as a credit servicer without registering in line with art 4.

is to *foster the market for NPLs*, which suggests consumer protection is at best a side-concern.[83] It goes without saying that the Directive does little to discourage turning consumer debt into profitable collection business. Within the Directive, however, perhaps most interesting from the perspective of consumer-debtors are two provisions which may delay or reduce the deployment of debt collection as such, namely amendments to the Consumer Credit and Mortgage Credit Directives aimed at the establishment of new information obligations and, most importantly, forbearance requirements in case of payment arrears.[84] In the Netherlands, the forbearance provisions are unlikely to be implemented in the WKI proposal, which has been re-presented to Parliament, with amendments, in November 2021.

To conclude: despite all its shortcomings, the proposed Dutch WKI seems to offer consumers better targeted and more comprehensive protection in respect of collection practices strictly intended, but something can still be expected in the way of consumer protection once the forbearance requirements in the 2021 Credit Servicers Directive are implemented. Given the overlaps and differences between the national and European interventions and several open or contested issues surrounding both, it seems easy to predict that we will see more twists and turns in debt collection rules in the years to come.

Legislation

European Union

Directive 2006/123/EC on services in the internal market

Directive (EU) 2019/2161 of the European Parliament and of the Council of 27 November 2019 amending Council Directive 93/13/EEC and Directives 98/6/EC, 2005/29/EC and 2011/83/EU of the European Parliament and of the Council as regards the better enforcement and modernisation of Union consumer protection rules (Text with EEA relevance)

Directive (EU) 2021/2167 of the European Parliament and of the Council of 24 November 2021 on credit servicers and credit purchasers and amending Directives 2008/48/EC and 2014/17/EU

The Netherlands

Article 6:96 BW (*Burgerlijk Wetboek, Dutch Civil Code*)

Article 21 Rv (*Wetboek van Burgerlijke Rechtsvordering, Dutch Code of Civil Procedure*)

Article 22 Rv

Article 111 Rv

Article 139 Rv

83 The proposal does specify that consumer protection rules apply and that the consumer can oppose to a purchaser/servicer all the defenses they would be able to use against the original creditor; however, little specific regulation is included in the Directive, to the exception of the exclusion of consumer credit from the extra-judicial enforcement of collaterals that the proposal seeks to introduce.

84 See Directive 2021/2167, art 27(2) and 28(2).

Wet van 11 mei 2022, houdende regels met betrekking tot de private buitengerechtelijke incassodienstverlening en wijziging van Boek 6 van het Burgerlijk Wetboek in verband met de aanpassing van de cumulatieregeling voor buitengerechtelijke incassokosten (Wet kwaliteit incassodienstverlening)

Other sources

The Netherlands

Redactieraad van het Landelijk Overleg Vakinhoud Civiel en Kanton & Toezicht (**LOVCK&T**), *Ambtshalve toetsing III. Herzien rapport van de LOVCK&T redactieraad*, May 2018, https://www.rechtspraak.nl/SiteCollectionDocuments/rapport-at-III-31-juli-2018.pdf

Rechtspraak.nl, Information form for monetary claims, https://www.rechtspraak.nl/SiteCollectionDocuments/landelijk-informatieformulier-ambtshalve-toetsen-consumentenzaken21.pdf

Kamerstukken II 2020-2021, 35733, nr. 3 (*Memorie van Toelichting*)

Kamerstukken 35733-5, 17 May 2021 (*Verslag*)

Besluit van 27 maart 2012, houdende regels ter normering van de vergoeding voor kosten ter verkrijging van voldoening buiten rechte (Besluit vergoeding voor buitengerechtelijke incassokosten)

Autoriteit Consumenten en Markt, advies over het wetsvoorstel kwaliteit incassodienstverlening, bijlage bij *Kamerstukken* II 2020-2021, 35733, nr. 3 (*Memorie van Toelichting*)

Judicial and administrative decisions

European Union

CJEU 9 November 2010 (Grand Chamber), Case C-137/08 VB *Pénzügyi Lízing v Ferenc Schneider* ECLI:EU:C:2010:65

CJEU 14 June 2012, Case C-618/10 *Banco Español de Crédito v. Calderón Camino ECLI*:EU:C:2012:349

CJEU 18 February 2016, Case C-49/14 *Finanmadrid v. Albán Zambrano and Others* ECLI:EU:C:2016:98

CJEU 17 May 2018, C-147/16 Karel de Grote – Hogeschool Katholieke Hogeschool Antwerpen v. Kuijpers ECLI:EU:C:2018:320

CJEU 13 September 2018, Case C-176/17 *Profi Credit Polska v. Wawrzosek* ECLI:EU:C:2018:711

CJEU 28 November 2018, Case C-632/17 *PKO Bank Polski v. Michalski* ECLI:EU:C:2018:963

CJEU 7 August 2018, Joined Cases C-96/16 and C-94/17 *Escobedo Cortés v. Banco de Sabadell*, ECLI:EU:C:2018:643

The Netherlands

Hoge Raad 13 September 2013, ECLI:NL:HR:2013:691

Hoge Raad 25 November 2016, ECLI:NL:HR:2016:2704

Rb. Amsterdam 16 October 2017, ECLI:NL:RBAMS:2017:7577

Rb. Amsterdam 21 October 2019, ECLI:NL:RBAMS:2019:7985

Rb. Amsterdam 7 November 2019, ECLI:NL:RBAMS:2019:8244
Hoge Raad 8 November 2019, ECLI:NL:HR:2019:1731
Rb. Noord-Holland 22 April 2020, ECLI:NL:RBNHO:2020:3155
Hoge Raad 10 July 2020, ECLI:NL:HR:2020:1276
Hoge Raad 10 July 2020, ECLI:NL:HR:2020:1274
Opinion of *Procureur Generaal bij de Hoge Raad* 16 August 2021, ECLI:NL:PHR:2021:757
Hoge Raad 12 November 2021, ECLI:NL:HR:2021:1677

Books, monographs, dictionaries

Dorien Thiescheffer, *E-court naast overheidsrechtspraak. Online rechtspraak als alternatieve geschilbeslechting en de garanties voor consumenten* (Celsus juridische uitgeverij 2018)

J.M.L. van Duin, *Effective Judicial Protection in Consumer Litigation* (Intersentia 2022)

Edited books

Burkhard Hess and Stephanie Law (eds), *Implementing EU Consumer Rights by National Procedural Law. Luxembourg Report of European Procedural Law: Volume II* (Beck 2019)

E.N. Verhage, 'The implementation of the Consumer ADR Directive in the Netherlands'. In: Cortes P. (ed.), *The New Regulatory Framework for Consumer Dispute Resolution.* Oxford: Oxford University Press 2016, pp. 229–250

Law journals and law reviews

B.B. Duivenvoorde, 'Oneerlijke handelspraktijken 2018–2019', *Tijdschrift voor Consumentenrecht en handelspraktijken* 2020/1, p. 23

C. Leone and J.M.L. van Duin, 'The real (New) Deal: levelling the odds for consumer-litigants', *European Review of Private Law* 2019/6, p. 1227

C. Seinen and A. Ancery, 'Vorderingen in b2c-verstekken: toetsen of toewijzen?', *Tijdschrift voor Civiele Rechtspleging* 2015/3, pp. 77–88

C. Seinen, 'De waarheidsplicht en de geraden gevolgtrekking anno 2020: een zoektocht naar proportionaliteit', *Tijdschrift voor Civiele Rechtspleging* 2020/2, p. 33

Emma van Gelder, 'Online Dispute Resolution: een veelbelovend initiatief voor toegang tot het recht?', *Maandblad voor Vermogensrecht* 2018/7–8, p. 262

J.M.L. van Duin, 'Wie betaalt de rekening? De kostenveroordeling in de context van het EU-consumentenrecht', *Tijdschrift voor Consumentenrecht en handelspraktijken* 2018/4, p. 180

J. Werbrouck and E. Dauw, 'The national courts' obligation to gather and establish the necessary information for the application of consumer law - the endgame?', *ELRev* 2021/3, p. 325

M. van Rossum and E. van der Minne, 'De (on)mogelijkheid van ambtshalve toetsing van het Unierecht in hoger beroep', *Tijdschrift voor de Procespraktijk* 2017, p. 98

M. van Zanten, 'Voorstel voor een nieuwe procedure bij onbetwiste vorderingen', *Beslag, executie & rechtsvordering in de praktijk* 2021/6, p. 15

M.K.M. Enderink and A. al Mansouri, 'Nieuwe regeling buitengerechtelijke kosten', *Tijdschrift voor de Procespraktijk* 2014/5, pp. 134–138

N.J.H. Huls, 'Hoe barmhartig is het burgerlijk recht voor de consument?', *Tijdschrift voor Consumentenrecht en handelspraktijken* 2019/2, p. 85

P.T. Dijkstra and A.A.M. Tuinstra-Karel, 'Toepassing van gedragsinzichten in het consumentenrecht door de Autoriteit Consument en Markt', *Tijdschrift voor Consumentenrecht en handelspraktijken* 2017/6, p. 279

R.P.J.L. Tjittes, 'De geest van het incassokortgeding terug in de fles', *RM Themis* 2002/3, pp. 161–163

R.R.M. de Moor, 'Wettelijke normering van buitengerechtelijke incassokosten: alleen maar 'voordeel' voor de consument?', *Tijdschrift voor Consumentenrecht en handelspraktijken* 2012/5

Newspaper articles

BBC, 'Dutch Rutte government resigns over child welfare fraud scandal', 15 January 2021, https://www.bbc.com/news/world-europe-55674146

Investico, *Dossier De Schuldenindustrie: wie verdient er aan mensen met schulden?* ('The debt industry: who profits from people in debt?') https://www.platform-investico.nl/dossiers/de-handel-schulden/

Karlijn Kuijpers, Thomas Muntz, and Tim Staal, 'Routinematige intimidatie', 37 De Groene Amsterdammer, 2017, https://www.groene.nl/artikel/routinematige-intimidatie ('Habitual harassment')

Karlijn Kuijpers, Thomas Muntz and Tim Staal, 'Vonnis te koop' ('Judgment for sale'), 3 De Groene Amsterdammer, 2018, https://www.groene.nl/artikel/vonnis-te-koop

Reports and industry publications

European Union

Study for the Fitness Check of EU Consumer and Marketing Law – Final Report Part 1: Main Report, European Commission, 29 May 2017, available at https://ec.europa.eu/newsroom/just/items/59332/en

The Netherlands

ACM, 'Incasso, Faciliterend of aggressief' (Debt collection: helpful or aggressive), 2017, https://www.acm.nl/nl/publicaties/onderzoek-naar-de-nalevingsbereidheid-de-incassosector

ACM/Motivaction, *Kwantitatief onderzoek naar de aard en omvang van incassoproblematiek onder consumenten*, 2014, https://www.acm.nl/sites/default/files/old_publication/bijlagen/14891_consumentenonderzoek-motivaction.pdf

Autoriteit financiële markten, *Consumenten en Incassotrajecten. De verantwoordelijkheden van aanbieders van consumptief krediet bij betalingsachterstanden*, 2016 (update: 19 december 2018), https://www.afm.nl/~/profmedia/files/wet-regelgeving/beleidsuitingen/leidraden/consumenten-incassotrajecten.pdf?la=nl-nl

De Rechtspraak, 'Rapport incassozaken', 2018, https://www.rechtspraak.nl/SiteCollectionDocuments/rapport-incassozaken-Rechtspraak.pdf

M.J. ter Voert and M.S. Hoekstra, *Geschilbeslechtingdelta* 2019, WODC I&O Research, Cahiers 2020-18

[Other] Internet-based sources

https://www.christenunie.nl/incassowet
https://www.nvio.nl/geschillenregeling
'Actieplan brede Schuldenaanpak,' https://www.rijksoverheid.nl/onderwerpen/schulden/schulden-aanpakken
https://www.socialevraagstukken.nl/driegesprek-rijksincassobeheer-wordt-menselijker-overheid/
https://www.rechtspraak.nl/Organisatie-en-contact/Organisatie/Raad-voor-de-rechtspraak/Nieuws/Paginas/Rechter-eist-meer-informatie-in-consumentenzaken.aspx
https://www.kbvg.nl/nieuws-en-opinie/kbvg-nieuws/kbvg-presenteert-rapport-over-de-ambtshalve-toetsing-door-de-rechtspraak

Authority for consumers and markets

https://www.acm.nl/nl/publicaties/publicatie/14892/Oneerlijke-praktijken-bij-incassobureaus
https://www.acm.nl/nl/publicaties/telecombedrijven-passen-incassopraktijk-aan-na-onderzoek-van-acm
https://www.acm.nl/nl/publicaties/nieuwe-toolkit-van-acm-maakt-actie-komen-tegen-oneerlijke-incassopraktijken-makkelijker
https://www.acm.nl/nl/onderwerpen-verkoop-aan-consumenten-toolkit-incasso-voor-schuldhulpverleners/foute-incassobrief
https://www.acm.nl/nl/publicaties/hendriks-incasso-past-agressieve-werkwijze-aan
https://www.acm.nl/nl/publicaties/incassobureau-intrum-nederland-niet-langer-onder-verscherpt-toezicht
https://www.acm.nl/nl/publicaties/acm-waarschuwt-voor-incasso-cc-jacobs-bemiddeling-en-herms-incasso
https://www.acm.nl/nl/publicaties/acm-waarschuwt-voor-incassobureaus-lootsma-en-partners-smits-en-co-en-inter-payment-service
https://www.acm.nl/nl/publicaties/acm-beboet-unitedcall-voor-agressieve-incassopraktijken
https://www.acm.nl/nl/publicaties/uitspraak-boetezaak-incassobureau-credit-invest
https://www.acm.nl/nl/publicaties/acm-beboet-dereisplanner-voor-incasso-onterechte-rekeningen-huur-vakantievillas
https://www.acm.nl/nl/publicaties/publicatie/12448/Consumenten-krijgen-geld-terug-voor-bellen-naar-0900-nummer-Corpus-Justitia

7 Regulation of abusive informal debt collection practices in Poland

*Jakub Kępiński**

7.1 Introduction

In Poland, as in other European Union (E.U.) Member States, **abusive informal (non-judicial) debt collection** practices are common and exceed acceptable limits. These practices are also referred to as harassing or intrusive debt collection.[1] It is important to notice that debts are not always pursued by the creditor himself. This role is often taken up by debt collectors who have purchased the debt from the creditor, and their aim is to recover it quickly and cheaply. Often, because of the higher costs involved, they do not find it expedient to pursue the debts in court. Instead, they resort to various informal means of debt recovery: sending letters, making phone calls, or conducting house visits. This, however, involves actions that are frequently out of proportion as they intimidate the debtors by exerting strong psychological pressure to make them, eventually, repay the debt.

Abusive informal debt collection practices have been reported in the Polish literature, but this issue has not been sufficiently analyzed.[2] These practices have also been investigated by the Office of Competition and Consumer Protection (hereinafter referred to by the abbreviation of the Polish name: UOKiK) and several rulings by Polish ordinary courts (civil and criminal).

In this chapter, I limit my considerations to the practice of debt recovery from consumers only. Therefore, no issues relating to the enforcement of debts from businesses will be examined here. The chapter is divided into three parts. In the first, I present certain possible ways of protecting consumer interests against abusive informal debt collection practices. In the second, I analyze several decisions

* Jakub Kępiński is a professor at Adam Mickiewicz Univeristy, Poznań, Poland, email; jakub.kepinski@amu.edu.pl

1 See: Krzysztof Mularski, „Nękająca windykacja" w perspektywie ochrony dóbr osobistych dłużnika", (2015) 2 Studia Prawa Prywatnego (STPP), pp. 23–39. Catalin Gabriel Stanescu, "Regulation of Abusive Debt Collection Practices in the EU Member States: An Empirical Account", (2021) 44 Journal of Consumer Policy, p. 179–216.

2 To date, only one major study has been published – see: Krzysztof Mularski, „Nękająca windykacja" w perspektywie ochrony dóbr osobistych dłużnika", (2015) 2 Studia Prawa Prywatnego (STPP), pp. 23–39, but also Grzegorz Grupa, „Windykacja należności jako przejaw uporczywego nękania z art. 190a § 1 KK", (2013) 5 Monitor Prawa Handlowego (MPH), pp. 30–40 and Aleksander Jakubowski, „Glosa do wyroku sądu apelacyjnego z dnia 10 czerwca 2011 r., VI ACa 84/11, (2011), Lex/el.

DOI: 10.4324/9781003343158-8

of Polish ordinary courts where such practices have, and sometimes have not, been found to infringe the debtor's personal rights. The third part is the summary of the findings.

7.2 Possible ways to protect the consumer-debtor

7.2.1 Introductory remarks

Poland has no sector-specific legislation that would directly address non-judicial debt collection practices aimed at consumers. There are, however, several ways in which consumers may seek restitution for loss or injury resulting from unfair practices of debt collectors. Apart from taking legal action suing for violation of their personal rights, they may seek justice in the criminal courts relying on the provisions of the Penal Code which defines the offence of persistent harassment.[3] A special role is also played by the UOKiK, which handles proceedings to determine whether the actions employed by debt collectors constitute practices infringing the collective interests of consumers.

7.2.2 Infringement of collective consumer interests

7.2.2.1 The Office of Competition and Consumer Protection

Article 24(1) of the Act on Competition and Consumer Protection[4] prohibits infringing the collective interests of consumers. A practice that infringes collective consumer interests is defined as conduct that is contrary to the law or good practice, such conduct including unfair market practices or acts of unfair competition.[5] When the President of the Office of Competition and Consumer Protection (hereinafter referred to President of UOKiK) establishes that a particular practice infringes the collective interests of consumers, he or she will issue a decision declaring the practice as infringing consumer interests and will order it to be discontinued.[6]

In examining whether a practice constitutes a violation of the collective interests of consumers, the President of UOKiK refers to two Acts: (i) the 1993 Act on Combating Unfair Competition[7] (CUC), and (ii) the 2007 Act on Combating Unfair Commercial Practices (CUCP)[8].

The purpose of CUC is to prevent and combat unfair competition. It contains a general definition[9] and individual acts of unfair competition.[10] In turn, CUCP defines the concept of unfair commercial practices and contains a catalogue of commercial

3 Article 190a § 1 of the Penal Code.
4 Dz. U. of 2021, item 275.
5 Article 24 (1)(2) of CCP.
6 Article 25 of CCP.
7 Dz. U. of 2020, item 1913.
8 Dz. U. of 2017, item 2070.
9 Article 3 of CUC.
10 Articles 5–17g of CUC.

practices deemed unfair in all circumstances ('blacklist'). This Act implements the Unfair Commercial Practices Directive (UCPD).[11] Therefore, it is reasonable to assert that CUCP also indirectly addresses unfair debt collection practices.[12]

These two Polish Acts are complementary in their primary goal to guarantee fair competition. However, each Act puts a different emphasis on securing the interests of certain market participants, which is reflected primarily in granting active court legitimacy over some entities.[13]

7.2.2.2 Selected decisions of the President of the Office for Competition and Consumer Protection (UOKiK)

The President of UOKiK addressed abusive debt collection practices employed by debt collectors against consumers on several occasions. Proceedings against debt collectors were initiated following consumer complaints received by the Office. Five decisions issued and published in the years 2011–2018 are addressed below.

In a decision of 13 May 2011,[14] which followed proceedings undertaken by the President of UOKiK after a complaint lodged by a group of consumers against a debt collecting company trading under the name SAF S.A., a handful of actions undertaken by the debt collector were found to infringe collective consumer interests. They included (i) letters calling for payment with multiple amounts of the debt claimed, which violated the obligation to provide consumers with reliable and complete information; (ii) letters sent to debtors about a possible visit of an 'on-site' debt collector who will visit them in order to establish their assets and/or start enforcement proceedings, which was misleading information since only a bailiff may initiate enforcement proceedings in debtors' homes; (iii) telling debtors that once the final judgment had been delivered, their personal data would appear in the Register of Insolvent Debtors, which would be detrimental to their reputation and violated the obligation to provide consumers with accurate and complete information; (iv) threatening debtors that a failure to repay the debt would be understood as a default on payment, an offence reportable to the police, possibly leading to a fine or detention. This practice was intended to cause fear in debtors for their personal assets and as such amounted to an illegal threat; (v) arrangements for debt settlement concluded with consumers, if any, contained clauses of standard contractual terms and conditions which were found illegal. In consequence of all the above infringements, a monetary penalty (fine) in the

11 OJ L 149, 11.6.2005, p. 22–39.

12 See: Catalin-Gabriel Stanescu, "Is the Unfair Competition Practices Directive Fit to Effectively Tackle Abusive Debt Collection?", (2020) EuCML, 235 and also "New Commission Notice on the interpretation and application of the Unfair Commercial Practices Directive ('the UCPD Guidance')", C/2021/9320, OJ C 526, 29.12.2021, pp. 29–30.

13 Jakub Kępiński, "Interests protected under the Polish Law on Combating Unfair Competition", (2020), 2 RPEiS, pp. 51–62.

14 Decision RKT-09/2011, dated 13.05.2011, <https://www.uokik.gov.pl/aktualnosci.php?news_id=2619>.

amount of PLN 70,000 (around 15,000 euro) was imposed on SAF, which eventually corrected its abusive practices.[15]

In a decision of 5 August 2011,[16] the practice followed by EURO BANK S.A. was also found to infringe the collective interests of consumers and the bank had to pay a high financial penalty (PLN 1,262,161, around 275,000 euro). It was established that the bank used various forms of pressure on consumers who were in arrears with their payments. How the bank conducted debt collection by telephone was also found to be abusive. Its representatives called debtors and, following their internal procedures, communicated the following message:

> If, despite the above position of Euro Bank, you still refuse to repay the money then we will have no other option. The Bank is now compelled to pass your dossier to the Street Collection Agency. An intervention unit of our enforcement officers will be sent to the addresses you have provided, and they will handle the negotiations with you at your home. Don't worry, our enforcement officers are specialists in recovering outstanding instalments that our customers do not want to pay back. They will come to your home in uniform and I am sure that after a quarter of an hour of negotiations despite all the problems in your life you will decide to pay the money back to the Bank!

Such communications were deemed to be contrary to good practice[17] and to contravene collective consumer interests. UOKIK also emphasized that while it did not question the creditor's right to seek recovery of the debt, such actions must respect good practice, the dignity and privacy of the consumer. The creditor must provide reliable information about the consequences of a debtor's failure to repay the debt.[18] In assessing the Bank's practice, the President of UOKiK referred to the 'Principles of Good Banking Practice'[19] and the 'Canon of Good Financial Market Practices,'[20] which, among other things, impose an obligation to respect the dignity of clients and provide them with accurate information.

In December 2017, UOKiK issued a decision in a case involving unfair practices employed by FOR-NET S.A.[21] which, in letters addressed to debtors

15 See: <https://www.uokik.gov.pl/komentarze_wyjasnienia_i_stanowiska.php?news_id=2619>.

16 Decision DDK-4/2011, dated: 5.08.2011, <https://www.uokik.gov.pl/aktualnosci.php?news_id=2972>.

17 Article 3 of CUC.

18 UOKIK, „Euro Bank złamał prawo – windykacja", Announcement of UOKIK, dated: 5.11.2011 r., <https://www.uokik.gov.pl/aktualnosci.php?news_id=2972>.

19 Związek Banków Polskich (ang. Association of Polish Banks), „Zasady dobrej praktyki rynkowej" – <https://www.zbp.pl/photo/prawo/ZDBP.pdf>.

20 Komisja Nadzoru Finansowego (ang. Financial Supervision Authority), „Kanon dobrych praktyk rynku finansowego" – <https://www.knf.gov.pl/knf/pl/komponenty/img/Kanon%20DPRF_51881.pdf>.

21 Decision RGD-8/2017, dated: 29.12.2017, <https://decyzje.uokik.gov.pl/bp/dec_prez.nsf/43104c28a7a1be23c1257eac006d8dd4/ccea49dfe0ed5508c1258271004c8e2b/$FILE/Decyzja%20RGD_8_2017%20BIP%20FOR_NET.pdf>.

(consumers) and their spouses, misled them by writing that: (i) a bailiff may be asked to instigate enforcement proceedings, which could be avoided if the debtor repaid the debt, and (ii) a notice of information about a potential offense by the debtor will be sent to the public prosecutor's office. Such practices were also found to be intimidating, causing consumers to fear for their personal assets and constituting a form of unjustified pressure to force a debtor to make a specific disposal of property. Consequently, they were found to infringe the collective interests of consumers and a fine in the amount of PLN 40,000 (around 8,500 euro) was imposed.

In July and November 2018, the President of UOKiK issued two decisions concerning the practices of two debt collecting entities: GetBack S.A.[22] and Vex Sp. z o.o.[23]

In the case involving GetBack S.A., its practices were challenged and found to have infringed the collective interests of consumers. It was established that, among other things, GetBack (i) failed, in correspondence addressed to debtors, to provide complete information necessary for the accurate identification of a monetary obligation (debt) claimed; (ii) added unjustified costs of court proceedings to the amount of the debt claimed; (iii) failed to inform consumers of their right to file a complaint provided it could be adequately substantiated; (iv) attempted to recover the debt by commissioning a court bailiff to send summons for payment, although court proceedings had not been instigated and an enforcement title issued against the debtor not obtained; (v) repeatedly sued the same consumer for the same alleged debt although the court had each time found the matter ungrounded and discontinued the proceedings; (vi) used unlawful pressure in debt collection practices to force consumers to pay their debts in the form of repeated telephone calls and text messages sent on the same day or on consecutive days; (vii) had 'on-site' debt collectors telephone or visit debtors' neighbors or members of their families and tell them about the debt; (viii) in communications sent to consumers, they were referred to as the Debtor's Rights Ombudsman Office or Debtor's Rights Ombudsman, falsely implying that the debtor could seek specialized help from them; (ix) failed to advise non-performing debtors about the adopted and applied principles of good practice and ethics applicable in the debt collection business. In light of the above abusive practices, GetBack was fined and had to pay a monetary penalty in the amount of PLN 5,045,045 (around 1,100,000 euro).

In the decision involving VEX Sp. z o.o., its practices were also found to infringe collective consumer interests and VEX Sp. z o.o. had to pay a penalty of PLN 20,122 (around 4,500 euro), too. It was established that the pressure exerted on consumers took the form of: (i) slogans and messages the content of which was intended to intimidate and frighten them and exert psychological pressure

22 Decision RLU-02/2018, dated: 23.11.2018, <https://www.uokik.gov.pl/aktualnosci.php?news_id =14986>.

23 Decision RGD-2/2018, dated: 12.07.2018, <https://www.uokik.gov.pl/aktualnosci.php?news_id =14986>.

to enforce the payment of the outstanding debt; (ii) contacting, without the consumer's prior consent, third parties who were asked to give the debtor's contact details; (iii) failure to provide complete data which would allow identification of the creditor and the debt, or to establish the legitimacy of the claim.

7.2.2.3 Codes of conduct

In the above decisions, the UOKiK also referred to corporate codes of conduct (also referred to as codes of good practice) which entrepreneurs voluntarily undertook to adhere to and applied, among other things, to certain market practices.[24]

Codes of good market practice have been adopted, *inter alia*, by the Association of Polish Banks[25] and by the Financial Supervision Authority[26] and the Association of Financial Enterprises (earlier the Confederation of Financial Entrepreneurs).[27]

The code of the Financial Supervision Authority and the Association of Financial sets out in detail the principles of good practice in debt management. Book III of that Code addresses the following issues: the relationship of a debt collector company with counterparties selling mass claims, rules for communicating with a debtor (correspondence, telephone conversations, and on-site debt collection), methods for handling complaints filed by debtors, procedures for dealing with complaints where the debtor asserts that the claim is time-barred or disputed, information protection, and personal data protection. The code also contains a list of prohibited and illicit practices.

An interesting example was the case of GetBack S.A.[28] GetBack was a member of the Confederation of Financial Entrepreneurs. However, the Ethics Commission of the Confederation found that its debt collection practices grossly violated the good practice principles. Abusive practices included: (i) negligent handling of complaints, (ii) conducting the recovery activities and communicating with debtors without respecting their rights; (iii) telephone calls before 6 a.m.; (iv) rude and impolite text messages sent by telephone; (v) too frequent telephone calls, intended to annoy or harass the debtor; (vi) failing to inform the debtor of his right to complain; (vii) failing to clarify with the creditor or the seller of the debt the objections raised by the debtor; (viii) using means designed to intimidate the debtor; (ix) disclosing information about the debt to unauthorized persons;

24 Article 2(5) of CUPC.

25 Związek Banków Polskich (ang. Association of Polish Banks), „Zasady dobrej praktyki rynkowej" – <https://www.zbp.pl/photo/prawo/ZDBP.pdf>.

26 Komisja Nadzoru Finansowego (ang. Financial Supervision Authority), „Kanon dobrych praktyk rynku finansowego" – <https://www.knf.gov.pl/knf/pl/komponenty/img/Kanon%20DPRF_51881.pdf>.

27 Związek Przedsiębiorców Finansowych w Polsce (ang. Confederation of Financial Entrepreneurs in Poland), „Zasady dobrych praktyk przedsiębiorstw zrzeszonych w Związku Przedsiębiorstw Finansowych w Polsce", (2020), <https://zpf.pl/pliki/etyka/ZPF_zasady_dobrych_praktyk_09.2020.pdf>.

28 Ruling of Komisja Etyki Konfederacji Przedsiębiorców Finansowych w Polsce, Case No. 13/2017, dated: 12.03.2018, <https://zpf.pl/orzeczenie-komisji-etyki-w-sprawie-132017/>.

(x) presenting false data concerning the debt. As a result, the Ethics Commission requested that the company be excluded from the Confederation's membership. This ruling was made public and the relevant authorities, including the UOKiK, were notified.

Expulsion from an industry organization or association may be onerous or not pleasant. However, in my opinion, it is not an effective way to address abusive or unfair practices used by creditors or by their debt collectors. I did not find any ruling of an ordinary court in Poland that would respond to complaints made by consumers about practices that failed to comply with the code of good market practices.

7.2.2.4 A guide to debt collection

To sum up these considerations it may be noteworthy to look at the recommendations contained in the short (one and a half pages) Guidelines for consumers[29] published by UOKIK. Their purpose is to advise debtors on what they should do if facing a debt claim and what a debt recovery or collection procedure should be like.

According to the Guidelines, first the legitimacy of the demand for payment of a debt must be checked and the debtor should make sure that the debt is not time-barred. There are also a few critical principles that debt collectors cannot breach. Firstly, they are not allowed to tell consumers that they will be charged the costs of court and enforcement proceedings although they may warn them that certain costs may be involved. Secondly, it is not allowed to send letters that intimidate consumers, create a feeling of fear or exert psychological pressure. Thirdly, debt collectors are not allowed to enter consumers' homes without their consent, to visit them at their place of work or to contact third parties. Fourthly, it is not permitted to charge exorbitant recovery costs. Charges for sending a letter or other notification must always correspond to the actual costs incurred by the debt collector. Fifthly, telephone and text message notifications should not be onerous. Sixthly, every debt collector should act within the limits of the law and good practice. Seventhly, debt recovery claims must not be pursued if a debt has arisen from a contract concluded due to unfair market practices.

7.2.3 Consumer protection under civil law

7.2.3.1 Personal rights in the provisions of the Civil Code

The Polish Civil Code (CC) provides for the protection of the personal rights of natural persons.[30] The Code offers a non-exhaustive list of personal rights,

29 UOKIK, „Poradnik na temat windykacji" (ang. "A Guide to Debt Collection") <https://www.uokik.gov.pl/aktualnosci.php?news_id=14986>.

30 Articles 23 and 24 of CC.

including health, freedom, dignity, freedom of conscience, name and nickname, a person's pictures or image, secrecy of correspondence, inviolability of the home, as well as artistic, inventive, and scientific activities. Case law has extended this list to include such interests as the memory of a deceased close relative or preservation of one's environment.

To facilitate the protection of these rights, the law provides for the presumption of illegality for violations of personal rights. This presumption obliges everyone who infringes a personal right to prove that the infringement was justified in the case. The justification of an infringement can arise from the consent of the right holder, from the application of a provision of the law (e.g. by a public authority), from exercising another person's conflicting moral right or the abuse of a particular personal right (e.g. if someone enters someone else's home, despite the protests of its owner in the event of an emergency where a phone call must be made to save somebody's life).[31]

Natural persons whose personal rights are breached may demand that the person who has infringed their rights cease the infringement and take necessary steps to remedy or mitigate the effects of the infringement. This most frequently entails the publication of appropriate apologies in the mass media to fulfill a court order.[32] Monetary compensation for moral damages caused by a breach of personal rights is also possible.[33] However, in most cases, it may only be granted when the right holder proves the fault of the infringer.

7.2.3.2 Case law of civil courts

Abusive debt collection practices have been recognized by ordinary courts of the first instance (the Regional Courts) and by the court of second instance (the Court of Appeal). The reasons these courts gave to justify their judicial decisions identify the type of practices that exceed the acceptable or permissible and the type of infringements of a debtor's personal rights.

The court rulings analyzed below concern two basic issues: (i) the infringement of the personal rights of natural persons as a result of abusive debt recovery practices employed by debt collectors, and (ii) public disclosure of debt by the creditor.[34]

According to the first one, actions taken by the creditor to recover the debt from the debtor do not constitute an infringement of the debtor's personal rights if they are purposeful and adequate. However, if the creditor uses excessive measures, intimidates, harasses, or unjustifiably creates the impression that failure to pay off the debt will generate financial consequences for the debtor beyond what

31 Zbigniew Radwański, Adam Olejniczak, „Prawo cywilne- część ogólna", (2021), 172–175.

32 Article 24(1) of CC.

33 Article 24(2) of CC.

34 Aleksandra Partyk, „Egzekwowanie należności przez wierzyciela a dobra osobiste dłużnika, Linia orzecznicza", (2019), Lex/el.

the law provides, such a practice may be unlawful and infringe the debtor's personal rights.

According to the other, it may be assumed that revealing information about the debt to the public or the unjustified disclosure of information about the debtor as an untrustworthy person constitutes a violation of the debtor's right to privacy and good name. Moreover, if a call for payment is improperly sent, whereby unauthorized persons may become aware of it, the personal good, such as the secrecy of correspondence, may also be infringed.

7.2.3.2.1 EXCESSIVE MEASURES

It may be useful to start the presentation of the various court decisions with the judgment of the Court of Appeal in Warsaw of 11 October 2018[35] in which the court explained the concept of 'harassing debt collection practices.' In its opinion, this meant

> excessive actions aimed at intimidating the debtor and exerting strong psychological pressure disturbing the his or her peace of mind, and aimed at arousing justified fear in the debtor about the safety of his or her home, on the principle that "the end justifies the means." The unlawfulness of such actions should be understood broadly, not only as a conflict with a specific legal norm, but also with the rules of social co-existence or even customs accepted in trading.

The court asserted that actions taken by a creditor in order to recover a debt was not an unlawful activity. However, when it involves the harassment or intimidation of a debtor, it should be regarded as an infringement of personal rights, such as: dignity, liberty, home inviolability, reputation, privacy, or secrecy of correspondence. In the case before the court, it was found that the actions of the debt collector's employees, consisting in repeated demands for payment sent in text messages and phone calls at night, violated the consumer's personal rights including freedom, which should be understood as a state free from fear and anxiety. It should be added that the amount claimed was only PLN 99.98 (less than 25 euro), the consumer disputed its legitimacy, and the creditor did not have an enforcement title.

In a judgment of 30 June 2016, the Court of Appeal in Warsaw[36] found that repeated phone calls, sending text messages to a person whose name was in the list of debtors because of a system error violated the personal rights of privacy. Whereas, threatening that the alleged debtor would be visited by 'on-site' inspectors amounted to the infringement of the right to the inviolability of the home.

35 Judgment of the Court of Appeal in Warszawa, dated: 11.10.2018, I ACa 387/18, Lex No. 2583324.
36 Judgment of the Court of Appeal in Warszawa, dated: 20.06.2016, VI ACa 403/15, Lex No. 2086195.

The same Court of Appeal in Warsaw, in its judgment of 25 April 2014,[37] found that it was a violation of the debtor's right to privacy to send him or her letters which specified the amount of court and enforcement costs. It was held that this was aimed at intimidating the debtor by making false implications that non-compliance with the demands specified in the letter would entail additional costs. The same also applied to letters sent in envelopes with overprints suggesting that the debtor had defaulted on the payment of the debt, not to mention harassment by telephone calls even though a final judgment had dismissed the action. To clarify, the claim was time-barred, which the debtor repeatedly argued.

In the judgment of 15 February 2013,[38] the Court of Appeal in Warsaw also found that the defendant used inappropriate measures which, in the Court's opinion, were 'letters addressed to the debtor informing him of the need to contact the creditor in order to prepare evidence, collect writing samples for examination by a graphologist or the announcement of a visit by debt collecting "on-site" officer.' Such actions performed by the creditor violated the debtor's right to privacy and the right to the inviolability of the home.

The courts did not always find that creditor's actions were unlawful and infringed the debtor's rights. Indeed, in some situations, it was held that the actions taken to enforce the debt and the measures used were appropriate and adequate. Such acceptable actions included: (i) summoning the debtor and his wife to repay the debt, visiting the debtor, or posting information about the debt in the National Debt Register and on the creditor's website, in a situation where the creditor had obtained a final order for payment;[39] (ii) calling the person in default of payment a debtor, even where the debt had become time-barred, because in the event of a time-barred payment even if the obligation becomes incomplete and (unenforceable which) cannot be enforced by state action, it continues to exist and is not extinguished;[40] (iii) informing the debtor about the status of the debt, the consequences of delays, and a demand for payment of the overdue amount in the form of letters, telephone calls, and text messages. In the court's view, such actions were permissible as to their form, content, and frequency, and they resulted from the loan agreement and did not exceed its limits.[41] Fortunately, not all creditors behave unfairly, and some of the court findings and rulings shown above also bear witness to this.

Excessive measures taken by creditors to recover debts may infringe the personal rights of debtors whose dignity, liberty, home inviolability, good name, privacy, or secrecy of correspondence are at stake. Fortunately, again, as can also be seen above, common courts usually resolve the disputes properly. The examples presented here, however, do not reflect the real scale of the phenomenon. In

37 Judgment of the Court of Appeal in Warszawa, dated: 25.04.2013, VI ACa 806/13, Lex No. 1506758.

38 Judgment of the Court of Appeal in Warszawa, dated: 15.02.2013, VI ACa 84/11, Lex No. 863322.

39 Judgment of the Court of Appeal in Katowice, dated: 16.01.2014, I ACa 941/13, Lex No. 1428071.

40 Judgment of the Court of Appeal in Warszawa, dated: 7.11.2014, VI ACa 140/14, Lex No. 1624059.

41 Judgment of the Court of Appeal in Katowice, dated: 23.06.2015, I ACa 232/15, Lex No. 1770667.

my opinion, only very few consumers (debtors) decide to take legal action against harassing debt recovery practices. Most of them will be subjected to abusive non-judicial debt collection practices and be forced to repay the debt.

7.2.3.2.2 PUBLIC DISCLOSURE OF DEBT BY CREDITOR

The other issue that the courts examined concerned information about the debtor's debt disclosed to the public. One of the first judgments in this matter was the ruling of the Court of Appeal in Białystok of 14 June 1995.[42] The dispute involved a housing association that posted a list of members who were in arrears with their rents on the notice board. The court held that such a practice by the creditor violated the debtor's right to privacy. It further argued that information about a person's degree of indebtedness belongs to the sphere of his or her privacy. No provision of the law authorizes a housing association to disclose on a notice board information about the outstanding or overdue rent owed by a defaulting tenant.[43]

In turn, the judgment of 7 November 1995 delivered by the Court of Appeal in Łódź[44] concerned a bank that was sending reminders to debtors by post. The reminders contained information about the debtor, the type of debt and the amount outstanding and were sent by registered mail, but without an envelope, so that anyone could read the content of the letter. The court held that the manner of sending the reminder violated the debtor's secrecy of correspondence which belongs to the category of personal rights.[45] According to the court, a creditor sending such a letter should use a form of mailing that will ensure the protection of its content. The court ruled that:

> the creditor's sending of a reminder to a debtor for payment of an overdue amount in a manner allowing persons other than the addressee to become acquainted with the content of the reminder constitutes a violation of the addressee's personal right, which is secrecy of correspondence, and which is subject to protection under Article 23 of CC.

Another practice considered by the courts was entering information about the debtor in various registers of debtors.

In the judgment of 28 November 2013, the Court of Appeal in Warsaw[46] held that information about an alleged debtor which a television services com-

42 Judgment of the Court of Appeal in Białystok, dated: 14.06.1995, I ACr 142/95, Lex no. 23659.

43 Also in: Judgment of the Court of Appeal in Białystok, dated: 25.01.2001, I ACa 4/01, Lex no. 48370, Judgment of the Court of Appeal in Gdańsk, dated: 24.11.2009 r., I ACa 1100/09, Lex no.1466758.

44 Judgment of the Court of Appeal in Łódź, dated: 7.11.1995, I ACr 529/95, Lex no. 23691.

45 Article 23 of CC.

46 Judgment of the Court of Appeal in Warszawa, dated: 28.11.2013, VI ACa 394/13, Lex no. 1480632, also Judgment of the Court of Appeal in Warszawa, dated: 30.06.2016 r., VI ACa 403/15, Lex no. 2086195.

pany entered in the National Debt Register violated the debtor's personal rights to a good name and credibility. The court held that the creditor's action was unlawful because there were no amounts overdue and outstanding. Moreover, the time limit of one month between the date of (sending) the call for payment with a warning of the intention to enter the information about the debt, if any, in the register was not preserved. The court also stressed that the creditor had failed to exercise due care and diligence in submitting the data to the register.

The Court of Appeal in Poznań came to a similar view in its judgment of 15 November 2007,[47] stating that entering information that a consumer and his wife were indebted to the Bank in the Consumer Credit Information Bureau, in a situation where a loan agreement had never been concluded, constituted an infringement of their personal rights: privacy, dignity, and a good name.

An infringement of a debtor's personal rights may also occur when a creditor fails to update the debtor's data in the debtor's register for several months. The Court of Appeal in Warsaw in its judgment of 12 December 2018[48] held that because of the creditor's failure to update the debt repayment information, the debtor was perceived by others as unreliable and not creditworthy. As a result, he was refused approval for a credit card. The court held that the creditor's failure to remove the entry about the previous debt violated the former debtor's personal rights such as dignity and privacy. The court explained further that the autonomy of information disclosure is an essential component of the right to privacy and implies the right to decide whether to disclose information about oneself to others and the right to exercise control over that information held by others.

Public disclosure of debt may violate the debtor's personal rights (privacy and dignity). Disclosure of such information should be done appropriately. Similarly, placing information on a debtor in various types of databases must comply with applicable law, and such information should also be updated without delay. Otherwise, the debtor's personal rights (dignity, privacy, and reputation) may be infringed.

7.2.3.3 Prescription of claims – amendments to art 117 of the Civil Code

It often happens that creditors try to recover a debt which the debtor claims to be time-barred. To address this problem art 117 of CC was amended and modified in 2018.

The amended article now states that all property claims are subject to prescription. The general prescription period is six years. However, it is three years for claims related to regular performances, i.e. payments, such as rent, or claims arising from business activity.[49] The prescribed period in the event of claims estab-

47 Judgment of the Court of Appeal in Poznań, dated: 15.11.2007, I ACa 825/07, Lex no. 370883.
48 Judgment of the Court of Appeal in Warszawa, dated: 12.12.2018, V Aca 651/17, Lex No 2613625.
49 Article 118 CC.

lished by a court decision, an arbitral award, or any other decision of a competent authority is six years.[50] The prescribed time limit may also be set differently by other provisions of CC. Therefore, it is always advisable to consult the provisions related to particular contracts to ensure that claims have not been prescribed, or time-barred before the party brings an action in court. For example, claims brought by businesses related to contracts of sale have a prescription period of two years.[51]

Provisions related to the prescription of claims are of a *stricti iuris* nature and consequently cannot be modified by agreement of the parties.

The prescription period starts to run when the claim comes into being. If the debtor is required to refrain from doing something, the prescription period starts to run upon the breach of that obligation. If a creditor cannot demand a performance until he or she has given notice to the debtor, the prescription period starts to run from when the notice can first be given.[52] The law provides for the suspension of the period of prescription[53] and the postponement of the expiry of that period.[54] However, the most important provisions apply to the interruption of the period of prescription or its renewal.[55] The new period of prescription starts to run again after such an interruption.

The interruption of the period of prescription may be a result of: (i) the acknowledgment of a claim by the debtor vis-a-vis the creditor (e.g. by confirmation of an invoice, partial payment, request for an extension of the payment term); or (ii) judicial enforcement, i.e. by bringing an action for debt recovery or satisfaction of a claim, for a declaratory judgment, or for securing measures; obviously, an action for execution or enforcement of a judgment equally interrupts the prescription period; or (iii) the commencement of mediation.

After the expiry of the period of prescription, the debtor is entitled to refuse performance. This means that the performance is still due but cannot be enforced without the debtor's consent. If an action is brought after the expiry of the period of prescription, the court will only take that expiry into consideration upon the debtor's request.[56]

The above provisions governing the prescription of claims were amended in 2018. Two important provisions were added: art 117 § 2^1 of CC and art 117^1 of CC. According to the explanatory memorandum, the purpose of these amendments was to introduce separate rules for the prescription of claims filed against consumers. It was argued that there was a need for ensuring better protection of consumers who are the weaker party to a legal relationship. Thus, in the case of claims against consumers, upon expiration of the prescribed time limit, the claim

50 Article 125 CC.
51 Article 554 CC.
52 Article 120 CC.
53 Article 121 CC.
54 Article 122 CC.
55 Article 123 CC.
56 Article 117 § 2 CC.

is transformed *ex lege* into an incomplete (natural) obligation, and thus cannot be enforced.[57] Before the 2018 amendment, the consumer had to raise a plea to the debt being time-barred. If the debtor failed to raise this plea, the creditor could claim a satisfaction against consumers.

Today, under the amended provisions, after the expiry of the prescription period, no satisfaction can be claimed against the consumer.[58] However, if performance is made voluntarily to satisfy a claim which has passed the prescription period, the debtor cannot reclaim such a performance.

The court may disregard the expiry of a prescribed time limit only when the debtor renounces the right to raise a defense based on a time-barred claim after the expiry of the prescription period for a claim. In exceptional cases, the courts may also refuse to consider such a motion if it is believed to violate the principle of equity,[59] i.e. when the debtor has fraudulently led the creditor to believe that his or her claim could be satisfied.

7.2.4 Criminal remedies – the offence of persistent harassment

Under Polish law, abusive debt recovery practices exceeding an acceptable level may also be treated as a crime. The Penal Code (PC) provides for criminal liability for a person who through persistent harassment of another person or a person close to him or her, considerably violates that person's privacy or induces threat or the feeling of anguish. The offence is punishable by imprisonment from six months to eight years.[60]

It has been pointed out in the literature on the subject that the PC's provisions may refer to several different factual states, and that overly intrusive debt recovery activities may also qualify as a crime of harassment. However, this will depend on the intensity and repetitiveness of these actions. The very undertaking of debt recovery activities is not a crime, if it falls within generally accepted limits, and the enforcement activities are devoid of hostility and aversion towards the debtor.[61] On the other hand, the offense of harassment may be regarded as committed if debt collectors contact debtors too frequently, threatening them with negative consequences if the debt is not paid.[62]

This opinion may be found in the ruling of 23 June 2015 of the Regional Court in Świdnica.[63] The defendant, in this case, was an intern of a debt collection

57 Sejm Rzeczypospolitej Polskiej, Print no 2216, dated: 22.01.2018 r., pp. 3–5. <https://www.sejm.gov.pl/sejm8.nsf/druk.xsp?nr=2216>.

58 Article 117 § 2^1 CC.

59 Article 117^1 CC.

60 Article 190a § 1 of PC.

61 Grzegorz Grupa, „Windykacja należności jako przejaw uporczywego nękania z art. 190a § 1 KK", (2013) 5 Monitor Prawa Handlowego (MPH), p. 36.

62 Magdalena Budyn-Kulik, „Kodeks karny. Komentarz do zmian wprowadzonych ustawą z dnia 25.02.2011. o zmianie ustawy – Kodeks Karny", LEX/el. 2011.

63 Judgment of the District Court in Świdnica, dated: 23.06.2015, IV Ka 394/15, Legalis.

agency. Within 14 days, he sent 253 messages to the debtor demanding repayment of the debt. The court held that such actions were objectively annoying in nature and their purpose was to intimidate the debtor. At the same time, the defendant claimed that the management fully approved of his actions. However, the court found that the intern was not acting in the interests of the company, which did not accept this type of behavior. What is more, he was subsequently fired. Eventually, the Regional Court found that the debtor's privacy was violated, and the defendant was guilty under art 190a § 1of PC.

Courts explain that the offence of harassment may only be committed if the perpetrator's action is of a persistent nature. The District Court in Dzierżoniów in its decision of 9 June 2015 reasoned that

> harassment is a conscious and intentional act of the perpetrator, which includes repeated acts of approaching the victim, e.g., following the person, contacting the person against his/her will, and in particular, making unwanted proposals, statements, declarations, and the like, etc. It must be stressed that these enforcement actions must also be characterised by persistence, they must be repeated. A single act will never be persistent. The victim of a criminal attack will always be 'another person'. This person may not necessarily be harassed directly, but also through the harassment of a person close to him or her.[64]

It should be added that criminal proceedings in this type of case are initiated relatively rarely, and, in some cases, the proceedings are dropped.[65]

7.2.5 Position of the Ministry of Justice

Even though the problem of abusive informal debt collection exists and is subject to court proceedings, the Minister of Justice, in his letter of 1 August 2017, stated that

> the legal regulations currently in place in the area of the jurisdiction of the Ministry of Justice, i.e., in civil and criminal law, provide sufficient grounds and measures to combat and defend against unlawful activities of debt collectors. Therefore, the Ministry of Justice … is not planning any legislative work in this area in the nearest future. Rather, the most important issue in the current state of affairs seems to be the lack of sufficient knowledge among the aggrieved parties of the legal measures and possibilities already provided by the existing provisions and the limited use of professional legal assistance, including free-of-charge legal assistance … It should therefore be recalled that consumers against whom debt recovery activities are conducted can also

64 Decision of the Regional Court in Dzierżoniów, dated: 9.06.2015, II Kp 149/15, Legalis.
65 Decision of the Regional Court in Dzierżoniów, dated: 9.06.2015, II Kp 149/15, Legalis.

> obtain free legal advice at district (municipal) consumer ombudsmen's offices … Free legal advice is also provided by the Polish Consumers' Association (e-mail advisory services) and by the Consumers' Federation (helpline). A consumer may also notify the President of the Office of Competition and Consumer Protection (UOKiK) of practices infringing collective consumer interests, which may then serve as the basis for the *ex officio* initiation of proceedings in this respect.[66]

Considering the above position, it should be assumed that no legislative initiatives aimed at 'sorting out' debt collection practices directed against consumers will be made in the near future. However, from the decisions of common courts analyzed above it follows that the consumer is powerless against the actions of the creditor in many cases. It is important to realize that the judgments discussed here only concerned those consumers who had sufficient legal awareness and financial means to take legal action. In my opinion, the number of consumers whose personal interests have been infringed by creditors' actions is certainly high. A cursory analysis of various types of postings of harassed debtors and ongoing discussions of debt collectors' practices that can be seen on the internet justify the assertion that the debtor-consumer needs protection. The Minister of Justice's stand in this matter seems too optimistic.

7.3 Conclusions

The CUCP enables the consumer to take legal action against a debt collector if his or her interest has been infringed or threatened because of an unfair commercial practice.[67] However, an analysis of the case law shows that there are relatively few decisions of the courts regarding actions brought by consumers under the CUCP. Thus, it can be inferred that the CUCP does not provide a sufficient basis for protecting consumers against unfair practices.

UOKiK uses the CUCP to determine whether a given market practice constitutes an unfair commercial practice within the meaning of the Act and whether it leads, in consequence, to an infringement of the collective interests of consumers (CCP).

Pursuing claims for infringement of a debtor's personal rights in civil proceedings currently seems to be the most effective method of combating unfair debt collection practices. As is apparent from the analysis of civil court rulings, the actions of debt collectors may infringe personal rights, such as the right to

66 Ministerstwo Sprawiedliwości, Letter no 13816 „w sprawie propozycji dotyczącej prawnego uregulowania działalności firm windykacyjnych, Pisma Urzędowe Ministerstw" (ang. on a Proposal for Legal Regulation of the Activities of Debt Collection Companies), dated: 1.08.2017 VIII/13816/2017, <https://www.sejm.gov.pl/sejm8.nsf/InterpelacjaTresc.xsp?key=18C007F8>.

67 Article 12 of CUCP, see also: Jakub Kępiński, "Interests protected under the Polish Law on Combating Unfair Competition", (2020), 2 RPEiS, pp. 51–62.

privacy, dignity, liberty, the inviolability of the home, reputation, privacy, or secrecy of correspondence.

An infringement of the debtor's personal rights such as dignity, freedom, and inviolability of the home occurs when the creditor acts abusively, intimidates the debtor, visits the debtor at home, sends debt collectors to the debtor's premises, harasses the debtor by letters or phone calls, or makes false implications that non-satisfaction of the debt will have financial consequences beyond what the law prescribes. An infringement of the debtor's personal interest such as the right to secrecy of correspondence occurs when the creditor sends the payment demand in a manner that allows unauthorized parties to become acquainted with its content. On the other hand, the spreading of false information about a debt publicly or failing to update information about the repayment of the debt may constitute a breach of the debtor's right to privacy, dignity, and good name.

The amendments to the civil law provisions on the prescription of claims were aimed at protecting the interests of consumers as the weaker party in legal relationships. Separate provisions that were introduced ensured that claims against consumers become time-barred by law upon the expiry of the prescription period. Hitherto, the consumer had to raise a defense of the statute of limitations. After the amendment, once the statute of limitations has expired, claims against consumers cannot be enforced.

There are no specific regulations under Polish law that address the activities of debt recovery companies. Nor are there any specific provisions regulating debt recovery, although there exist codes of good practice that should be observed in debt recovery practices. Still, however, determining whether the actions taken by debt collectors are excessive or inadequate may not be so straightforward and may cause doubt. There is a need for a legislative initiative taken with a view to defining precisely how consumer debts may be pursued and recovered.

Nevertheless, according to the Ministry of Justice, such a legislative initiative is not necessary, but this stance does not seem to be justified given the practices adopted by many creditors, which in consequence lead to numerous infringements of debtors' personal rights. What is more, the scale of these abusive practices needs to be researched and established. As for now only a small proportion of consumers are fully aware of their rights, including personal rights, which they seek to exercise in various ways (sadly not always with success).

Articles/chapters

Aleksander Jakubowski, "Glosa do wyroku s.apel z dnia 10 czerwca 2011 r., VI ACa 84/11", (2011), Lex/el.

Aleksandra Partyk, "Egzekwowanie należności przez wierzyciela a dobra osobiste dłużnika, Linia orzecznicza", (2019), Lex/el.

Catalin-Gabriel Stanescu, "Is the Unfair Competition Practices Directive Fit to Effectively Tackle Abusive Debt Collection?", (2020) 9 (6) Journal of European Consumer and Market Law 235–247.

Catalin Gabriel Stanescu, "Regulation of Abusive Debt Collection Practices in the EU Member States: An Empirical Account", (2021) 44 Journal of Consumer Policy 179–216.
Grzegorz Grupa, "Windykacja należności jako przejaw uporczywego nękania z art. 190a § 1 KK", (2013) 5 Monitor Prawa Handlowego (MPH), 30–40.
Jakub Kępiński, "Interests Protected under the Polish Law on Combating Unfair Competition", (2020) 2 RPEiS 51–62.
Janina Panowicz-Lipska, "Glosa do wyroku s.apel z dnia 7 listopada 1995 r., I ACr 529/95", (1996) 7–8 OSP 143.
Krzysztof Mularski, "Nękająca windykacja" w perspektywie ochrony dóbr osobistych dłużnika", (2015) 2 Studia Prawa Prywatnego (STPP) 23–39.
Magdalena Budyn-Kulik, "Kodeks karny. Komentarz do zmian wprowadzonych ustawą z dnia 25.02.2011 r. o zmianie ustawy – Kodeks Karny", LEX/el. 2011.
Zbigniew Radwański, Adam Olejniczak, "Prawo cywilne- część ogólna", (2021).

Decisions/judgments

- UOKIK
  - Decision RKT-09/2011, dated: 13.05.2011, https://www.uokik.gov.pl/aktualnosci.php?news_id=2619.
  - Decision DDK-4/2011, dated 5.08.2011, https://www.uokik.gov.pl/aktualnosci.php?news_id=2972.
  - Decision RGD-8/2017, dated: 29.12.2017r., https://decyzje.uokik.gov.pl/bp/dec_prez.nsf/43104c28a7a1be23c1257ea c006d8dd4/ccea49dfe0ed5508c1258271004c8e2b/$FILE/Decyzja%20RGD_8 _2017%20BIP%20FOR_NET.pdf.
  - Decision RGD-2/2018, dated: 12.07.2018 r., https://www.uokik.gov.pl/aktualnosci.php?news_id=14986.
  - Decision RLU-02/2018, dated: 23.11.2018 r., https://www.uokik.gov.pl/aktualnosci.php?news_id=14986.
- Courts
  - Judgment of the Court of Appeal in Białystok, dated: 14.06.1995, I ACr 142/95, Lex No. 23659.
  - Judgment of the Court of Appeal in Łódź, dated: 7.11.1995, I ACr 529/95, Lex No. 23691.
  - Judgment of the Court of Appeal in Białystok, dated: 25.01.2001, I ACa 4/01, Lex No. 48370.
  - Judgment of the Court of Appeal in Poznań, dated: 15.11.2007, I ACa 825/07, Lex No. 370883.
  - Judgment of the Court of Appeal in Gdańsk, dated: 24.11.2009 r., I ACa 1100/09, Lex No.1466758.
  - Judgment of the Court of Appeal in Warszawa, dated: 15.02.2013, VI ACa 84/11, Lex No. 863322
  - Judgment of the Court of Appeal in Warszawa, dated: 25.04.2013, VI ACa 806/13, Lex No. 1506758.
  - Judgment of the Court of Appeal in Warszawa, dated: 28.11.2013, VI ACa 394/13, Lex No. 1480632.

- Judgment of the Court of Appeal in Katowice, dated: 16.01.2014, I ACa 941/13, Lex No. 1428071.
- Judgment of the Court of Appeal in Warszawa, dated: 7.11.2014, VI ACa 140/14, Lex No. 1624059.
- Decision of the Regional Court in Dzierżoniów, dated: 9.06.2015, II Kp 149/15, Legalis.
- Judgment of the District Court in Świdnica, dated: 23.06.2015, IV Ka 394/15, Legalis.
- Judgment of the Court of Appeal in Katowice, dated: 23.06.2015, I ACa 232/15, Lex No. 1770667.
- Judgment of the Court of Appeal in Warszawa, dated: 20.06.2016, VI ACa 403/15, Lex No. 2086195.
- Judgment of the Court of Appeal in Warszawa, dated: 30.06.2016 r., VI ACa 403/15, Lex No. 2086195.
- Judgment of the Court of Appeal in Warszawa, dated: 11.10.2018, I ACa 387/18, Lex No. 2583324.
- Judgment of the Court of Appeal in Warszawa, dated: 12.12.2018, V Aca 651/17, Lex No 2613625.

* Others
  - Ruling of Komisji Etyki Konfederacji Przedsiębiorców Finansowych w Polsce, Case 13/2017, dated: 12.03.2018 r., https://zpf.pl/orzeczenie-komisji-etyki-w-sprawie-132017/.

Documents

* UOKiK:
  - UOKiK, "Euro Bank złamał prawo – windykacja", Announcement of UOKIK, datek: 5.11.2011 r., https://www.uokik.gov.pl/aktualnosci.php?news_id=2972.
  - UOKIK, "Poradnik na temat windykacji" (ang. "A Guide to Debt Collection") https://www.uokik.gov.pl/aktualnosci.php?news_id=14986.
* Codes of Conduct
  - Komisja Nadzoru Finansowego (ang. Financial Supervision Authority), "Kanon dobrych praktyk rynku finansowego" - https://www.knf.gov.pl/knf/pl/komponenty/img/Kanon%20DPRF_51881.pdf
  - Związek Banków Polskich (ang. Association of Polish Banks), "Zasady dobrej praktyki rynkowej" - https://www.zbp.pl/photo/prawo/ZDBP.pdf.
  - Związek Przedsiębiorców Finansowych w Polsce (ang. Confederation of Financial Entrepreneurs in Poland), "Zasady dobrych praktyk przedsiębiorstw zrzeszonych w Związku Przedsiębiorstw Finansowych w Polsce", (2020), https://zpf.pl/pliki/etyka/ZPF_zasady_dobrych_praktyk_09.2020.pdf.
* Others
  - Ministerstwo Sprawiedliwości, Letter no 13816 "w sprawie propozycji dotyczącej prawnego uregulowania działalności firm windykacyjnych, Pisma Urzędowe Ministerstw" (ang. on a Proposal for Legal Regulation of the Activities of Debt Collection Companies), dated: 1.08.2017 VIII/13816/2017, https://www.sejm.gov.pl/sejm8.nsf/InterpelacjaTresc.xsp?key=18C007F8.

- Sejm Rzeczypospolitej Polskiej, Print no 2216, dated: 22.01.2018 r., p. 3-5. https://www.sejm.gov.pl/sejm8.nsf/druk.xsp?nr=2216.
- "New Commission Notice on the interpretation and application of the Unfair Commercial Practices Directive ('the UCPD Guidance')", C/2021/9320, OJ C 526, 29.12.2021.

8 Romania's struggle to regulate abusive debt collection practices

Cătălin-Gabriel Stănescu and Albert Albanezi

8.1 Introduction

Informal (non-judicial) debt collection is one of Romania's most profitable and dynamic markets, recording substantial revenue from year to year.[1] According to empirical data from the National Agency for Consumer Protection (NACP), a total of RON 1.2 billion (approximately 250 million euro) were recovered from consumer debt portfolios in 2017, RON 1.4 billion in 2018, RON 1.1 billion in 2019, and RON 1.2 billion in 2020. The exponential growth of the debt collection market has attracted an increasing number of entities[2] involved in the process, which have generated a growing number of abusive practices[3] and the need for adequate regulatory solutions to tackle them.[4]

This need became more pressing after 2008–2010 as the economic crisis dramatically increased debt ratios in the consumer-credit sector. Between 2010 and

1 For instance, the value of the claims managed by Romanian companies in the domestic market increased by 45% in 2016 compared to 2015. <https://www.profit.ro/povesti-cu-profit/financiar/piata-de-colectare-a-creantelor-a-inregistrat-o-crestere-de-45-in-2016-fata-de-anul-precedent-16998922> accessed 15 November 2021. The growing trend was also confirmed in 2017, with a 14% increase compared to the previous year, the total market value reaching approximately RON 400 million (90 million euro). <https://www.zf.ro/banci-si-asigurari/eos-piata-de-colectare-de-creante-a-crescut-cu-15-anul-trecut-la-400-milioane-de-lei-16763436> accessed 15 November 2021.

2 From the data provided by the Romanian National Consumer Protection Agency, answering our request for information – Request No. 8161/ 11.10.2021, we can confirm the following number of debt collectors per year: 2017 – 52; 2018 – 71; 2019 – 79; 2020 – 82; 2021 – 80.

3 Information regarding abusive debt-collection practices can often be found in the press. To offer a few examples: <https://economie.hotnews.ro/stiri-finante_banci-21081044-domnul-popescu-darea-plata-firmele-recuperare.html>; <http://www.ziare.com/bani/imprumut/datoria-ta-pe-maini-straine-cum-te-aperi-de-abuzurile-recuperatorilor-sfatul-specialistului-1232663>; <https://jurnalul.antena3.ro/special-jurnalul/anchete/cum-sa-scapi-de-firmele-de-recuperari-de-credite-622970.html>; <https://infoploiesticity.blogspot.com/2015/08/atentie-nu-va-lasati-intimidati-de.html>; <https://www.conso.ro/info-banci/anpc-incearca-sa-stopeze-abuzurile-recuperatorilor-de-creante> accessed 15 November 2021.

4 T.W. Bank, 'Romania. Diagnostic Review of Consumer Protection and Financial Literacy. Vol II Comparison against Good Practices' (*TW* Bank, 2009) 7. In the report, the World Bank calls for the protection of debtors against the abusive debt collection practices of banks and other specialized entities, pointing out an almost complete lack of protection mechanisms.

DOI: 10.4324/9781003343158-9

2016, five legislative projects were promoted to regulate the activity of debt collectors and prohibit the use of abusive practices against the consumer debtor. Nonetheless, the implementation process was burdensome and lengthy due to a lack of political drive and strong lobbying from the financial sector.[5] For instance, in 2014, the Romanian Government decided to refrain from implementing any legislation that might affect credit discipline or the informal recovery of non-performing loans (NPLs)

> Because preserving credit discipline among debtors contributes significantly towards enhancing financial stability, we will take all efforts to avoid the adoption of legislative initiatives dealing with personal insolvency that create a moral hazard and are open to widespread abuse by debtors as this would undermine credit discipline. Furthermore, in order to avoid threats to financial stability from the new provisions on abusive clauses … we will … take all necessary measures to ensure a harmonized application of these provisions, such as the training of judges. If the new institutional arrangement of this specialized court does not succeed in avoiding financial stability threats, we will consult extensively with all relevant stakeholders as well as with the IMF and EC to come up with alternative solutions. Given the substantial NPL overhang, the authorities will remove, where possible, impediments to … household out-of-court debt restructuring and NPL resolution.[6]

Despite these aspects, Romanian academia largely ignores the subject of debt recovery and the abusive practices of debt collectors. Information on the matter is found mainly in the press or on the social media pages of politicians claiming to be preoccupied with finding solutions. However, the lack of academic debate should not be construed to mean that Romania's informal debt collection phenomenon is without practical difficulties.

This chapter aims to fill the knowledge gap and critically assess the legal framework for informal debt collection. On the one hand, it addresses in chronological order the legislative projects regarding debt recovery, highlighting the connections between the proposed solutions and the final versions adopted. On the other hand, the chapter undertakes an analysis based on a series of *sine qua non* building blocks for efficient regulation of debt collection and tests GEO No.

5 Intricately connected to debtor protection measures, the Government assumed on numerous occasions its commitment not to promote legislative projects that could undermine 'credit discipline' or 'maintaining payment discipline.' Although the two letters of intent were used in connection with the adoption of the law regarding the insolvency of natural persons, in certain sectors, consumer-debtor protection measures are viewed as encouraging the debtor not to pay. See Government's point of view, p. 2, n 1 and 2 <http://www.cdep.ro/proiecte/2014/500/70/9/pvg823.pdf> accessed 15 November 2021.

6 Romania: Letter of Intent, Memorandum of Economic and Financial Policies, and Technical Memorandum of Understanding (March 05.2014) para 37 <https://www.imf.org/External/NP/LOI/2014/ROU/030514.pdf> accessed 3 December 2021.

52/2016[7] on consumer credit relating to residential immovable property (the law currently in force) on this basis. To illustrate this, the chapter also employs a comparative approach by juxtaposing other U.S. or European solutions with the Romanian ones.

As far as terminology is concerned, the chapter refers strictly to informal debt recovery, meaning debt collection without the involvement of state authorities. It uses the terms 'debt collection' and 'debt recovery' interchangeably to avoid repetitions.

We limited our analysis to sector-specific legislation, with references to existing soft law[8] (when applicable), without expanding to the provisions of the Civil or Criminal Code and European instruments such as Directive 2005/29/EC concerning unfair business-to-consumer commercial practices (UCPD)[9] transposed into national law.

The chapter is structured as follows. The first section describes our analysis matrix and its building blocks. The second section presents chronologically the legislative projects aimed at tackling informal debt recovery. The third section evaluates the legislation in force through the lens of our analysis matrix. Finally, we present our conclusions.

8.2 Analysis matrix: the building blocks of an efficient regulatory system for debt collection practices

Instead of a black-letter law approach, we decided that using a matrix of analysis containing the building blocks of efficient regulation would be more helpful in evaluating the potential success of a legal framework applicable to informal debt collection. Three reasons justify this approach. First, there are differences between national legislative and institutional approaches to regulating informal debt recovery. These differences must be considered and surmounted when

7 Ordonanţă de urgenţă 52/2016 privind contractele de credit oferite consumatorilor pentru bunuri imobile, precum şi pentru modificarea şi completarea Ordonanţei de urgenţă a Guvernului nr. 50/2010 privind contractele de credit pentru consumatori (GEO No. 52/2016 on credit agreements for consumers relating to residential immovable property and amending GEO No. 50/2010) Official Gazette of Romania 727 (20 September 2016).

8 The Commercial Claims Management Association (CCMA) is a Romanian association of debt collectors and a member of the Federation of European National Collection Associations (FENCA). Although it currently has only 15 members, these are the most representative entities operating on the market. Their Code of Conduct is available at < https://www.amcc.ro/en/code-of-conduct/> accessed 16 November 2021.

9 The Directive had been transposed into national legislation by Legea 363/2007 privind combaterea practicilor incorecte ale comercianţilor în relaţia cu consumatorii şi armonizarea reglementărilor cu legislaţia europeană privind protecţia consumatorilor (Law No. 363/2007 concerning unfair business-to-consumer practices) Official Gazette of Romania 899/28 (December 2017) part I. Regarding the effects of the UCPD on debt collection, see Cătălin-Gabriel Stănescu, 'Is the Unfair Commercial Practices Directive Fit to Effectively Tackle Abusive Debt Collection?' (2020) 6 Journal of European Consumer and Market Law 235–247.

regulation is adopted. Hence, an analysis matrix could overcome the systemic differences in existing legislation. Second, a mere mechanical description of the relevant legislation would not offer helpful answers for less-developed legislative systems looking for inspiration. Finally, an analysis matrix would also be useful in assessing future projects or amendments, irrespective of the time, placement, or content of such projects or modifications.

The chapter employs a matrix of analysis consisting of six building blocks previously identified by one of the authors.[10] The building blocks are: (1) the definition of debt collectors; (2) the existence of a licensing system; (3) the presence of legal requirements concerning (a) communication with the debtor and third parties, (b) harassment of the debtor or third parties, (c) using misrepresentation or misleading information, (d) validation of the debt, and (e) costs and additional charges; (4) open-end definitions; (5) enforcement via private action; and (6) enforcement via state action.

We do not argue that the regulation of informal debt collection based on these building blocks will automatically be successful. Other circumstances should be considered, such as the precise substance of the legal provisions, their correlation with other existing legal requirements, the efficiency and professionalism of the supervisory authorities/consumer-protection agencies, the presence of qualified personnel in these agencies and the judicial system, the debtor's access to information, the extent of the banking sector's influence, and the degree of regulatory capture or systemic corruption.

8.3 A chronology of failure? Proposals and efforts to regulate informal debt collection in Romania

Informal debt collection practices are currently covered by GEO No. 52/2016 on consumer credit relating to residential immovable property, which amended GEO No. 50/2010 on consumer credit. The Romanian legislator used the implementation of Directive 2014/17/EU[11] to introduce, for the first time, several legal provisions concerning informal debt recovery. However, the process was lengthy and sinuous, as illustrated below.

8.3.1 The 2010 legislative project concerning the debt collection procedure

The year 2010 saw the first legislative proposal to regulate informal debt collection in Romania, inspired by American federal legislation.[12] It is noteworthy that

10 Cătălin-Gabriel Stănescu, *Self-Help, Private Debt Collection and the Concomitant Risks. A Comparative Law Analysis* (Springer 2015) 230–231.

11 Directive No. 2014/17/EU of the European Parliament and of the Council of 4 February 2014 on credit agreements for consumers relating to residential immovable property and amending Directives 2008/48/EC and 2013/36/EU and Regulation (EU) No. 1093/2010 [2014] OJ L 60/34.

12 For a detailed analysis of the FDCPA, see Stănescu (note 10).

the project's initiator, Mr. Iulian Urban, was the majority shareholder of one of the largest debt collection companies.

In the explanatory memorandum, the initiators claimed that because of the pressure exercised by creditors or debt collection companies or departments, 'consumers were abused in their capacity as debtors.'[13] It was highlighted that 'there is no legal framework to regulate the activity of the companies that provide amicable debt collecting services, although the majority of Member States have dedicated legislation.'[14] Consequently, 'natural person debtors … are abused or harassed by the actions of the personnel in debt collecting companies or departments.' Therefore, a legal framework was needed to organize this activity strictly.[15]

Additionally, the project included detailed provisions for debt collection (Chapter II), the prerogatives of debt collectors (Chapter III), debtor protection mechanisms (Chapter IV), as well as disciplinary, administrative, and criminal fines (Chapter VI).[16] However, the legislative proposal contained a series of questionable definitions of debtor, communication, internal collecting department, debt collector, debtor's assets, order of payment, debt collection, creditor, and claim.[17]

The project received a favorable opinion from the Legislative Council, conditioned, among others, on amendments clarifying the problematic definitions of debt, debt collectors, communications, the legal nature of the companies offering such services, the services offered, and administrative and criminal liability.[18]

The Government's position was similar, highlighting the need to adequately define amicable debt collection, creditors, debt collectors, debt, and notifications regarding abusive practices. Most notably, the Government recommended the introduction of provisions about informing consumers, challenging the debt, the nature of the debt itself, and the prerogatives of the supervisory authority, namely, NACP.[19]

Regardless, the version adopted by the Senate[20] did not contain the requested adjustments. Consequently, the project received a negative opinion from the Budget, Finance, and Banking Committee and was never subjected to a plenary

13 Legislative Proposal No.PL-x 691/2010, explanatory memorandum, issued 22.11.2010 <http://www.cdep.ro/proiecte/2010/600/90/1/em691.pdf> accessed 16 November 2021.

14 Directive No. 2014/17/EU (note 11).

15 Ibid.

16 Ibid.

17 Legislative proposal on the debt collection procedure, No.PL-x 691/2010, art 3 <http://www.cdep.ro/proiecte/2010/600/90/1/se691.pdf> accessed 16 November 2021.

18 Advisory Notice of the Legislative Council issued 22.11.2010 <http://www.cdep.ro/proiecte/2010/600/90/1/cl691.pdf> accessed 16 November 2021.

19 Government's opinion No. 396/ 22.11.2010<http://www.cdep.ro/proiecte/2010/600/90/1/pvg691.pdf> accessed 16 November 2021.

20 Legislative project in the version adopted by the Senate on 15.11.2010 <http://www.cdep.ro/proiecte/2010/600/90/1/se691.pdf> accessed 16 November 2021.

debate.[21] The Chamber of Deputies eventually rejected the proposal because of its inherent shortcomings and legal inconsistencies.[22]

8.3.2 The 2014 amendment project: the conversion mechanism for foreign currency loans

The legislative project of 2014 aimed to amend GEO No. 50/2010[23] on consumer credit by introducing a conversion mechanism for foreign currency loans. According to the explanatory memorandum,[24] a 2013 report of the National Bank of Romania revealed that approximately 70% of non-performing debtors in mortgages failed to make payments for at least a year. Furthermore, it highlighted that bank generally used two methods to redress the debtor's situation, namely, loan restructuring and foreclosure, both equally inefficient in assisting the debtor. On the one hand, restructuring was far too ambitious because low-income households could not improve their income level. On the other hand, foreclosure meant that banks could not cover their initial loan due to the price drop in the real-estate market. Moreover, debtors faced several risks: (a) losing their home, (b) low chances of acquiring another one, and (c) deficiency payments. The explanatory memorandum stressed that 'the social repercussions deriving from these household dramas are of the most profound nature.'[25]

The initiators thought that a fairer option was to share the credit and currency risk between the debtor and the bank. Thus, the consumer should have the opportunity to request a loan conversion at the rate of conversion practiced at the moment of signing. The mechanism was designed to redress the imbalance caused by the volatile nature of the Swiss franc (CHF).

Although the project was initiated in 2014, it was not until 2016 that the legislative procedure resumed, with several amendments proposed by the Budget, Finance, and Banking Committee.[26] One of the envisioned changes stated that in the case of Swiss franc loans, creditors were obliged to convert the debt into the national currency, under penalty of administrative fines.

The Chamber of Deputies adopted the updated version in October 2016, but the Government contested it on constitutional grounds. The Romanian Constitutional

21 The negative advisory opinion from the Budget, Finance, and Banks Committee is not publicly available. However, the recordings of the meeting of the Deputies Chamber that took place on 18 September 2012 can be consulted at <http://www.cdep.ro/pls/steno/steno.stenograma?ids=7157&idm=18> accessed 16 November 2021.

22 The result of the vote is available at <http://www.cdep.ro/pls/steno/eVot.Nominal?idv=9448> accessed 16 November 2021.

23 Ordonanţă de urgenţă Nr. 50/2010 privind contractele de credit pentru consumatori (GEO No. 50/2010 on consumer credit) Official Gazette of Romania 389 (11 June 2011).

24 Explanatory memorandum concerning Legislative Proposal No. PLX 337/2014, <http://www.cdep.ro/proiecte/2014/300/40/5/em345.pdf> accessed 16 November 2021.

25 Ibid.

26 Proposal from the Budget, Finance and Banking Committee, No.4c-2/662/10.10.2016 <http://www.cdep.ro/comisii/buget/pdf/2016/rp345_14;2.pdf> accessed 16 November 2021.

Court (RCC) held that the legislative procedure did not respect the bicameralism principle and that the proposal was thus unconstitutional.[27] The RCC further argued that a conversion mechanism was already available to debtors in light of GEO No. 52/ 2016 on consumer credit relating to residential immovable property.[28]

8.3.3 Law No. 77/2016 on Datio in Solutum[29]

The 2016 *Datio in Solutum* law undertook to 'protect debtors from abusive practices in cases of assignment of debt'[30] and ensure the equal distribution of the real-estate devaluation risk between debtor and creditor. The project received a favorable opinion from the Legislative Council, with observations and proposals, none of which tackled the issue of abusive informal debt-collection practices or regulating companies that provide such services.[31] The Budget, Finance, and Banking Committee gave a similarly favorable opinion.[32] However, the President requested a reexamination, and the Government issued a point of view supporting a revision of the text.[33] Following the reexamination request, the Judiciary, Disciplinary, and Immunities Committee granted a favorable opinion conditioned on several changes in the law.[34]

Nonetheless, despite its stated purpose, the *Datio in Solutum* Law did not address informal debt collection practices. The explanatory memorandum did not clarify the notion of abuse by debt collectors, and the law did not contain any provisions in this regard. For this reason, we will not discuss it any further.

27 Romanian Constitutional Court Decision No. 62 [2017] Official Gazette of Romania 161 (3 March 2017) <https://www.ccr.ro/wp-content/uploads/2020/07/Decizie_62_2017.pdf> accessed 16 November 2021.

28 For a detailed analysis of the ruling, see Marieta Avram, 'Battlefield Journal: Legislative Decisions and Counter-Decisions with Impact in the Financial and Banking Environment' (2019) Romanian Rev Priv L 312.

29 Legea 77/2016 privind darea în plată a unor bunuri imobile în vederea stingerii obligaţiilor asumate prin credite, (Law No. 77/2016 Datio in Solutum of immovable property to settle debts), published in the Official Gazette of Romania No. 330 of 28.04.2016.

30 Explanatory memorandum concerning Legislative Proposal No. PL-x 743/2015 issued 02.11.2015 available at <http://www.cdep.ro/proiecte/2015/700/40/3/em951.pdf> accessed 16 November 2021.

31 Legislative Council's notice, No. 675/ 20.06.2015, available at <http://www.cdep.ro/proiecte/2015/700/40/3/cl951.pdf> accessed 16 November 2021.

32 Favorable opinion of the Budget, Finance and Banking Committee, No. 4c-2/967/10.11.2015, available at <http://www.cdep.ro/comisii/buget/pdf/2016/rp345_14;2.pdf> accessed 16 November 2021.

33 Government's point of view, No. 2573/15.03.2016, <http://www.cdep.ro/proiecte/2015/700/40/3/pvg743.pdf> accessed 16 November 2021.

34 Judiciary, Disciplinary, and Immunities Committee, 'Report', No. 4c-11/243/05.04.2016, (*Romanian Parliament Chamber of Deputies*, 2016) <http://www.cdep.ro/comisii/juridica/pdf/2016/rp743_15.pdf> accessed 16 November 2021.

8.3.4 GEO No. 52/2016 on credit agreements for consumers relating to residential immovable property

The 2016 GEO on credit agreements for consumers relating to residential immovable property ticked two boxes: it transposed Directive 2014/17/EU and amended the existing consumer-credit regime instated by GEO No. 50/2010 on consumer credit. This section only highlights the novelties of the ordinance in connection with informal debt collection before we evaluate them at length in the next one.

GEO No. 52/2016 on consumer credit relating to residential immovable property is the first regulatory tool to implement an authorization procedure for debt collection companies and prohibit certain abusive debt recovery practices. The explanatory memorandum stated that clear licensing criteria are needed since 'debt collection activities have seen quite a surge in recent years, without an overall perspective on the actual number of such companies, nor their activities.'[35]

The ordinance has one major flaw, its applicability in time: it states that its provisions do not apply to ongoing credit contracts.[36] This limitation implies that the mechanisms designed to protect consumer debtors can only be used for future contracts, even though pending contracts can also be affected by abusive collection practices. Furthermore, without justification, the law discriminates between two classes of debtors – those with ongoing contracts (although they might not be in the debt recovery stage yet) and those who signed their contract after the entry into force of GEO No. 52/2016[37] – and protects only the latter.

8.3.5 The 2018 amendment project on limiting the possibility of speculation in case of debt assignment

The 2018 project targeted a recurring theme,[38] namely, limiting the extent of speculation by debt collectors in the assignment of debt. However, in its one-page monolithic structure, the explanatory memorandum failed to highlight the legal reasoning behind the legislative project, merely stating that debtors are often 'packed in portfolios, without regard of their financial state or their conduct

35 Explanatory memorandum concerning Legislative Proposal No. PL-x 511/2016, issued 13.12.2016, <http://www.cdep.ro/proiecte/2016/500/10/1/em749.pdf> accessed 16 November 2021.

36 GEO No. 52/2016 (note 7) art 135.

37 For a detailed analysis, see Radu Rizoiu, 'The Light Comes from the West: The Applicability of Government Emergency Ordinance No. 52/2016 to Existing Contracts' (2016) Romanian Rev Priv L 161.

38 For instance, another 2015 legislative project aimed to tackle the issue of limiting the possibility of speculation from debt collectors in case of debt assignment, Legislative Proposal No. Pl-x nr. 290/2015. Explanatory memorandum issued 24.03.2015 <http://www.cdep.ro/proiecte/2015/600/90/4/em883.pdf> accessed 17 November 2021.

towards the debt … a situation which dangerously escalates into an unlawful detainment of the debtor by a dominant creditor for extended periods.'[39]

In the Senate's version,[40] the legislative proposal indicated that if a debt is assigned, the consumer could satisfy the claim by paying double the amount at which the assignee acquired the NPL without additional costs.

The CCR held that although it intended to empower the consumer with an effective tool, the project suffered from procedural shortcomings:[41] the advisory opinion of the Economic and Social Council was not requested during the legislative procedure, which rendered the law unconstitutional in its entirety.

8.3.6 The 2019 amendment project on limiting excessive interest rates

Finally, a 2019 legislative project attempted to tackle the issue of excessive interest rates charged during debt recovery. The explanatory memorandum contains 11 pages of explanations concerning alarming interest rates, with several links to articles and studies published by academics. The following statement emphasizes the underlying motivation: 'excessive interest rates practiced by creditors in relation to consumers cause loss of money, resources, and energy, not to mention the loss of the opportunity to channel these resources towards more legitimate and rational objectives than the excessive and unjustified profit of a small number of corporate entities.'[42]

The version adopted by the Senate[43] hesitantly defined the notion of excessive interest rates and tried to impose caps. For instance, art 6 stated that for consumer loans not exceeding RON 15,000 (approximately EUR 3,000), the total amount paid by the consumer cannot surpass double the amount loaned. The total amount owed was defined as the principal plus interest rates, commissions, and any other costs generated by the loan as stated in the contract.

This project, too, was challenged on constitutional grounds. In its reasoning, among several inconsistencies identified, the CCR pointed out the definition of the annual percentage rate of charge, which, although inspired by the provisions of GEO No. 52/2016 on consumer credit relating to residential immovable

39 Explanatory memorandum concerning Legislative Proposal No. PL-x 85/2018 issued 07.03.2018 <http://www.cdep.ro/proiecte/2018/000/80/5/em113.pdf> accessed 17 November 2021.

40 Senate's version, 26.02.2018 <http://www.cdep.ro/proiecte/2018/000/80/5/se113.pdf> accessed 17 November 2021.

41 Romanian Constitutional Court Decision No. 140 [2019] Official Gazette of Romania 377 (14 May 2019) <https://www.ccr.ro/wp-content/uploads/2020/07/Decizie_140_2019.pdf> accessed 17 November 2021.

42 Explanatory memorandum concerning Legislative Proposal No. PL-x 664/2019 issued 19.12.2019 <http://www.cdep.ro/proiecte/2019/600/60/4/em883.pdf> accessed 17 November 2021.

43 Senate' s version, 11.12. 2019 <http://www.cdep.ro/proiecte/2019/600/60/4/se883.pdf> accessed 17 November 2021.

property, managed to contradict them. Unsurprisingly, the project was judged unconstitutional.[44]

The deficiencies of the last regulatory project reveal the common denominator of all listed projects: despite tackling essential consumer-protection issues, they were affected by either provisional inconsistencies or procedural blunders, raising the question of whether the legislators were honest about their intent to pass them or only pretended for publicity reasons.

8.4 Assessing the legal provisions regulating informal debt collection in Romania

This section evaluates the legal provisions of GEO No. 52/2016 on consumer credit relating to residential immovable property through the lens of the proposed analysis matrix, with references to *soft law*. Where relevant, we adopted a comparative approach by pointing to solutions implemented by other jurisdictions.

8.4.1 Defining debt collectors

The starting point in regulating informal debt collection is determining to whom the law applies, that is, defining debt collectors. Should original creditors be included or only the assignees and third parties? Are lawyers who mainly oversee debt recovery covered or not? As we show, the answer is not always clear-cut, and national approaches vary significantly in their scope and coverage.[45]

For instance, the definition of debt collectors in the Fair Debt Collection Practices Act (FDCPA) (at the federal level) only covers third parties – firms specialized in debt recovery,[46] their agents or employees, and lawyers active mainly in this field.[47] Original creditors fall within the law's ambit only if they operate

44 Romanian Constitutional Court Decision No. 69 [2021] Official Gazette of Romania 492 (12 May 2021) <https://www.ccr.ro/wp-content/uploads/2021/05/Decizie_69_2021.pdf> accessed 17 November 2021.

45 For a detailed presentation of the scope and coverage of the E.U.'s informal debt collection sector-specific laws, see Cătălin-Gabriel Stănescu, 'A Critical Assessment of the Need for Harmonization of the Legal Framework Concerning Abusive Informal Debt Collection Practices in the European Union: Is Harmonization Possible and How Can it Best Be Attained?' (2021) 44 Journal of Consumer Policy 531–537.

46 *Cirkot v. Diversified Systems Inc.* [1993] 839. Supp. 941 (D Conn).

47 *Heintz v. Jenkins* [1995] 514 U.S. 291; *Garret v. Derbes* [1997] 1110 F. 3d 317 (5th Cir). In the latter, the attorney at law oversaw 639 debt-collection claims, amounting to merely 1% of his total activity. Regardless, the courts deemed that given the recurrence of his activity, he should be considered a debt collector. Similarly, in *Scott v. Jones* [1992] 964 F.2d 314, 316 (4th Circ), given that 70–80% of the lawyer's income was generated by debt collection, with approximately 4,000 requests per year over a period of four years, the court ruled that the lawyer had to be classified as a debt collector. Since the FDPCA does not define 'regularly,' the evaluation standard varies from case to case, with numerous factors to be considered. For details, see Daniel A. Edelman The Fair Debt Collection Practices Act – Recent Developments, 8 Loy. Consumer L. Rev. 303 (1996), 9–15 <http://www.edcombs.com/wp-content/uploads/2013/08/Fair-Debt-Collection-Practices-Act/July /2013.pdf> accessed 17 November 2021.

under a different name.[48] The situation of assignees remains questionable as not all U.S. courts agree that they are concerned by the provisions of the law.[49]

At the state level, the approach is more extensive, with original creditors and assignees included in the definition of debt collectors. This approach is logical as laws regarding fair debt collection practices aim to prevent and discourage abusive debt recovery. Furthermore, given that the effect on the consumers is the same, the abusive practices of the original creditors should fall along the same line as the practices of specialized debt collection agencies. Therefore, the definition of debt collector should be clear and all-encompassing.

The definition chosen by GEO No. 52/2016 on consumer credit relating to residential immovable property is somewhat confusing at first glance. It states that a debt collecting entity is a legal person 'other than the creditor' that must meet specific licensing requirements (to be covered extensively in the next section).[50] However, upon closer inspection,[51] the definition also encompasses the original creditors. It is stated that debt collection can only be practiced by specialized entities registered as such, as well as creditors. In this respect, art 3, point 2, corroborated by art 2 para 1 of GEO No. 52/2016 defines creditors as legal persons granting consumer credits for the sale or purchase of residential immovable property or loans related to such assets secured by a mortgage.

The definition also covers personnel, defined as 'any natural person that works for a designated representative and is in contact with the consumers in the interest of the activities regulated by the ordinance'[52] and 'any natural person that coordinates or supervises the aforementioned employees.'[53] Lawyers are only incorporated in the definition if they act as *in-house* counsel for debt collection companies, that is, as part of the personnel. In other cases, the situation remains unclear because external lawyers are not considered debt collectors under the ordinance's provisions.

In conclusion, it can be argued that despite some unclarities, as far as the first component in the analysis matrix is concerned, GEO No. 52/2016 defines debt collectors.

48 *Orenbuch v. North Shore Health Systems Inc.* [2003] 250 F. Supp. 2d 145 (e.D.N.Y). In this case, the internal debt collection department of a hospital operated under a different name, leading the court to deem that the department functioned as a separate entity.

49 *Munoz v. Pipestone* [2005] 397 F Supp. 2d 1129, 1133 (D Minn). The court ruled that the assignee, who never notified the debtor, was to be considered a debt collector as long as there was a prior agreement with a debt collection agency, especially as the assignee's main activity was debt collection. However, the court's rationale suggests that if the assignee's main activity had been financial investment, the outcome would have been different. For example, see *Scally v. Hilco Receivables* [2005] LLC, 392 F. Supp. 2d 1036, N.D. Ill. For details, see Edelman (note 48) 7–9.

50 GEO no 52/2016 (note 7) art 3 point 29.

51 Ibid, art 128 para 11.

52 Ibid, art 3 point 10(b).

53 Ibid, (c).

8.4.2 Authorization procedure

Most jurisdictions regulating debt collection (the U.S. at the state level, Norway, the U.K., Belgium, Denmark, Finland, Germany, Greece, Latvia, and Sweden) have implemented an authorization or registration system.[54] Generally, an operating license is issued upon request, provided that the company meets the regulatory requirements.[55] Debt collectors must observe these conditions at the moment of authorization and throughout their activity. Failure to do so can result in criminal sanctions[56] or administrative measures such as warnings, orders to desist, fines,[57] suspension of activity, revocation[58] of the operating license, or permanent termination of the activity.

Nevertheless, the efficiency of licensing systems varies. For instance, in the absence of open-end clauses, practices that do not breach specific provisions cannot be considered when implementing temporary or permanent measures to stop debt collectors' illegal activities during administrative or judiciary procedures.[59] Some jurisdictions, such as several U.S. states,[60] the Scandinavian countries, Belgium, and Latvia, have imposed a financial guarantee. This measure is necessary to ensure that the recovered claims will be transferred to the creditor or that the debt collector has sufficient funds to cover potential financial fines or damages resulting from abusive practices. In the same line of thought, other U.S. states[61] and European countries such as France, Denmark, and Norway require fiduciary accounts to guarantee a separation between the funds belonging to the debt collectors and those recovered to the creditors' benefit. Finally, Germany and France also impose professional insurance.

An authorization system could be considered the first step in creating an efficient regulatory system of debt-collection activities. Thus, it is surprising that

54 For details, see Cătălin-Gabriel Stănescu, 'Regulation of Abusive Informal Debt Collection Practices in the European Union. An Empirical Account' (2021) Journal of Consumer Policy 44(2) 179–216.

55 For example, in the U.K., the requirements are known as a 'fitness test.' See Dennis Rosenthal, *Consumer Credit Law and Practice. A Guide* (4th edn Bloomsbury Professional 2013) 326.

56 Operating without authorization is considered a criminal offence in the U.K. See Steven Finlay, *Consumer Credit Fundamentals* (2nd edn Palgrave Macmillan 2009) 79. Criminal liability deriving from failure to respect the obligations imposed by the authorization is applicable in Idaho. See Stănescu (note 10) 236 note 136.

57 Section 39A of the Consumer Credit Act 1974 in the U.K. or s 20 of the Rechtsdienstleistungsgesetz (Out-of-Court Legal Services Act) – RDG of 12 December 2007 (Federal Law Gazette I, p. 2840) in Germany.

58 Sections 52 and 53 of the Consumer Credit Act 1974 in the U.K. or s 14 of the RDG in Germany.

59 This issue was widely debated in the U.K., where the powers of the former Office for Fair Trading were expressly extended to allow the suspension of the authorization, effective immediately, in urgent matters where consumer protection dictates it. See Rosenthal (note 55) 332.

60 For instance, in Colorado.

61 For example, Idaho, Michigan, Nevada, and Washington. Without the requirement of a fiduciary account, in Arkansas, the authorization will be suspended or revoked if the recovered amount is not transferred to the original creditor. In Idaho, the same situation is a criminal offence punishable by up to five years of imprisonment.

Romania only chose to implement such a system starting in 2017, via GEO No. 52/2016 and Order No. 1/2017 issued by the NACP.[62]

The authorization procedure set by GEO No. 52/2016 on consumer credit relating to residential immovable property does not require a fiduciary account or other financial guarantees. Instead, a minimum share capital of approximately 100,000 euro[63] is necessary to protect the interests of creditors or debtors and deter rogue operators from entering the market. In addition, debt collectors must have a registered office, a subsidiary, or a representative in Romania to resolve legal disputes and face potential administrative or criminal liability.[64] Additional documentation, such as the article of incorporation and the director or legal representative's criminal record, is required under the provisions of Order No. 1/2017 of the NACP. However, it remains questionable whether these criteria are sufficient to cover the potential liability of the debt collectors as well as protect creditors in case of insolvency of the debt collector.

Article 128 para 3 letter d) of GEO No. 52/2016 contains a unique requirement. The remuneration of the employees of debt-collection companies cannot be conditioned exclusively by the amount recovered or the objectives established. Order No. 1/2017 of the NACP even requires the manager(s) of the legal person to give an affidavit stating this limitation. One may wonder whether this provision was included to deter employees from engaging in abusive practices to maximize their income or reiterate Romanian labor law provisions requiring the payment of a minimum hourly wage.[65] While it is possible to include a target/objective clause in the labor agreements, in such cases, conditioning remuneration on reaching said targets is strictly prohibited. In our view, the second interpretation is more likely.

Having introduced an authorization system, the Romanian legislator ticked another box on the list of building blocks of an efficient regulatory system of debt collection, taking a major step forward in protecting consumers' interests. If supported by active supervision and the possibility to impose administrative and criminal sanctions, such a system could be the first line of defense against abusive debt collection practices and rogue debt collectors.

8.4.3 Abusive practices

There are numerous methods of abuse in informal debt collection and analyzing each in detail would exceed the objective of this chapter. Thus, we propose to

62 Ordinul Nr. 1 din 2017 privind documentația și informațiile necesare înregistrării precum și modalitatea și termenele de raportare pentru entitățile de recuperare de creanțe (Order No. 1/2017 of the NCPA regarding the documents required for licensing and reporting deadlines for debt collectors) Official Gazette of Romania 33 (11 November 2017).

63 GEO No. 52/2016 (note 7) art 3 point 29.

64 Ibid, art 128 para 3(a).

65 Law No. 53/2003 (Romanian Labor Code) Official Gazette of Romania 345 (18 May 2011) art 164 para 2.

classify abusive practices based on their effect or scope, distinguishing between (a) practices that affect communication with the debtor and third parties and (b) practices that harass and mislead. However, each jurisdiction approaches these practices differently.

GEO No. 52/2016 on consumer credit relating to residential immovable property contains several limitations concerning abusive debt collection. The ordinance progresses from general terms such as 'harassing or abusive practices' to specific methods such as 'the posting of notifications on the apartment door, or the apartment building door,' which reflects the concern of the legislator with some of the most egregious tactics employed by debt collectors in Romania. The following analysis is based on the elements described in the analysis matrix.

8.4.3.1 Communication with the debtor and third parties

The importance of regulating communication is supported by the fact that all legislation regulating debt collection contains provisions relating to this matter (although the exact details vary). Romania is no exception.[66]

Communication with the debtor or third parties can be justified by the need to gather information on the debtor's whereabouts or assets and specific data relating to debt collection (e.g., income level and payment capacity). Hence, restrictions connected to communication can be divided into two categories: the first refers to direct or indirect contact with the debtor, while the second concerns approaching third parties. Thus, on the one hand, regulating communication aims to protect the intimacy and private life of the debtor and related third parties (extended family, emotionally attached persons, and close friends) and limit the possibility of invasion. On the other hand, regulating the content of communication protects the debtor's dignity by avoiding exposure to public shame or abusive language or behavior.

Another rather unique trait of the Romanian regulation is the inclusion of specific rules concerning communication that address the form of written notifications, such as a requirement to use a font of at least Times New Roman 12 point, and an obligation to transmit information clearly and understandably. As for content, elements such as the identification and contact information of the debt collector, the name of the original creditor in case of assignment, the date of the assignment, and the exact amount owed must be disclosed to the debtor.[67]

Regarding restrictions, Romanian law prohibits contacting the debtors at their workplace, contacting third parties other than the debtor's legal successors, attorney, or legal representative, posting notifications on the apartment or building door other than documents issued by judiciary authorities, and contacting the debtor between 8 p.m. and 9 a.m.[68]

66 Stănescu (note 54).
67 GEO No. 52/2016 (note 7) art 59 paras 4, 5.
68 Ibid, art 60.

On this subject, the Commercial Claims Management Association (CCMA)'s Code of Conduct – a soft law mechanism – hardly offers further guarantees. The only noteworthy addition are the recommendation that written correspondence be sent in a sealed envelope devoid of signs or writing that would indicate its content except the sign or mark of the debt-collection company.[69] Nevertheless, in practice, these would suffice to reveal the correspondence's purpose because many debt collectors mention their business activity in their name. Furthermore, the Code of Conduct limits the frequency of phone calls to no more than two per week unless there is active, ongoing negotiation with the debtor.[70]

In addition to mandatory requirements regarding the content of written communication, GEO No. 52/2016 on consumer credit relating to the residential immovable property also confers on the debtor the right to challenge the claim. Express or tacit refusal to communicate with the debt collector does not entail admittance, nor can it hinder the consumer's right to challenge the claim.

Regardless, provisions on communication remain insufficient as there is no reference to notification via modern means,[71] such as the internet or social media, nor of unconventional methods such as house visits, public approaches, or calls with a concealed caller ID. There is also no mention of the means of proof at the debtor's disposal in matters of abusive practices in verbal communication.

4.3.2 Harassment

Debt collectors must refrain from using practices that harass or oppress the debtor or related third parties (spouses, partners, parents, children, other relatives, and even close friends). Extending the level of protection to third parties is vital because, otherwise, the debtor could easily be constrained to act contrary to their will to protect others.

Romanian law stipulates a general ban on harassment, threats, and aggressive techniques to physically or psychologically harm the consumer or their relatives, or which could affect the debtor's reputation.[72] Although the text covers relatives, the provisions do not extend to other third parties such as partners and close friends. Furthermore, it is difficult to understand why, according to the ordinance's requirements, only the debtor's reputation is mentioned, while damaging that of relatives falls outside the scope of the law.

69 CCMA's Code of Conduct art 5 paras 1, 2, available at <https://www.amcc.ro/wp-content/uploads/2021/06/CODE-OF-CONDUCT-1.pdf>, last accessed 18 November 2021.

70 Ibid, art 6 para 6.

71 This is all the more surprising as representatives of debt collectors praise themselves on using voice analytics in debt-collection activities <https://www.zf.ro/banci-si-asigurari/marilena-popovici-b2holding-pe-zona-de-recuperare-a-creantelor-de-retail-ne-bazam-foarte-multpe-voice-analytics-18214402> accessed 19 November 2021.

72 GEO No 52/2016 (note 7) art 60(e), (f).

8.4.3.3 Misleading practices

Closely tied to the rule's governing communication is the matter of the use of misleading or false information. A textbook example is creditors creating collection departments with distinct identification to give the impression that there was an assignment of debt. This gives two advantages to the original creditor: (a) they send a clear message to the debtor that the debt collection procedure has entered a new phase handled by a specialized team and (b) they protect their image from any negative associations.[73] Misleading practices can be divided into two categories: false or deceiving information relating to the claim (with limitations already covered when discussing communication requirements) and misleading tactics during the debt collection procedure, presented below.

GEO No. 52/2016 on consumer credit relating to residential immovable property prohibits the creditor or debt collectors from using terms such as 'counseling,' 'counsel,' and other similar words.[74] In this case, the CCMA's Code of Conduct is more revealing. For instance, threats of inexistent sanctions are prohibited,[75] as well as sending documents or letters that appear to come from a courthouse or public institution or use characteristic information belonging to such institutions.[76] Moreover, debt collectors must not supply any false information on the status, qualification, expertise, and professional attributions of the collecting agent or lead to such an assumption.[77]

It is safe to say that the Romanian legislator failed to include specific provisions regarding misleading communication practices. Whether this was due to a certain tolerance for such practices or because the UCPD's implementing act[78] or criminal provisions relating to fraud and deception offer the necessary protection remains to be determined. What can, however, be concluded is that the absence of specific requirements relating to this matter is a substantial gap in the current regulation on debt collection.

8.4.3.4 Validation of the debt

In an attempt to prevent debt recovery, from the wrong person, of a claim that has already been satisfied, or simply as a means of deterrence against false information about the claim, laws regulating debt collection contain procedures intended to validate the debt.[79] Consequently, the following section does not discuss an abusive practice but a positive obligation of debt collectors to prove diligence, ascertain that the claim is genuine and valid, and identify the actual debtor.

73 See Finlay (note 56) 213.
74 GEO no 52/2016 (note 7) 66 para 1.
75 CCMA Code of Conduct (note 69) art 11 para 1(a).
76 Ibid, art 11 para 1(e).
77 Ibid, art 11 para 1(g).
78 Ibid, note 9
79 See Stanescu (note 54).

Moreover, debt validation expresses the debtor's right to challenge any aspect of the claim, from its existence to its amount. Thus, the possibility to challenge a claim is an important defense mechanism at the consumer's disposal, without which no regulation of debt collection is complete.

As mentioned in the section on communication, the first written notification must specify the total amount owed and contain the documents certifying the debt. However, the possibility to request additional documentation is uncertain because legal provisions do not expressly grant such a right. According to GEO No. 52/2016 on consumer credit relating to residential immovable property, the debtor has the right to challenge the claim's existence, or the amount owed within 30 days of receiving the written notification, and the debt collector is obligated to provide a formal reply within 30 days.[80] During the validation period, no debt collection activities can be conducted.

Accordingly, the CCAM's Code of Conduct[81] states that the first notification should enclose the documents that certify the amount, the original creditor, and the assignee (if relevant). Subsequent notifications should only mention the number and status of the debt collection file and the updated amount.

In their current version, the legal provisions reproduce U.S. law. Thus, they create a good opportunity for the parties involved to clarify certain problematic aspects of the claim, such as the pursuit of the wrong debtor or recovery of a claim that has already been satisfied entirely or partially.

8.4.3.5 Additional charges and costs

Closely tied to the issue of debt validation is the matter of debt collectors' attempts to artificially augment the claim with additional charges and costs. Given that such tactics are common practice, efficient regulation of debt collection must tackle them specifically.

In Romania, additional charges and interest rates are limited by legal caps. For instance, penalty interests cannot exceed the total amount owed.[82] Furthermore, it is specified that commissions, additional fees, and interests cannot exceed legal caps, and imposing collection fees other than those strictly necessary for the foreclosure procedure is prohibited.[83] As mentioned in section 8.3.6, limiting excessively high rates has been a recurring theme in the amendment projects, with the latest attempt made in 2019, although none of the projects materialized.

Without further details concerning the nature and extent of penalty interest, the Romanian legislator's intent to clarify the circumstances under which one can charge penalty interest in case of default and the express ban of any other debt recovery related costs are salutary.

80 GEO No. 52/2016 (note 7) art 59 para 5(b).
81 CCMA's Code of Conduct (note 70) art 5 para 3.
82 GEO No. 52/2016 (note 7) art 54 para 2.
83 Ibid, art 60(b), (c).

8.4.4 Open-end definitions

Given the incredible speed of technological advances and debt collectors' highly innovative abusive practices, a swift reaction from lawmakers is essential. One potential solution is to grant supervisory bodies the prerogative to adopt rules and best-conduct guidelines, as in the US with the adoption of the Dodd-Frank Act of 2010.[84] A similar approach is found in the U.K. with the Consumer Credit Sourcebook issued by the Financial Conduct Authority. Thus, the definitions and practices adopted by the law are constantly reviewed and updated, resulting, at least on paper, in a proactive attitude towards new challenges.

Another solution consists in using functional open-end definitions, which could adapt the existing legal provisions to emerging practices by analogy. Given that lawmakers need time to acknowledge a current problem and search for a remedy, this building block of a functional regulatory regime of debt collection is essential and represents a true challenge for civil law systems.

In this context, GEO No. 52/2016 on consumer credit relating to residential immovable property notably uses broad-spectrum definitions with non-exhaustive examples, for instance, when referring to harassment. Regardless, none of these definitions seem to consider the use of technology – namely the internet, mobile communications, web pages, or social media – in debt collection. Hence, we conclude that general definitions in the dedicated Romanian legislation are deficient, with potentially uncertain and contradictory results, because the law must be interpreted by the courts blindly, without clear guidelines to accompany the judge through the process.

8.4.5 Enforcement via private action

The success of debt collection legislation does not solely depend on identifying the positive and negative obligations of those involved in the procedure but also on the possible sanctions against abusive practices and the available remedies. For instance, the most significant achievement of the U.S. FDCPA and its distinctive feature is that it gives consumers several alternative legal grounds for private action and efficient implementation mechanisms.

U.S. federal law is primarily focused on prosecuting actions that attract civil, administrative, or criminal liability to deter debt collectors from using abusive practices. The FDCPA centers on what is *not allowed* in debt collection and provides the consumer with many individual remedies and incentives to act. In other words, the law compels debt collectors to observe it or pay for non-compliance. This feature is unmatched by other administrative sanctioning systems like those of the U.K. or other European states. For these reasons, we deem enforcement via private action the most efficient enforcement mechanism.

84 The primary functions of the Bureau are issuing rules, orders, and guidance implementing Federal consumer financial law. U.S. Code Title 12, Chapter 53, Subchapter V, Part B, Section 5511, para (c), letter (5).

Civil liability is at the heart of the system created by the FDCPA to protect consumer debtors. Any debt collector resorting to abusive practices can be held accountable, provided that the debtor files a case against them. The U.S. regulator considered that simply compensating the debtor for the damages incurred is insufficient to discourage abusive debt collection practices. Consequently, the U.S. consumer is incentivized to act on their own. Accordingly, debt collectors may have to pay a fine directly to the consumer for every action that breaches the law. Moreover, consumers can file class-action lawsuits, request damages and/or the compensation of legal fees – including representation fees – and can choose to file a case in front of both state and federal courts (or only the most advantageous one).[85]

Except for repairing damages, no other system applicable to debt collection provides a solution similar to the FDCPA concerning civil liability.[86] In other systems, Romania included, civil action follows general procedural norms, with no financial or procedural stimulant encouraging the debtor to take matters into their own hands. On the contrary, in the U.K., the debtor can use an alternative dispute-resolution mechanism through the Financial Ombudsman, but only after trying to resolve the dispute amicably directly with the debt collector. The objective appears to be to relieve courts of futile and expensive lawsuits concerning small claims or matters that could be directly addressed by the parties involved. Regardless, unsatisfied consumers have the right to take matters before a court, a minimal advantage deriving from E.U. legislation. Despite the shortcomings of litigation, it is self-explanatory that the possibility of taking the debt collector to court constitutes a significant hindrance for those who engage in abusive practices.

Romania did not provide for a particular cause of action or civil fines. However, it should be mentioned that the alternatives introduced by the FDCPA in the U.S. are not all essential in the Romanian context. For instance, a consumer debtor would be exempted from paying the judicial fee.[87] Moreover, litigation fees and attorney costs are awarded to the debtor if their claim is upheld.[88]

However, we consider that the introduction of civil fines in favor of the abused consumer debtor would be more efficient in tackling abusive practices. Such remedies are not entirely unfamiliar to Romanian legislation. For instance, in the case of self-help repossession of mortgaged assets,[89] the New Civil Code provides for such fines.[90] Hence, in instances where a creditor breaches the law during self-

85 For a detailed analysis of civil liability and the stimulants used by the FDCPA, see Stănescu (note 10) 267–272.

86 For details, see Stănescu (note 54).

87 OUG Nr. 80/2013 privind taxele judiciare de timbru, (GEO No. 80/2013 regarding judiciary stamp taxes) Official Gazette of Romania 392 (29 June 2013) art 29 para 1(f).

88 New Civil Procedure Code art 453 para 1, art 451 para 1.

89 New Civil Code art 2440.

90 Such sanctions were first introduced in Romanian legislation by Legea 99/1999 privind unele măsuri pentru accelerarea reformei economice, publicată în Monitorul Oficial al României, Partea

help repossession, they must return the asset, cover the damages, and pay the debtor a third of the repossessed asset's value.[91]

Introducing such civil fines in favor of the consumer would deter abusive debt collectors and incentivize debtors to address the courts. This is especially noteworthy as the damage caused is often insignificant compared to the time and cost of litigation, leaving many abusive practices unprosecuted. Furthermore, the introduction of civil fines would ease the burden of proof and the assessment of damages by the courts. Finally, this approach would reduce the number of complaints brought before the supervisory bodies, which could invest their efforts and resources into sanctioning entities that systematically engage in abusive debt collection practices.

8.4.6 Enforcement via state action

Administrative fines are an alternative to individual lawsuits favored by most European states that regulate informal debt collection. However, it should be noted that enforcement via private action and enforcement via state action are not mutually exclusive. Instead, they have converging effects, which is why, in our view, efficient regulation of debt collection should include both mechanisms.

GEO No. 52/2016 on consumer credit relating to residential immovable property presents a generous list of administrative fines and contraventions that the NACP can impose in its capacity as a supervisory body, either *ex officio* or based on prior complaints by aggrieved consumers or organizations representing their interests. Administrative fines could be levied for engaging in prohibited practices (as covered by section 8.4.3), operating without authorization, breaching the terms of the authorization, or violating the complementary sanctions applied. The legal regime for contraventions is covered by GO No. 2/2001.[92] Meanwhile, administrative sanctions such as suspending or revoking the authorization (by order of the NACP President) are covered by Law No. 554/2004.[93]

As evidenced by previous comparative analysis,[94] administrative sanctions are embraced by all legislation applicable to abusive debt collection, becoming an essential element of the regulatory regime. Regardless, their efficiency remains

---

I nr 236/27 mai 1999 (Law No. 99/2019 regarding the acceleration of economic reform) Section VI – Security interests in movable assets, which was inspired by U.S. legislation, namely the Uniform Commercial Code art 9. Radu Rizoiu classifies them as 'damages' awarded to the debtor and rightfully, with great intuition, notes the courts' hesitancy to award them. See Radu Rizoiu, *Garantiile reale imobiliare. O abordare functionala. Analiza economica a dreptului garantiilor reale - Introducere in regimul juridic al ipotecilor mobiliare* (1st edn Universul Juridic 2011) 668–669.

91 New Civil Code art 2474. The version of this remedy in Law No. 99/1999 art 87 was harsher, providing for at least 30% of the value of the guaranteed claim.

92 Ordonanța Nr. 2/2001 privind regimul contravențiilor (G.O. No. 2/2001 regarding the legal regime of contraventions), Official Gazette of Romania No. 410 (25 July 2001).

93 Legea 554/2004 a contenciosului administrative (Law No. 554/2004 regarding administrative law) Official Gazette of Romania No. 1154 (7 December 2004).

94 Stănescu (note 54).

fluctuating and questionable[95] given the limited resources of the NACP and the multitude of activities that need to be covered. Moreover, administrative fines should be constantly updated to preserve their deterrence. Lastly, only judicial practice will prove how effective these measures are should the creditor or debt collector become insolvent.

8.5 Conclusions

This chapter provided a chronological overview of the regulatory projects impacting debt collection in Romania and the currently applicable legislation, that is, GEO No. 52/2016 on consumer credit relating to residential immovable property. Given the numerous regulatory attempts since 2010, we conclude that the Romanian legislator is aware of the problems arising from abusive debt collection practices. On the one hand, this is a positive aspect that requires acknowledgment. On the other hand, because it took almost six years for basic legislation addressing the issue to be adopted, we conclude that the legislative process was a long and treacherous road, which was negatively impacted by numerous failures. While causes vary from the legislator's incapacity to design a viable and functional project to the influence of the financial lobby and (potential) regulatory capture, they all converge into the shortcomings of GEO No. 52/2016 on consumer credit relating to residential immovable property.

Putting the emergency ordinance through the test of our analysis matrix, we conclude that the current legislation features, at least partially, most of the building blocks. GEO No. 52/2016 defines debt collectors, introduces a relatively simple authorization procedure, contains a list of abusive practices, appears to use open-end definitions (but not functional ones), and provides for supervisory mechanisms supported by administrative sanctions.

The adopted solution is decent; however, it could have been much better. Of the building blocks in our analysis matrix, private action is missing. Nevertheless, the feature that undermines the efficiency of GEO No. 52/2016 the most is its starting point because it excludes from its coverage contracts that were ongoing when it entered into force. Another significant constraint is that GEO No. 52/2016 transposes the provisions of Directive 2014/17/EU and, thus, inherits its limitations. Like the directive, GEO No. 52/2016 only applies to credit agreements secured via a mortgage or whose purpose is to acquire or retain property rights for land or an existing or projected building. Significant categories of consumer vulnerability, such as debts relating to overdraft facilities or credit cards and obligations of contracts concluded with service providers, are outside the scope of the

95 Based on the information gathered from the NACP, the numbers of complaints against debt collectors are: 2017 – 359; 2018 – 175; 2019 – 257; 2020 – 258; 2021 – 221. Out of these, the number of complaints solved in favor of the debtor is miniscule: 2017 – 17; 2018 – 29; 2019 – 22; 2020 – 28; 2021 – 12. When discussing the fines applied, the numbers do not inspire confidence in their deterrent effect: three fines of approximately 6,000 euro, one fine of approximately 4,000 euro, one fine of approximately 500 euro, and numerous written notices.

national legislation. Therefore, since the protection offered by GEO No. 52/2016 is available only for specific contracts concluded after its entry into force, many consumer debtors are left out.

Bibliography

Books

Finlay, S., *Consumer Credit Fundamentals* (2nd ed. Palgrave Macmillan, UK 2009)

Rizoiu, R., *Garantiile reale imobiliare. O abordare functionala - Analiza economica a dreptului garantiilor reale - Introducere in regimul juridic al ipotecilor mobiliare* (1st ed. Universul Juridic, Bucharest 2011)

Rosenthal, D., *Consumer Credit Law and Practice - A Guide* (4th ed. Bloomsbury Professional, Great Britain 2013)

Stănescu, C.G., *Self-Help, Private Debt Collection and the Concomitant Risks. A Comparative Law Analysis* (Springer, Switzerland 2015)

TW Bank, *Romania. Diagnostic Review of Consumer Protection and Financial Literacy. Vol II Comparison against Good Practices* (The World Bank, Washington, DC 2009)

Journals

Avram, M., Battlefield Journal: Legislative Decisions and Counter-Decisions with Impact in the Financial and Banking Environment (2019) Romanian Rev Priv L 312

Rizoiu, R., The Light Comes from the West: The Applicability of Government Emergency Ordinance No. 52/2016 to Existing Contracts (2016) Romanian Rev Priv L 161

Stănescu, C.-G., Is the Unfair Commercial Practices Directive Fit to Effectively Tackle Abusive Debt Collection? (2020) Journal of European Consumer and Market Law, vol 9, (6), 235

Stănescu, C.-G., A Critical Assessment of the Need for Harmonization of the Legal Framework Concerning Abusive Informal Debt Collection Practices in the European Union: Is Harmonization Possible and How Can it Best Be Attained? (2021) Journal of Consumer Policy, 44 (4), 531

Stănescu, C.G., Regulation of Abusive Informal Debt Collection Practices in the European Union. An Empirical Account (2021) Journal of Consumer Policy, 44(2), 179

Legislation

Directive 2014/17/EU of the European Parliament and of the Council of 4 February 2014 on credit agreements for consumers relating to residential immovable property and amending Directives 2008/48/EC and 2013/36/EU and Regulation (EU) No 1093/2010 [2014] OJ L 60/34

Consumer Credit Act [1974]

Dodd-Frank Act [2010]

Ordinul Nr.1 din 2017 privind documentația și informațiile necesare înregistrării precum și modalitatea și termenele de raportare pentru enitățile de recuperare de creanțe (Order No. 1/2017 of the NCPA regarding the documents required for licensing and the reporting deadlines for debt collectors), published in the Official Gazette of Romania, No, 33 of 11.01.2017

Ordonanţă de urgenţă 52/2016 privind contractele de credit oferite consumatorilor pentru bunuri imobile, precum şi pentru modificarea şi completarea Ordonanţei de urgenţă a Guvernului nr. 50/2010 privind contractele de credit pentru consumatori (GEO 52/2016 on credit agreements for consumers relating to residential immovable property and amending GEO 50/2010)

Legea 77/2016 privind darea în plată a unor bunuri imobile în vederea stingerii obligaţiilor asumate prin credite (Law No. 77/2016 Datio in Solutum of immovable property to settle debts) published in the Official Gazette of Romania No. 330 of 28.04.2016

OUG nr 80/2013 privind taxele judiciare de timbru, publicată în Monitorul Oficial al României, Partea I, nr 392/29 iunie 2013 (GEO No. 80/2013 regarding judiciary stamp taxes), published in the Official Gazette of Romania No. 392 of 29.06.2013.

Ordonanţă de urgenţă Nr. 50/2010 privind contractele de credit pentru consumatori, (Government Emergency Ordinance - G.E.O. No. 50/2010 on consumer credit) published in the Official Gazette of Romania, No. 389 of 11.06.2011

Legea 363/2007 privind combaterea practicilor incorecte ale comercianţilor în relaţia cu consumatorii şi armonizarea reglementărilor cu legislaţia europeană privind protecţia consumatorilor, publicată în Monitorul Oficial al României, Partea I nr 899/28 decembrie 2017 (Law No. 363/2007 Concerning unfair business-to-consumer practices

Legea 554/2004 a contenciosului administrative a fost publicată în Monitorul Oficial al României, Partea I, nr 1154/07 decembrie 2004 (Law No. 554/2004 regarding administrative law).

Law No. 53/2003, Romanian Labour Code, republished in the Official Gazette of Romania, No. 345 of 18.05. 2011

Ordonanţa Nr. 2/2001 privind regimul contravenţiilor a fost publicată în Monitorul Oficial al României, Partea I, nr 410/25 iulie 2001 (GO No. 2/2001 regarding the legal regime of contraventions).

Case law

Romanian Constitutional Court Decision [2017], No. 62 of 07.02.2017, published in the Official Gazette of Romania, No. 161 of 03.03.2017

Romanian Constitutional Court Decision [2019], No. 140 of 13.03.2019, published in the Official Gazette of Romania, No.377 of 14.05.2019

Romanian Constitutional Court Decision [2021], No. 69 of 28.01.2021, published in the Official Gazette of Romania, No. 492 of 12.05.2021

Scott v. Jones [1992] 964 F.2d 314, 316 (4th Circ.)

Cirkot v. Diversified Systems Inc. [1993] 839. Supp. 941 (D.Conn.).

Heintz v. Jenkins [1995] 514 U.S. 291

Garret v. Derbes [1997] 1110 F. 3d 317 (5th Cir.)

Orenbuch v. North Shore Health Systems Inc. [2003] 250 F. Supp. 2d 145 (e.D.N.Y)

Munoz v. Pipestone [2005] 397 F Supp. 2d 1129, 1133 (D. Minn.)

Scally v. Hilco Receivables [2005] LLC, 392 F. Supp. 2d 1036, N.D. III

9 Regulation of abusive informal debt collection practices in Sweden

Hajo Michael Holtz

This chapter gives an overview of the Swedish regulation of informal debt collection practices. In this context, the term 'informal debt collection practices' means debt recovery practices where the state apparatus is not yet involved, but where the debt is recovered by either the creditor him- or herself or a third party, both as a service provider or a new creditor. Hence, informal debt collection has to be distinguished from 'formal debt collection' where the state apparatus is involved, that is, either general courts (*allmänna domstolar*) or the Swedish Enforcement Authority (*Kronofogdemyndigheten*). Nevertheless, informal debt collection is considered a legal, pre-step of formal debt collection. Sweden represents one of the countries in the European Union where informal debt collection practices are highly regulated by law. This chapter aims to contribute to the question on how informal debt collection practices, in general, may be regulated and whether the Swedish model may serve as an inspiration for European regulation or regulation in other Member states. This chapter is structured in the following way: at first, the background and the scope of the applicable laws are described, including the supervisory authority and competent courts; secondly, the licensing system and requirements are laid out; thirdly and most importantly, this chapter deals with the material rules concerning informal debt collection practices in Sweden, including examples of banned practices; then, the validation of debts and the costs of debt collection are described; and finally, the enforcement mechanisms for good debt collection practices are explained. The chapter concludes with some observations and reflections on the Swedish regulatory model of informal debt collection practices.

9.1 Overview of debt collection regulation in Sweden

9.1.1 Applicable laws

Informal debt collection – and, even formal debt collection – is highly regulated in Sweden by several laws. The primary law covering informal debt collection is the Swedish Debt Recovery Act, henceforth referred to as SDRA.[1] Section 1.1 of

1 Act 1974:182 (*Inkassolagen*). Please observe that the Swedish Authority for Privacy Protection, *Integritetsskyddsmyndigheten*, henceforth referred to as 'IMY,' translates the Swedish term

DOI: 10.4324/9781003343158-10

the SDRA defines the term 'debt collection measure' as meaning every measure that involves some pressure on the debtor other than an indication of the time for payment or an indication that the claim, if not paid, will be handed over to someone else for debt collection.[2] Consequently, mere payment reminders by creditors are not considered to be a debt collection measure, are not part of the debt collection process, and are not subject to the SDRA. Payment reminders constitute a preliminary stage of the debt collection process in Sweden. However, payment reminders are covered indirectly by informal debt collection; namely, the costs for payment reminders are usually part of the debt that shall be recovered. There exists administrative practice and case law on the issue of costs for payment reminders.[3] At the same time, actual measures or actions such as suspending the provision of a service, terminating an agreement or filing for bankruptcy are generally not considered a debt collection measure either. Threatening the debtor with such measures to recover a debt falls within the scope of the SDRA.[4] Most other actions taken by the creditor or a commissioned third party to pressurize the debtor with the aim of payment may therefore be considered debt collection measures. Consequently, the threshold for actions falling within the scope of the law is relatively low.

Besides the definition of the term 'debt collection measure,' s 1 of the SDRA stipulates the material scope of the law. Accordingly, the SDRA applies to collecting one's own or someone else's claims through formal debt collection letters (*inkassokrav*) or other debt collection measures. According to s 1.1, the SDRA applies in the following cases:

a) A business collecting own claims (so-called self-collection);
b) Debt collection using debt collection agencies;
c) Debt collection through banks, lawyers, and other actors under the supervision of a supervisory authority other than the Swedish Authority for Privacy Protection; and
d) Debt collection by other means if the claim has arisen in a business or has been transferred for recovery (e.g. factoring).

It has to be observed that the SDRA applies even if no license for the debt collection activities is required.[5] Similarly, it can be noted that in case (d), the SDRA even

'*inkasso*' to 'debt recovery,' whereas in this chapter, the term 'debt collection' is preferably used. The terms are considered synonyms.

2 The type and level of 'pressure' that is allowed by law will be described in the main section of this chapter, see section 9.3 below. In short, debt collection in Sweden is primarily about demanding payment in the form of a formal debt collection letter in combination with the threat of further legal processing of the claim.

3 See more below, section 9.3.2.

4 IMY, *Tillämpning av inkassolagen – allmänna råd* (General Guidelines of the Swedish Authority for Privacy Protection on the Application of the SDRA, 2011) at p. 11. See further concerning filing for bankruptcy Högsta domstolen (Swedish Supreme Court) judgment 9 October 1990 in case T30-90, referred to as NJA 1990 p. 585.

5 See more below, section 9.2.

applies if the debt collection as such is not being conducted as a business activity, e.g. by private individuals.[6] The SDRA applies to debt collection measures taken by foreign creditors against debtors located in Sweden and debt collection businesses situated in Sweden but directly targeting foreign debtors in other countries.[7] At the same time, the SDRA does not apply to private individuals collecting own, non-business related claims; private individuals collecting non-business related claims of relatives; and estates collecting own, non-business related claims.[8] In addition, providing simple assistance in connection with debt collection activities, e.g. offering forms, drafts, or printing, is not covered by the SDRA either.[9]

An interesting question is whether the SDRA applies to the Swedish state and the recovery of state-owned claims. The law explicitly does not apply to the Swedish Enforcement Authority.[10] *Argumentum e contrario*, the act applies to all other governmental authorities and agencies, e.g. the Swedish Tax Authority (*Skatteverket*), when conducting debt collection measures against debtors. This also follows from other special regulations.[11] The Swedish Legal, Financial and Administrative Services Agency (*Kammarkollegiet*) even receives assignments as a debt collection service provider for other governmental agencies and authorities.

Besides the Swedish Debt Recovery Act, there exist some other relevant laws and regulations that apply to informal debt collection. These are mainly the Debt Recovery Ordinance,[12] the Act on Debt Collection Costs,[13] Binding Rules of the Swedish Authority for Privacy Protection,[14] as well as General Guidelines of the Swedish Authority for Privacy Protection on the Application of the SDRA.[15] The latter document plays a central role in interpreting the material rules in the SDRA. Formally, these General Guidelines constitute non-binding soft law. Nevertheless, it seems that, in practice, debt collectors have no real choice other than to follow these recommendations by the competent supervisory authority.[16] Even administrative practice of the supervisory authority and case law of the competent courts serve as important sources of law regarding informal debt collection in Sweden.

In addition, numerous other Swedish laws and regulations exist that either apply indirectly to informal debt collection or if informal debt collection turns

6 Proposition 1974:42 (governmental proposition of the SDRA), at p. 14.
7 Ekelund, *Inkasso – Regelverket och marknaden* (Avthentes 2000), at p. 14.
8 See s 1.2 of the SDRA, where also the term 'relatives' is defined.
9 IMY, *Tillämpning av inkassolagen – allmänna råd* (2011), at p. 10.
10 According to s 1.3 of the SDRA.
11 See Ordinance on Handling of Governmental Claims 1993:1138, ss 10–12, as well as Administrative Rules KAMFS 2006:1 by the Legal, Financial and Administrative Services Agency (*Kammarkollegiet*).
12 Ordinance 1981:956 (*Inkassoförordningen*).
13 Act 1981:739 (*Lag om ersättning för inkassokostnader m.m.*).
14 DIFS 2011:1 (*Föreskrifter om tillstånd enligt 2 § inkassolagen*).
15 IMY, *Tillämpning av inkassolagen – allmänna råd* (2010).
16 See Förvaltningsrätten i Stockholm (Administrative Court in Stockholm) judgment 16 May 2013 in case 10125-12.

into a formal debt collection process. Some of those laws and regulations include the Swedish Act on Interest Payments,[17] the Swedish Act on Payment Orders and Enforcement[18] or the Swedish Code of Judicial Procedure,[19] to name a few.

9.1.2 Competent supervisory authority and courts

As already mentioned above, the competent supervisory authority for informal debt collection is the Swedish Authority for Privacy Protection (*Integritetsskyddsmyndigheten*), henceforth referred to as 'IMY,' which, amongst other areas, is also responsible for oversight of the General Data Protection Regulation (GDPR) in Sweden. Besides the Swedish Authority for Privacy Protection, two other supervisory authorities may be competent in relation to informal debt collection issues, namely the Swedish Financial Supervisory Authority (*Finansinspektionen*) and the Swedish Bar Association (*Sveriges advokatsamfund*) concerning debt collection by banks, other financial market actors and fully qualified lawyers. Even the Swedish Consumer Agency (*Konsumentverket*) may be competent, however, only with regards to consumer credit legislation if the debt being collected originates from a consumer credit contract. The Swedish legislator selected the Swedish Authority for Privacy Protection as a supervisory authority since informal debt collection is not only about protecting consumers and the law is also applicable in B2B-relationships; another reason is the proximity of debt collection to credit information.[20] The Swedish Authority for Privacy Protection is similarly the competent supervisory authority for the Swedish Credit Information Act.

Regarding the court system in Sweden, it is mainly administrative courts (*Förvaltningsrätt, Kammarrätt, Högsta förvaltningsdomstolen*) that are dealing with laws and regulations on informal debt collection, since they are competent for appeals against decisions by the Swedish Authority for Privacy Protection as well as the Swedish Financial Supervisory Authority. Nevertheless, general courts (*Tingsrätt, Hovrätt, Högsta domstolen*) also play a role in this field when it comes to the debt that is being collected in case it is contested by the debtor, as well as regarding criminal sanctions or damages due to a breach of good debt collection practices.[21] Other than that, the Swedish Patent- and Market Courts (*Patent- och marknadsdomstolen, Patent- och marknadsöverdomstolen*) can be named as special courts for intellectual property law and market law disputes. These courts are competent concerning unfair commercial practices, consumer protection as well as consumer credit.[22] Swedish case law is, therefore, relatively

17 Act 1975:635 (*Räntelagen*).
18 Act 1990:746 (*Lag om betalningsföreläggande och handräckning*).
19 Code 1942:740 (*Rättegångsbalken*).
20 Proposition 1974:42, at p. 31.
21 See more below, section 9.5.
22 The Swedish Patent and Market Courts may deal with debt collection issues indirectly, for instance with regards to late payment fees in general contract terms. See for example Patent- och marknadsdomstolen (Patent and Market Court) judgment 21 October 2021 in case PMT 9984-20.

scattered. In general, the amount of court decisions, especially of the higher courts and regarding the interpretation of the central concept of good debt collection practices, appears to be limited.[23]

9.1.3 Debt collection in Sweden

Below is an overview of the different stages of the debt collection process in Sweden concerning informal and formal debt collection. Please observe that the creditor is typically entitled to compensation for costs of informal debt collection only with regards to one single payment reminder, one single debt collection letter, and, where applicable, an instalment plan.[24]

- Contract
- Invoice
- Payment reminder
- Informal debt collection measures
  - Debt collection letter
  - Other written communication, e.g. email
  - Communication via telephone
  - Other forms of contact (visits)
  - Other kinds of measures, e.g. threat of filing for bankruptcy
  - Instalment plan
- Formal debt collection
  - Swedish Enforcement Authority (undisputed claims)
  - Court of law (disputed claims)
- Enforcement of payment order, judgment or other execution titles by the Swedish Enforcement Authority

9.2 Licensing system and requirements

The starting point for the Swedish licensing system is that all debt collection operations that relate to the collection of claims on behalf of someone else or claims that have been transferred for collection may only be conducted with the permission (license) of the Swedish Authority for Privacy Protection.[25] Consequently, the licensing requirement applies to classical debt collection agencies and cases in which claims are sold and formally transferred to a new creditor for collection. However, there exist several important exceptions to

23 Cf. Karlsson-Tuula, *Inkassolag (1974:182)*, 4 §, nr. 8, Karnov (Juno), accessed 17 September 2021. Under an earlier version of the SDRA, appeals against decisions by the Swedish Authority for Privacy Protection were restricted.

24 See more regarding compensation for costs below, section 9.4. Formal debt collection and the process of enforcement have their own rules on costs and compensation which are not dealt with in this context.

25 According to s 2.1 of the SDRA.

this rule. The main rationale behind most exceptions is to avoid unnecessary bureaucracy.[26] A debt collection license is not required under the following circumstances:[27]

a) Self-collection that is, businesses recovering own business-related claims;
b) Operations under the supervision of the Swedish Financial Supervisory Authority;[28]
c) Debt collection conducted by fully qualified lawyers;[29]
d) Debt collection within a group of companies for group-internal claims;
e) Debt collection by non-profit organizations on behalf of their members;
f) Debt collection by municipalities on behalf of companies owned by municipalities or debt collection by companies owned by municipalities on behalf of municipalities or other companies owned by municipalities.[30]

Regarding the license requirements, a license may only be granted if the business can be assumed to be conducted in a competent (*sakkunnigt*) and prudent manner (*omdömesgillt*).[31] These requirements may be described as a sort of 'worthiness test.' The requirements of competence and prudence have to be met by a natural person who shall be in charge of the debt collection activities, i.e. the CEO, a corporate legal counsel or some other employee who will oversee the activities.[32] According to the official application form, documentation has to be handed in concerning: (a) the responsible person's theoretical education and professional experience in debt collection activities; (b) certificates proving that he or she has not been subject to personal insolvencies; (c) whether he or she has debts with the Swedish Enforcement Authority; or (d) whether he or she is banned from certain professions. A license may be issued for a maximum period of ten years.[33] In

26 Ekelund, *Inkasso – Regelverket och marknaden* (Avthentes 2000), at p. 17.
27 According to ss 2.2 and 2.3 of the SDRA as well as s 1 of the Binding Rules DIFS 2011:1.
28 This applies to banks, other credit market operators, as well as insurance companies. With regards to factoring companies, the license requirement applies only if the company is not already considered a credit market operator under the supervision of the Swedish Financial Supervisory Authority. Please observe that, in some cases, companies may have to register with the Swedish Financial Supervisory Authority without being subject to its supervision. In such cases, the licensing requirement according to the SDRA may apply.
29 However, lawyers may have the right to apply for a license; see Kammarrätten i Stockholm (Administrative Court of Appeal in Stockholm) judgment 3 April 2018 in case 7539-17. A license may come along with benefits, such as access to a database at the Swedish Enforcement Authority. Lawyers, however, do not appear to be the most active actors in the debt collection sector in Sweden.
30 For example, local energy companies.
31 According to s 3.1 of the SDRA.
32 See for detailed information IMY, <https://www.imy.se/verksamhet/inkasso/ansok-om-inkassotillstand/> accessed 2 December 2021.
33 According to s 3.2 of the SDRA.

practice, it appears that licenses are issued for a period not exceeding five years, in some cases even for shorter periods.[34]

9.3 Banned informal debt collection practices

9.3.1 General rules in the SDRA

The core of the Swedish regulation of informal debt collection measures constitutes ss 4–8 of the Swedish Debt Recovery Act, containing material rules on debt collection activities. The general clause in s 4 of the SDRA is one of the most essential rules on debt collection practices. It stipulates that all debt collection operations must be conducted following good debt collection practices (*god inkassosed, sed* meaning custom). The term 'good debt collection practices' in the debt collection sector in Sweden may be compared to the general term 'professional diligence' as referred to in art 2(h) in the Unfair Commercial Practices Directive 2005/29/EC (UCPD), although there is no direct connection between the two concepts. Section 4 of the SDRA further states that, in doing so, the debtor shall specifically not be caused unnecessary damage or inconvenience or be subjected to undue pressure or other improper debt collection measures. The term 'good practices' is then specified in the following sections in the SDRA as well as in case law.[35] The primary source for interpretation is the administrative practice of the Swedish Authority for Privacy Protection.[36]

Section 5 of the SDRA regulates the formal requirements of a debt collection letter: a letter of demand in combination with information that the claim has been handed over to a debt collection agency or is processed for self-collection. Accordingly, formal debt collection letters must be made in writing and must contain certain mandatory information. Among other things, the debt collection letter has to separately specify the different parts of the claim: the principal, the interest, and the costs for the debt collection procedure. The latter part does not contain reminder fees, invoice fees, or other administrative fees unrelated to the debt collection process. Thus, the SDRA does not require separately denoting such fees in the debt collection letter.[37] It is further required that the debtor is given reasonable time to voluntarily pay.[38] According to administrative practice, deadlines should not be less than eight days from the date when the letter was sent, so that the debtor at least has four days to make the payment from the date when the letter has been received.[39] The requirement that letters have to be sent 'in writ-

34 Karlsson-Tuula, *Inkassolag (1974:182)*, 3 §, nr. 7, Karnov (Juno), accessed 17 September 2021.

35 See more below, section 9.3.2.

36 See for example IMY, *Tillämpning av inkassolagen – allmänna råd* (2011).

37 See Kammarrätten i Stockholm (Administrative Court of Appeal in Stockholm) judgment 30 March 2015 in case 4369-15.

38 According to s 5.3 of the SDRA.

39 IMY, *Tillämpning av inkassolagen – allmänna råd* (2011), at p. 26. In addition, no other debt collection measures should be taken at least for four days after the deadline for payment has expired, see ibid.

ing' does not prohibit digital debt collection letters *per se*. However, the Swedish Authority for Privacy Protection may only accept digital letters that have been sent via a digital mailbox provider for official letters (such as *Kivra* in Sweden), not via regular email providers, if the debtor has voluntarily joined such a service and has not objected to such letters.[40] Sections 6 and 7 of the SDRA concern legal action within the meaning of formal debt collection measures in connection with the claim. Such legal action may not be taken until the debtor has received a formal debt collection letter according to s 5 unless it is evident that the debtor is unwilling to pay the debt or special reasons justify a different approach.[41]

A practically important provision constitutes s 8 in the SDRA, which regulates the debt collector's duty to investigate the claim. Before taking measures, the debt collection agency must investigate whether probable reasons exist that the claim may not be legally justified. This obligation does not amount to conducting a comprehensive investigation.[42] However, the debt collection agency must not purely rely on guarantees or other kinds of assurances by the creditor.[43] Typical examples of probable reasons are statutory limitation or invalid contracts.[44] Another example of probable reasons is when the creditor already makes claims that are obviously not covered by the contract between the creditor and the debtor, such as default interest rates.[45] Probable reasons may arise from the information presented by the creditor, from other information as part of the investigation by the debt collection agency, or from objections raised by the debtor. As can be understood from s 5.3 in combination with s 8 in the SDRA, the debtor has a legal right to raise objections against the claim. The debt collection agency has a corresponding duty to investigate whether an objection is based on legitimate reasons or not. Such reasons for an objection by the debtor may be fraud, breach of contract, payment, or other kinds of wrongdoing on the part of the creditor, on the other hand, not the mere inability to pay.[46] If legitimate reasons for the non-payment are probable (not proven), then, further debt collection measures should not be taken, and the claim has to be materially investigated and assessed in a general court of law. A particular category in this context concerns cases where the debtor is a

40 IMY, <https://www.imy.se/verksamhet/inkasso/digitala-inkassokrav/> accessed 2 December 2021. The problem with regular email is that there does not exist an official register and, thus, email addresses cannot be equated with physical addresses. See further IMY, decisions in cases DI-2019-11314 and DI-2019-5660.

41 Examples where s 7 in the SDRA may be applied are recurring claims such as regarding payment for rent or subscriptions. In such cases, legal action may be taken for the latest monthly payment even if no letter has been sent for this specific payment, see IMY, *Tillämpning av inkassolagen – allmänna råd* (2011), at p. 29.

42 Karlsson-Tuula, *Inkassolag (1974:182)*, 8 §, nr. 14, Karnov (Juno), accessed 17 September 2021.

43 IMY, *Tillämpning av inkassolagen – allmänna råd* (2011), at p. 19.

44 IMY, *Tillämpning av inkassolagen – allmänna råd* (2011), at p. 18.

45 Karlsson-Tuula, *Inkassolag (1974:182)*, 8 §, nr. 14, Karnov (Juno), accessed 17 September 2021.

46 IMY, *Tillämpning av inkassolagen – allmänna råd* (2011), at p. 37.

minor (under 18). In such cases, it is presumed that the claim is unjustified if not confirmed otherwise.[47]

9.3.2 Examples of measures contrary to 'good practices'

It is impossible for the law to specify all potential types of pressure that creditors or debt collectors may use to recover debts in advance.[48] The following examples are therefore not exhaustive. The primary source for the specification of good debt collection practices, and therefore examples, is the administrative practice of the Swedish Authority for Privacy Protection (IMY) and its General Guidelines on the Application of the SDRA from 2011. To begin with, and unsurprisingly, it is contrary to good practices to conduct debt collection measures concerning claims that are not yet due.[49] In the same way, as already discussed above, it is against good practices to threaten with debt collection measures or legal action via the Swedish Enforcement Authority when probable reasons point to the fact that the claim may not be justified, e.g. due to legitimate objections by the debtor.[50]

Another question that regularly comes up in case law and administrative practice is the costs for payment reminders. Although such reminders are not directly covered by the SDRA, claiming fees for payment reminders as part of the principal claim is.[51] Examples of practices contrary to professional diligence in connection with payment reminders are: (a) claiming fees for a reminder without a corresponding contractual right; (b) claiming fees for more than one payment reminder; (c) falsely calling a formal debt collection letter a 'reminder'; or (d) falsely claim that a reminder fee is 'statutory' when, in fact, it is contractual.[52]

An additional example of an unfair debt collection practice is to take legal action when the debtor has not received the formal debt collection letter due to a mistake by the creditor or the debt collection agency.[53] This may be the case if the debt collection letter has been addressed wrongfully, either sent to the wrong

47 See IMY, decision in case 1891-2014. According to Chapter 9 of the Swedish Parental Code 1949:381, minors can, as a basic rule, not take on any debt by themselves.

48 Ekelund, *Inkasso – Regelverket och marknaden* (Avthentes 2000), at p. 23.

49 IMY, *Tillämpning av inkassolagen – allmänna råd* (2011), at p. 15.

50 IMY, *Tillämpning av inkassolagen – allmänna råd* (2011), at p. 19 and 37. It is also forbidden to accept objections by the debtor only in writing, see IMY, *Tillämpning av inkassolagen – allmänna råd* (2011), at p. 23. In a current case from 2022, IMY stated that threatening with an entry in the debt information registry is, as well, against good practices if the requirements for such an entry are not met, see IMY, decision in case IMY-2022-1292.

51 Reminder fees are covered by s 2 of the Act on Debt Collection Costs.

52 See IMY, *Tillämpning av inkassolagen – allmänna råd* (2011), at pp. 15–18. See also for reminder fees Svea hovrätt (Court of Appeals in Stockholm) judgment 10 April 1997 in case FT1659-96, referred to as RH 1997:41. More than one payment reminder may be sent but not associated with costs. There does not exist a strict obligation to send a payment reminder, however, unless the debt concerns penalty fees for illegal parking. In that case, Act 1984:318 requires a prior payment reminder.

53 See ss 5 and 6 of the SDRA.

address, wrong debtor or otherwise wrongfully addressed due to incomplete information about the debtor's identity.[54] To correctly identify the debtor may also be relevant in cases where minors are involved in a debt collection process. In such cases, the debt collection agency needs to investigate whether the debtor is the child or rather the parents; either way, debt collection letters should always be addressed to the parents.[55]

Other classical examples of measures contrary to good practices or professional diligence concern the fees for debt collection letters. Fees may not be claimed for debt collection letters that do not meet the formal requirements set out in the SDRA.[56] According to administrative practice, fees for debt collection letters may not be claimed: (a) if payment has already been made before the letter was sent; (b) if the debtor did not have the actual possibility to pay the debt after a payment reminder was sent; or (c) for more than one debt collection letter.[57] It is also considered contrary to good practices to send different debt collection letters from the same creditor for different claims against the same debtor, separately, without justification, just to induce costs.[58]

Following from s 4 of the SDRA, debt collection measures shall not cause the debtor unnecessary inconvenience. For that reason, personal visits at home or at work by debt collection agents are strictly forbidden unless the debtor explicitly consented to such visits.[59] Contact via telephone may be permissible, but only if the debtor did not object to being contacted in this way, only after the payment period in the debt collection letter has expired and in any way not after 9 p.m.[60] Similarly, regarding certain types of claims from long-term contracts, mainly electricity, telephone, and internet, threatening to cut off the service may be against good debt collection practices if the requirements for cutting-off such services are not met.[61] It can also be argued that claiming costs for debt collection measures can cause the debtor unnecessary inconvenience if the costs are

54 IMY, *Tillämpning av inkassolagen – allmänna råd* (2011), at p. 17. Consequently, the creditor has the obligation to correctly identify the debtor.

55 IMY, *Tillämpning av inkassolagen – allmänna råd* (2011), at p. 28.

56 According to s 3 of the Act on Debt Collection Costs and s 5 of the SDRA.

57 IMY, *Tillämpning av inkassolagen – allmänna råd* (2011), at pp. 27–29. As a basic rule, fees may be claimed if the debt collection letter was sent, at the latest, the same day when the payment was credited. Two debt collection letters may be sent for recurring claims such as regarding payment for rent or subscriptions. In other cases, more than one debt collection letter may be sent but not associated with costs.

58 See Förvaltningsrätten i Stockholm (Administrative Court in Stockholm) judgment 16 May 2013 in case nr. 10125-12.

59 IMY, *Tillämpning av inkassolagen – allmänna råd* (2011), at p. 31.

60 IMY, *Tillämpning av inkassolagen – allmänna råd* (2011), at p. 32.

61 There exist special rules in Sweden on when certain services may be cut off, see e.g. Chapter 11 of the Swedish Act on Electricity 1997:857, which *inter alia* requires a substantial breach of contract, a notice period of three weeks and a notification to the competent municipality. See concerning electronic communication services Chapter 5, s 19 in the Swedish Act on Electronic Communication 2003:389 and concerning rental contracts Chapter 12 of the Swedish Code on Land Law 1970:994.

unproportionate to the capital claim (*de minimis* claims).[62] Another example of an unfair debt collection practice is conducting debt collection measures when the debtor has entered into an instalment plan as long as the instalment plan is valid.[63]

9.3.3 Some further sections in the SDRA

The Swedish Debt Recovery Act contains some other sections on debt collection activities that are worth mentioning. These include s 9, which stipulates that payments made by the debtor to the debt collector are valid against the creditor. Consequently, it does not matter for the debtor if he or she makes payments to the debt collector or the creditor, as long as the claim was not legally transferred to a new creditor (e.g. factoring), and it is up to the debt collector to have routines in place to be notified if payments are being made to the creditor.[64] Other provisions in the SDRA are s 10 on the management of funds (*inter alia*, funds that have been collected on behalf of others must be kept separate), s 10(a) on the sale of a debt collection agency's registry of debtors (requires consent by the Swedish Authority for Privacy Protection) and s 11, which regulates a duty of confidentiality in debt collection activities.

9.4 Validation of debts and costs of debt collection

With regards to the question whether national law provides for an obligation of the creditor/debt collector to verify if the debt is accurate and, concurrently, if the debtor has the right to challenge the existence and the amount of the debt, the answer from a Swedish perspective is affirmative. As shown above, the debt validation is part of the debt collection procedure according to s 8 of the SDRA and the legal duty to investigate the claim. Should probable reasons indicate that the claim may not be legally justified, debt collection measures should not be taken.[65] Such probable reasons may arise from information already presented by the creditor, from other information as part of the investigation (e.g. claims against minors) or from objections by the debtor. As long as the investigation is ongoing, the debt collection agency should not take any further debt collection measures.[66] In other words, the debt collection process can be considered suspended during the validation/challenge. If the investigation shows that

62 See Ekelund, *Inkasso – Regelverket och marknaden* (Avthentes 2000), at p. 29. However, there does not exist case law or administrative practice on this question. The legal situation concerning such claims must, therefore, be considered unclear.

63 IMY, *Tillämpning av inkassolagen – allmänna råd* (2011), at p. 34.

64 See Swedish Debt Collection Board (*Inkassonämnden*), decision in case 191-2020, <https://svenskinkasso.se/ansokan-om-forelaggande-avseende-fordran/> accessed 2 December 2021.

65 Formally, s 8 of the SDRA is constructed as a recommendation ('should'); see Högsta förvaltningsdomstolen (Swedish Administrative Supreme Court), judgment 6 April 1992 in case 886-1991, referred to as RÅ 1992 ref. 38. Nevertheless, the duty to investigate is considered by the Swedish Authority for Privacy Protection as part of good practices in the debt collection sector.

66 IMY, *Tillämpning av inkassolagen – allmänna råd* (2011), at p. 19.

probable reasons are present, a civil lawsuit must be filed in a general court of law if the creditor wishes to uphold the claim against the debtor. The debtor, consequently, has not only the right to object but, in doing so with legitimate reasons, he or she also has the power to end the informal debt collection process.

Even the costs of informal debt collection are strictly regulated by law in Sweden.[67] Accordingly, the creditor is eligible for compensation of the following costs in connection with informal debt collection procedures:

- The creditor is eligible for the costs of one payment reminder, at most 60 SEK, see s 4 of the Act on Debt Collection Costs, provided that the parties have agreed on a reminder fee, see s 2 of the Act on Debt Collection Costs;
- The creditor is eligible for costs of one debt collection letter, at most 180 SEK, see s 4 of the Act on Debt Collection Costs, provided that the debt collection letter meets the legal requirements, see s 3 of the Act on Debt Collection Costs;
- The creditor may be eligible for the costs of an instalment plan, at most 170 SEK, see s 4 of the Act on Debt Collection Costs, provided that the instalment plan meets the requirements in s 3 of the Act on Debt Collection Costs; extra reasonable costs for notification and accounting in connection with an instalment plan may be reimbursable, if the parties have agreed on such costs;[68]
- Alternatively, in B2B relationships, the creditor may be eligible for 450 SEK delay compensation, see ss 4(a) and 5 of the Act on Debt Collection Costs (according to late payment Directive 2011/7/EU);[69]
- The creditor is eligible for payment of default interest which is either 8% per annum, or the contractually agreed amount.[70]

These costs for the informal debt collection procedure, although not directly connected to the actual costs, appear to be reasonable and not placing a to high cost burden on the debtor. At the same time, the amount stipulated by law may probably not create an incentive for payment either. The reason is that, according to the administrative practice of the supervisory authority, these costs can normally only be claimed once. Whether creditors or debt collection actors may abuse the regulatory system by inflating the debt through costs is not known in this context and would require further research.[71]

67 According to s 12 of the SDRA in combination with the Swedish Act on Debt Collection Costs.

68 IMY, *Tillämpning av inkassolagen – allmänna råd* (2011), at p. 36.

69 Directive 2011/7/EU on Combating Late Payment in Commercial Transactions may serve as a starting point for E.U. regulation concerning the collection of consumer debts.

70 See s 6 of the Swedish Act on Interest Payments. The default interest rate is formally the general reference interest rate plus eight percentage points. However, the general reference rate in Sweden is 0% at the time of writing. According to s 19(a) of the Act on Consumer Credit 2010:1846, the contractual default interest rate regarding consumer credit agreements shall not exceed the general reference interest rate plus 40 percentage points per annum. In other cases, contractual default interest rates must be reasonable according to s 36 of the Swedish Act on Contracts 1915:218.

71 See for some critical reflections below, section 9.6.2. It cannot be excluded that debtors, in breach of good debt collection practices, are charged several times for the costs of informal debt collection. As long as the debtor does not object, these cases will not become known to the public.

9.5 Enforcement mechanisms

The enforcement of good debt collection practices in Sweden consists of administrative, criminal, civil, and even ethical mechanisms. First and foremost, the responsibility for enforcing good debt collection practices lies with the supervisory authority, the Swedish Authority for Privacy Protection, through general oversight.[72] The Swedish Authority for Privacy Protection has the right to inspect debt collection businesses, to get access to documentation and request other information from businesses; the authority's requests may be combined with the threat of a fine in case of non-compliance.[73] Moreover, the supervisory authority may issue rules on how the debt collection activities are to be conducted that may be combined with the threat of a fine in case of non-compliance.[74] The Swedish Authority for Privacy Protection may even revoke the debt collection license if a business does not correct its behaviour or if, otherwise, the requirements for a license are no longer present.[75] Debtors have the possibility to file complaints with the Swedish Authority for Privacy Protection concerning good debt collection practices. However, the authority is not taking a stance on questions about the legality of claims or costs in individual cases.[76] According to their annual report for 2020, the Swedish supervisory authority has during the year processed 271 complaints relating to debt collection, started two supervisory cases as a consequence of complaints, and concluded three supervisory cases that were initated earlier.[77]

Besides administrative remedies, certain behaviour is even criminalized as part of the enforcement mechanism. Those who are guilty by intent or through negligence of the following conduct may be sentenced to a fine or jail for a maximum of one year, namely: (a) conducting debt collection without a license; (b) violating the duty to report changes of facts relevant for the business; (c) violating the duty to apply for consent if a register may be sold; or (d) providing false information in supervisory cases.[78] For example, in a case from 2006, two men were sentenced to a fine in the amount of 16,000 SEK and 12,000 SEK respectively for showing up at a debtor's combined home and workplace to collect a debt without having a debt collection license.[79]

72 According to s 13 of the SDRA.

73 According to s 14 of the SDRA.

74 According to s 15.1 of the SDRA. See for example Högsta förvaltningsdomstolen (Swedish Administrative Supreme Court) judgment 6 April 1992 in case 886-1991, referred to as RÅ 1992 ref. 38.

75 According to s 15.2 of the SDRA.

76 IMY, <https://www.imy.se/privatperson/utfora-arenden/klagomal-om-inkasso/> accessed 2 December 2021.

77 See IMY, Annual Report 2020 <https://www.imy.se/globalassets/dokument/arsredovisningar/imy-arsredovisning-2020.pdf>, p. 62, accessed 2 December 2021.

78 According to s 17 of the SDRA.

79 See Svea hovrätt (Court of Appeals in Stockholm) judgment 23 October 2006 in case B9210-05, referred to as RH 2007:70.

In addition to the administrative and criminal legal consequences of conduct in breach of the rules and regulations concerning informal debt collection, the law provides for a right of the debtor to claim damages (civil litigation). The person who carries out debt collection activities shall compensate the debtor for any inflicted damage resulting from undue pressure or other improper debt collection measures.[80] The right to claim damages includes pecuniary as well as non-pecuniary damage for suffering and the like. In a 1985 case, a company that was wrongfully considered a debtor of a claim, which was sued in court and, consequently, received an entry in the debt information registry, was awarded 30,000 SEK in damages for lost profits and their efforts in connection with defending the claim.[81] However, the Swedish Supreme Court ruled in that case that companies are not eligible for non-pecuniary damages for suffering and the like. In contrast, the natural person who was subject to a debt collection attempt without a license in the case mentioned above from 2006 was awarded damages for suffering in the amount of 7,000 SEK.[82]

Lastly, ethical self-regulation exists, which is quite common in Sweden, even in other sectors of the economy.[83] Swedish debt collection stakeholders have formed the Swedish Association of Debt Collection Agencies (*Svensk inkasso*), which in turn has set up a debt collection board that takes care of complaints and decides whether professional diligence has been followed or not (*Inkassonämnden*). Nevertheless, the debt collection board has no authority to make any legally binding decisions, e.g. award damages or take other kinds of actions. It appears that the debt collection board processes about 25 cases per year that lead to a decision.[84] Another side of ethical self-regulation represents internal procedures for handling complaints by debtors. According to the Swedish Authority for Privacy Protection, 'good debt collection practice' requires debt collection agencies to implement routines for handling complaints by debtors as well as a complaint policy as part of their governance.[85]

In summary, the central part of the enforcement of professional diligence in debt collection activities in Sweden constitutes the administrative oversight by the supervisory authority, the Swedish Authority for Privacy Protection. It can be assumed that the potential threat of revocation of the debt collection license functions as a deterrent in many cases. It can be assumed that the possibility of filing complaints with the supervisory, too, is vital for creditors – complaints can

80 According to s 18 of the SDRA.

81 See Högsta domstolen (Swedish Supreme Court) judgment 19 February 1985 in case T303-83, referred to as NJA 1985 p. 143.

82 See Svea hovrätt (Court of Appeals in Stockholm) judgment 23 October 2006 in case B9210-05, referred to as RH 2007:70.

83 An example is the Swedish advertising industry, which has set up a self-regulatory organisation in the form of the Swedish Advertising Ombudsman (*Reklamombudsmannen*).

84 See Swedish Association of Debt Collection Agencies <https://svenskinkasso.se/category/inkassonamnden/> accessed 2 December 2021.

85 IMY, *Tillämpning av inkassolagen – allmänna råd* (2011), at p. 48.

quickly be filed via an online form. The number of complaint errands that are being processed every year by the supervisory authority could indicate the relevance of the complaint mechanism. Even complaints with the industry organization, *Svensk inkasso*, based on business ethics, may, to some extent, function as a way of enforcing professional diligence in the debt collection sector. In contrast, it appears that criminal charges and civil litigation are only filed in severe cases of misconduct or damage.

9.6 Some observations and reflections

9.6.1 Relationship between debt collection and commercial practices

As already mentioned, it can be noted that there exists some overlap between rules and regulations relating to debt collection practices and commercial practices in general. One interface in this regard is the common concept of good practices or professional diligence, which functions as a general clause in both areas. One difference, however, may be that good practices in the debt collection sector are, at least in Sweden, mainly defined and interpreted by the competent supervisory authority, in contrast to commercial practices in general, where ethical self-regulation (*inter alia*, by means of the International Chamber of Commerce) and the competent courts play a slightly more important role than the supervisory authority (the Swedish Consumer Agency) in defining standards of behaviour.

Although there might exist an overlap between debt collection law and the law on unfair commercial practices, including consumer protection law, the UCPD is not applied to unfair debt collection practices in Sweden, at least as far as can be assessed in this context.[86] The main reason is most likely the fact that unfair debt collection practices already are regulated by sectorspecific legislation. Another explanation might be the choice of the supervisory authority and the choice of the competent courts. Decisions by The Swedish Authority for Privacy Protection are appealed in Administrative courts, not in the Swedish Patent and Market Courts, which are responsible for commercial practices, including consumer protection. At the same time, the Swedish Consumer Agency, which is responsible for overseeing unfair commercial practices harming consumers' economic interests, has no direct competency in debt collection matters. Nevertheless, it does not appear implausible to argue that debt collection practices may fall within the scope of the UCPD as some kind of after-sales commercial practice.[87] In that case, one may ask the interesting question of whether an infringement of good debt collection

86 This is confirmed by Stănescu, *Regulation of Abusive Debt Collection Practices in the EU Member States: An Empirical Account*. Journal of Consumer Policy 44, pp. 179–216 (2021), at p. 188.

87 This view appears to be supported by the European Commission's Guidance On The Implementation/Application Of Directive 2005/29/EC On Unfair Commercial Practices, SWD(2016) 163 final, p. 6. See also Stănescu, *Is the Unfair Commercial Practices Directive Fit to Tackle Effectively Abusive Debt Collec-tion? A Critical Evaluation*. European Consumer and Market Law Review, Volume 9, Issue 6, pp. 235–247 (2020).

practices may, simultaneously, constitute an infringement of professional diligence in the meaning of the UCPD and the Swedish Marketing Act.[88] This question requires further research.

9.6.2 Some critical reflections

Both advantages and disadvantages may accompany the strict regulation of informal debt collection. On the one hand, the Swedish model provides relatively simple rules for creditors, debtors, and debt collection businesses and, thus, contributes to clear and foreseeable results. On the other hand, one might argue that the Swedish model at the same time guarantees creditors and debt collection businesses a right to generate "income" from debt collection activities irrespective of actual costs. It might be assumed that creditors or debt collection agencies generally claim the maximum amount of compensation for costs allowed by law. Consequently, the strict regulation of debt collection costs may, in some way, foster the development of a debt collection industry, that is debt collection conducted on a massive scale, potentially to the detriment of the debtor collective.[89] No signs in administrative practice or case law were found that the maximum amount of compensation for debt collection costs allowed by law if claimed, is being questioned. A solution might be to put a stricter burden of proof onto the creditor when it comes to the actual costs concerning the allowed maximum amount.

Another critical reflection concerns self-collection as part of the informal debt collection process. Firstly, it could be seen as problematic that creditors have the unrestricted right to claim compensation for costs for collecting their own debts. In Sweden, the Act on Debt Collection Costs does not differentiate between self-collection and debt collection on behalf of someone else. One might argue that collecting one's debt and the costs associated with it constitutes an intrinsic risk of entering into contracts. For that reason, compensation for personal efforts in connection with recovering a debt should not be granted unless the creditor has suffered some kind of provable damage. Secondly, self-collection may be problematic when companies collect their own debts but use a secondary company or business name for their debt collection activities. In Sweden, companies may register a secondary name for parts of their business (*särskilt företagsnamn*). Using a secondary company name when collecting own debts may appear to debtors as if the debt collection process already involves an external party as a debt collector. Besides the fact that such a procedure might potentially be misleading and thereby constituting an unfair commercial practice, it may open the possibility for an unnecessarily prolonged debt collection process. Companies may first attempt to collect debts in-house and then, if it fails, hand the process over to a third-party debt collection agency. It cannot be ruled out that such a prolonged process

88 Act 2008:486 (*Marknadsföringslagen*).

89 However, the costs regulated by law are not unreasonably high and it is not impossible that a lack of regulation would lead to higher costs for debtors.

may increase the debtor's risk of being charged for debt collection costs several times.[90]

9.7 Final remarks

In conclusion, as shown above, debt collection activities are highly regulated in Sweden. Although the Swedish model is not free from criticism, it appears that the Swedish Debt Recovery Act achieves its purpose, for the most part, namely protecting debtors against unnecessary damage, inconvenience, undue pressure, or other improper debt collection measures.[91] One of the strengths of the Swedish model can be considered to be the material rules in the SDRA. Those are the general clause on good debt collection practices (professional diligence) in combination with more specific rules on the standards for good behaviour regarding certain aspects of the debt collection process. In this way, the SDRA offers the possibility to prohibit specific unfair practices, but, at the same time, the law establishes a measurement or standard for debt collection practices to be deemed 'good' practices to begin with. An important part within the regulatory framework is the debt collector's legal duty to investigate the claim before taking measures, as well as the corresponding legal right of the creditor to raise objections to the claim. The Swedish model, thus, strikes what may be considered a fair balance between the parties and provides the debtor with the power to take control of the process by raising an objection based on probable and legitimate reasons, and, in doing so, forcing the creditor to turn to the state apparatus for further processing of the claim (employing formal debt collection).

Likewise, the clarity of the rules, leading to foreseeable results and legal certainty, may be considered another strength of the Swedish model. A central aspect in this regard represents the clear distinction between disputed and undisputed claims together with the clear distinction between informal and formal debt collection. That is to say only undisputed claims shall be subject to informal debt collection. In contrast, disputed claims need to be brought up in a general court of law and shall not be referred to the Swedish Enforcement Authority for obtaining payment orders. Consequently, under the Swedish model, the risk of the system being abused to collect or enforce illegitimate or even fraudulent claims may be considered limited, although not excluded.[92]

Even the mixture of administrative, criminal, civil, and ethical enforcement mechanisms in Sweden appears to be an appropriate way of enforcing professional diligence in the debt collection sector. As mentioned above, the focus in

90 In this context, this is merely considered a theoretical risk. No indications have been found for this actually being the case. A more definitive answer would require further research.

91 Cf. s 4 of the SDRA.

92 An example for a potential abuse of the system may be oversight case DI-2021-7660. The case concerns a foreign company sending fraudulent contract offers disguised as invoices to consumers. The supervisory authority is now investigating the Swedish debt collection agency cooperating with this company. A more concrete statement on the risk for abuse would require further research.

Sweden lies on governmental oversight by the supervisory authority. However, the administrative powers of the Swedish Authority for Privacy Protection do not imply a right to impose administrative fines on companies engaged in unfair debt collection practicesas compared to art 83 of the General Data Protection Regulation (EU) 2016/679. Such administrative fines, based on a company's turnover, may serve as an even more effective deterrent as the potential threat of revocation of the debt collection license.[93] Should the Swedish law be amended in the future, it would be welcomed if the introduction of such GDPR-like administrative fines would be considered.

E.U. law

Directive 2005/29/EC of the European Parliament and of the Council of 11 May 2005 On Unfair Commercial Practices.
Directive 2011/7/EU of the European Parliament and of the Council of 16 February 2011 on Combating Late Payment in Commercial Transactions.

Statutory laws Sweden

Swedish Act on Contracts 1915:218 (*Avtalslagen*).
Swedish Code of Judicial Procedure 1942:740 (*Rättegångsbalken*).
Swedish Parental Code 1949:381 (*Föräldrabalken*).
Swedish Code on Land Law 1970:994 (*Jordabalken*).
Swedish Debt Recovery Act 1974:182 (*Inkassolagen*).
Swedish Act Interest Payments 1975:635 (*Räntelagen*).
Swedish Act on Debt Recovery Costs 1981:739 (*Lag om ersättning för inkassokostnader m.m.*).
Swedish Act on Fees for Illegal Parking 1984:318 (*Lag om kontrollavgift vid olovlig parkering*).
Swedish Act on Payments Orders and Enforcement 1990:746 (*Lag om betalningsföreläggande och handräckning*).
Swedish Act on Electricity 1997:857 (*Ellagen*).
Swedish Act on Electronic Communication 2003:389 (Lag om elektronisk kommunikation).
Swedish Marketing Act 2008:486 (*Marknadsföringslagen*).
Swedish Act on Consumer Credit 2010:1846 (*Konsumentkreditlagen*).

Sub-statutory laws Sweden

Debt Recovery Ordinance 1981:956 (*Inkassoförordningen*).
Ordinance on Handling of Governmental Claims 1993:1138 (*Förordning om hantering av statliga fordringar*).
Administrative Rules KAMFS 2006:1 by the Legal, Financial and Administrative Services Agency (*Kammarkollegiets föreskrifter om hantering av statliga fordringar*).

93 The potential threat of revocation requires that a license is needed in the first place, which is not always the case.

Binding Rules of the Swedish Authority for Privacy Protection DIFS 2011:1 (*Föreskrifter om tillstånd enligt 2 § inkassolagen*).

Preparatory works Sweden

Proposition 1974:42 (governmental proposition of the SDRA).

Soft law

European Commission, Guidance On The Implementation/Application Of Directive 2005/29/EC On Unfair Commercial Practices, SWD(2016) 163 final.
Integritetsskyddsmyndigheten (IMY), *Tillämpning av inkassolagen – allmänna råd* (General Guidelines of the Swedish Authority for Privacy Protection on the Application of the SDRA, 2011).

Court cases Sweden

Högsta domstolen (Swedish Supreme Court) judgement 19 February 1985 in case T303-83, referred to as NJA 1985 p. 143.
Högsta domstolen (Swedish Supreme Court) judgement 9 October 1990 in case T30-90, referred to as NJA 1990 p. 585.
Högsta förvaltningsdomstolen (Swedish Administrative Supreme Court), judgment 6 April 1992 in case 886-1991, referred to as RÅ 1992 ref. 38.
Svea hovrätt (Court of Appeals in Stockholm) judgement 10 April 1997 in case FT1659-96, referred to as RH 1997:41.
Svea hovrätt (Court of Appeals in Stockholm) judgement 23 October 2006 in case B9210-05, referred to as RH 2007:70.
Förvaltningsrätten i Stockholm (Administrative Court in Stockholm) judgement 16 May 2013 in case 10125-12.
Kammarrätten i Stockholm (Administrative Court of Appeal in Stockholm) judgement 30 March 2015 in case 4369-15.
Kammarrätten i Stockholm (Administrative Court of Appeal in Stockholm) judgement 3 April 2018 in case 7539-17.
Patent- och marknadsdomstolen (Patent- and Market Court) judgement 21 October 2021 in case PMT 9984-20.

Administrative practice Sweden

Integritetsskyddsmyndigheten (IMY), Decision in case 1891-2014.
Integritetsskyddsmyndigheten (IMY), Decision in case DI-2019-5660.
Integritetsskyddsmyndigheten (IMY), Decision in case DI-2019-11314.
Integritetsskyddsmyndigheten (IMY), Decision in case IMY-2022-1292.
Integritetsskyddsmyndigheten (IMY), Request for comment in case DI-2021-7660.

Books

Ekelund, Tom, *Inkasso – Regelverket och marknaden* (Avthentes 2000).

Articles

Stănescu, Catalin-Gabriel, Is the Unfair Commercial Practices Directive Fit to Tackle Effectively Abusive Debt Collection? A Critical Evaluation. *European Consumer and Market Law Review* 9(6), pp. 235–247 (2020).

Stănescu, Catalin-Gabriel, Regulation of Abusive Debt Collection Practices in the EU Member States: An Empirical Account. *Journal of Consumer Policy* 44, pp. 179–216 (2021).

Databases

Karlsson-Tuula, Marie, *Inkassolag (1974:182)* (digital commentary to the SDRA), Karnov (Juno), accessed 17 September 2021.

Other internet-based sources

Integritetsskyddsmyndigheten (IMY), https://www.imy.se/verksamhet/inkasso/ansok-om-inkassotillstand/ accessed 2 December 2021.

Integritetsskyddsmyndigheten (IMY), https://www.imy.se/verksamhet/inkasso/digitala-inkassokrav/ accessed 2 December 2021.

Integritetsskyddsmyndigheten (IMY), Annual Report 2020, https://www.imy.se/globalassets/dokument/arsredovisningar/imy-arsredovisning-2020.pdf, p. 62, accessed 2 December 2021.

Swedish Debt Collection Board (*Inkassonämnden*), decision in case 191-2020, https://svenskinkasso.se/ansokan-om-forelaggande-avseende-fordran/ accessed 2 December 2021.

Swedish Association of Debt Collection Agencies, https://svenskinkasso.se/category/inkassonamnden/ accessed 2 December 2021.

10 Regulation of abusive informal debt collection practices

The U.K. debt collection industry: why regulation isn't enough

Jodi Gardner and Mia Gray

In January 2021, the Financial Conduct Authority (FCA) wrote an open letter to the United Kingdom's debt collection industry highlighting numerous poor practices and demanding immediate improvements. The letter outlines the extent of the unfair treatment being experienced and the disproportionate impact of this treatment on vulnerable consumers. This situation exists despite decades of industry regulation from the FCA and its predecessor, the Office of Fair Trading (OFT). The U.K. is unusual in being one of the few countries in Europe with a regulatory regime for private sector debt collection. The FCA regulates the informal collection of consumer debts, and there are specific restrictions on these practices in the regulator's Consumer Credit Sourcebook (CONC) and the FSMA (Regulated Activities Order) 2001. Despite these regulatory restrictions, there have been increased reports of exploitative and inappropriate informal debt collection practices (IDCPs) in the U.K., something which the Covid-19 pandemic has exacerbated.[1] As an example of the extent of the issues experienced as a result of the global situation, the number of people in severe problem debt has risen dramatically from 1.7 to 2.4 million from March 2020 to January 2021.[2]

This chapter explores the UK regime on IDCPs, arguing that instead of being seen as a 'model' for regulation, other countries should learn from the mistakes and gaps in the U.K.'s approach. *First*, we outline the legal obligations of debt collectors. This section shows that *in theory* the U.K. provides a relatively robust form of protection. It also highlights the relationship between the U.K.'s 'hidden problem of household bill debt,'[3] the distinction between private sector and public sector debt collection regulation, which allows government bodies to engage in unfair IDCPs. The *second* section examines the limitations of these regulations.

1 See, for example, Jillian Ambrose, 'UK energy firms using debt collectors despite coronavirus agreement' *The Guardian* (London, April 2020).

2 Step Change Debt Charity, 'Statistics Yearbook: Personal Debt in the UK' (January–December 2020).

3 See Mia Gray, Jodi Gardner and Katherine Moser, 'Low-Income Debt in High Income Countries' in Jodi Gardner, Mia Gray and Katharina Moser (eds), *Debt and Austerity: Implications of the Financial Crisis* (Edward Elgar 2020).

DOI: 10.4324/9781003343158-11

The section highlights the lack of clarity of the processes utilized by private sector debt collectors. It examines a range of terms and conditions from telecommunications providers and banks (the main service providers who utilize debt collectors in the U.K.), emphasising that the relevant contractual provisions are complex, often legally incorrect, and potentially breach the unfair terms provisions of the Consumer Rights Act 2015. We then explore the ineffective enforcement mechanisms for breaches of regulations relating to IDCPs, highlighting the need for proactive and accessible enforcement processes. Without an effective way for consumers to complain and penalties for firms that breach the restrictions, a debt collecting regulatory regime provides little if any practical benefits for vulnerable parties. The *third* section questions whether there should be any role for IDCPs of small consumer debts. If consumers are in financial hardship, is it morally justified to refer them to a debt collector in the first place? *Finally*, the chapter concludes and makes several recommendations for how to strengthen the U.K.'s regulation in this area.

10.1 Debt collection in the U.K.

The first part of the chapter outlines the process and environment of IDCPs in the United Kingdom (U.K.). The discussion explores the size and scale of the industry and the legal entitlements and obligations of debt collectors.

10.1.1 Legal regulation of informal debt collection

Debt collection is a significant – and fast growing – industry in the U.K., in 2018 it had a revenue of £2 billion and deals with £200 billion in loans annually.[4] We refer to the constellation of private and public sector organizations involved in debt collection as an 'industry' to highlight the interdependence of the actors around the collection of unpaid debts. The industry is comprised not just of the initial creditors but is enlarged to include private sector firms and enforcement agents and bailiffs, debt advice charities, private IVA firms, an ombudsman (and woman), and the courts. Whilst any overdue account can be passed to a debt collector (subject to legal restrictions on the assignment), certain industries are more likely to utilize these services. For example, the financial sector has used IDCPs for consumer debts like those arising from contracts for telecoms and utilities services.[5] The industry grew by a third from 2013 to 2018 and is likely to continue experiencing significant growth as a result of the economic ramifications of the global pandemic.[6]

Given the significant commercial value of the industry, it has been analyzed from a political-economy perspective. In her discussion of debt collection and

4 Apex Insight, *UK Consumer Debt Collection and Debt Purchase* (2018) <www.credit-connect.co.uk/wp-content/uploads/2018/02/1259-Apex-Insight-UK-Consumer-debt-purchase-and-debt-collection-2018-summary-Credit-Connect.pdf>.

5 Ibid.

6 Apex Insight, *UK Consumer Debt Collection and Debt Purchase* (2018) <www.credit-connect.co.uk/wp-content/uploads/2018/02/1259-Apex-Insight-UK-Consumer-debt-purchase-and-debt-collection-2018-summary-Credit-Connect.pdf>.

non-performing loans, Montgomerie highlights the exceptional treatment of discharged debt.

> The debt collection industry exists because of a simple political loophole that treats debt differently from any other commodity bought and sold in markets. Imagine this scenario. You go shopping, buy a designer T-shirt on sale, originally £250, and pay £25 instead. The next day you return to the shop and demand a full-redemption rate refund of £250, on the grounds that this is the item's original retail price. No business would grant such a refund. Yet this is exactly what debt collection agencies do. Thanks to a political and regulatory exemption, debt collectors can buy discharged debt at a discount, from lenders, and turn around to borrowers and demand the full amount of the loan. These are the same borrowers identified as unable to repay (otherwise the debt would not be discharged).[7]

As this suggests, IDCPs often involves a legal or statutory assignment of an outstanding debt from the original creditor to the debtor-collector.[8] This process has many advantages: it allows businesses to avoid the risk and practical burden of seeking repayment of outstanding amounts and to clear balance sheets. It also raises large legal and ethical issues with the structure and conduct of debt collection. There is a wide range of legal and ethical challenges, particularly in collecting outstanding money from individuals as opposed to businesses. Despite this, there is very little research on the regulation of debt collectors, the legal mechanisms involved in assigning a debt, and what specific rights and liabilities arise.[9]

10.1.1.1 Industry regulation

The U.K. is one of a few countries in Europe with a regulatory regime for IDCPs.[10] Since 2014, the collection of consumer debts falls under the auspices of the FCA, and there are specific restrictions on debt collection practices in the FCA's Consumer Credit Sourcebook (CONC)[11] and the FSMA (Regulated Activities

7 Johnna Montgomerie, *Should We Abolish Household Debts?* (Polity, 2019) pp. 114–115.

8 There are a number of different legal mechanisms used to collect debts, all with different legal consequences. For a full discussion on this see Jodi Gardner and Chee Ho Tham, 'Debt Collection and Assignment of Debts: Navigating the Legal Maze' in Paul Davies and Tan Cheng-Han (eds) *Commercial Law Intermediaries* (Hart Publishing, 2022).

9 See, for example, ibid.

10 Cataline Stănescu, 'Regulation of Abusive Debt Collection Practices in the EU Member States: An Empirical Account' (2021) 44 *Journal of Consumer Policy* 179.

11 CONC is a combination of Standards, General Principles for Businesses (CONC 1.1.4), guidance for businesses and specific rules. For more information about its application and purpose, see CONC 1.1. Unless stated otherwise, all references in this chapter are to specific rules in CONC. CONC can be accessed from <https://www.handbook.fca.org.uk/handbook/CONC/>.

Order) 2001.[12] Notably, taking steps to procure the payment of a debt due under a credit agreement is a regulated activity under the latter regulation. The FCA views debt collection as a *high-risk activity*, which means that conducting this activity without a relevant permission is a breach of the general prohibition even where a firm is permitted to carry on other regulated activities.[13]

The regulatory structure is meant to protect the consumer and limit the most egregious aspects of IDCPs. The first obligation is found under Principle 7 of the FCA's Principles for Businesses and requires all debt collectors to 'communicate information … in a way which is clear, fair and not misleading.' Coupled with this obligation is the requirement under CONC for firms not to misrepresent their legal position regarding the debt or debt recovery process.[14] Together, these obligations prohibit activities such as sending letters that look like court claims, using intimidating legal language, contact debtors at unreasonable times, and requiring debtors to use premium rate phone numbers. In addition, debt collectors are required to make it clear who they are and what their role is, give balance statements about the debt when asked, and inform debtors of the outcome of disputed or queried debts.

In fact, consumers who are in default or arrears have specific legal rights under CONC 7.3. This includes the requirement that firms, including debt collection firms, deal with them fairly,[15] and with adequate forbearance and due consideration.[16] The firm must allow the consumer reasonable time and opportunity to repay their debt[17] and is even required to consider 'suspending, reducing, waiving or cancelling any further interest or charges' when a consumer is in financial difficulties.[18] The FCA has taken a number of regulatory actions to enforce these obligations, including a recent action against Barclays Bank for failing to show forbearance and due consideration to 1.5 million business and retail customers who fell into arrears or experienced financial difficulties, which resulted in a financial penalty of £26,000,000.[19]

One major issue with problem debt is the speed with which a small debt can escalate because of fees and charges associated with IDCPs. The FCA's regulation of the industry also restricts the fees and charges levied against consumers. Under CONC 7.7.2, debt collectors cannot claim any costs if there is no contractual right to do so. This includes situations such as claiming collection costs that were not outlined in the

12 The FSMA (Regulated Activities Order) 2001 can be accessed from <https://www.legislation.gov.uk/uksi/2001/544/contents/made>.

13 Article 39F; debt collectors are also considered 'credit intermediaries' under art 3(f) of Parliament and Council Directive 2008/48/EC1 (Directive on credit agreements for consumers) and are therefore subject to the requirements of this Directive: *Verein fr Konsumenteninformation v. INKO, Inkasso GmbH* (Case C-127/15).

14 CONC 7.11.1.

15 CONC 7.3.2.

16 CONC 7.3.2A.

17 CONC 7.3.6.

18 CONC 7.3.5(1).

19 FCA, 'FCA fines Barclays £26 million over treatment of customers in financial difficulty', Media Release on 15 December 2020.

original agreement or adding unreasonable charges.[20] However, as will be discussed below, very few contractual terms outline the costs consumers must pay to debt collectors, which leaves this aspect of the collection process open to exploitation.

There are additional obligations in place if a debt collector visits a consumer's property. The FCA states that 'A firm must ensure that all persons visiting a customer's property on its behalf... do not... act in a threatening manner towards a customer.'[21] This requires the debt collector to provide notice of the time and day they will visit and explain the reason for their visit. They are not entitled to visit consumers who are vulnerable and must leave if a consumer is unwell or distressed. The debt collector is also not entitled to come into the home if the consumer does not want them to do so and is not entitled to visit the consumer at work.

There are further obligations on debt collectors when dealing with consumers who are vulnerable. The FCA defines vulnerability as those experiencing physical or mental health issues, learning disabilities or dementia, drug or alcohol addiction, or traumatic life events (such as bereavement or relationship breakdown). The Vulnerability Registration Service, a charity providing an independent register of vulnerable people, estimates that over a third (34%) of the UK population considered themselves vulnerable under this definition in 2021.[22] Disclosing 'vulnerable status' to debt collectors means they may have to suspend or curtail certain collection practices. For example, debt collection visits are prohibited where a firm knows or suspects that a customer may be particularly vulnerable[23] and the CONC 7.10 requires firms must suspend recovery action from customers lacking sufficient mental capacity to make relevant financial decisions.[24]

10.1.1.2 Unfair terms and regulation of fees and charges

In addition to the specific industry regulation, there is general legislation that could impact the contractual rights of consumers. Contracts with debt collection assignment terms *and* debt collection contracts are subject to the Consumer Rights Act 2015.[25] Any unfair terms in these contracts will therefore not be binding on the consumer.[26] A clause could be considered 'unfair' under the Consumer Rights Act 2015 if it causes a significant imbalance in the parties' rights and obligations to the detriment of the consumer.[27] When coming to a decision on this matter, the

20 There are further restrictions on fees and charges, and these are discussed in below.
21 CONC 7.9.14(1).
22 Vulnerability Registration Service, Press Release on 11 August 2021.
23 CONC 7.9.14(2).
24 CONC 7.10.
25 See definitions in Consumer Rights Act 2015, ss 2(2) and 2(3); <https://www.legislation.gov.uk/ukpga/2015/15/contents/enacted>.
26 Consumer Rights Act, s 62(1).
27 Consumer Rights Act, s 62(4).

courts examine a wide range of factors, including the nature of the subject matter of the contract and the circumstances in which the contract was entered into.[28]

The fees that debt collectors can charge are also subject to significant general regulation. In addition to CONC 7.7.2 (discussed above), there is common law on penalty clauses and, potentially, the 'unfair terms' regime in the Consumer Rights Act with various outcomes. The legitimacy of fees and charges was expanded in *Cavendish v. Makdessi*[29] where the Supreme Court amended the scope of liquidated damages clauses from the previous 'genuine pre-estimate of loss'[30] to the more generous 'legitimate interest in performance' test. Unless the fees are particularly unconscionable or extortionate, it may be difficult to have the fees and charges levied against consumers held to be unfair penalties. That said, while businesses are allowed to 'fund [their] own business activities and make a profit,'[31] it could be argued that, as the debt collectors purchase the debts for a fraction of their full value, *any* additional fees and charges levied beyond the principal debt would not meet the 'legitimate interest in performance' test. While detailed analysis of this point is beyond the scope of the current chapter, it is likely that a determination would depend on the circumstances of the specific case and an analysis of the amount of debt, what it had been purchased for, and the time/resources spent liaising with the consumer in question.

As this suggests, the analysis of 'fair' IDCPs is particularly difficult, as the debts are generally combined with many others and sold 'in bulk' by the service providers. One approach would be for courts to consider the average costs charged in the industry to determine what is 'fair' – but that is assuming that the industry as a whole is acting fairly and charging reasonably. The experiences of the sale of Personal Protection Insurance and payday lending shows that this assumption is often unfounded.[32]

Another approach would be to exclude fees and charges from the fairness analysis of the CRA as they are the 'price payable under the contract.'[33] This is in line with the wide approach taken by the House of Lords in *Office of Fair Trading v. Abbey National Plc*.[34] There are significant similarities between fees for unauthorized overdrafts and debt collecting fees and charges such that the decision in *OFT v. Abbey National Plc* would arguably also apply to debt collecting contracts. This case was however decided under the previous regulatory regime of the Unfair Terms in Consumer Contracts Regulations. There are potentially addi-

28 Consumer Rights Act, s 62(5). For an example of the application of unfair terms on credit and debt collection processes, see *Radlinger v. Finway* (Case C-377/14).

29 [2015] UKSC 67, [2016] AC 1172.

30 *Dunlop v. New Garage* [1915] AC 79.

31 [2015] UKSC 67, [2016] AC 1172 at [286].

32 See Jodi Gardner, 'High-Cost Credit in the United Kingdom: A Philosophical Justification for Government Intervention' in Karen Fairweather, Paul O'Shea and Ross Grantham (eds), *Credit, Consumers and the Law: After the global storm* (Ashgate Publishing 2016); Sara Williams, 'The rise and rise of affordability complaints' in Jodi Gardner, Mia Gray and Katharina Moser (eds) *Debt and Austerity: Implications of the Financial Crisis* (Edward Elgar, 2020).

33 Consumer Rights Act 2015, s 64(1).

34 [2009] UKSC 6, [2009] 3 WLR 1215.

tional protections in place under the CRA 2015, which require these terms to be both 'transparent and prominent.'[35] It is possible that the fees and charges clauses under the contracts reviewed would not pass either of these requirements. As discussed above, the clauses are often expressed in difficult and legally complex language.[36] Moreover, the clauses are sub-clauses in long and complicated standard form contracts and therefore are not presented in such a way that an average consumer would be aware of the term.[37]

10.1.1.3 Financial Ombudsman Service

The actions of *private sector* debt collectors are also regulated by the Financial Ombudsman Service (FOS). FOS is a free service that has jurisdiction over IDCPs, based on legal regulations and best practice guidance, and is generally considered consumer friendly.[38] FOS's review of IDCPs revealed that in 2018, the Ombudsman received 3,300 enquiries about debt collection and took over 1,000 new complaints for investigation. Complaints included consumers being asked to repay incorrect amounts of money (21%), consumer service issues (including being contacted excessively) (13%), and being chased for debts that did not belong to them (13%). As a result of this review, the FOS called on all debt collecting firms to improve their practices, particularly in relation to dealing with vulnerable customers.[39] Thus, altogether with the legal framework, regulatory structure and Ombudsman service, the U.K. has what looks like a wide array of regulatory oversight mechanisms both in formal law and in organizational structures to stop the worst excesses of the debt collection industry. However, the next section highlights why this legal and regulatory oversight is not sufficient to protect debtors in arrears.

10.1.2 Debt collection and inequality

The increased use of debt collectors is inherently linked with issues of poverty and inequality in the U.K., both of which have been exacerbated by the austerity measures implemented since the Global Financial Crisis and by the impact of the pandemic.[40] The U.K. is no stranger to inequality and division. Britain has long had one of the highest measures of income and wealth inequality among developed nations.

35 Consumer Rights Act 2015, s 64(2).

36 A term is 'transparent' if 'it is expressed in plain and intelligible language': Consumer Rights Act 2015, s 64(3).

37 A term is 'prominent' if is brought to the consumer's attention in such a way that a reasonably well-informed, observant and circumspect consumer would be aware of the term': Consumer Rights Act 2015, ss 64(4) and 64(5).

38 Elaine Kempson, Sharon Collard and Nick Moore, 'Fair and reasonable: An assessment of the Financial Ombudsman Service' (Personal Finance Research Centre, 2004).

39 Financial Ombudsman Service, 'Dealing with Debt' (*Ombudsman News issue 147*, February 2019) <www.financial-ombudsman.org.uk/news-events/ombudsman-news-issue-147-dealing-debt>.

40 See discussion in Mia Gray, Katharina Moser and Jodi Gardner, 'Understanding low-income debt in a high-income country' in Jodi Gardner, Mia Gray and Katharina Moser (eds), *Debt and Austerity: Implications of the Financial Crisis* (Edward Elgar 2020).

A decade of austerity policies has worsened inequality in the country – with poorer households bearing the largest burden of changes to the system of public spending, tax and benefit system,[41] and with poorer local governments experiencing the largest cuts from central government.[42] Austerity budget cuts have increased both income and wealth inequality. The ONS reported that by 2016, the top 10% of households had an income 6.8 times higher than those in the lowest 10%. *Wealth* inequality is even worse, with increased inequality in property, financial, and total wealth, although pension wealth inequality actually decreased.[43]

The situation has become so concerning that, in May 2019, Great Britain and Northern Ireland was visited by Philip Alston, the United Nations Special Rapporteur on extreme poverty and human rights. Whilst the report's findings are clearly the basis for concern, the mere fact that Alston, whose job is to investigate 'extreme poverty,' felt that a visit to the U.K. was justified, highlights just how dire inequality and extreme poverty have become. The subsequent report was strongly (and unsurprisingly) critical of the decade of austerity measures, stating that despite the U.K. being the world's fifth largest economy and having a 'fundamentally strong' economy, one-fifth of the population lives in poverty and approximately 5% are in extreme destitution. An additional 2.5 million people are no more than 10% above the poverty line, just one financial hiccup away from falling into poverty. The Special Rapporteur also criticized the 'shocking increase in the number of food banks and major increases in homelessness and rough sleeping; a growing number of homeless families,' concluding that due to austerity measures 'great misery has been inflicted unnecessarily' on the most vulnerable people in the U.K.[44]

Poverty, inequality, and over-indebtedness are all clearly linked to IDCPs. Therefore, it is crucial to keep the background of British politics and impact of austerity in mind when analyzing the problem of, and potential solutions to, abusive IDCPs in the country.

10.1.3 Hidden problem of household debt collection

The nature and composition of debt in the U.K. has changed fundamentally during the decade since the global financial crash. Debt in the U.K., and particularly low-income debt, is shaped by new actors and new regulations. The enforcement of commercial consumer credit, particularly credit card and payday lending, has

41 Christina Beatty and Stephen Fothergill, 'The uneven impact of welfare reform: the financial losses to places and people' *Project Report* (Sheffield, Sheffield Hallam University 2016)

42 Mia Gray and Anna Barford, 'The depths of the cuts: the uneven geography of local government austerity' (2018) 11 *Cambridge Journal of Regions, Economy and Society* 3, 541.

43 Office of National Statistics, 'Wealth in Great Britain Wave 5: 2014 to 2016' (1 February 2018) <www.ons.gov.uk/peoplepopulationandcommunity/personalandhouseholdfinances/incomeandwealth/bulletins/wealthingreatbritainwave5/2014to2016#total-wealth>.

44 Philip Alston, 'Visit to the United Kingdom of Great Britain and Northern Ireland. United National General Assembly Report A/HRC/41/39/Add.1' (2019).

received considerable attention in policy, academia, and the media.[45] However, debt advice charities have found that the nature of problem debt is changing, and that credit card debt is declining while debt to the state (local and national) has become a key area of problem debt for many. Strikingly, austerity measures have seen the growth of problem debt owed to the state – mostly for tax credit and benefit overpayments and council tax arrears.[46]

Citizens Advice has recently highlighted what they call the 'the hidden problem of household bill debt.' In 2017–2018, Citizens Advice received almost 700,000 complaints about these debts – nearly double the number of complaints it received about consumer credit. The increase in household bill debt stems from five key debts – council tax arrears, rent arrears, tax credit overpayment, unpaid parking fines, and Magistrate fines.[47] Out of these, council tax arrears were by far the largest cause of concern, making up approximately one-third of all the complaints about household bill debt. Whilst there are no overall statistics on the total amount of this type of debt in the U.K., the Citizens Advice Bureau estimated that in 2017 over £19 billion was owed to government and essential services providers, a 34% increase from 2010.[48] The main sources of this debt were tax credit overpayments, council tax arrears and benefit overpayments – again reinforcing the point that the state (at a national and local level) is playing the role of dispenser of welfare, while at the same time becoming a major creditor.[49]

Household bill debt creates a number of specific challenges for regulators. They are overwhelmingly considered 'priority debts,' that is debts that have severe consequences if they are not paid – including cutting off essential services, eviction, future benefit reduction, or even bankruptcy.[50] Crucially, the main sources of debt, the creditors, are the government and not private institutions. Much of the legal reasoning behind the current regulation of debt is about 'fairness,' transparency, and protecting the vulnerable. This reflects the legal mechanisms and regulatory structure of debt collection origins in the OFT (regulation of IDCPs was then transferred to the FCA in 2014). This meant that the regulatory emphasis wasn't on 'debt'

45 See, for example, Amelia Gentleman 'Wonga: the real cost of a payday loan' *The Guardian* (1 March 2012); Rupert Jones and Hilary Osborne, 'Crackdown on payday loans advertising' *The Guardian* (2 July 2013); Hilary Osborne, 'Rise in consumer borrowing is fastest since pre-crisis, says Bank of England' *The Guardian* (4 January 2017).

46 Mia Gray, 'Debt begets debt: public and private debt in austerity Britain' in Jodi Gardner, Mia Gray. and Katherine Moser (eds), *Debt and Austerity, Implications of the Financial Crisis* (Edward Elgar, 2020).

47 Joe Lane, Barney McCay and Marini Thorne, *Hidden Debts: The growing problem of being behind on bills and in debt to the government* (Citizens Advice Bureau 2018) 8.

48 Ibid, 13.

49 Mia Gray, 'Debt begets debt: public and private debt in austerity Britain' in Jodi Gardner, Mia Gray and Katherine Moser (eds), *Debt and Austerity, Implications of the Financial Crisis* (Edward Elgar, 2020).

50 The Centre for Social Justice, *Collecting Dust: A path forward for government debt collection* (April 2020), 17; For further analysis, see Joseph Spooner, 'The Local Austere Creditor' in Saul Schwartz (ed), *Oppressed by Debt: Government as a Creditor of the Poor* (Routledge, 2022).

per se, but on private sector actors' fair competition and trade practices. Thus, debt was wrapped up in the language of the 'consumer' and the 'customer' – not the 'citizen,' 'benefit recipient,' or 'resident' which may be more attuned to public sector debt issues. Fairness of market-based practices calls for different parameters and discourses than fair treatment of a citizen in relationship to their local government.

Crucially, the state finds itself in an invidious position as welfare provider, creditor *and* regulator. This creates an inherent conflict of interest when determining how to regulate the creation and collection of these types of debts. As welfare provider, it should be concerned with ensuring that all citizens are provided with the social minimum, and that this is protected from IDCPs.[51] As creditor, the state needs to ensure high rates of collection as a matter of fairness of funding public services and ensure the public entity's long-term survival. As regulator, the state needs to ensure fair treatment of those bound up in problem debt and proportionate collection measures. Does the state protect the most vulnerable and insist on high standards or 'best practice' in debt collection – regulating itself to ensure high standards are upheld? Or does it actively and aggressively pursue debt owed to the public sector, in an age where public budgets have been wracked by austerity and Covid-19? These are impossible trade-offs for the regulator-creditor in the public realm. The tension in these roles highlights how the creditor-debtor relationship can distort the social contract and the relationship between resident and the local state.[52]

One might imagine that the government as creditor may show more leniency than the private sector in debt recovery. However, U.K. local state utilizes heavy-handed and exploitative mechanisms to recoup as much money as possible out of those who can least afford it when it comes to debt enforcement. As local governments become more prominent in the role of creditors under austerity, they are also more prominent in using bailiffs for debt enforcement. The use of bailiffs is now the most common mechanism of collection of household debts.[53] Money Advice Service estimated that in 2017, the majority of debt collection contracts (£2.3 million out of £2.5 million of debt) passed to bailiff firms originated from local government. The extent and severity of this was recently outlined by the Centre for Social Justice, which provided a number of disturbing examples of how 'government debt collection continues to lag significantly behind that of the private and regulated sector.'[54]

Finally, the use of bailiffs is also a costly form of enforcement for the debtor. It has a different commercialization model to private debt collecting activities, where the debts are sold for a fraction of the value and the 'profit' comes from the debtor paying more to the collector than was paid for the debt. In contrast, enforcement

51 Jodi Gardner, 'Austerity, inequality and high-cost credit: understanding the role of the social minimum' in Jodi Gardner, Mia Gray and Katharina Moser (eds), *Debt and Austerity: Implications of the Financial Crisis* (Edward Elgar, 2020).

52 Maurizio Lazzarato and Joshua David Jordan, *The Making of the Indebted Man: Essay on the Neoliberal Condition* (MIT Press, 2012).

53 Ed McDonagh, Rosie Derricourt and Thelma Baker, *The rules of enforcement: Making a complaint about the behaviour of bailiffs in a self-regulated system* (Citizens Advice Bureau, 2019).

54 Ibid.

by bailiffs results in significant costs being added to the outstanding debt. In 2021, bailiffs who are not High Court enforcement officers are entitled to charge £110 for writing to an individual about a debt owed, £235 for visiting a debtor's house, and £110 for taking and selling belongings. A single debt enforcement process could cost an individual who is already struggling with debt an additional £455 before paying off any of the pre-existing debt.[55] High Court enforcement officers charge even more – £75 for a notice of enforcement letter, £190 for the first visit, £495 if the consumer refuses to make an arrangement to pay or breaks a payment arrangement, and £525 for removal of goods. StepChange estimates that if an individual has a £1,000 debt, it will total at least £2,285 when all enforcement fees are added.[56] In total, Citizen's Advice estimates that in 2019, bailiff fees added an additional £200 million of fees on top of households' existing debts.[57] This is of particular concern, as even before the added stress of the pandemic, many low-income debtors were already in a financially precarious situation.

10.2 Limitations on effective regulation

Clearly, effective regulation is lacking in the debt collection industry – whether in the more regulated collection of private sector debt or debt to the more lightly regulated public sector. Regulations in both suffer from profound limitations, which make abusive IDCPs common. This section outlines two key limitations that undermine the regulation's effectiveness outlined in Section 10.1: the lack of clarity and the difficulties enforcing the obligations on debt collectors.

10.2.1 Lack of clarity

A lack of clarity undermines the consumer protection afforded by the regulations outlined above. To examine this, we analyzed a selection of contracts that referred to debt collection processes in the United Kingdom. This involved reviewing 28 consumer contracts in the banking and utility sectors. These contracts highlighted a significant lack of clarity about the legal mechanism associated with the assignment of debt. The complexity of IDCPs is highly likely to create significant confusion for debtors. First, it is common for the contract to refer to multiple terms denoting different legal concepts, further adding to the complexities. One contract reviewed utilized eight separate legal concepts in their debt collection discussion (agency, assign, transfer by

55 Citizens Advice Bureau, <www.citizensadvice.org.uk/debt-and-money/action-your-creditor-can-take/bailiffs/how-bailiffs-should-treat-you/check-bailiffs-fees/>. If the debt over £1,500, additional fees of 7.5% of the debt will also be charged.

56 StepChange Debt Charity, 'High Court enforcement officers. What can they do?' <https://www.stepchange.org/debt-info/debt-collection/high-court-enforcement-officers.aspx>. If the debt over £1,000, additional fees of 7.5% of the debt will also be charged.

57 Citizens Advice, '1.3 million households have fallen behind on council tax due to coronavirus' (25 June 2020) <https://www.citizensadvice.org.uk/about-us/our-work/policy/policy-research-topics/debt-and-money-policy-research/13-million-households-have-fallen-behind-on-council-tax-due-to-coronavirus/>.

novation, pass, transfer, sub-contract, grant security, and declare a trust over). This creates significant confusion, as the multiple assignment methods can have different rights and responsibilities for parties and it is highly unlikely that any consumer reading these terms would have a clear understanding of the legal consequences of non-payment of their debts. In fact, only six out of the 28 contracts reviewed specified a single method by which the debt was assigned. This lack of clarity is confusing for debtors without commercial legal advice or experience and exacerbates the unequal power in the creditor-debtor relationship.[58]

Second, the fees charged by debt collectors are also opaque. Of the 28 contracts reviewed, only two contracts specifically stated what fees and charges would apply if the account was sent to a debt collector. A further eight contracts did not make any specific references to how much the customer would be charged in the event of non-payment. The remainder of the contracts had general clauses stating that, if the consumer did not pay their bills, they would be subjected to a number of financial penalties and/or the service provider would be entitled to pass on any third-party charges to the consumer. Therefore, it is difficult, if not impossible, for most people who find themselves in debt arrears to understand how much the IDCPs will cost them. The lack of clarity is particularly a problem with private sector debt, when consumers agree to the terms and conditions of the contract in question before the company can provide services. In contrast, with household debt, most local residents do not sign a contract to pay local taxes and only find themselves immersed in legal documentation when unable to make payments.

10.2.2 Enforcement difficulties

The protections in place are also undermined by a lack of effective enforcement of breaches by debt collecting firms – something that happens with both the collection of private-sector and household debt.

10.2.2.1 Collection of private sector debt

The FCA has, on occasion, undertaken investigations into different debt collectors. In 2014, the regulator required Wage Payment and Payday Loans Ltd to enter into an agreement not to engage in outcome collection of debts after it was determined that the firm prioritized the collection of debts over fair treatment of its customers.[59] The firm did not adhere to this agreement and in 2016 the company's permission to work in the industry was revoked.[60] The regulator also required the company CFO Ltd to suspend all debt collection activities (including all outbound collection

58 Samuel Kirwan, 'On 'those who shout the loudest': Debt advice and the work of disrupting attachments' (2019) 98 *Geoforum* 318.

59 FCA, 'Application for Imposition of Requirements: Wage Payment and Payday Loans Limited' (2014) <www.fca.org.uk/publication/requirement-notices/wppl-vreq.pdf>.

60 FCA, 'Final Notice, Wage Payment and Payday Loans Limited' (28 September 2016) <www.fca.org.uk/publication/final-notices/wage-payment-payday-loans-limited-2016.pdf>. As a result, the

calls, mail, email, and text message communications/campaigns) while it made any necessary changes to its policies, procedures and staff incentive schemes to ensure that those activities were conducted in compliance with FCA requirements. This was after the FCA became concerned that the company potentially misused banking information provided by customers, including via affiliated websites, to repay outstanding debts of existing CFO customers who are in arrears. The company was later required to pay customers over £34 million in redress for unfair practices.[61]

In another example, the FCA fined Barclays Bank £26 million for failures in relation to their treatment of consumer credit customers who fell into arrears or experienced financial difficulties. Barclays had identified a number of failings with their treatment of customers as early as 2014 but these were not fully rectified because of a number of errors. In 2020, the FCA determined that the financial institution had failed to: (1) follow its customers' contact policies for customers who fell into arrears; (2) have appropriate conversations with customers to help understand the reasons for the arrears; and (3) properly understand customers' circumstances leading it to offer unaffordable, or unsustainable, forbearance solutions.[62]

However, despite these high-profile successes, many problems remain with enforcing the existing regulations on IDCPs. Research from the Vulnerability Registration Service highlights the extent that debt collecting activities have impacted those who can afford it the least. Despite FCA guidance for creditors to help identify vulnerable customers and regulation to curtail some collection practices, 41% of people who fall under the FCA's 'vulnerable customer' definition say they have been mistreated by organizations in both the private and public sectors. This includes banks/financial services, housing and local government. The research shows that in 2021, 18% of vulnerable customers have missed payments or gone into arrears and one in five (20%) have continued to receive calls, emails, or visits chasing up payments or for debt collection. Furthermore, when these consumers get into financial difficulties, they find it difficult to get the right support from the creditor or debt collection agency. 29% found it difficult to locate the right person to talk to and 37% found it difficult to have to keep repeating their circumstances to different departments within different organizations.[63]

10.2.2.2 Collection of household debt

A fundamental part of the infrastructure that has sprung up around debt is the change in practices of debt collection, which can be aggressive, lacking in dignity, and

---

company went into liquidation the following year: <https://www.fca.org.uk/news/news-stories/cfo-lending-limited-enters-administration>.

61 FCA, 'Payday Firm CFO Lending to pay £34 million redress' (19 September 2016) <www.fca.org.uk/news/press-releases/payday-firm-cfo-lending-pay-34-million-redress>.

62 FCA, 'FCA fines Barclays £26 million over treatment of customers in financial difficulty' (December 2020).

63 Rozi Jones, '41% of vulnerable customers say they have been treated unfairly by providers', *Financial Reporter* (12 August 2021).

exploitative. In particular, the use of mostly private sector bailiffs as the most common mechanism of collection of household debts is troubling.[64] Enforcement of debts by bailiffs is of particular concern, given that many low-income debtors are often already vulnerable and can easily be coerced into unaffordable and unreasonable repayment agreements.[65] While the regulatory structure outlined above stops the most egregious examples in the private sector, it does little to control the excessive zeal of public sector debt collection. Thus, as local governments become more prominent as debt collectors under austerity, they are also more prominent in using bailiffs for debt enforcement.[66] Money Advice Service estimated that in 2017, 2.3 million of the 2.5 million debts that were passed to bailiff firms were from local governments.[67] Citizens Advice estimates that one in three people contacted by bailiffs have grounds for a complaint regarding breaches of applicable rules. The main basis of complaints is refusal to accept affordable payment offers, misrepresentation of rights of entry (for example, by threatening to break into the house), taking control of goods inappropriately, acting aggressively towards people in debt, and finally, acting unsympathetically towards vulnerable people, especially people with illnesses and disabilities.[68]

Many of these issues are long-standing. In 2014, the U.K.'s Ministry of Justice created additional obligations on bailiffs and provided clarity on maximum bailiff fees. Whilst the rules themselves were a step forward, enforcing these rules, making complaints, and ultimately taking the bailiffs to court remain exceptionally difficult and complex.[69] In reality, vulnerable debtors who do not have the funds to pay outstanding debts and are being hounded by bailiffs, rarely have the financial and practical means (or emotional energy) to pursue redress. In the first four years after the 2014 obligations were imposed, the Ministry of Justice reported only 56 complaints through the new court-based process – a tiny proportion of the estimated 1,600,000 rule infringements during this period.[70]

Unlike the consumer friendly and free to access Financial Ombudsman Service for private debts and enforcement, there is no equivalent independent regulator for bailiff activity on debts to the public sector. The public sector does have the Local Government Ombudsman (LGO), which examines complaints about councils and

64 Joe Lane, Barney McCay and Marini Thorne, *Hidden Debts: The growing problem of being behind on bills and in debt to the government* (Citizens Advice Bureau 2018) 18.

65 The Centre for Social Justice, *Collecting Dust: A path forward for government debt collection* (April 2020).

66 Mia Gray, 'Debt begets debt: public and private debt in austerity Britain' in Jodi Gardner, Mia Gray and Katherine Moser (eds), *Debt and Austerity, Implications of the Financial Crisis*, (Edward Elgar, 2020).

67 Ed McDonagh, Rosie Derricourt, and Thelma Baker, *The Rules of Enforcement: Making a complaint about the behaviour of bailiffs in a self-regulated system* (Citizens Advice Bureau, 2019).

68 Joe Lane, Barney McCay and Marini Thorne, *Hidden Debts: The growing problem of being behind on bills and in debt to the government* (Citizens Advice Bureau 2018).

69 The Centre for Social Justice, *Collecting Dust: A path forward for government debt collection*, (April 2020) 58.

70 Ed McDonagh, Rosie Derricourt, and Thelma Baker, *The Rules of Enforcement: Making a complaint about the behaviour of bailiffs in a self-regulated system* (Citizens Advice Bureau, 2019) 17.

some other authorities' actions. The LGO can support a complaint – often about failure to assess affordability, not checking for vulnerability indicators, and delay or bad communication on the part of the council – but not about bailiff activity itself. Bailiffs have obligations to undertake affordability assessments and check for vulnerable debtors. However, there is significant evidence that they are failing in their duties, similar to commercial credit providers. Unfortunately, the debtors who suffer from these breaches have restricted enforcement mechanisms, meaning that bailiffs have little incentive to change their behaviour. This creates a regulatory gap between the rights that debtors have in theory and the rights that they can enforce in practice; a gap that is exacerbated by the austerity cuts to legal aid and the uneven access to justice.[71]

The Covid-19 pandemic has brought many of these issues to a head in the U.K. Due to the increased attention on the actions of bailiffs during the pandemic, an agreement has been made to set up a new independent body – the Enforcement Conduct Authority (ECA). This is designed to ensure unfair treatment by bailiffs is 'stamped out' and to help vulnerable people reset their finances. The ECA was developed as a result of the Centre for Social Justice bringing together bailiff firms and debt advice charities to tackle rising complaints about bailiff enforcement and to create the Enforcement Oversight Working Group. The body will replace the current focus on self-regulation in the bailiff industry and replace it with (1) clear rules for bailiffs and sanctions for firms and individual who breach the rules, (2) a two-stage complaints process, with the ECA acting as an independent adjudicator, and (3) protocols to allow vulnerable people fair and affordable repayment plans.

The ECA aims to 'protect the vulnerable and achieve fairness' and has been described as a 'win win' in terms of customer experience, maximizing repayment, and reputation management.[72] The development has been welcomed by businesses and charities, such as the Money Advice Trust.[73] However, there are some significant limitations. First, it is funded by the bailiff industry and will not be entirely compulsory. Second, the vast majority of people who bailiffs visit are vulnerable – it is implausible that the consumer would be unable to pay their household bills if there were no evidence of financial distress. In light of this, it remains unclear how the ECA is going to 'protect' all of these individuals whilst also maximizing repayment. Third, the process relies on consumers actively making complaints against bailiffs who breach their legal obligations. Again, due to

71 See discussion in Mia Gray, Jodi Gardner and Katherine Moser, 'Low-Income Debt in High Income Countries' in Jodi Gardner, Mia Gray and Katharina Moser (eds), *Debt and Austerity* (Edward Elgar 2020) and Jodi Gardner and Mary Spector, 'Austerity and Access to Justice: Exploring the Role of Clinical Legal Education in Cambridge' in Dan Wei, James Nehf and Claudia Lima Marques (eds), *Innovation and the Transformation of Consumer Law* (Springer Publishing, 2020).

72 Alan Hamblett, 'The new ECA could be the good press debt collection desperately needs', *The MJ* (9 August 2021).

73 Money Advice Trust, 'Money Advice Trust Welcomes Proposals for New Enforcement Conduct Authority' (25 July 2021) <moneyadvicetrust.org/latest-news/money-advice-trust-welcomes-proposals-new-enforcement-conduct-authority/>.

the nature of the people whom bailiffs visit, we remain unconvinced that this will offer any additional protection or regulatory oversight. Instead, a full statutory regime with a completely independent enforcement body should be enacted. Until then, bailiff activities should be completely suspended.

10.3 Is consumer debt collection ever fair?

As discussed in Section 10.1, the Unfair Terms Regime applies to debt collection contracts. This section discusses whether the assignment of consumer debts is, in and of itself, a potential unfair term. Under *Aziz v. Catalunyacaixa*[74] when determining whether a clause is unfair, it must be considered if the consumer is being deprived of an advantage that they would have had under national law in the absence of the contractual provision in question.[75] If so, is it ever fair to assign debts of consumers who are in financial distress? Service providers have significant obligations when dealing with vulnerable consumers, with the FCA recently providing additional guidance to firms on how these matters should be dealt with.[76] A vulnerable consumer is defined as 'somebody who, due to their personal circumstances, is especially susceptible to harm, particularly when a firm is not acting with appropriate levels of care.'[77] The FCA states that there are four key drivers that increase consumer vulnerability: (1) health conditions or illnesses; (2) major life events (such as bereavement, job loss or relationship breakdowns); (3) the inability to withstand emotional or financial shocks; and (4) low knowledge of financial matters.[78]

The OFT specifically notes that Covid-19 is likely to significantly exacerbate many issues already affecting consumers, such as ill health, bereavement, and job loss.[79] A survey of over 16,000 individuals in February 2020 estimated that approximately 24 million people in the U.K. have characteristics of vulnerability, 10.7 million of whom have low financial resilience. Out of these people, 7.2 million are over-indebted and 3.8 million are in severe financial difficulty.[80] There is significant overlap between individuals in severe financial difficulty and those subject to debt collection processes. People in financial distress are more likely to be constantly or usually overdrawn, have persistent credit card debt, and/or utilize high-cost credit to cover day-to-day expenses.[81] This has only worsened with Covid-19, with an additional 3.5 million adults now having low financial

74 Case C-415/11; [2013] 3 CMLR 5.

75 This approach was confirmed by the House of Lords in *OFT v. Abbey National* [2009] UKSC 6, [2009] 3 WLR 1215 [105].

76 FCA, *Guidance for firms on the fair treatment of vulnerable customers* (GC20/3, 2020) <www.fca.org.uk/publications/finalised-guidance/guidance-firms-fair-treatment-vulnerable-customers>.

77 Ibid [1.1].

78 Ibid [2.1].

79 Ibid [1.15b].

80 FCA, *Financial Lives 2020 Survey: the impact of coronavirus* (2021), <www.fca.org.uk/publications/research/financial-lives-2020-survey-impact-coronavirus>.

81 StepChange Debt Charity, *Life on the Edge: Towards more resilient family finances* (2014).

resilience. Despite this, service providers are continuing to use debt collectors for overdue debts, including energy companies.[82]

Research from StepChange Debt Charity further confirms the unequal impact of Covid-19. In the 2020 Statistics Yearbook the charity highlights that among the new clients accessing debt advice in the last 12 months:

- Three in five (60%) were women;
- Half (50%) were in a vulnerable situation, up from 44% in 2019;
- Almost one-quarter (22%) were single parents, compared to 6% of the wider UK population;
- One-third (33%) were in receipt of Universal Credit;
- More than one-third (34%) were renting privately.

The average amount of debt also increased significantly, from £2,137 in 2019 to £2,453 in 2020. This is mirrored by the substantial increases in the proportion of clients behind on many different types of household bill, as well as rises in average monetary amounts for individual bill types.[83]

There are significant legal obligations when dealing with customers who are in financial difficulties.[84] On top of the specific legal obligations, vulnerable consumers must be treated appropriately and with best practice or service providers risk an adverse finding by FOS. One of the key advantages of referring an outstanding account to a debt collector is that the business can avoid the risk and practical burden of seeking repayment of outstanding amounts. For example, due to the burdensome nature of the tasks, in early-2021, certain banks proposed creating an industry-wide debt collection service to chase unpaid Covid-19 support loans.[85] Financial institutions, understandably, do not want to engage in these types of activities.

Debt collectors do have legal obligations when dealing with vulnerable consumers (as discussed above). However, individuals will likely receive more empathetic and understanding treatment from the service providers (i.e. the initial creditor), who have an ongoing relationship with the consumer. This can be contrasted with debt collectors, which, whilst subject to largely the same regulatory obligations, have a limited relationship and are focused solely on extracting maximum payment from the individual in question. Therefore, referring unpaid accounts to a debt collector allows service providers to avoid, or at least pass on, the legal obligations they owe to consumers in financial difficulties. This could arguably contravene the concern emphasized in *Aziz v. Catalunyacaixa* that consumers ought not to be denied advantages they would have

82 Jillian Ambrose, 'UK energy firms using debt collectors despite coronavirus agreement' *The Guardian* (26 April 2020).

83 StepChange Debt Charity, *Statistics Yearbook: Personal Debt in the UK* (January–December 2020).

84 See discussion in: FCA *FG21/1 Guidance for firms on the fair treatment of vulnerable customers* (2021) <www.fca.org.uk/publication/finalised-guidance/fg21-1.pdf>.

85 Stephen Morris and Daniel Thomas, 'Talks stall on shared Covid loan debt collector for UK banks', *Financial Times* (7 February 2021).

under national law because of the contractual provision allowing the service provider to assign the debt to another party.

Therefore, it is worth considering whether the assignment of debts in consumer contracts[86] are, in general, unfair contract terms. They clearly fulfill the criteria of creating a significant imbalance in the parties' rights and obligations to the consumer's detriment, as the service provider benefits at the consumer's disadvantage. Since a consumer's inability to pay sums owed is *prima facie* evidence of financial vulnerability, is it fair to sell such indebtedness (at a fraction of a price) to a business that makes a profit from extracting a maximum level of payment from parties already struggling?[87] The harms of debt collection have been outlined by Montgomerie, who states

> When lenders decide that an outstanding loan is not going to be paid … they can discharge these debts, and the lender is given a tax break equivalent to the value of the loss against an asset. Lenders have made a practice of selling these loans to debt collection agencies, often for 2 per cent to 10 per cent of their face value. Debt collectors … try to make a profit by extracting payment from the borrowers that lenders have long given up on. Debt collection agencies are well known for causing emotional and even economic and physical harm to people.[88]

In light of these characteristics, it is arguable that terms allowing for consumer debt collection are unfair contract terms. The authors recognize that this would change the landscape of how consumer debts are collected. It is however one that is worthy of further consideration. If firms were prevented from referring consumer debts to debt collectors, they would have to consider the approach taken to outstanding accounts more broadly and flexibly. This could include processes such as payment holidays, repayment plans, downgrading services to more affordable levels, and working closely with consumer welfare organizations, such as StepChange Debt Charity. Considering that debts are sold for such a small fraction of their face value, it is highly likely that these alternative processes will not be excessively financially detrimental to the service provider but will bring significant benefits for the indebted consumer.

86 This discussion is limited to debt collection of consumer contracts and the authors recognize that debt collection has a valid and important role in many other scenarios.

87 It is recognized that there will be some consumers who refuse to pay outstanding amounts but who are not in financial difficulties. As outlined by the recent FCA research discussed above, these people will be in the minority. The service provider will still however have significant legal rights to enforce payment of the outstanding amount against these parties and, as they are not financially struggling, it will be a much simpler process.

88 Johnna Montgomerie, 'Relief from austerity: the case for a targeted write-off of the UK's household debt stock' in Jodi Gardner, Mia Gray and Katharina Moser (eds), *Debt and Austerity* (Edward Elgar, 2020) 286.

Debt to the public sector also needs fundamental restructuring. The public sector, and particularly local government, needs to reshape its approach to debt collection. In many other aspects of society, such as public sector employment, the government promotes and follows 'best practice' in equal pay, union recognition, and parental rights. This approach can and should be extended to debt collection mechanisms, which is clearly not happening. It is crucial that the government rethinks its processes. The Centre for Social Justice recommendations designed to 'Embed fairness across all of government debt collection' are an excellent starting point for this discussion.[89]

10.4 Conclusion and recommendations

There is not much that is clear in the world of abusive IDCPs, but in the UK two things are obvious: (1) these issues arise in both private and public debt and (2) existing regulation prohibiting these practices is not enough. Despite having one of the strictest and most heavily regulated regimes for debt collection activity, there is still unacceptable, and increasing, reports of exploitative and unfair tactics used to extract payment from financially vulnerable individuals. Local authorities in the U.K. are currently the most frequent users of expensive and exploitative bailiff services for the recovery of unpaid council tax and rent arrears. Therefore, it is also apparent that whilst the existing regulation covers the collection of debt from *private* companies, regulation of *household* and *government debts* is also crucial. The situation is however even more complex. The impacts of austerity have resulted in an unprecedented reduction in funding for these authorities. As a result, many have engaged in aggressive debt collection techniques to balance their books and keep vital community services open. Therefore, the state is struggling to navigate a path through its position as welfare provider, creditor, and regulator. It is struggling with impossible trade-offs between pursuing debts owed to the public sector and ensuring fair and compassionate treatment of individuals weighted down by problem debt.

Finding solutions to these multifaceted problems is essential, but unfortunately beyond the scope of this chapter. They will require detailed analysis, including a reconsideration of the nature of public debt and the justification of the consumer debt collection industry. However, a few recommendations can be made, looking at the informal debt collection practices on temporary and longer-term measures.

Temporary measures must be implemented relatively quickly to address some of the more acute consequences of debt collection practices. The pandemic has increased inequalities on a number of levels, and the financial complications of Covid-19 are likely to remain as part of the social fabric for years to come. Until these are addressed, firms and government should temporarily freeze any fees charged or other negative consequences for unpaid debts, and the previous prohibition on bailiff activities and other debt collection activities should be reinstated.

89 The Centre for Social Justice, *Collecting Dust: A path forward for government debt collection* (April 2020) 62. Whilst it is beyond the scope of this chapter to analyze this issue any further, there is a clear need for further research on the fairness of household debt enforcement activities.

Finally, the ECA should be closely monitored to ensure that it is fit for purpose, and that it is making decisions not just on legal obligations, but also one the basis of what is fair and in accordance with 'best practice.'

On a longer-term basis, the recommendations can be divided on the basis of whether the debt is public or private. For public sector debt, the industry must be regulated more broadly and more thoroughly. The ECA is not sufficient to address the many exploitative and questionable aspects of public debt collection. Preferably, the prohibitions on evictions and bailiff activity that were enacted as part of the pandemic response should be made permanent and other, less exploitative and expensive, mechanisms should be utilized. It is unacceptable that bailiff activities added £200 million worth of fees to the existing debts of those who were already the most vulnerable. If enforcement action continues, the ECA should be restructured to be completely statutory and independent from the bailiff industry and work alongside a more general, independent, and accessible government dispute resolution process. Finally, it is also essential to treat the cause not the symptoms of public debt collection. It is crucial that more funding is provided to local governments, so that the support for council tax and other household bills can be continued. This will help address the impossible trade-offs currently experienced at the local government level.

For private debt, it seems trite to say that all businesses should also be required to rethink their debt collection processes and enact a more fair and flexible method of recovering arrears, ensuring affordability assessments of all repayment plans. The issues are however much deeper, and the very existence of the debt collection industry must be questioned. We currently have a situation where a legal and regulatory loophole has allowed the creation of an exploitative and predatory industry that receives revenue of over £2 billion per year – money that is taken directly out of the pockets of people who are already financially stretched. If creditors could no longer assign debts to debt collectors, they would be required to work directly with consumers to determine appropriate and affordable repayment processes. This is preferable to selling the debt for a fraction of its value, throwing the debtors to the mercy of such a vulture-like industry. Finally, the mere fact that so much profit is to be made from the carcasses of indebted households raises fundamental questions about welfare and the social contract. In reality, the main solution for the multiple problems we are currently experiencing with austerity-related debt will be to tackle the underlying issues of inequality and poverty. It is unacceptable that such a wealthy, developed country with a proud history of welfare and assisting those in need has ended up with such inconceivable levels of inequality and poverty.

Bibliography

Apex Insight, *UK consumer debt collection and debt purchase* (2018) <www.credit-connect.co.uk/wp-content/uploads/2018/02/1259-Apex-Insight-UK-Consumer-debt-purchase-and-debt-collection-2018-summary-Credit-Connect.pdf>

Catalin Stănescu, 'Regulation of abusive debt collection practices in the EU member states: An empirical account' (2021) 44 *Journal of Consumer Policy* 179

Christina Beatty and Stephen Fothergill, 'The uneven impact of welfare reform: The financial losses to places and people' *Project Report* (Sheffield Hallam University, 2016)

Citizens Advice, '1.3 million households have fallen behind on council tax due to coronavirus' (25 June 2020) <https://www.citizensadvice.org.uk/about-us/our-work/policy/policy-research-topics/debt-and-money-policy-research/13-million-households-have-fallen-behind-on-council-tax-due-to-coronavirus/>

Citizens Advice Bureau, <www.citizensadvice.org.uk/debt-and-money/action-your-creditor-can-take/bailiffs/how-bailiffs-should-treat-you/check-bailiffs-fees/>

Ed McDonagh, Rosie Derricourt and Thelma Baker, *The rules of enforcement: Making a complaint about the behaviour of bailiffs in a self-regulated system* (Citizens Advice Bureau, 2019)

Financial Conduct Authority, *FCA fines Barclays £26 million over treatment of customers in financial difficulty*, Media Release on 15 December 2020 (2020)

Financial Conduct Authority, *FG21/1 guidance for firms on the fair treatment of vulnerable customers* (2021) <www.fca.org.uk/publication/finalised-guidance/fg21-1.pdf>

Financial Conduct Authority, *Financial lives 2020 survey: The impact of coronavirus* (2021) <www.fca.org.uk/publications/research/financial-lives-2020-survey-impact-coronavirus>

Financial Conduct Authority, *Guidance for firms on the fair treatment of vulnerable customers* (GC20/3, 2020) <www.fca.org.uk/publications/finalised-guidance/guidance-firms-fair-treatment-vulnerable-customers>

Joe Lane, Barney McCay and Marini Thorne, *Hidden debts: The growing problem of being behind on bills and in debt to the government* (Citizens Advice Bureau, 2018)

Jodi Gardner, 'Austerity, inequality and high-cost credit: Understanding the role of the social minimum' in Jodi Gardner, Mia Gray and Katharina Moser (eds), *Debt and austerity: Implications of the financial crisis* (Edward Elgar, 2020)

Jodi Gardner, 'High-cost credit in the United Kingdom: A philosophical justification for government intervention' in Karen Fairweather, Paul O'Shea and Ross Grantham (eds), *Credit, consumers and the law: After the global storm* (Ashgate Publishing, 2016)

Jodi Gardner and Chee Ho Tham, 'Debt collection and assignment of debts: Navigating the legal maze' in Paul Davies and Tan Cheng-Han (eds.), *Intermediaries in commercial law* (Hart Publishing, 2022)

Jodi Gardner and Mary Spector, 'Austerity and access to justice: Exploring the role of clinical legal education in Cambridge' in Dan Wei, James P. Nehf and Claudia Lima Marques (eds), *Innovation and the transformation of consumer law* (Springer Publishing, 2020)

Johnna Montgomerie, 'Relief from austerity: The case for a targeted write-off of the UK's household debt stock' in Jodi Gardner, Mia Gray and Katharina Moser (eds), *Debt and austerity: Implications of the financial crisis* (Edward Elgar, 2020)

Johnna Montgomerie, *Should we abolish household debts?* (Polity, 2019)

Joseph Spooner, 'The local austere creditor' in Saul Schwartz (ed.), *Oppressed by debt: Government as a creditor of the poor* (Routledge, 2022)

Maurizio Lazzarato and Joshua David Jordan, *The making of the indebted man: Essay on the neoliberal condition* (MIT Press, 2012)

Mia Gray, 'Debt begets debt: Public and private debt in austerity Britain' in Jodi Gardner, Mia Gray and Katherine Moser (eds), *Debt and austerity, implications of the financial crisis* (Edward Elgar, 2020)

Mia Gray and Anna Barford, 'The depths of the cuts: The uneven geography of local government austerity' (2018) 11 *Cambridge Journal of Regions, Economy and Society* 3

Mia Gray, Jodi Gardner and Katherine Moser, 'Low-income debt in high income countries' in Jodi Gardner, Mia Gray and Katharina Moser (eds), *Debt and austerity: Implications of the financial crisis* (Edward Elgar, 2020)

Money Advice Trust, 'Money advice trust welcomes proposals for new enforcement conduct authority', (25 July 2021) <moneyadvicetrust.org/latest-news/money-advice-trust-welcomes-proposals-new-enforcement-conduct-authority/>

Office of National Statistics, 'Wealth in Great Britain wave 5: 2014 to 2016' (1 February 2018) <www.ons.gov.uk/peoplepopulationandcommunity/personalandhouseholdfinances/incomeandwealth/bulletins/wealthingreatbritainwave5/2014to2016#total-wealth>

OFT v Abbey National [2009] UKSC 6, [2009] 3 WLR 1215

Philip Alston, 'Visit to the United Kingdom of Great Britain and Northern Ireland. United National General Assembly Report A/HRC/41/39/Add.1' (2019)

Samuel Kirwan, 'On 'those who shout the loudest': Debt advice and the work of disrupting attachments' (2019) 98 *Geoforum* 318

Sara Williams, 'The rise and rise of affordability complaints' in Jodi Gardner, Mia Gray and Katharina Moser (eds), *Debt and austerity: Implications of the financial crisis* (Edward Elgar, 2020)

StepChange Debt Charity, 'High Court enforcement officers. What can they do?' <https://www.stepchange.org/debt-info/debt-collection/high-court-enforcement-officers.aspx>

StepChange Debt Charity, *Life on the edge: Towards more resilient family finances* (2014)

StepChange Debt Charity, 'Statistics yearbook: Personal debt in the UK' (January–December 2020)

The Centre for Social Justice, *Collecting dust: A path forward for government debt collection* (April 2020).

11 Can the Representative Actions Directive combat abusive debt collection practices in the E.U.?

Agnes Horvath

11.1 Introduction

The legislative bodies of the E.U. have adopted Directive 2020/1828 on representative actions for the protection of the collective interests of consumers[1] ('RCRD'). The act imposes the obligation on all Member States to provide procedural remedies against breaches of the law that would be able to affect the consumers collectively. Thanks to the RCRD, consumers can bring action in all Member States for redress remedies through a representative body called a 'qualified entity' ('QE'). It is important to note that the RCRD can affect the debt collection industry: it is meant to apply to existing E.U. legislative acts provided in Annex 1 of the RCRD.[2] Annex 1 includes acts such as E.U. Directive 2014/17/EU on credit agreements for consumers relating to residential immovable property,[3] Directive 2008/48/EC about unfair terms in consumer contracts,[4] or Directive 2005/29/EC on unfair business-to-consumer commercial practices in the internal market.[5] These are all pieces of legislation which bear importance to debt collection.

The possibility of fighting abusive debt collection practices collectively can have a significant impact. The importance of combatting abusive practices is highlighted in studies showing that abusive practices are widely present in the

1 Directive 2020/1828 on representative actions for the protection of the collective interests of consumers [2020] OJ L 409/1.
2 See para 1 of art 2 of the Directive provides the scope of application as applying 'to representative actions brought against infringements by traders of the provisions of Union law referred to in Annex I, including such provisions as transposed into national law, that harm or may harm the collective interests of consumers. This Directive is without prejudice to the provisions of Union law referred to in Annex I. It applies to domestic and cross-border infringements, including where those infringements ceased before the representative action was brought or where those infringements ceased before the representative action was concluded.'
3 E.U. Directive 2014/17/EU on credit agreements for consumers relating to residential immovable property [2014] OJ L 060/34.
4 Directive 2008/48/EC about unfair terms in consumer contracts [2008] OJ L 133/66.
5 Directive 2005/29/EC on unfair business-to-consumer commercial practices in the internal market [2005] OJ L 149/22.

DOI: 10.4324/9781003343158-12

Member States of the E.U.[6] It is high time for legislative efforts to provide better protection to consumers, given that the E.U. is expecting an increase in the number of non-performing loans due to the Covid-19 pandemic.[7] It has been suggested that consumers in the E.U., together with investors, many of whom are consumer investors, are not strong enough to initiate legal action when it comes to unfair contract terms.[8] It was observed in regards to the sub-prime crisis that debtors or consumer-debtors form a 'herd,' showing close similarities to the 'class' in class actions.[9] Therefore, protecting debtors collectively can be considered an appropriate response. An example of best practices for collective debt collection litigation is the U.S. Fair debt Collection Practices Act, which explicitly allows for class action litigation to be pursued by claimants together.[10] The E.U. is making steps in a similar direction with the RCRD. Since only six of the E.U. Member Stats provide collective actions remedies, this chapter carries importance for most E.U. Member States.[11]

The chapter will present the changes that can affect those Member States who have no or minimal tradition in collective consumer protection. The chapter employs a doctrinal methodology through analyzing legal texts, doctrinal sources, cases, and other written sources. As a methodological caveat, I must put forward the scarcity of legal sources available on informal debt collection. Where definitions for informal debt collection are included in the sector-specific regulation of the industry, it has been suggested that 'informal debt collection could be a *sui generis* category of independent professional services.'[12] While legal sources often do not explicitly mention private or abusive debt collection, most court

6 Giulia Porino, 'Debt collection: Europe could end unjustifiable and wide-spread malpractices,' (*Finance Watch*, 19 February 2020) <https://www.finance-watch.org/debt-collection-europe-could-end-unjustifiable-and-wide-spread-malpractices/>, accessed 26 August 2021.

7 Elizabeth McCaul, Speech by Elizabeth McCaul, Member of the Supervisory Board of the ECB, at the NPL Summit 2021, Athens European Central Bank. 'NPL Management and the COVID-19 Crisis', 18 March 2021. <https://www.bankingsupervision.europa.eu/press/speeches/date/2021/html/ssm.sp210318~a0a512f98b.en.html>.

8 Cristina Amato, Chiara Perfumi, 'Financial Investors as Consumers,' in James Devenney, Mel Kenny (eds.) *Consumer Protection in Europe: Theory and Practice*. New York: Cambridge University Press, 2012 viii, 279–305, 296.

9 Micklitz, Hans-W, 'Herd Behaviour and Third Party Impact as a Legal Concept'. In Stefan Grundmann, Florian Möslein, Karl Riesenhuber (eds.) *Contract Governance*, 106–46. Oxford University Press, 2015. <https://doi.org/10.1093/acprof:oso/9780198723202.003.0006. 112>.

10 See s 813(a)2(b) of '*Fair Debt Collection Practices Act*', 12 August 2013.

11 Stanescu, Catalin, 'Regulation of Abusive Debt Collection Practices in the EU Member States: An Empirical Account.' *Journal of Consumer Policy*. 44. 1–38. 10.1007/s10603-020-09476-8., p. 22 figure 13.

12 Stănescu, Catalin, 'A Critical Assessment of the Need for Harmonization of the Legal Framework Concerning Abusive Informal Debt Collection Practices in the European Union'. *Journal of Consumer Policy* 44, no. 4 (1 December 2021): 531–57. <https://doi.org/10.1007/s10603-021-09495-z>.

cases concern judicial debt collection. Unfortunately, finding informal debt collection cases in the Central and Eastern European regions is much more difficult.[13]

Firstly, the provisions of the RCRD will be addressed. Secondly, the chapter will show how abusive debt collection practices qualify as breaches of the law that allow consumers to engage the help of a QE. Member States where representative actions for collective consumer protection were not the norm before are especially important to discuss. Finally, the chapter will establish a connection between the efficiency of the RCRD and the existence of sector-specific regulation concerning informal debt collection.

Romania is one of the Member States where collective consumer protection actions are uncommon.[14] A few notable cases from Romania clarify how Member States without collective actions tackled litigation that would have required them. Cases were fought against Volksbank[15] and against the Romanian Commercial Bank,[16] where several consumers decided to fight collectively against the two banks regarding abusive clauses in contracts. Attorneys taking part in consumer protection collective action litigation in Romania have suggested that the Romanian judicial system is still uncertain about handling and adjudicating collective actions and the possibility of separation of the claims by the court brought by the claimants or members of the class is persistent.[17] Due to the novel possibility of providing redress measures as a remedy, representative actions have the potential to be widely used. This change in procedural possibilities for Member States who have little experience with collective actions requires an analysis.

11.2 The novelty of the RCRD

The RCRD requires Member States to adopt national laws and transpose its provisions by 25 December 2022,[18] with the measures applying from 25 June 2023.[19] The implementation dates give little time for consumers to get informed and start

13 Tajti, Tibor, 'A Holistic Approach to Extra-Judicial Enforcement and Private Debt Collection – A Comparative Account of Trends, Empirical Evidences, and the Connected Regulatory Challenges – PART ONE' (December 30, 2019). *Pravni Zapisi vol. X*, No. 2, pp. 275-331, (2019) at . DOI: 10.5937/pravzap0-24140. Available at SSRN: <https://ssrn.com/abstract=3512798>.

14 Alexandra Popescu, 'Collective actions – a solution for realizing civil rights. How it was. (Procesele colective – o solutie pentru realizarea drepturilor cetatenesti. Cum a fost)'. (*Juridice*, 21 February 2011) <htps://www.juridice.ro/136000/procesele-colective-o-solutie-pentru-realizarea-drepturilor-cetatenesti-cum-a-fost.html>, accessed 27 August 2021.

15 Mihai Banita, 'Volksbank loses first collective action with clients. The court abolishes abusive clauses. (Volksbank pierde primul proces colectiv cu clienţii. Instanţa desfiinţează clauzele abuzive)', (*Economica*, 20 March 2012). <https://www.economica.net/90-de-romani-pagubiti-de-volksbank-castiga-procesul-cu-banca_19336.html>, accessed 27 August 2021.

16 Decision nr. 2123 from October 20, 2015 (Decizia nr. 2123/20.10.2015) ICCJ.

17 Piperea and Associates, 'Collective actions' (Piperea si Asociatii: Procesele colective,) <https://www.piperea.ro/upload/file/procesele-colective.pdf>, accessed 27 August 2021.

18 See art 24 of Directive.

19 Ibid.

organizing their actions. The keyword of the RCRD is 'representative,' and at the center of the proceedings are not attorneys hired by the class, but QE, who represent the consumers when litigating their collective interests. The RCRD comes as an extension and replacement of Directive 2009/22/EC on injunctions to protect consumers' interests which allowed for collective representation seeking injunctions for the benefit of consumers.[20] The RCRD incorporates injunctions from Directive 2009/EC for consumers, and also provides redress measures, thus, potentially becoming a much widely used means of consumer protection and litigation.

It is important to note that the RCRD has E.U.-wide scope and applies to cross-border E.U. representative actions, as well.[21] This is a vital aspect because it is not uncommon for E.U. citizens to relocate within the Union, especially since the pandemic has proven that mobility is valuable for workers all around Europe,[22] and the globe.[23]

Even though, the EC has declared its intention to distance the E.U. solution from the U.S. class actions, the U.S. being a leading jurisdiction for class action consumer protection, some comparison between U.S. class actions and E.U. representative actions is beneficial for identifying the potential weaknesses of the E.U. solution.[24] As a comparison, a first-order difference between the U.S.-type class action and actions regulated by the RCRD is that the latter gives less collective power to the consumers themselves and can be seen as less effective towards defendants.[25] The relevant actors of the RCRD are the QEs who may initiate action against the defendants, or traders.

11.2.1 Relevant actors

The RCRD relies on QEs to action the traders on behalf of consumers. The RCRD defines QE as 'any organization or public body representing consumers' interests which has been designated by a MS as qualified to bring representative actions in accordance with' the RCRD.[26] Therefore, a QE will be an administrative body or non-governmental entity, who has received the designation by the national

20 Directive 2009/22/EC on injunctions for the protection of consumers' interests [2009] OJ L 110/30.

21 See art 2(1) of Directive.

22 Marcu, S. 'Towards Sustainable Mobility? The Influence of the COVID-19 Pandemic on Romanian Mobile Citizens in Spain.' *Sustainability* 2021,13,4023. <https:// doi.org/10.3390/su13074023>.

23 MBO Partners. 'Digital Nomads: How COVID-19 Impacted Digital Nomads'. <https://www.mbopartners.com/state-of-independence/2020-digital-nomads-report/> accessed 13 December 2021.

24 Manning Gilbert Warren III, 'The U.S. Securities Fraud Class Action: An Unlikely Export to the European Union', 38 Brook. J. Int'l. L. 1075 (2012), pp. 1075 – 1076.

25 Martin & Hutten, 'Comparing the EU's Representative Action Directive to US Class Action Procedures'. <https://www.lexology.com/library/detail.aspx?g=d56786ed-a883-4f46-806e-bfc09ba61118> (Lexology, 14 April 2021) accessed 10 November 2021.

26 Article 3 para 4 of Directive.

authorities to represent collective consumer interest, and not a law firm. The RCRD explicitly provides that consumer organizations, mainly, should be granted the QE status if they represent consumers from more than one MS.[27]

Member States can choose to designate the same QE for the purposes of the RCRD who already serve as designated QEs for the injunctions Directive 2009/22/EC.[28] Since the two Directives are interconnected, it is logical that the RCRD provides redress measures before it substitutes itself for the 2009/22/EC Directive. In Romania, for example, according to Government Decision 1553/2004 to transpose Directive 2009/22/EC, the National Authority for Consumer Protection[29] ('NACP') is the QE and the responsible governmental administrative agency[30] to initiate injunctive actions.[31] It is unsure whether new QEs will be appointed in the future, maybe even due to the implementation of the RCRD, or if the NACP will remain as QE for the RCRD. The NACP, if designated, will have an active role and duty in protecting the collective interests of consumers. According to the NACP's 2020 Report, 1,268 claims were made by consumers against financial service providers, with 18 fines being instated by the NACP as a result, amounting to RON 170,000.[32] This suggests an average of less than RON 9,000 for each fine (approximately 2,000 euro). It is the aim of the RCRD that more representative actions be introduced in the future, thus, it is expected that QEs like the NACP will be more active in the future.

It should be mentioned that there can be disadvantages to naming public bodies as QEs, such as inefficiency of the implemented measures by the public bodies, or possible regulatory capture.[33] Understanding that only QEs can bring actions is crucial. QEs will be in the position to first assess whether consumer interests are affected negatively by the trader's actions, or not. Most probably, if the QE does not see merit in bringing action, the consumers will remain with the possibility to only action the debt collector in court individually, without the QE's help. Since the RCRD relies on QEs representing consumers' interests, leading

27 Article 4(2) of Directive.

28 Directive 2009/22/EC on injunctions for the protection of consumers' interests [2009] OJ L 110/30.

29 Romanian National Authority for the Protection of Consumers, Autoritatea Nationala pentru Protectia Consumatorilor, <https://anpc.ro>, accessed 27 August 2021.

30 It should be mentioned that it was once listed as the qualified entity by the Commission as 'Asociatia pentru Protectia Consumatorilor din România (APC – România)' in Notices from MS, Notification from the Commission concerning Article 4(3) of Directive 2009/22/EC of the European Parliament and of the Council on injunctions for the protection of consumers' interests, which codifies Directive 98/27/EC, concerning the entities qualified to bring an action under Article 2 of this Directive, (2019/C 237/03), <https://eur-lex.europa.eu/legal-content/EN/TXT/PDF/?uri=CELEX:52019XC0715(01)&from=EN>.

31 Government Decision nr. 1553 of September 23, 2004, M. Of. nr. 695 of 30 September 2011 (Hotărâre nr. 1.553 din 23 septembrie 2004 (republicată) M. Of. nr. 695 din 30 septembrie 2011).

32 NACP Report for 2020 (Raport ANPC 2020), <https://anpc.ro/galerie/file/544/2021/RAPORT_ANPC_2020_-.pdf>.

33 Christopher Hodges, '*The Reform of Class and Representative Actions in European Legal Systems: A New Framework for Collective Redress in Europe*', London: Bloomsbury Publishing (UK), 2008. 231.

plaintiffs, or class representatives, who would be just as well members of the class of consumers, are not mentioned. Leading plaintiffs are part of the procedure in some European jurisdictions, for example Denmark allows class representatives to be appointed.[34] On the other hand, an advantage of litigation led by QEs is that judges will probably be less inclined to sever the cases in court, as they would do prior to the application of the RCRD.[35]

Traders are defined as 'any natural person, or any legal person irrespective of whether privately or publicly owned, that acts, including through another person acting in that person's name or on that person's behalf, for purposes relating to that person's trade, business, craft or profession.'[36] The definition is quite broad and would easily encompass most business or commercial activities, including financial services. As Annex 1 to the RCRD provides a list of legislation that includes financial services, one can conclude that traders would include banks and debt collectors, therefore, private informal debt collectors as well. The definition is broad enough to allow the inclusion of informal debt collectors as 'independent professional services.'[37] Whether done for the benefit of the collector themselves ('in that person's name') or as agents to somebody ('on that person's behalf') the definition incorporates informal debt collection.

Additionally, the definition requires that traders be 'privately or publicly owned.' The phrasing of the definition of traders seems to exclude state or juridical entities, for example bailiffs – since they are not 'owned' in the legal sense of the word. Also, members of the judicial enforcement apparatus of Member States would not qualify as having a 'trade, business, craft.' Their activity could be seen as being connected to their 'profession,' if the term 'profession' is understood broadly. However, the phrasing of the definition suggests that it is intended to concern businesses in the private sphere. This interpretation is validated by the Hungarian ('*kereskedő*') and Romanian ('*comerciant*') translations as well, which both concern business activities. According to the 2021 Guidelines for the application of the Unfair Commercial Practices Directive, public authorities, for example municipalities, can be considered 'traders' only in regard to profit-making activities, like selling tickets for an art exhibition.[38] Bailiffs' main role is not to

34 Alsøe, Gorrissen Federspiel-Christian, Morten Melchior Gudm, sen, and Søren Henriksen. *'Class Action Procedure in Denmark'*. (*Lexology*, 28 May 2019.) <https://www.lexology.com/library/detail.aspx?g=26a50777-3279-46fd-b24c-5bdaa5faa239>.

35 Piperea and Associates: Collective actions (Piperea si Asociatii: Procesele uropaive,) <https://www.piperea.ro/upload/file/procesele-colective.pdf>, accessed 27 August 2021.

36 Article 3(2) of Directive.

37 Stanescu, Catalin, 'A Critical Assessment of the Need for Harmonization of the Legal Framework Concerning Abusive Informal Debt Collection Practices in the European Union' (2021) *Journal of Consumer Policy* 44, no. 4 (1 December 2021): 531–557. <https://doi.org/10.1007/s10603-021-09495-z>.

38 Commission Notice – Guidance on the interpretation and application of Directive 2005/29/EC of the European Parliament and of the Council concerning unfair business-to-consumer commercial practices in the internal market (Text with EEA relevance) (2021). <https://eur-lex.europa.eu/legal-content/EN/TXT/?uri=CELEX%3A52021XC1229%2805%29>.

make profit but to enforce the law. They are different from the private debt collectors, whose main commercial purpose would be for profit activity via collecting debt. Therefore, the RCRD is intended to apply to private debt collection by virtue of the definition of 'trader.'

11.2.2 Applicable remedies

Injunctions are provided as a possible solution to representative collective consumer actions by Directive 2009/22/EC.[39] The RCRD amended and repealed it and added redress measures. Suspension of debt collection in judicial cases is already an option in many Member States, for example Romania.[40]

Unfortunately, an EC report states that the injunction Directive's success is questionable.[41] According to the report, due to a lack of requirement for Member States to keep a record of the number of injunctions sought, we cannot know for sure how many actions were initiated. It also shows that from implementation until 2012, 5,632 actions for injunction were reported. Three thousands of these were reported in Germany.[42] This number is relatively low, considering it includes all types of injunctive measures sought, not just against debt collection. This suggests that the 2009/22/EC Directive still left room for improvement. To that end, the RCRD requires Member States to provide the Commission with information about the number and type of representative actions concluded, the infringements concerned, the parties of the actions, and the representative actions' outcomes for issuing an E.U.-wide Commission report.[43] In this way, there will be relevant and reliable data to assess whether the RCRD is successful, and whether consumers can rely on it for injunctive or redress measures.

The RCRD provides a suspension or interruption of the limitation period for redress claims as an additional measure, to allow consumers to seek an injunction.[44] The initiation of collective actions suspends or interrupts ongoing limitation periods to benefit the consumers.[45] This enables the consumers to commence a separate action for seeking redress after the injunction has been adjudicated.

The **redress measures** are the true novelty of the RCRD. Remedies such as 'compensation, repair, replacement, price reduction, contract termination or reimbursement of the price paid' are introduced by the RCRD.[46] Repair and

39 Directive 2009/22/EC on injunctions for the protection of consumers' interests [2009] OJ L 110/30.
40 Article 719 of the Romanian Code of Civil Procedure.
41 COM(2012)635 – Report Application of Directive 2009/22/EC on injunctions for the protection of consumers' interest, <https://eur-lex.europa.eu/legal-content/EN/TXT/?uri=celex%3A52012DC0635>.
42 Ibid.
43 See art 23 para 2 of RCRD.
44 See art 16 of RCRD.
45 See art 16(1) of Directive, also, see Annexes to COM(2012)635 – Application of Directive 2009/22/EC on injunctions for the protection of consumers' interest, <https://www.eumonitor.eu/9353000/1/j4nvirkkkr58fyw_j9vvik7m1c3gyxp/vj4dt9rd9cwd>, accessed 25 August 2021.
46 Article 9 of Directive.

replacement are not remedies that concern debt collectors. However, compensation, price reduction, contract termination may be sought by consumers against debt collectors.

As a key to informing the consumers involved, **post-solution information** will have to be provided by the debt collectors who are targeted by the representative action. The debt collector is required to inform all consumers affected about the final decisions or settlement reached with the QE.[47] The RCRD allows Member States to regulate a **consultation mechanism** between the QE and the debt collector on consumers' behalf.[48] The consultation will take place before bringing the representative action before courts or administrative bodies and is meant to offer a chance to end the infringement before legal action is initiated. The consultation in its basic form is phrased to precede representative actions for an injunction. However, Recital 41 of the RCRD provides that filing representative actions for redress measures can also be preceded by consultation.[49] Since the phrasing of the RCRD explicitly requires settlements to be approved by the court or administrative body presiding over the issue, traders might be able to reach settlements during the two-week consultation period granted and to present their settlement offer afterwards.

11.2.3 Possible problems

One of the main shortfalls of the RCRD is not *prima facie* apparent. The RCRD requires Member States to regulate penalties for failure to comply with injunctions, with orders to provide information to consumers, or failure or refusal to provide evidence.[50] Unfortunately, there is no explicit penalty imposed by the RCRD for failure to comply with a redress measure. This can have adverse effects, where in case of **non-compliance** with a redress measure, the consumer will either be expected to

a) action the debt collector in court individually, or
b) inform the QE about the non-compliance with the decision for redress.

The consumer will be required to act alone in case (a) because the RCRD does not provide remedies for non-compliance with redress decisions. The debtor will not be able to inform the QE to initiate a separate representative action even if none of the group members have received compensation or the compensation is unduly delayed. Annex I does not seem to include any legal acts referring to this possibility. It should be mentioned that the RCRD does establish a penalty for failure to

47 See art 13(3) of Directive.
48 See art 8(4) of Directive.
49 See Recital 41 of Directive.
50 See art 19 of the Directive.

inform about a settlement or that a group of consumers with claims is formed.[51] But this is a different kind of non-compliance with the judicial or administrative decision than not complying with the redress measures themselves.

As a Directive mainly adopted for redress measures, the RCRD puts forward a **settlement** mechanism. It must be mentioned that Italy has initiated the implementation of a settlement structure that would make it compulsory to at least try to settle before the collective action can be initiated.[52] In the RCRD, the possibility of settlements relies on the 'court's or administrative' body's decision.[53] Settlements between the trader and the QE can only be reached if the court or the administrative body hearing the action approves the settlement. Otherwise, the proceedings must continue before the court, and the settlement will not prevail. The settlement may be either jointly proposed by the trader and the QE, or by the court or administrative body hearing the action.[54]

This suggests that the procedural framework for settlements makes out-of-court settlements without approval of the court or administrative body impossible. This is different from the U.S. class action system, where the court can certify the class for the settlement in case of agreement. This practice has received some criticism because it favors the defendant, who may be able to settle and escape an otherwise more expensive class action without any investigations into the merits of the claims by a court.[55] Even if the Federal Rules of Civil Procedure requires settlement procedures to be initiated by notice to the absent class members who might be affected by the settlement, certifying for the sake of settlement might still mean a lesser involvement of the court.[56] The RCRD does not allow for settlements to surpass judicial review. Also, non-compliance with national law, or the impossibility of enforcement of the settlement will represent causes to refuse the settlement between the traders and the QE.[57] It is not entirely sure how compensation will be quantified by courts for cases where the abusive collection was proven. Consequently, the settlement mechanism is probably even more critical since settlements would have the advantage of providing a possibly favorable solution to both parties without the burden of quantifying damages to fall on the courts.

51 See art 19(1) b) of RCRD.

52 Cristina Amato, Chiara Perfumi, 'Financial Investors as Consumers,' in James Devenney, Mel Kenny (eds.) *Consumer Protection in Europe: Theory and Practice*. New York: Cambridge University Press, 2012 viii, 279–305, 304.

53 See art 11(2) of Directive.

54 See art 11 of RCRD.

55 Erichson, Howard M., 'The Problem of Settlement Class Actions' (June 14, 2013). 82 *George Washington Law Review* 951 (2014), Fordham Law Legal Studies Research Paper No. 2243155, Available at SSRN: <https://ssrn.com/abstract=2243155 or http://dx.doi.org/10.2139/ssrn.2243155>.

56 Rule 23 of Federal Rules of Civil Procedure.

57 Article 11(2) of RCRD

11.3 Abusive behavior defined and sector specific regulation

11.3.1 Abusive behavior and harm to consumers

Annex 1 contains several E.U. legislative acts transposed into national legislation (directives) or directly applicable (regulations), including numerous financial legislative acts. Some of the legislation, for example[58] Directive 2008/48/CE[59] or Directive 2014/17/EU[60] have generally been transposed into national law by Member States for whom collective actions are still a novelty.[61] The CJEU held that debt collectors must be considered 'credit intermediaries,' for example in regard to the provision of repayment plans.[62] This conveys that debt collectors can be considered liable for consumer credit protection breaches.

Additionally, art 2 states that the RCRD 'applies to representative actions brought against infringements by traders of the provisions of Union law referred to in Annex I, including such provisions as transposed into national law, that **harm or may harm** the collective interests of consumers' (emphasis added).[63] It is not yet sure how the probability of harm is meant to be established or what can be considered harmful for the consumers. While injunctive relief might as well be sought collectively by consumers who experience harm in the form of abuse by debt collectors, redress in the context of abusive debt collection will probably be sought only for compensation, due to the nature of the claims that could be formulated against debt collectors. Seeking moral damages or price reduction is also a possibility – if the amount to be enforced upon the debtor is perceived to be illegitimate, the debtor may claim a reduction.

The abusive manner in which debt collection occurs is generally difficult to spot and is rarely mentioned directly in court cases. There is evidence of abusive debt collection in such unverifiable and non-judicial sources as websites of lawyers offering services to counteract abusive debt collectors or on public forums on the internet.[64] It is much more difficult to find evidence in court decisions. The

58 Annex 1 to Directive, 19.

59 Directive 2008/48/EC of the European Parliament and of the Council of 23 April 2008 on credit agreements for consumers [2008] OJ L 133/ 66.

60 Directive 2014/17/EU of the European Parliament and of the Council of 4 February 2014 on credit agreements for consumers relating to residential immovable property [2014] OJ L 60/ 34.

61 In Romania for example, Directive 2008/48/CE has been transposed into Romanian law through the Government Emergency Ordinance (hereinafter 'GEO') 50/2010 about credit contracts for consumers. GEO 50/2010 explicitly mentions the obligation of debt collectors to not collect any interest on loans during the enforcement procedure. Similarly, Directive 2014/17/EU transposed to Romanian legislation by GEO 52/2016 about credit contracts offered to consumers for immovable goods, which explicitly mentions 'entities which engage in debt recovery activities.'

62 C-127/15 *Verein für Konsumenteninformation* ECLI:EU:C:2016:934.

63 See art 2(1) of Directive.

64 Avocat Cululis Adrian, 'Sunteti Hartuit De Recuperatorii De Creante?Anulati-le Executarea Silita, (Indrumari juridice, 14 June 2019), (Are you harassed by debt collectors? Get their enforcement acts annulled (Legal guidance)' <https://indrumari-juridice.eu/indrumarijuridice/sunteti-hartuit-de-recuperatorii-de-creanteanulati-le-executarea-silita/>, accessed 14 november 2021.

situation is well exemplified by the one described about Hungary, where proof of abusive debt collection is primarily available as anecdotal evidence and less in reported cases.[65] Some judicial debt collection court cases concerning abusive collection will also tackle private debt collection. For example, in a recent Romanian case, the plaintiff actioned the defendant in tort law for 'causing moral and material harm by exercising its right to enforcement, leading to unjust enrichment … in an abusive, excessive, perpetual and unreasonable manner' (translation by the author).[66] This in one example of abusive debt collection which could be remedied with the help of QEs.

The **remedy** of collective actions for consumers all over the E.U. against the harms that they may suffer is related to the small claim nature of the debt.[67] Simply put, consumer debtors might not consider the monetary gains of an individual action against the debt collector to be advantageous considering the costs. This is especially so when considering that the judiciary might decide against the consumer debtor, and the legal fees will be costly above the debt itself. In these cases, debtors will be inclined to decide against individual legal action even if the debt collection was indeed abusive. Debtors can become discouraged and give in to abusive informal collection without a fight even if it is not lawful.

One of the cases when debt collection may be unlawful concerns time-barred debts, which is explicitly unlawful in some Member States like Romania, for example. Quite often, debt collectors' abusive behavior entails the use of harassment or other abuses to collect time-barred debts that are not legally enforceable at the moment of collection due to the passing of the statute of limitations.[68] After the statute of limitations has passed, the debt can be enforced legally only if the debtor amicably agrees to enforcement, but enforcement is not lawful of time-barred debts without the debtor's consent. This is a crucial fact that debtors might not realize when met with the notification about the collection. However, the debtors are not necessarily cognizant of the procedural aspects of debt collection and might not know that the collection happens abusively.

Another possibility for deciding against rightful individual litigation with the debt collector would be if the debtor's income is already subject to illegal garnishment for previous debts. In Romania, for example, garnishment is allowed

65 Tajti Tibor, 'A Holistic Approach to Extra-Judicial Enforcement and Private Debt Collection – A Comparative Account of Trends, Empirical Evidences, and the Connected Regulatory Challenges – PART ONE' (December 30, 2019). *Pravni Zapisi vol. X*, No. 2, pp. 275–331, (2019) 309.

66 Hotărâre nr. 159/2021 din 03/02/2021 – Civil – actiune in raspundere delictuala Curtea de Apel Bucuresti – Secţia a III-a civilă şi pentru cauze cu minori şi de familie (S3-Completul nr.11 Apel) .

67 Class actions in the U.S. are considered to be the appropriate remedy for small claims. See, for example, Pato, Alexia, '*Jurisdiction and Cross-Border Collective Redress: A European Private Ibternational Law Perspective*' (2019) Hart Publishing, Studies in Private International Law, Bloomsburry Collections, 12.

68 Bierens Debt Recovery Lawyers. 'Debt Collection in Romania – No Cure No Pay | Bierens (Tip!)'. <https://www.bierensgroup.com/en-gb/debt-collection-romania/> accessed 7 January 2022.

for only half of the income if several garnishments are placed on the income.[69] Because a significant amount of the income is already under abusive deduction the debtor might consider that additional garnishments have only a small effect on their income. In other words, if the debtor is already losing a big amount each month, losing a little more might not be a big enough incentive to spend time and legal fees on fighting the collection. The enforcement process does become longer due to the capped amount that can be enforced monthly, but in situations when the debtor is already losing money unlawfully, losing a little more to additional garnishment because of the enforcement by the debt collector might not make a difference.

In these cases, when individual actions are not considered worth the investment of time and legal fees, collective actions can represent a possibility to counter abuses by informal debt collectors. Therefore, harm can be interpreted differently in the context of individual actions and collective actions. While individual actions might not be introduced for minor harm, if a QE initiates action against an abusive debt collector, debtors may be more inclined to join even if they only experienced what they may consider minor harm.

11.3.2 Interpreting harm

The challenge for the QE will be to demonstrate that the manners of the collection are abusive and violating one or more legislative acts mentioned in Annex I. Abusive methods or means of debt collection will be subject to interpretation by the QE and, finally, by the courts or administrative bodies hearing the claim. Interpreting abusive behavior can represent less of a difficulty if some legal guideline exists which can be followed, for example in the form of sector specific regulation. This would allow QE and courts to look at the facts of the case and decide whether collection was abusive or not, based on the sector-specific regulation which interprets what can be considered harmful.

To exemplify this, Romania is one of the few MS where a sector-specific regulation covers the activity of debt collectors. At the same time, Hungary does not operate with sector specific regulation.[70] Romania specifically has transposed legislation explicitly regulating abusive behavior of debt collectors.[71] Directive 2014/17/EU, a legislative act listed in Annex I, refers to 'credit intermediaries,' a term which the CJEU has interpreted as covering debt collectors, for example in cases when they provide repayment plans.[72] Directive 2014/17/EU was transposed

69 Article 728 Romanian Code of Civil Procedure (Noul cod de procedura civila, M. Of. 545 of 2012).

70 Tajti Tibor, A Holistic Approach to Extra-Judicial Enforcement and Private Debt Collection – A Comparative Account of Trends, Empirical Evidences, and the Connected Regulatory Challenges – PART ONE (December 30, 2019). *Pravni Zapisi vol. X*, No. 2, pp. 275–331, (2019) 308.

71 Emergency Ordinance 52 of 2016, art 60.

72 C-127/15 *Verein für Konsumenteninformation* ECLI:EU:C:2016:934.

into Romanian law by GEO 52 of 2016,[73] explicitly mentioning 'entities for debt collection.' These entities include informal debt collectors. According to the GEO, debt collectors are forbidden from, for example, using threats or harassment, physical or mental harm, or even damaging the 'consumers' reputation.[74] The above are abusive methods that debt collectors are forbidden from using during recovery. Therefore, by using the examples given in the GEO, QEs will be granted the legal interpretation of what abusive collection can be. The QE will be able to acknowledge that the abuses mentioned in the legislation are against the interest of consumers and will have to do a factual analysis of the case in two steps. Firstly, does the behavior described by consumers fit into the abusive categories in the law? And secondly, did the abuse occur in the way that the consumers describe?

In Member States without sector-specific regulation, like Hungary, QEs will be required to analyze the claim brought before them more deeply and rely on their own abuse concepts. QEs will have to evaluate whether the described way the debt collection occurred was abusive or not, without the guidance of any hard law instrument. In the absence of regulation interpreting abuses in this way can become more difficult. Thus, the lack of sector-specific regulation for some Member States will require the additional step of interpreting and deciding what is abusive and what is not. Informal debt collectors incur the added difficulty that their actions do not have clear definitions of what abusive actions are. Clearly established rules and definitions by regulation of the activity of debt collectors aid all the relevant actors to avoid possible confusion during the representative action. This situation may be solved with the implementation of Directive 2021/2167 on credit servicers and credit purchasers.[75]

11.3.3 Cross-border actions against abusive debt collection

Judicial precedent in the E.U. already exists for a government agency to pursue consumer protection claims against a service provider located in a different Member State. The CJEU has established that surveillance proceedings will be in the competence of authorities of the Member State in which the consumers who receive the service reside.[76] The RCRD defines cross-border actions in reference to the establishment of the QE as 'a representative action brought by a QE in a MS other than that in which the QE was designated.'[77] The RCRD is supposed to offer solutions to EU citizens seeking national representative actions and cross-border

73 Emergency Ordinance 52 of 2016, art 60.

74 Ibid.

75 Directive (EU) 2021/2167 of the European Parliament and of the Council of 24 November 2021 on credit servicers and credit purchasers and amending Directives 2008/48/EC and 2014/17/EU, 438 OJ L § (2021). <http://data.europa.eu/eli/dir/2021/2167/oj/eng>.

76 C-475/12 *UPC DTH Sàrl v Nemzeti Média- és Hírközlési Hatóság Elnökhelyettese* ECLI:EU:C:2014:285.

77 Article 3(7) of Directive.

injunctions or redress, especially if the consumers live in a different MS than the debt collector.[78] According to the Recital, established rules of private international law and Union law govern the procedural aspects of the representative actions.[79] However, the competence of administrative authorities or enforcement of decisions by these authorities will be settled by national law.[80] This latter provision allows the MS to decide according to their legislative structure.

Since sector-specific regulation can be absent at MS level in the E.U., or it can differ from Member State to Member State, the issue of cross-border representative actions against abusive informal debt collection practices is especially problematic. The E.U. solution begs the question: how does a QE initiate cross-border representative actions if in some Member States abusive behavior is regulated, and in others it is regulated differently or not at all? Also, how will compensation be established as a redress measure if the Member States regulate compensation differently,[81] or if the regulation of debt collection remains heterogeneous, as it was observed, across Member States?[82]

The RCRD attempts to make it impossible for a domestic representative action to become a cross-border representative action while the administrative body or the courts hear it.[83] The 'deciding criterion for determining the type of representative action brought' will be the Member State that designated the QE who initiates action.[84] Even if the debt collector or the consumers are domiciled in different Member States, the determining factor will be the place of establishment of the QE. Such measures can easily give significant power to Member States who do not have representative actions regulated or do not habitually rely on representative collective actions structure for consumer protection. Member States who do not have an already established legal framework for collective actions can introduce new legal solutions, or transplant already working solutions from other jurisdictions, as long as the RCRD is respected. This might also suggest a possibility for becoming a preferred jurisdiction for forum shopping if the regulatory standards introduced are less demanding.

78 See Recital 20 of the Directive.

79 See Recital 21 of the Directive about Regulation (EC) No 864/2007 of the European Parliament and of the Council of 11 July 2007 on the law applicable to non-contractual obligations (Rome II) [2007] OJ L 199/ 40, Regulation (EC) 593/2008 or the Rome I Regulation on the law applicable to contractual obligations [2008] OJ L 177/6, and Regulation (EU) 1215/2012 on jurisdiction and the recognition and enforcement of judgments in civil and commercial matters [2012] OJ L 351/1.

80 See Recital 22 of the RCRD.

81 Helmut, Koziol, 'Harmonising Tort Law in the European Union: Advantages and Difficulties', (2013) ELTE Law Journal, <https://eltelawjournal.hu/harmonising-tort-law-in-the-european-union-advantages-and-difficulties/>.

82 Stanescu, Catalin. 'Does the European Union Need a Regulation of Unfair Debt Collection Practices?' (2016) *RRDE* 135. P. 145.

83 See Recital 23 of the RCRD.

84 See Recital 23 of the RCRD.

11.4 Conclusions

As it is dawning on Europe that consumer protection is often more effective when done for a collectivity of people, it appears that the debt collection industry in the E.U. will need to adjust to the RCRD. QEs will be required to decide whether abusive practices are actionable in a representative manner for redress measures to consumers. Their work will be less difficult if regulation defines or at least describes what abusive debt collection is. Having sector specific regulation can provide guidance in establishing the abusive nature of the collection and can facilitate the work of QEs and the courts or administrative bodies that must reach a decision. Even if the RCRD has its faults, an increase in litigation for debt collectors with QEs is probable in the future.

While debtors could be disinterested in individually pursuing justice against abusive debt collection after balancing the harm of collecting against litigation costs, relying on the help of a QE that will see that their interest prevail is an encouragement. If their claims are presented in a Member State where sector-specific regulation clearly defines the forms of abusive collection, the QE will easily be able to initiate actions and to help debtors collectively in front of a court or administrative body.

The RCRD represents a possibility of redress, an unprecedented remedy for consumers who have experienced unjust behaviors in the past but felt too powerless to act. How the procedure for establishing if a collection was abusive or not will be structured without sector-specific regulation, or how the calculation of appropriate redress in court will happen are still not clear. To make a difference and serve the consumers efficiently, it will be the job of the legislators, QEs, and courts to look to other jurisdictions to guide them with possible interpretations and precedents.

Legislation

Annexes to COM (2012) 635 - Application of Directive 2009/22/EC on injunctions for the protection of consumers' interest, https://www.eumonitor.eu/9353000/1/j4nvirkkkr58fyw_j9vvik7m1c3gyxp/vj4dt9rd9cwd.

Directive 2005/29/EC concerning unfair business-to-consumer commercial practices in the internal market, OJ L 149, 11.6.2005, p. 22–39.

Directive 2008/48/EC on credit agreements for consumers and repealing Council Directive 87/102/EEC, OJ L 133, 22.5.2008, p. 66-92.

Directive 2009/22/EC on injunctions for the protection of consumers' interests OJ L 110, 1.5.2009, p. 30–36.

Directive 2014/17/EU on credit agreements for consumers relating to residential immovable property and amending Directives 2008/48/EC and 2013/36/EU and Regulation (EU) No 1093/2010, OJ L 60, 28.2.2014, p. 34–85.

Directive 2020/1828 on representative actions for the protection of the collective interests of consumers and repealing Directive 2009/22/EC, OJ L 409, 4.12.2020, p. 1–27.

Directive (EU) 2021/2167 of the European Parliament and of the Council of 24 November 2021 on credit servicers and credit purchasers and amending Directives 2008/48/EC and 2014/17/EU, 438 OJ L § (2021). http://data.europa.eu/eli/dir/2021/2167/oj/eng.

Emergency Ordinance 50/2010 (Ordonanţa de urgenţă 50 din 2010), published in M. Of. 389 from June 11, 2010.
Emergency Ordinance nr. 52/2016 about credit contracts offered to consumers for immovable goods (Ordonanţa de urgenţă 52 din 2016),), M. Of. 727 of September 20 2016.
'Fair Debt Collection Practices 'Act'', August 12 2013. https://www.ftc.gov/enforcement/rules/rulemaking-regulatory-reform-proceedings/fair-debt-collection-practices-act-text.
Federal Rules of Civil Procedure, Rule 23. Class Actions.
Government Ordinance 1553/2004 (Hotărârea Guvernului nr. 1553 din 23 septembrie 2004) (republicată) M. Of. nr. 695 of 30 September 2011.
New Civil Code of Romania (Noul cod civil), M. Of. 505 of 2011.
New Civil Code of Procedure of Romania (Noul cod de procedura civila), M. Of. 545 of 2012.
Regulation (EC) No 593/2008 on the law applicable to contractual obligations (Rome I) OJ L 177, 4.7.2008, p. 6–16.
Regulation (EC) No 864/2007 on the law applicable to non-contractual obligations (Rome II), OJ L 199, 31.7.2007, p. 40–49.
Regulation (EU) 1215/2012 on jurisdiction and the recognition and enforcement of judgements in civil and commercial matters, OJ L 351, 20.12.2012, p. 1–32.

Cases

CJEU Case C-127/15.
CJEU Case C-475/12.
Decizia nr. 2123/20.10.2015, Inalta Curte de Casatie si Justitie.
Hotărâre nr. 159/2021 din 03/02/2021 – Civil – actiune in raspundere delictuala Curtea de Apel BUCUREŞTI - Secţia a III-a civilă şi pentru cauze cu minori şi de familie (S3-Completul nr.11 Apel.

Reports

Alsøe, Gorrissen Federspiel-Christian, Morten Melchior Gudm, sen, and Søren Henriksen. 'Class Action Procedure in Denmark'. *Lexology*, 28 May 2019. https://www.lexology.com/library/detail.aspx?g=26a50777-3279-46fd-b24c-5bdaa5faa239.
COM(2012)635 – Report Application of Directive 2009/22/EC on injunctions for the protection of consumers' interest, https://eur-lex.europa.eu/legal-content/EN/TXT/?uri=celex%3A52012DC0635.
Commission Notice – Guidance on the interpretation and application of Directive 2005/29/EC of the European Parliament and of the Council concerning unfair business-to-consumer commercial practices in the internal market (Text with EEA relevance) (2021), https://eur-lex.europa.eu/legal-content/EN/TXT/?uri=CELEX%3A52021XC1229%2805%29.
Giulia Porino, 'Debt Collection: Europe Could End Unjustifiable and Wide-Spread Malpractices' (*Finance Watch*, February 19 2020), https://www.finance-watch.org/debt-collection-europe-could-end-unjustifiable-and-wide-spread-malpractices/.
Notices from MS, Notification from the Commission concerning Article 4(3) of Directive 2009/22/EC of the European Parliament and of the Council on injunctions for the

protection of consumers' interests, which codifies Directive 98/27/EC, concerning the entities qualified to bring an action under Article 2 of this Directive, (2019/C 237/03), https://eur-lex.europa.eu/legal-content/EN/TXT/PDF/?uri=CELEX:52019XC0715(01)&from=EN.

Raport ANPC 2020, https://anpc.ro/galerie/file/544/2021/RAPORT_ANPC_2020_-.pdf.

Books and articles in books

Amato, Cristina, Perfumi Chiara, 'Financial Investors as Consumers' in James Devenney, Mel Kenny (eds), *Consumer Protection in Europe: Theory and Practice*. New York: Cambridge University Press, 2012, viii, 279–305.

Hodges, Christopher, *The Reform of Class and Representative Actions in European Legal Systems: A New Framework for Collective Redress in Europe*. London: Bloomsbury Publishing (UK), 2008.

Micklitz, Hans-W., 'Herd Behaviour and Third Party Impact as a Legal Concept' in Stefan Grundmann, Florian Möslein, Karl Riesenhuber (eds), Contract Governance. Oxford: Oxford University Press, 2015, 106–146.

Pato, Alexia, Jurisdiction and Cross-Border Collective Redress: A European Private International Law Perspective. Oxford: Hart Publishing, 2019. Studies in Private International Law. Bloomsbury Collections. https://doi.org/10.5040/9781509930326.ch-001.

Articles

Erichson, Howard M., 'The Problem of Settlement Class Actions' (2014) 82 *George Washington Law Review* 951. Fordham Law Legal Studies Research Paper No. 2243155. https://doi.org/10.2139/ssrn.2243155.

Koziol, Helmut, 'Harmonising Tort Law in the European Union: Advantages and Difficulties' (2013) *ELTE Law Journal*. https://eltelawjournal.hu/harmonising-tort-law-in-the-european-union-advantages-and-difficulties/.

Marcu, S., 'Towards Sustainable Mobility? The Influence of the COVID-19 Pandemic on Romanian Mobile Citizens in Spain' (2021) 13 *Sustainability* 4023. https://doi.org/10.3390/su13074023.

Stănescu, Catalin, 'A Critical Assessment of the Need for Harmonization of the Legal Framework Concerning Abusive Informal Debt Collection Practices in the European Union' (2021) 44(4) *Journal of Consumer Policy* 531–557. https://doi.org/10.1007/s10603-021-09495-z.

Stanescu, Catalin, 'Does the European Union Need a Regulation of Unfair Debt Collection Practices?' (2016) 4(11) *R.R.D.E.* 135.

Stanescu, Catalin, 'Regulation of Abusive Debt Collection Practices in the EU Member States: An Empirical Account.' (2021) 44 *Journal of Consumer Policy* 1–38. https://doi.org/10.1007/s10603-020-09476-8.

Tajti Tibor, A., 'Holistic Approach to Extra-Judicial Enforcement and Private Debt Collection - A Comparative Account of Trends, Empirical Evidences, and the Connected Regulatory Challenges - PART ONE' (December 30, 2019). Pravni Zapisi, vol. X, no. 2, pp. 275–331. https://doi.org/10.5937/pravzap0-24140.

Warren III, Manning Gilbert, 'The US Securities Fraud Class Action: An Unlikely Export to the European Union' (2012) 38 *Brook. J. Int'l. L.* 1075, pp. 1075–76.

Online sources

Adrian, Avocat Cululis, 'Sunteti Hartuit De Recuperatorii De Creante? Anulati-le Executarea Silita' (*Indrumari juridice*, 14 June 2019), available at https://indrumari-juridice.eu/indrumarijuridice/sunteti-hartuit-de-recuperatorii-de-creanteanulati-le-executarea-silita/, accessed 14 November 2021.

Autoritatea Nationala pentru Protectia Consumatorilor, available at https://anpc.ro, accessed 27 August 2021.

Banita, Mihai, 'Volksbank pierde primul proces colectiv cu clienţii. Instanţa desfiinţează clauzele abuzive' (*Economica.net*, 20 March 2012), available at https://www.economica.net/90-de-romani-pagubiti-de-volksbank-castiga-procesul-cu-banca_19336.html, accessed 26 August 2021.

Bierens Debt Recovery Lawyers, 'Debt Collection in Romania – No Cure No Pay' *Bierens (Tip!)*, available at https://www.bierensgroup.com/en-gb/debt-collection-romania/, accessed 7 January 2022.

Martin, Linda, Hutten, Henry, 'Comparing the EU's Representative Action Directive to US Class Action Procedures' (*Lexology*, April 14, 2021), available at https://www.lexology.com/library/detail.aspx?g=d56786ed-a883-4f46-806e-bfc09ba61118, accessed 10 November 2021.

MBO Partners, 'Digital Nomads: How COVID-19 Impacted Digital Nomads', available at https://www.mbopartners.com/state-of-independence/2020-digital-nomads-report/, accessed 13 December 2021.

McCaul, Elizabeth, Speech by Elizabeth McCaul, Member of the Supervisory Board of the ECB, at the NPL Summit 2021, Athens European Central Bank. 'NPL Management and the COVID-19 Crisis' (18 March 2021), available at https://www.bankingsupervision.europa.eu/press/speeches/date/2021/html/ssm.sp210318~a0a512f98b.en.html.

Piperea si Asociatii, 'Procesele colective', available at https://www.piperea.ro/upload/file/procesele-colective.pdf, accessed 27 August 2021.

Popescu, Alexandra, 'Procesele colective – o solutie pentru realizarea drepturilor cetatenesti. Cum a fost' (*Juridice.ro*, 21 February 2011), available at https://www.juridice.ro/136000/procesele-colective-o-solutie-pentru-realizarea-drepturilor-cetatenesti-cum-a-fost.html, accessed 22 July 2021.

Index

For Product Safety Concerns and Information please contact our EU
representative GPSR@taylorandfrancis.com
Taylor & Francis Verlag GmbH, Kaufingerstraße 24, 80331 München, Germany

www.ingramcontent.com/pod-product-compliance
Ingram Content Group UK Ltd.
Pitfield, Milton Keynes, MK11 3LW, UK
UKHW020142200926
475702UK00005B/870

* 9 7 8 1 0 3 2 3 8 0 3 3 9 *